This book is a study of the spatial distribution of Frankish settlement in the Latin Kingdom of Jerusalem at the time of the Crusades, and of the spatial and social interrelation between the Franks and the indigenous population. It is based on an unprecedented field study of more than two hundred Frankish rural sites and on a close reexamination of the historical sources.

The book shows that the country was divided between local Muslim and Christian populations. The Franks refrained almost completely from settling the purely Muslim regions of the country, establishing their settlements only in Christian areas. The historical and geographical explanation for the division of the country between Christian and Muslim populations lies in a far-reaching social process of nomadization and sedentarization which began with the Muslim conquest in the seventh century and which reached its zenith before the Frankish conquest of the country.

The author reexamines some of the basic assumptions of standard recent scholarship, and advocates a new model of the nature of Frankish settlement, as a society of migrants who settled in the Levant, had close relations with Eastern Christians, and were almost completely shut off from the Muslim society which lived elsewhere in the country.

FRANKISH RURAL SETTLEMENT
IN THE
LATIN KINGDOM OF JERUSALEM

FRANKISH RURAL
SETTLEMENT
IN THE
LATIN KINGDOM
OF JERUSALEM

RONNIE ELLENBLUM

The Hebrew University of Jerusalem

CAMBRIDGE
UNIVERSITY PRESS

PUBLISHED BY THE PRESS SYNDICATE OF THE UNIVERSITY OF CAMBRIDGE
The Pitt Building, Trumpington Street, Cambridge, United Kingdom

CAMBRIDGE UNIVERSITY PRESS
The Edinburgh Building, Cambridge CB2 2RU, UK
40 West 20th Street, New York NY 10011–4211, USA
477 Williamstown Road, Port Melbourne, VIC 3207, Australia
Ruiz de Alarcón 13, 28014 Madrid, Spain
Dock House, The Waterfront, Cape Town 8001, South Africa

http://www.cambridge.org

First published 1998
First paperback edition 2002

Typeface Bembo 10½/12½ pt.

A catalogue record for this book is available from the British Library

Library of Congress Cataloguing in Publication data
Ellenblum, Ronnie.
Frankish rural settlement in the Latin Kingdom of Jerusalem / Ronnie
Ellenblum.
p.   cm.
Includes bibliography and index.
ISBN 0 521 55401 2 (hc)
1. Jerusalem – History – Latin Kingdom, 1099–1244. 2. Land
settlement – Jerusalem – History. 3. Human settlements – Jerusalem –
History. 4. Jerusalem – Population – History. 5. Jerusalem – Ethnic
relations.
D179.E44 1996
956.94'03–dc20 96-32621 CIP

ISBN 0 521 55401 2 hardback
ISBN 0 521 52187 4 paperback

CONTENTS

ILLUSTRATIONS

TABLES

ACKNOWLEDGMENTS

I wish to express my heartfelt thanks and gratitude to the various institutions, teachers, colleagues, and friends who helped me throughout the years to complete this book.

In the years of my doctoral research in Jerusalem and in Paris I received financial aid and generous grants from the Hebrew University of Jerusalem, from the French government, and from the Nahmias Foundation. A research grant from the National Council for Research and Development and a scholarship of the Inter-University Committee for Distinguished Doctoral Students enabled me to dedicate one semester each year for three years to fieldwork. In the post-doctoral year I spent in Paris I enjoyed a grant from the Lady Davies Foundation. In the last two years I was helped by the Alon Foundation and I was a fellow of the Yad Hanadiv Humanities Fellowships. Finally, a research grant of the Israel Science Foundation enabled the completion of the work.

In Jerusalem and Paris many helped me during the years of research and writing. My teachers Prof. Shlomo Hasson and Amiram Gonen discussed with me the findings in the light of current thinking in social sciences. Prof. Israel Finkelstein and Mr. Mordechai Aviam shared with me some of their archeological findings and, more important, their vast knowledge of the archeology of Palestine. The late Prof. Shalom Reichman read the manuscript of this work and my gratitude to him is immense. Dr. Rehav Rubin and Architect Giora Solar excavated with me a Frankish manor house, an excavation which contributed greatly to the understanding of such sites.

Numerous scholars made suggestions, passed on references, pointed out my mistakes, and induced me to revise my interpretations. I must thank Prof. Hans E. Mayer, Prof. Robert Fossier, Prof. Michel Balard, Prof. Jacques Le-Goff, Prof. Paul Claval, Prof. Jonathan Riley-Smith, Prof. Jean-Marie Pesez, Prof. Martin Biddle, Prof. Leon Pressouyre, and many others.

During the more than two hundred days I spent in field work I was accompanied by more than one hundred friends, students, colleagues, photographers, and surveyors. Many of them joined me for only a day or two and I cannot mention them all. Nevertheless, I would like to thank my students at the Avshalom Institute in Tel Aviv who accompanied me for six years, my students at the Hebrew University in Jerusalem, and the staff of various field study centers of the Society for the Protection of Nature in Israel. Ariel Vago, Boaz Buki, Gil Kovo, Ora Kerman, David Huli, and Yevgeni Mirman were among those who spent more time than the others studying the Frankish ruins. Boaz Buki and Dov Tal accompanied me in the flights above the sites. I owe much to their photographic talents.

My friends in Israel, Paris, and England were kind enough to listen to my endless discussions of my work. They encouraged me in every possible way. I would like to thank in particular Dr. Reuven Amitai-Preiss, Dr. Miri Rubin, and Dr. Naomi Tadmor.

Tamar Soffer produced the best possible maps and illustrations from my data. My mother-in-law Doris Lankin translated the manuscript into English. Shosh Zilberberg, the secretary of the Department of Geography of the Hebrew University, was also a true friend and helped me a lot in any possible way.

I owe a great debt to my supervisors Prof. Y. Ben-Arieh and Prof. B.Z. Kedar for their interest, criticism, and friendship. Prof. Ben-Arieh introduced me into the fascinating field of historical geography. I wish that I were able to be as dedicated to my students as he was and still is to me. Prof. Kedar was my first teacher in the history of the Middle Ages. His vast knowledge, his openmindedness, and the way he encouraged me to write and think in an unorthodox way are a model for university teaching.

To my children, Gali, who was born when this work was started, Yuval, for whom the Frankish sites were a fascinating play ground, and my younger daughter Maya, who was born when the work was finished, and to my wife Lenore, who helped me in every possible way and who was the best critic of any new idea, this book is dedicated with love.

Ronnie Ellenblum

ABBREVIATIONS

AAS	*Asian and African Studies*
AOL	*Archives de l'Orient latin*, 2 vols., Paris, 1881–1884
BEC	*Bibliothèque de l'ècole des chartes*
BSNAF	*Bulletin de la Société nationale des antiquaires de France*
BSOAS	*Bulletin of the School of Oriental and African Studies*
CCSL	*Corpus Christianorum, Series Latina*, Turnhoult, 1953–
CSCO	*Corpus Scriptorum Christianorum Orientalium*, Louvain, 1903–
DB	*Domesday Book*, 2 vols., Public Office Commission, 1783–1814
DOP	*Dumbarton Oaks Papers*
DRHC	*Documents relatifs à l'histoire des croisades*
EHR	*English Historical Review*
EI²	*Encyclopaedia of Islam*, 2nd edn.
IEJ	*Israel Exploration Journal*
IHC	*Itinera Hierosolymitan Crucesignatorum (saec. XII–XIII)*, ed. S. de Sandoli, 4 vols., Stadium Biblicum Franciscanum, Collectio maior, XXIV, Jerusalem, 1978–1984
JA	*Journal Asiatique*
JESHO	*Journal of the Economic and Social History of the Orient*
JPOS	*Journal of the Palestine Oriental Society*
JRAS	*Journal of the Royal Asiatic Society of Great Britain and Ireland*
JSAI	*Jerusalem Studies in Arabic and Islam*
OC	*Oriens christianus. Römische Halbjahreshefte für die Kunde des christlichen Orients*
PEFQS	*Palestine Exploration Fund Quarterly Statements*
PG	*Patrologia Cursus Completus, Series Graeca*, ed. J.P. Migne, 161 vols., Paris, 1857–

PL	*Patrologia Cursus Completus, Series Latina*, ed. J.P. Migne, 221 vols., Paris, 1844–1864
QDAP	*Quarterly of the Department of Antiquities in Palestine*
QFIAB	*Quellen und Forschungen aus italienischen Archiven und Bibliotheken*
RA	*Revue archéologique*
RB	*Revue biblique*
RBe	*Revue bénédictine*
RH	*Revue historique*
RHC	*Recueil des Historiens des Croisades*, ed. Académie des Inscriptions et Belles-Lettres, Paris, 1841–1906
RHC, Arm.	*RHC, Document arméniens*, 2 vols., Paris, 1869–1906
RHC, Grec.	*RHC, Historiens Grecs*, 2 vols., Paris, 1875–1881
RHC, Lois	*RHC, Les Assises de Jérusalem*, 2 vols., Paris, 1841–1843
RHC, HOcc.	*RHC, Historiens occidentaux*, 5 vols., Paris, 1844–1895
RHC, HOr.	*RHC, Historiens orientaux*, 5 vols., Paris, 1872–1906
RHDFE	*Revue historique de droit français et étranger*
ROL	*Revue de l'Orient latin*
RS	*Rerum Britannicarum medii aevi scriptores or Chronicles and Memorials of Great Britain and Ireland during the Middle Ages Published under Direction of the Master of the Rolls* (Rolls Series), 99 vols., London, 1858–1897
ZDPV	*Zeitschrift des deutschen Palästina-Vereins*

Primary sources appear in abbreviated forms in the footnotes (see pp. 288–295).

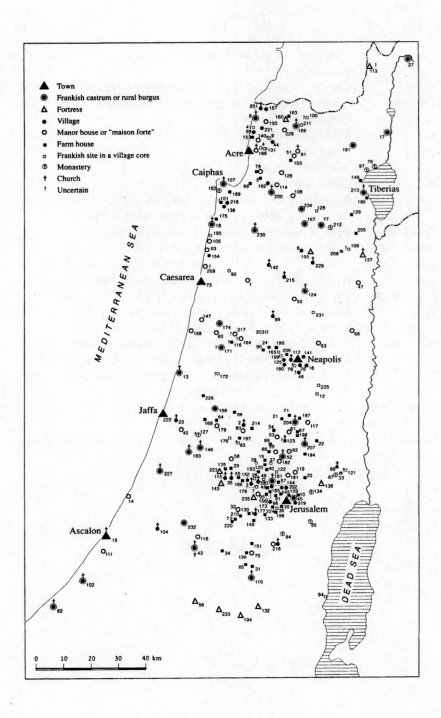

Town

Frankish castrum or rural burgus

Fortress

Village

Manor house or "maison forte"

Farm house

Frankish site in a village core

Monastery

Church

Uncertain

MEDITERRANEAN SEA

DEAD SEA

Acre

Caiphas

Tiberias

Caesarea

Neapolis

Jaffa

Ascalon

Jerusalem

0   10   20   30   40 km

Map 1   Frankish rural sites in Palestine
castri, castelli, villages, farm houses, manor houses, mills, isolated buildings, and
unknown sites

1 'Aara (Castellum Arearum), 157/212
2 'Abud (Casale Sancte Marie), 156/158
3 Abu Ghosh (Emaus Fontenoid), 160/134
4 Abu Sinan (Busenen), 166/262
5 Afeq (Kurdana, Recordana), 160/250
6 'Afula, 177/223
7 Kh. al-'Ajab, 163/138
8 Akhziv (al-Zib, Casale Humberti de Pace),
159/272
9 'Amqa (Ancra), 166/264
10 'Anatā (Aneth, Anathoth), 175/135
11 'Aqaba (Aila), 150/881
12 'Aqraba, 182/170
13 Tell Arshaf (Arsuf, Arsur), 132/178
14 Ashdod-Yam (Mina al-Qal'a, Castellum
Beroart), 114/132
15 Ashqelon (Ascalon), 177/180
16 'Askar (Aschar), 177/180
17 'Ateret (Bayt al-Akhzan, Le Chastelez),
209/267
18 'Atlit (Castellum Peregrinorum), 144/234
19 'Ayn 'Arik, 164/146
20 'Ayn Fara (Farafronte), 178/137
21 'Ayn Mushariqa, 169/159
22 'Ayn Samiya, 181/135
23 Azor (Yazur, Casel des Plains), 131/159
24 Kh. Babriya (near Sabastiyya), 166/186
25 al-Ba'ina, 175/258
26 Balata (Balathas), 177/179
27 Baniyas (Belinas), 215/294
28 Bauwariya, 151/142
29 Bayt 'Anan (Bethanam), 160/139
30 Kh. Bayt Arza, 167/126
31 Bayt 'Aynun, 162/108
32 Bayt 'Itab (Bethaatap), 155/126
33 Bayt Jubr, 191/139
34 Bayt Nasib (Bethenase), 151/111
35 Bayt Nuba (Bethnoble), 153/140
36 Bayt Safafa (Bethafava?), 169/128
37 Bayt Sila, 164/142
38 Bayt Surik (Bethsurit), 164/136
39 Baytuniya (Beitiumen), 166/143
40 Bayt 'Ur al-Fawqa (Vetus Bethor), 161/144
41 Ben-'Ammi (Umm al-Faraj, Le Fierge),
161/267
42 Bet-Dagan (Bayt Dajan, Casal Maen),
134/156
43 Bet-Guvrin (Bayt Jibrin, Bethgibelin),
140/112
44 Bet-Ha'emeq (Mimas), 164/263

45 Bethany (Ayzariya, St. Lazarus), 174/131
46 Betheri (Kh. al-Tira?), site unknown
47 Bet-She'an (Baysan, Bethsan), 197/211
48 Bet-Telem (Bayt Tulma), 166/134
49 Biddu, 164/138
50 Bil'ama (Castellum Beleismum), 177/205
51 Bi'na, 260/175
52 al-Bira (Magna Mahomeria), 170/146
53 Bir Zayt, 169/153
54 Budd al-Burj, 167/157
55 al-Burayj, 158/140
56 al-Burj (Castrum Ficuum), 141/095
57 al-Burj, 167/132
58 al-Burj (Burj al-Habis, Qal'at al-Tantura,
Gith), 152/145
59 al-Burj, 168/137
60 al-Burj al-Ahmar (Le Tour rouge),
146/182
61 Burj Bardawil, 173/156
62 Burj Baytin (Bethel), 172/148
63 Burj al-Far'ah, 183/188
64 Burj al-Haniya, 147/159
65 Burj al-Haska, 159/108
66 Kh. Burj Kafriya, 166/148
67 Burj al-Lissana, 175/156
68 Burj al-Malih, 193/193
69 Burj al-Sahal, 162/248
70 Burj Sansan, 153/123
71 Burj Sinjil, 174/161
72 Burj al-Sur (Bethsura), 159/110
73 Caesaria (Cesaire), 140/212
74 Casale Album, site unknown
75 Castrum Feniculi, site unknown
76 Capernaum, 204/254
77 Dabburiya (Buria), 185/233
78 Da'uq (Casale Doc, Castiel Doc), 161/253
79 Dawarta, 177/179
80 Dayr Abu Mash'al (Bellifortis?), 156/156
81 Dayr al-Asad (St. George de La Baena),
175/259
82 Dayr al-Balah (Darom), 088/092
83 Dayr al-Jidi, 154/151
84 Dayr Kharitun, 172/117
85 Dayr Mar Saba (St. Sabbas), 181/123
86 Dayr al-Mir, 153/162
87 Dayr al-Qilt (St. George de Choziba),
190/139
88 Dayr al-Quruntal (Quarantene), 190/142
89 Dayr Sa'ida, 167/152
90 Dayr Sarur, 162/187

Hallward Library - Issue Receipt

Customer name: Hill, Claire Victoria

Title: Frankish rural settlement in the Latin
kingdom of Jerusalem / Ronnie Ellenblum.
ID: 1003513839
Due: 14/05/2007 23:59

Total items: 1
18/03/2007 19:00

All items must be returned before the due date
and time.

WWW.nottingham.ac.uk/is

PART ONE

PRESENTATION OF THE PROBLEM

CHAPTER ONE

A SEGREGATED SOCIETY OR AN
INTEGRATED SOCIETY?

In many studies published in the last forty years the common analysis concludes that Frankish rural settlement in the Levant was very limited. The Franks, it was argued, confined themselves almost exclusively to the large cities and fortresses and engaged to a very limited extent in agricultural activities.[1] "Let it be stated from the beginning," says Joshua Prawer, "the Crusaders' society was predominantly, almost exclusively, an urban society."[2] The Frankish urban society and the Muslim rural one were depicted as being almost totally segregated and as having very limited social, cultural, and geographical relations.

The interpretation which had prevailed until the end of the 1940s presented, while relying on the same sources, a totally different picture of Frankish society and of its relations with the local communities.[3] This interpretation assumed that the Franks had become highly assimilated with the local Oriental communities and that an integrated "Franco-Syrian society" consisting of the ruling Franks and of their autochthonous subjects was created during the period of the Crusades. As E. G. Rey wrote, the Franks and their indigenous subjects lived together not only in the countryside, but in the cities, in the mountains, in the ports, and even in the ranks of the Occidental army.[4]

---

[1] Cahen, 1950–1951, 286; Smail, 1956, 57–63; Prawer, 1980c, 102–142; Richard, 1980, 655; Hamilton, 1980, 90; Pringle, 1986a, 12; Pringle, 1989, 18–19; Benvenisti, 1970, 219 and 233, distinguished between Frankish villages, the number of which being "very small, less than ten." and manor houses which were quite numerous. Cf. Benvenisti, 1982. Cf. also Smail, 1973, 80; "Professor Prawer considers that nearly all Syrian Franks were townees, without roots in the countryside and, as always, his arguments are well grounded . . . The conclusion seems irresistible that Europeans were rare exceptions among a rural peasantry composed almost entirely of indigenous Syrians."   [2] Prawer, 1980c, 102–103.

[3] Rey, 1866, 17–19; Dodu, 1914, 42–75; Madelin, 1916, 258–314; Madelin, 1918; Duncalf, 1916, 137–145; Grousset, 1934–1936, I, 287, 314; II, 141, 225, 264, 518, 615, 754–755; III, Intro. xiv–xv, and 57–59, 61–62; Johns, 1934.   [4] Rey, 1866, 17.

The basic assumptions of this interpretation were rejected already in the 1950s by R. C. Smail and J. Prawer. Smail was the first to oppose the basic assumptions of the new model and those of the earlier model. In his famous *Crusading Warfare 1097–1193*, he wrote:

> The student is left to choose between two sharply differing conceptions of the nature of Franco-Syrian society. On the one hand are the scholars who have regarded the orientalizing of Frankish manners in Syria, and the instances which appear in the sources of friendly relations between Franks and Muslims, as evidence of the creation of a Franco-Syrian nation and civilization; on the other hand are those who have assigned greater importance to other aspects of social organization in the Latin states, and to the instances of hostile relations between Franks and Muslims. They consider that the Franks remained a ruling class, separated from their Syrian subjects by language and religion, with force as the ultimate sanction of their dominion.[5]

Smail did not challenge the information presented by the proponents of the former school, maintaining that the difference between the two approaches arises not from the uncovering of new information unbeknown to his predecessors but from different methods of interpreting the same information. His school attributed great importance to evidence of strained intercommunal relations and minimized the importance of evidence hinting at the assimilation of the Franks with the Oriental communities. The earlier school favored a completely different interpretation of the same facts and emphasized evidence of the good relations which purportedly existed between the Franks and the inhabitants of the occupied countries. Smail accepted, for example, that the Franks did employ Syrian doctors, cooks, servants, and artisans; that they "clothed themselves in eastern garments" and included "fruit and dishes of the country" in their diet; that their houses were planned according to Syrian style; that they "had dancing girls at their entertainments; professional mourners at their funerals; [that they] took baths; used soap [and] ate sugar."[6] However, according to Smail, all these habits were not indicative of cultural assimilation and did not testify to anything more than accommodation to the external conditions of life.

Smail argued that the historical interpretation of his predecessors was influenced by the expansionist ambitions of France on the eve of World War I and was aimed at proving the existence of the French "special genius" for colonial rule. The so called enlightened rule of the Franks in the Levant during the Middle Ages was purportedly one of the manifestations of this "genius." The basic assumptions on which both methods of interpretation are

---

[5] Smail, 1956, 40; cf. 62–63.   [6] Smail, 1956, 43.

founded are called "conceptions" by Smail. According to him, it is the "conception" which establishes the relative importance of known facts, connects them, and vests them with social, economic, cultural, and political significance. In short, Smail's "conception" is the "model" of today.

Models, says Haggett, are a network of theories, laws, equations, or assumptions which indicate our attitude towards a world which we think we see. The construction of such models, he adds, "is inevitable because there is no fixed dividing line between facts and beliefs."[7] The term "model" is therefore used in this study even though many of the originators of the two contradictory approaches did not use it and that it is doubtful if they would have claimed to have developed "models" at all. Nonetheless it is a fact that more or less the same data led to the creation of two radically opposed interpretations, each of which was supported by the most prominent scholars of the relevant period: the one propounding the integration of the Franks into eastern society and the other, their total segregation.

Smail analysed the overt and covert basic assumptions of the "French model"; however, the model which he developed, together with Joshua Prawer, arguing that there was cultural and geographical segregation between the Franks and the local inhabitants, is explained by a series of assumptions each emerging from a previous assumption and sustaining all the others.

Therefore, the first aim of the present study will be to define the basic assumptions underlying the model developed by Smail and Prawer (called here for the sake of convenience the "existing model") which concludes that Frankish settlement in the Levant was of very limited scope.

The existing model – a segregated society

An "urban society"

The proponents of the existing model maintain that the Frankish settlement in the Levant was accompanied by a radical social metamorphosis which changed a largely rural society into an urban one. In accordance with this approach, the Crusaders preferred, or were forced to prefer, life in the cities or fortresses rather than in villages; and the Frankish society underwent, in fact, an accelerated process of urbanization. Prawer describes this change in the following words:

The castle and the countryside, the two dominant features of the early Middle Ages that prevailed well into the central period . . . did not play the same role in the Latin

[7] Haggett, 1965, 23.

Near East . . . The new perspective [called here "the existing model"] . . . describes [the] Crusader society as mainly urban and the Syro-Palestinian cities not only as centers of urban, royal or seigniorial administration but also as the principal habitat of the Western conquerors and immigrants.[8]

The existence of large and well-protected cities in the Eastern Mediterranean, which were larger and better protected than most contemporary cities in the Latin West, enabled according to this model, the process of accelerated urbanization. The Eastern cities are perceived as having provided conditions of security and convenience which were preferable to the hard physical conditions and the shaky security which were the lot of the rural population. The Franks may not have been capable of building new cities, but they could appreciate the advantages of settling in the existing cities. Prawer claims that "The creation of the Crusaders' city-settlement and city population was conditioned and defined by the intrusion of a mainly agricultural and village-dwelling society into a country where the city had been for centuries an established and central institution."[9] The Levantine cities, which continued to serve during the whole course of history as centers of habitation and commerce, enabled and encouraged in their very existence this process of urbanization.

The lack of security: the external danger

The external and internal dangers are perceived as being the all-important element. It is assumed that the Franks were exposed to perpetual Muslim attacks which threatened their very existence and forced them to find shelter behind the fortified walls of the cities and fortresses: "the threat of invasion [was] almost continuous, but many of the subject peoples never fully consented to Latin rule, and on important occasions were to show themselves either doubtfully loyal or actively hostile."[10]

It should be noted that the exponents of the existing model were well aware of the fact (which will be discussed in full in the chapter dealing with criticism of the model) that the attacks from the external borders were not unremitting and certainly did not threaten the whole kingdom. Therefore they stressed another aspect of the security threat: the threat from within.

---

[8] Prawer, 1977, 179; cf. Smail, 1973, 67.   [9] Prawer, 1980c, 102.
[10] Smail, 1956, 204. Cf. Cahen, 1940, 327: "Les caractères de l'occupation franque découlent essentiellement d'un fait, leur petit nombre. Se disperser au milieu de populations neutres ou hostiles eût constitué pour les Francs un danger de mort; aussi se groupent-ils dans un petit nombre de localitès. La masse des petites gens reste dans quelques villes . . . Dans les campagnes, l'occupation franque est totalement dèpourvue de base rurale."

Collaboration between the local population and the external enemy

According to the supporters of the existing model, the state of insecurity which compelled the Franks to settle in the fortified cities and fortresses emanated also from the fact that the autochthonous population was mainly Muslim and tended to collaborate with their fellow-religionists across the borders. The Franks, therefore, could not find peace even in the heart of their own Kingdom since the decisive majority of the country's inhabitants were Muslims. The protagonists of the existing model assumed, as a self-evident fact, that the process of Islamization of the local population had already reached such a stage by the twelfth century that the country was inhabited mainly by Muslims. Prawer writes: "The countryside was settled in an overwhelming majority by Muslims, but with a fair sprinkling of Oriental Christians of different denominations, whereas in Galilee there were additional Jewish agglomerations and in Samaria autochthonous Samaritan villages."[11]

The local Christians also preferred, according to this theoretical framework, to collaborate with the Muslims with whom they shared a common language and culture. Smail argues:

All Syrian Christians, orthodox and monophysite, had lived for centuries under the generally tolerant Muslim rule of the caliphs . . . Between them and their Latin overlords there was the bond of a common faith, but they were tied also to the Muslims by history, language and habits. They gave the Franks no trouble, but they could regard the prospect of Muslim rule with equanimity . . . It would therefore appear that the native Christians provided no firm basis for Latin rule, and that they increased rather than alleviated the Franks' military problems.[12]

Even Claude Cahen, who accepted only part of these basic assumptions, tended to ascribe the existence of some of the Frankish fortresses to the internal danger. From the architectural structure of some of them he concluded that they were intended to serve as observation posts in the areas that were occupied by the Franks themselves:

Les spécialistes de l'architecture militaire des Croisés n'ont peut-être pas porté une attention suffisante à la signification des châteaux qu'ils étudiaient. Implicitement, ils les considèrent comme destinés tous d'abord à la défense du territoire contre des ennemis extérieurs. Tel est évidemment le cas de ceux qui se trouvent aux points stratégiques des frontières successives. Mais beaucoup ne peuvent avoir eu d'autre fonction (comme aussi en Occident) que de surveiller des districts de l'intérieur.[13]

---

[11] Prawer, 1980e, 201.   [12] Smail, 1956, 52.   [13] Cahen, 1983, 169.

The tendency of the Oriental Christians to cooperate with the Muslims is attributed also to the Latin priests' taking the place of the Greek Orthodox clergy in the ecclesiastical hierarchy. The Muslim rulers, it is claimed, had vested the Oriental Christians with broad autonomy in matters of religious rites and had allowed them to appoint their own religious leadership. Additional reasons for the probable tendency of the local Christians to co-operate with the Muslims were found in the fact that a not inconsiderable part of the Eastern Christian communities continued to live, during the whole course of the Frankish regime, in areas which were under Muslim control. The Eastern Christians had also probably felt humiliated because their legal status was inferior to that of the Franks, who had a separate legal system from that of the local Christians.[14]

The assumption that the Christian population shared a common language and culture with the Muslims within and across the border is actually composed of two additional assumptions, first that the Arabization of the Christian population of the Levant had been completed before the Frankish occupation[15] and second that the Arabization of the Turkish tribes, which constituted an appreciable part of the forces against whom the Franks had fought, had also been completed by the twelfth century, so that differences of language, culture, and customs between the local Christian population and the Muslim Turks were almost non-existent.[16]

The existing model does not excel in details concerning the processes of Islamization and Arabization of the local population, but the picture it presents does include two elements: first, that the local population had been subjected since the middle of the seventh century to a process of cultural assimilation into the ruling Arab-Muslim culture, a process which caused many of them to embrace Islam. Secondly, those local Christians who had not become Muslims by then had adopted the Arab-Muslim culture and the

---

[14] On the ousting of the Greek ecclesiastical hierarchy and for the confiscation of property belonging to the Greek church, see Raymond of Aguilers, 154; Matthew of Edesse, ed. *RHC*, ch. 21, 54–55; William of Tyre, 6, 23, 340. For the transfer of Greek property to the Latin monastery of Mt. Tabor, see Hospital, II, AI, 897–898. For the separate judiciary of Latins and local Christians, see Jean of Ibelin, I, ch. 4, 26. Cf. Hamilton, 1980, 161–163; Mayer, 1977, 1–33. The break between the Greek and the Latin clergy was apparently expressed also in the fact that only very few of the Latins knew Greek. See William of Tyre, 15, 21, 703. For the claim that the Muslims vested the Eastern churches with religious autonomy, see Sivan, 1967a.

[15] Hamilton, 1980, 159–169; Cahen, 1971, 285–292; Cahen, 1972, 62–63; Riley-Smith, 1977, 9–22.

[16] Prawer finds no substantive differences between Turkish Muslims and other Muslims. One can gather from his writings that he does not ascribe great importance to the Turkish influence, particularly within the boundaries of the Kingdom. See for example: "Within the frontiers of the Latin states there were virtually no turks or nomadic Turcomans . . . During the last quarter of the eleventh century when the Selchükid Turks, the secular arm of the 'Abbasids, pushed the Fatimids out of Syria and Palestine, there probably followed some strengthening of the Sunnah." Prawer, 1985b, 62.

use of the Arab language. It transpires from this approach that even if the Franks were not exposed to the risk of daily attacks from external enemies, those who dared to settle in the rural areas were exposed to danger from the potential hostility of the Arabized inhabitants – both Muslims and Christians.

The demographic ratio

According to the exponents of the existing model, the precarious existence of the Frankish states was still further aggravated by the demographic ratio which clearly favored the Muslim inhabitants of the country, whose numbers, although considerably depleted before and during the conquest, far exceeded those of the Frankish population. When they produce figures, some of these scholars maintained that the Frankish population constituted between 15% to 25% of the total population.[17]

The Crusader fortresses

The proponents of the existing model repeatedly emphasize the defensive or offensive role of the fortresses which were built by the Franks. Frankish settlement outside the bounds of the big cities is considered by them to be mainly of strategic value. The assumption that there was no Frankish rural settlement ruled out, in practice, any serious examination of the economic, administrative and symbolic roles of the fortresses:

Ce qui caractérisé cette société féodale [wrote Jean Richard] c'est son caractère médiocrement rural . . . La population militaire du royaume, de la principauté, des comtés, est une population surtout urbaine. Elle reside soit dans les châteaux dont, très vite, les états latins se sont herissés: en effet, conscients de la faiblesse des effectifs qu'ils pouvaient opposer aux Musulmans, les Croisés ont mis sur pied tout un réseau de forteresses, quelques-unes formidables, d'autres plus modestes, qui garantissaient les territoires contre les invasions. Les seigneurs de ces châteaux, avec leurs propres vassaux, y resident pratiquement en permanence pour en assurer la garde.[18]

Even Smail, who conceded that the fortresses had administrative and economic roles in the organization of rural estates, considered these roles to be secondary to their strategic value.[19]

---

[17] Prawer, 1975, I, 570–571; Prawer, 1980c, 102–103, 117; Russell, 1985, 295–314; Benvenisti, 1970, 25–28. [18] Richard, 1980, 556.

[19] Compare Smail, 1956, 204–244, with Smail, 1951, 133–135, 143. It should be noted, however, that even though Smail does focus primarily on the military functions of the castle he makes the point (Smail, 1956, 60–62 and 209) that castles had other functions too as "the physical basis of overlordship" (Smail, 1956, 61).

The previous model – an integrated society

The former model, which was rejected by Smail and Prawer at the beginning of the fifties, presented, while relying on the very same sources, a totally different picture of Frankish society and of its relations with the local communities.[20] The proponents of this model claimed that the Crusades created an integrated society which consisted of the Franks and of their subjects. The Franks, they argued, were deeply influenced by the Oriental habits and were responsible for the unprecedented atmosphere of law, order, and tolerance which prevailed in Palestine during the twelfth and the thirteenth centuries. They claimed that the Frankish regime was a "régime de la tolérance en matière religieuse"; and that there was "résolution des vainqueurs de n'imposer aux anciens habitants de la contrée, en dehors des obligations féodales, l'humiliation d'aucune servitude politique."[21] Rey, Dodu, Madelin, Hayek, and Grousset idealized this alleged friendly relationship and did not make any distinction between the relations of the Franks with the local Christians and their relations with the Muslims. "Une seule chose est certaine," wrote Dodu, "c'est que, la race n'ayant pas été plus que la religion un obstacle, la fusion des deux sociétés s'opéra sous la sceptre des rois francs avec une rapidité à peine contrariée par l'état de guerre."[22] This idealization of the intercultural relationship, which Smail labeled "something more than [French] propaganda written with reference to a peace treaty,"[23] facilitated the creation of the existing model, which, in its turn, told a completely different story of social, political, and geographical segregation.

Smail's assumption that the previous model was influenced by French colonialistic sentiments is certainly feasible. The discussion of the sociological and intellectual background of the scholars is as legitimate as the discussion of their sources. Smail, who was very much ahead of his times, paved the way for a discussion of similar questions concerning himself and his co-thinkers. Is it possible, for example, that Prawer's dichotomous approach was influenced also by the manner in which Zionism interpreted the relations between the European immigrants and the local Muslim population? Similarly could some of the conceptions accepted today by the scholars have been influenced by the atmosphere of de-colonization in Britain after World War II? The idea that every model is influenced to a greater or lesser extent by the contemporary cultural and political background is certainly true with respect to every study, including the present one.

---

[20] See n. 3.   [21] Dodu, 1914, 75.   [22] Dodu, 1914, 52–53; Cf. also Hayek, 1925.
[23] Smail, 1956, 41.

The existing model, developed by Smail and Prawer, sounds convincing and reasonable and has continued to influence scholarly thinking since it was formulated. The great influence of this model on the historiography of the Crusades and on the historical analysis of Frankish settlement in the Levant justifies a closer examination of each of its components.

CHAPTER TWO

CRITICISM OF THE EXISTING MODEL

An "urban society"?

The settlement of the Franks in cities and the creation of a Frankish "urban society" are presented as "exceptional phenomena," which makes examination of their nature all the more difficult.[1] It is not easy to define a Frankish "city" or a Frankish "town" and it is even harder to define an "urban society" of the twelfth century, the difficulties emanating from the absence of clear criteria, and the lack of any parallel to so dramatic a process of urbanization. The terms "town" or "city" might refer to a certain type of spatial organization, to a minimal number of people living on the same site, or to the existence of an encircling wall. It might also refer to a place where certain occupations are practiced or indicate the volume of trade and services. The term "city" might also be used as an historical reference to a Roman "civitas." It might indicate the existence of a bishopric see or of a certain legal status.

There is no doubt that Antioch, Edessa, Acre, and Jerusalem were cities in the twelfth century, even though we know practically nothing about their urban structure. However, can we define the other "cities" of the Latin Kingdom as such? Was Nablus a city or a village? And what about Nazareth, Le Safforie, Bethsan, Sebaste, Gaza (Gadres), Hebron, and the other major Frankish settlements? Do we know anything about their geographical structure or about their services, and volume of trade? Was there any real difference in the size and in the historical, legal, and ecclesiastical status, between the "cities" and some of the "villages" of Frankish Palestine? Were there differences in the kind of economic functions of the "city" and the "village"? Did the inhabitants of even the largest cities engage in agriculture?

It can only be noted that till today no study has been made of the size of

---

[1] Prawer, 1980c.

12

the non-built-up areas of the "Crusader city," even though a superficial examination of the sources will testify to the importance of agriculture in places like Jerusalem, Nablus, Tyre, Tripoli, and other "urban" settlements.[2] The research on Frankish cities in Palestine (with the exception of Jerusalem and Acre) is still at its very beginning.[3]

Indeed, medieval chroniclers tended to divide the Frankish settlements into "cities" and "fortresses" but their criteria might not be relevant to our discussion. The term "city" is applied sometimes to a bishopric see, and it does not necessarily have a geographical sense. The same might also be true of the terminology used by modern scholars. Places such as Saffuriya (Le Safforie), Nazareth, Sebaste, and St. Abraham (Hebron) appear in Prawer and Benvenisti's map of Crusader Palestine as "unfortified towns" only, so it seems, because they had actual or historical bishopric sees.[4] In any event, the various concepts relating to city and fortress apparently cover a whole spectrum of settlement types.

No lesser a difficulty arises in the very use of the term "urban society." An "urban society" is not created merely by lumping a population together in a settlement surrounded by a wall. The process by which a "rural society" becomes an "urban society" is a major sociological change which engulfs all human, cultural, economic, geographic, and psychological domains. The process of historical urbanization creates new types of mentality and values and its stages of development can be determined only retroactively. I am not sure it is possible to speak about the existence of an "urban society" in settlements about which we know very little and where the economic and social structure of its inhabitants is almost completely unknown.

At the basis of this book is the conception that the study of medieval settlement cannot rely on the division of settlement types into "agricultural settlements" and "urban" ones – terminology which, for the most part, cannot be proved. The types of settlement are, first and foremost, the spatial manifestation of social structures. One cannot fix boundaries between, and separate artificially, the social structure and its spatial elements. Similarly one cannot ignore the social and spatial background which the Franks brought with them from their countries of origin.

There is no doubt that the Frankish society created in the Levant was not

---

[2] About the agricultural pursuits of the inhabitants of Jerusalem, see Holy Sepulcher, no. 96, 1126–1130, 213–214; no. 161, 1176, 313; no. 163, 1177, 316; Kohler, no. 17, 1125, 125–127; Hospital, no. 84, 1129, 78; no. 138, 1141, 113–114; no. 150, 1143, 121–122. For the intensive agricultural activity of the inhabitants of Sidon, see Strehlke, no. 62, Feb. 11, 1128, 51. For agricultural pursuits within the confines of the urban security set-up, see Holy Sepulcher, no. 28, 1125, 90.   [3] Cf. Bahat, 1990; Prawer, 1977; Prawer, 1985a.

[4] Prawer & Benvenisti, 1970.

an exact copy of any contemporary European society and that it was influenced by the special conditions of life existing there. It can be assumed that the pattern of Frankish settlement was also influenced by social changes and different styles of living. However, the assumption that the Franks abandoned almost completely their rural way of life in favor of an "almost exclusive urban society," while at the same time retaining an appreciable number of the social and political elements which they brought with them from Europe, is difficult to accept without better founded evidence than that produced till now.

The external danger

Did the actual extent and frequency of Muslim raids on the Latin Kingdom justify a Frankish reluctance to settle in rural areas? Conder, who dealt with this question at the end of the nineteenth century, maintained that during most of the twelfth century the Frankish Kingdom enjoyed comparative peace and prosperity: "the Latins in Syria enjoyed, for nearly a century, an amount of peace and prosperity greater than that of most European lands during the same period, and that often for many years they were untroubled by war, while for the first sixty years their contests were all on the boundaries of the kingdom."[5]

Apparently several parts of the Kingdom did enjoy comparative peace and quiet, at least from the 1120s onwards. It would appear also that there were regions, such as the lordships of Arsur, Caesarea, and the royal domain of Acre, which did not suffer from any Muslim attack until the end of Saladin's offensive in the 1180s.

The spatial distribution of Muslim raids is important to our discussion because, when compared to the spatial distribution of Frankish castles, it testifies to the weak link between the construction of fortresses and the external danger. Many castles and fortified towers were built in the comparatively safe regions of Caesarea and the Western Galilee (Calansue, Caco, the Red Tower, Castellum Arearum, Castellum Rogerii Longobardi, Turris Salinarum, Castrum Feniculi, Merle, Castellum Regis, Le Saffran, Caymont, and many more), whereas in the very regions which were attacked several

---

[5] Conder, 1897, 161. Razi, 1970, 30, also pointed out this fact: "In the period between 1120 and 1163 the military superiority of the Kingdom of Jerusalem over its northern neighbors became more and more obvious. And before the conquest of Damascus by Nur al-Din they were not divested of this superiority. As a result most of the conflicts between the Crusaders and the Muslims occurred beyond the borders of the Galilee. The number of Muslim incursions into the Galilee were few and of limited exent, and the inhabitants enjoyed a long and continuous period of peace and security" (my translation). Cf. Rheinheimer, 1990, 228–229.

times, such as the mountains of Nablus (besides the city of Nablus itself), there were practically no Frankish fortresses. Though it is possible to claim that Calansue, Caco, and the Red Tower were built when Muslim raids from Ascalon were still a perceived threat, Ascalon never endangered such distant localities. In any case we do not have any testimony of such farreaching attacks.

Thus, if there were any connection between the construction of fortresses and the external danger then at least in the twelfth century that connection was an inverse one. In other words, the number of so-called fortresses constructed in the comparatively safe areas was much greater than the number of fortresses actually constructed in areas exposed to continuous danger.

As stated before, the region which was exposed more than the others to Muslim military incursions was the region which faced Ascalon. William of Tyre points out on many occasions, and very explicitly, that the fortresses erected in this area were intended to prevent incursions by the Ascalonites.[6] However, an examination of the history of military confrontations between the two rivals reveals difficulties even with respect to this commonly cited example.

It is important to point out that in this region, too, no fortresses were constructed during the first decades of the Frankish state. The first fortress – that of Bethgibelin – was built only in the 1130s.

The military relationship between Ascalon and the Kingdom of Jerusalem can be divided, in accordance with the frequency and multiplicity of the hostilities between them, into two main stages: in the first stage, between 1099 and the mid-twenties of the twelfth century, the military confrontations between the two were almost incessant. In the second period, which started apparently in the mid-twenties of the twelfth century and continued until the conquest of the city in 1153, there is no mention of any major confrontation between the two rivals. The hostilities between Ascalon and the Kingdom of Jerusalem were of limited scope and hardly digressed beyond the vicinity of Ascalon. Both sides suffered losses of life and property, but it would appear that in the second period it was the people of Ascalon who were exposed to danger rather than their opponents.

Even William of Tyre, who stressed again and again the danger from Ascalon, noted that already in 1137 only new recruits dared to attack the Franks, while the veteran soldiers who had already tasted the effects of combat with the Franks desisted from doing so.[7] Nevertheless, almost all the

---

[6] William of Tyre, 14, 22, 659–660; 15, 21, 306–307; 15, 25, 707–708; 14, 8, 640.
[7] William of Tyre, 14, 22, 659–660.

Frankish fortresses of this region were erected in the very period which was more secure than the previous one.

The dividing line between the two periods is not sharply defined and does not begin at some fixed date. The beginning of the period during which the barbs from Ascalon were blunted can be found already in the first two decades of the twelfth century. Even at this early stage, the Franks were victorious in an appreciable number of battles, and even then they had succeeded, time and again, in damaging the rural infrastructure of the Muslim city. Evidence of early Frankish incursions testifies to the havoc which the Franks wrought on Ascalon's agricultural hinterland. This havoc caused the governor of Ascalon to sign, already in 1111, a peace treaty with the Franks, despite the overt objections of the rulers in Egypt.[8]

The buds of Ascalon's military weakness can be found also in the fact that its defenders were not able to stop the Frankish attempt to conquer Egypt in 1118. It would appear that Ascalon's last serious attack against Frankish territory occurred in 1124, and even then, according to William of Tyre, the Ascalonites dared to attack Jerusalem only because they discovered that the entire Frankish army was occupied with the siege of Tyre.[9]

During the second period, which began in the twenties and ended with the final conquest of Ascalon in 1153, the military strength of the Frankish regime was consolidated and Ascalon was no longer able to endanger the Kingdom. The written sources show explicitly that the danger from Ascalon did not pass completely but that it decreased to the extent that Frankish agricultural settlement near the newly built fortresses became possible.[10]

---

[8] Already in 1102, Albert of Aachen, in describing the Crusader attack on the agricultural surroundings of Ascalon, wrote that "they destroyed vineyards and crops and all the produce of that year." Albert of Aachen, IX, 15, 599. He tells us also that in 1106 Baldwin's men "destroyed vineyards, fig trees and every other kind of tree." Albert of Aachen, IX, 51, 624. For the peace agreement which the governor of Ascalon sought to sign with the Crusaders in 1111, see Ibn al-Qalanisi, trans. Gibb, 108–109; Ibn al-Athir, ed. *RHC*, IV-1, 277; Albert of Aachen, XI, 35–37, 680–681; Cf. Prawer, 1956, 231–240. On the other hand, for the attack by Ascalon and the Fatimid army on the Christians near Ramla in 1107, in which 400 people were killed, see Albert of Aachen, X, 8, 636–638. For the unsuccessful attack by Ascalon against the Mt. Hebron area in 1109, which reached the gates of Jerusalem, see Albert of Aachen, X, 33–35, 646–647; for another attack against the Crusaders on the Jaffa–Jerusalem road in 1109, which apparently originated from Ascalon, see Fulcher of Chartres, II, 37, 514–518.

[9] For the last serious attack by Ascalonites, carried out in 1124, which reached Bira, see Fulcher of Chartres, II, 731–732; William of Tyre relates that the people who remained in the city and its environs were fully capable of repulsing the attack. William of Tyre, 13, 8, 595.

[10] In their guerrilla attacks the Ascalonites took advantage of exceptional periods of weakness suffered by the Frankish army as, for example, in the attack on Teqo'a in 1139, when the Frankish army was engaged in besieging the Cave Fortress in the Gilead. The attack ended with the approach of the Frankish army. William of Tyre, 15, 6, 682–683. For a similiar event, see William of Tyre, 11, 20, 525. In 1141 William of Tyre still ascribed the construction of Ibelin to the need for defense against Ascalon. William of Tyre, 15, 24, 706–707. But even in his opinion the danger

It is worthwhile to note what Prawer, who relied on William of Tyre, had to say about the construction of fortresses around Ascalon:

During the reign of Fulk of Anjou [1132 – 41] the power of the Crusader State was on a permanent incline . . . The whole of the southern coast line was in ruins because *the Crusaders* [my emphasis] would invade and destroy the fields. But the Egyptian city maintained its artificial existence thanks to the continuous assistance of the Egyptian rulers . . . The Crusaders designed a new plan for solving the problem of Ascalon. During a period of four years they surrounded the city with a network of fortresses, built on the main invasion and infiltration routes, and at the same time worked out a plan for self-defence which was something of a revolutionary novelty in border defence: the creation of a Crusader agricultural settlement which the deeper its roots were implanted, the more it strengthened the military power.[11]

Prawer did not try to reconcile the contradiction between the obvious Frankish military superiority, as reflected in the damage inflicted on the region of Ascalon, and the Franks' need to protect themselves against an aggressive enemy. This contradiction is accentuated by the presentation of the Frankish agricultural settlers as "fighting farmers," enlisted to safeguard the country. However, the contradiction can be resolved, in my opinion, by separating the Frankish military superiority, which enabled the establishment of rural settlements and castles, from the fact that these settlements endured, from time to time, hostilities from Ascalon, and thus required the aid of the troops stationed in the fortresses. The need for protection of this nature disappeared completely in the second half of the twelfth century, after the fall of Ascalon to the Franks.

The castles of the south-eastern part of the Kingdom were used, as elsewhere in Europe, as settlement kernels, and their establishment testified to Frankish military supremacy and not to its weakness.

The construction of the castles without any apparent Ascalonite objection and their lengthy deployment without any serious attempt on the part of Ascalon to conquer them, testify to this superiority. Although the very

---

from Ascalon subsided during the course of the thirties and it was this lesser danger which led to the construction of an additional fortress of Blanchegarde in 1142. William of Tyre, 15, 25, 707–708. One can learn about the decreased danger in the forties from the fact that the Franks were able, in 1150, to construct a fortress and city in Gaza, between Ascalon and Egypt, without any real opposition. William of Tyre, 17, 12, 775–777. That the construction of fortifications did not completely eliminate the danger of guerrilla attacks can be learnt from the descriptions of Usama Ibn al-Munkidh. He describes two attacks at the beginning of the 1150s: one against Bethgibelin and one against Ibelin and its environs. In the first incursion the Ascalonites set fire to the granaries of Bethgibelin and immediately retired, after the Franks stormed out of their fortifications "next to one another." The attack against Ibelin ended with the death of 100 men of Ascalon and the capture of a similar number of prisoners. Usama, trans. Hitti, 41–42. See also Hoch, 1992.   [11] Prawer, 1956, 238 (my translation).

construction of the fortifications increased the day-to-day feeling of security
and the power of attraction of the new settlement nuclei, it did not apprecia-
bly change the basic balance of power in the south. The rulers of Ascalon did
not succeed in challenging the military superiority of the Franks even when
the Frankish army was busy beyond the borders of the Kingdom but they did
not cease to harass the Franks even after the fortifications had been constructed. William of Tyre attributed the weakening of the threat from Ascalon
to the construction of the fortifications, as did the other chroniclers of his
generation. But it would appear that, as in contemporary Europe, the improvement in the security situation preceded the construction of the fortifications.[12]
This explanation is consistent with that given by Smail, according to whom
"the Frankish castles built near Ascalon were intended to support attacks
against the Egyptian garrison . . . The castles of southern Palestine were not,
therefore, established for general purposes of frontier defence. During the
period of their construction the political state of Egypt was such that there was
no danger of the Fatimids renewing their earlier invasions."[13]

There were other regions which suffered from sporadic Muslim aggres-
sions during the twelfth century, such as the district of Nablus (in 1113,
1137, and apparently also in 1152)[14] and the eastern part of Lower Galilee
and Bethsan (mainly at the end of the twelfth century).[15] The mountain area
of Jerusalem was raided only twice before the ascendance of Salah al-Din:
the first time, as already mentioned, was in 1124, and the second raid, a very
unsuccessful one, took place in 1152.[16] Western Galilee was attacked for the
first time in 1169.[17] There is no record of Muslim attacks on the coastal plain

---

[12] "Avec une surprenante cohérence, les sources ecclésiastiques, chroniqueurs italiens et chartes
languedociennes, évoquent la crainte des incursions quent la crainte des incursions sarrazines. On
a déjà fait justice de cette interprétation: P. Toubert pour le Latium, J. P. Poly pour le littoral de
la France méditerranéenne et E. Magnou-Nortier pour la Septimanie, ont montré là le topos, que
dément un examen des faits. Ce ne sont pas des dangers extérieurs qui ont conduit à la pro-
lifération des châteaux: l'incastellamento biterrois commence d'ailleurs au moment où disparait
la Garde-Freinet." Bourin-Derruau, 1987, I, 87.   [13] Smail, 1956, 211–213.

[14] For the raid of 1113, see Ibn al-Qalanisi, trans. Gibb, 186; Usama, trans. Hitti, 138–140; Fulcher
of Chartres, II, 565–572; William of Tyre, 11, 19, 523–525; Albert of Aachen, XII, 9–10,
694–695. For the raid of 1137, see Kedar, 1989, 91–92. For the unsuccessful raid of 1152, see
William of Tyre, 17, 20, 787–789. Cf. Grousset, 1939, 637–639.

[15] The Galilee was raided only once between 1121 and 1169. For the raid of 1121, see William of
Tyre, 12, 16, 565–566; Ibn al-Qalanisi, trans. Gibb, 86–87; Fulcher of Chartres, 643–644. For
the raid of 1134, see Ibn al-Qalanisi, trans. Gibb, 216–218; Ibn al-Athir, ed. RHC. IV-1,
392–397. For the raid of 1169, see: Hospital, 404, 279–280, 1169.

[16] For the raid of 1124, see n. 9. For the raid of 1152, see n. 14.

[17] A battle in which the Franks were defeated and the Muslims reached the gates of Acre was
described in a letter sent by Patriarch Aimaricus to the princes of the West in 1169, Hospital, 404,
1169, 279–280.

north of the River Yarkon before the battle of Hattin. It would appear that there were not many additional attacks which were not described in the contemporary chronicles, as the Arabic and Latin chroniclers, who dealt mainly with such events, had no reason to ignore them.

If, therefore, we regard the acknowledged accounts as indicative of the real situation, it would appear that the lapses of time between the incursions were sometimes that of a generation. In such a span of years, the Franks could establish a whole network of rural settlements. In other words, in a period of from thirty to fifty years, during which the security and political structure of the Crusader Kingdom was molded, one cannot speak of any danger or real security threat to that Kingdom. On the contrary, during that period Palestine enjoyed comparative peace and quiet, in contradistinction to the turbulent period of the eleventh century. The "unremitting pressure" on some of the Frankish settlements began only with the offensives of Nur al-Din and Salah al-Din.[18]

One cannot conclude from this relative peace that the safety of the local inhabitants or of itinerants was always ensured. We have quite a few descriptions of bandits and hostile nomads in regions such as Hebron, east of the Jordan and perhaps also in the eastern Lower Galilee and the coastal plain.[19] But this insecurity, which was characteristic mainly of the first decades of the Kingdom, must be examined within the context of the period and not according to modern criteria. The state of security of the itinerants and farmers in the Latin Kingdom was not much different from the state of security on the roads and in the rural areas of contemporary Europe. From all practical viewpoints the danger from the external borders could not constitute the reason for the ostensible tendency of the Franks to enclose themselves in fortresses and large cities.

---

[18] Until the middle of the seventies Salah al-Din's and Nur al-Din's attacks were aimed at the periphery of the Kingdom. For the attack on Gaza and the south, see: Abu Shama, ed. *RHC, HOr.,* 489; William of Tyre, 20, 19, 936–939; For the conquest of 'Aqaba, see al-Maqrizi, *Khitat,* I, 185; Abu Shama, *Raudatayn,* 489; al-Qalqashandi, VII, 27. For the attack on Monreal in 1172, see William of Tyre, 20, 27, 950–951. For another attack on the southern part of the Kingdom in 1173, see William of Tyre, 20, 28, 951–952. The attacks on the heart of the Kingdom began before the battle of Gezer in 1177, and in the first of them Lydda and Ramle were destroyed and villages "of our people" were also harmed. William of Tyre, 21, 20 (21), 998–999, and 21, 23 (24), 993. At the beginning of the eighties the intensive attacks against the Galilee commenced. In the middle of the eighties Salah al-Din's attacks reached central Samaria, see Lyons & Jackson, 1982, 201–241.

[19] See, for example, Fulcher of Chartres, 373–374; Abert of Aachen, VII, 39; William of Tyre, 10, 25, 485; Raba, Russians, 54; William of Tyre, 21, 25, 997–998; Fulcher of Chartres, II, 37, 514–518; Ibn al-Furat, trans. Lyons, 50–51; al-Qalqashandi, IV, 155.

Internal insecurity

The third assumption, alleging internal insecurity caused by the subject peoples, is actually composed of three interrelated assumptions.

In the first it is assumed that the countryside of the Kingdom was settled by an "overwhelming majority" of Muslims and, therefore, that the local population was almost totally Islamized. The proponents of the existing model evidently took it for granted that the Muslim inhabitants preferred to collaborate with their fellow-Muslims instead of with the Christian Franks.

The second assumption, and hence the second reason for internal insecurity, is that the local Christians were totally Arabized and therefore bound to the Muslims by history, language, and social connections. Even the local Christians preferred, according to the existing model, these historical and cultural connections to connections with the Latin Franks. The third assumption, emanating from the second, maintains that the enemies of the Latin Kingdom were also Arabized Muslims, as there is no way of explaining how "cultural, language and historical ties" could have existed between the enemies of the Kingdom and the local Christian inhabitants unless one assumes that "the culture, language and history" referred to a Semitic and probably Arabic culture. This assumption ignores the possibility that the enemies of the Franks might have been Turkish tribes which had not yet absorbed the Arabic culture which was widespread among the local inhabitants of the Kingdom.

A Muslim majority

The argument that the majority of the population of Palestine was Muslim already in the eleventh century is based on the existing scholarly consensus regarding the main period of Islamization. Recently, many scholars of Islamic history tend to date the critical stage of Islamization to the tenth century and the beginning of the eleventh.[20] It should be remembered, however, that some prominent Islamists are of the opinion that the local Christian population at the time of the Crusades was very large. M. Gil actually thinks that on the eve of the twelfth century there was a Christian major-

---

[20] For the assumption that the critical stage of Islamization occurred within a century or two of the conquest, see Arnold, 1913, 9–10, 81–82; Gottheil, 1908; Dennett, 1950, showed that the abstention from paying the poll tax could not be a sufficient reason for earlier conversion. For the assumption, which prevailed until the 1970s, that the major part of the population was already converted in the ninth century, see Brett, 1973; Lapidus, 1972, 256–257. For the assumption that the process was completed by the eleventh century, see Bulliet, 1979a, 44, 50–51; Bulliet, 1979b; Frye, 1984, 86; Bloom, 1987; Lev, 1988. For the actual state of the research, cf. Morony, 1990, 135–150.

ity in Palestine,[21] while Cl. Cahen and P. Hitti estimate that at the end of the
eleventh century the population of the Levant was evenly divided between
Christians and Muslims.[22] But these scholarly estimations too are based
essentially on intuition and incomplete texts.[23] No definite dating on the
process of Islamization of the Palestinian and Syrian populations has as yet
been established, and it is doubtful whether the existing sources allow of the
conduct of such a study.[24]

Many scholars refrain from attempting to assess the comparative sizes of
the Muslim and Eastern Christian populations and regard it as sufficient to
emphasize the fact that a major phase of Islamization took place after the
expulsion of the Franks from the Holy Land and Syria. Other studies dealing
with the process of Islamization of the Copts in Egypt maintain that even
during the first half of the fourteenth century there was still a very influen-
tial Coptic community in Egypt.[25] However, can one rely on studies dealing
mainly with the process of Islamization in Egypt, Iran, and Asia Minor in
order to draw conclusions concerning the Islamization of Palestine and
Southern Syria? Can one assume that in Southern Syria and Palestine there
remained as substantial an Eastern Christian minority at the beginning of the
twelfth century as in Egypt, Northern Syria, and Lebanon? Or was the
process of Islamization faster in the former countries, with the result that a
definite majority of their populations had become Islamized by that time?

It is difficult to find answers to these questions as an important aspect of
the Islamization process lies in its geographical diversity. The process was
probably faster in Persia and in Iraq than it was in Northern Syria, Lebanon,
or Egypt, and the differences are still apparent in the respective sizes of the
Christian communities. In Lebanon, for example, the Christians still claimed
to be a majority in 1932 and the Copts are still a substantial minority in
Egypt.[26]

Furthermore, this regional diversity characterizes not only large provinces
and regions but sub-regions too. The Copts are still more numerous in

---

[21] Gil, 1992, 170–172; see also Mayer, 1988, 154: "The greater part of the native population consisted of Christian Syrians, themselves divided into several religious groups" Mayer is one of the
only historians of the Crusades who claims that the majority of the native population consisted
of Syrian Christians.   [22] Cahen, 1954, 6–7; Hitti, 1972, 212.

[23] Cf. Friedmann, 1982.

[24] See Levtzion, 1990. Many scholars confined themselves with the description of the local
Christian communities. See, among many others, Poliak, 1938; Charon (=Korolevskij), 1908;
Bar-Asher, 1976; Duncalf, 1916; Every, 1946; Every, 1947; Hamilton, 1980, 159–211, 310–331.

[25] Wiet, 1924, 990–1003; Perlmann, 1942; Little, 1976; Little, 1990; Bosworth, 1979; Leiser, 1985;
Morony, 1990.

[26] According to the census of 1932 there were 338,802 Muslims and 417,656 Christians of various
sects in French Lebanon.

Upper Egypt than they are in Lower Egypt; in Lebanon, there are still Christian provinces, and most of the Christian villages in Palestine are concentrated in three regions – the Western Galilee and the regions of Ramallah and Bethlehem, which were historically inhabited by the members of their faith.[27] The causes of this regional diversity are poorly understood and it is difficult, therefore, to draw analogies between one region and another insofar as the path of Islamization is concerned.

No one can describe clearly the decline of Christianity in the Islamic countries. Hence, it is very difficult to establish to what extent the Muslims were a majority in the Levant or in parts thereof in the twelfth and thirteenth centuries.

I do not intend to try and decide so weighty an issue, which deviates in many aspects from the subject of this study, and shall content myself with the observation that the degree of Islamization of wide areas of the Levant at the end of the eleventh century has still not been examined; and that the argument about the tempo of the process, even in the regions which were studied, has still not been decided. This being so, I do not think that it is possible to assume, without additional research, that the process of Islamization of Palestine attained its final phase already in the twelfth century and, therefore, that the majority of the population at the time was already Muslim. The difficulty of accepting the current hypothesis is aggravated by the fact that part of the Muslim population was either expelled or slaughtered by the Frankish conquerors during the First Crusade and immediately thereafter.[28]

As the assumption that already in the twelfth century an absolute majority of the Palestinian population was Muslim, and therefore hostile to the Franks, has not been proved as yet, the claim which derives from this assumption, that the Franks refrained from settling in rural areas because of the danger emanating from the local population, must also still be proved.

The local Christians and their relationship with the Franks and with the Muslims

Scholars who dealt with the relations between the Franks and the "Oriental Christians" emphasize the multiplicity of sects and the existence of theological differences amongst Eastern Christians.[29] Nevertheless, even though the ethnic, cultural, and political schism amongst the various Christian commu-

---

[27] Local Christians constituted almost 20% of the rural population in the sub-district of Ramallah and less than 1% in the sub-district of Nablus. See Barron, 1923.

[28] See Sivan, 1967b; Prawer, 1980b, 85–86.

[29] Prawer, 1985b, 60–61; Prawer, 1972, 214–232; Hamilton, 1980, 156–211; Smail, 1956, 40–63; Richard, 1979, 131–143.

nities was obvious to all, the exponents of the existing model still tried to find a common denominator in the relations between the various "Oriental Christian" communities and the ruling Franks. The most common characteristic was their alleged absence of loyalty to the Frankish regime. Smail maintained that even the Armenians did not excel in their loyalty to the Frankish rulers. They participated, he argued, in the battles against the Turks and even rescued, at personal and collective risk, Frankish knights who fell into the hands of the Turks, but they often betrayed the Latins. Such acts of treason justify, in his opinion, the following conclusion: "There were enough instances of Armenian disloyalty to show that the people, whose ties with the Franks were closer than those of any other Syrian people, could not always be fully trusted, and it is significant that the weakness often revealed itself when the Franks were facing military difficulties."[30]

The relations between the "local Christians" and the Franks are generalized and are usually examined as reflecting common interests such as: the diplomatic relations with Byzantium, the attitude of orthodox Islam towards the Dhimmi, or the military strength of the local communities.[31]

There were two ostensible reasons for the hostility of the "local Christians" towards the Franks: first, the fact that the Latins had taken the place of the Greeks in the ecclesiastical hierarchy. This fact is considered to be a result of the hostile attitude shown by the Franks, already during the First Crusade, towards "Eastern Christianity."[32] Secondly, the "local Christians" had no reason to prefer the Franks over their former Muslim rulers, as the Muslim religion prohibited many kinds of offences against the Christians. The "local Christians" maintained their autonomy during 500 years of Muslim rule, and this autonomy was limited during the Frankish regime.[33] As Smail argues: "They had, after all, enjoyed toleration and the protection of the Byzantine emperor in the days of Muslim rule, and they had little incentive to help maintain the domination of the Franks."[34]

Sivan was of a similar opinion: "Cet état de choses s'explique sans doute par le fait que les chrétiens orientaux fasaient preuve d'une grande indifférence à l'égard des croisés, leurs soi-disant libérateurs; parfois même,

---

[30] Smail, 1956, 48.   [31] See, for example, Sivan, 1967a; Rose, 1987; Mayer, 1978.

[32] See chapter 1 n. 14. It is difficult to establish to what extent the Franks discriminated against the local Christians as there is no suitable yardstick for measuring against whom they discriminated and where and when. The proponents of the dichotomous approach find the roots of the negative attitude of the Franks towards the local Christians already in 1098. In a letter sent by the leaders of the First Crusade to Urban II they define all the local Christians as heretics. Hagenmeyer, *Kreuzzugsbriefe*, no. 16, 164; Fulcher of Chartres, 264. It is important to note that according to Fulcher of Chartres Urban II disagreed with this definition, see Fulcher of Chartres, 135–136.   [33] Sivan, 1967a; Cahen, 1958; Cahen, 1964; Fattal, 1958.

[34] Smail, 1956, 51.

ils leur témoignaient de l'hostilité à cause des atteintes graves portées par les Francs aux rites non latins."[35]

This approach which paints, almost in ideal colours, the mutual relations between the Muslims and the local Christians caused Smail to find evidence of the good relations between the Muslims and the vanquished Christians even in the description of the meeting between Zanki and the Jacobite metropolitan of Edessa, a meeting which took place after the conquest of the city:

> Zanki . . . had shown no mercy to the Franks, but he treated the Syrian Christians with marked clemency . . . [the anonymous Syrian chronicler who described the conquest of Edessa] not only described Zanki's forbearance towards the eastern Christians, but was at pains to record his visits to their churches and his friendly relations with the Jacobite metropolitan. The tone of such historians has its value as evidence of the state of mind of the people to whom they belong.[36]

I think that Smail went rather too far in his interpretation of an isolated occurrence taken out of context. It is difficult to find evidence of the good relations between the Jacobite Syrians and Zanki and his Turkish allies in the events that occurred after the conquest of Edessa: a conquest which involved horrifying slaughter of the local population, the destruction of churches, and the conversion of other churches to mosques. This is particularly so if we recall that a short time later the local Christians collaborated with the Franks in an attempt to liberate the city which resulted in an additional massacre even greater than the first.[37]

The alleged tendency of the local Christians to collaborate with the Muslims is based, as stated above, on the fact that Muslim law reveals a preferential attitude towards Christians and Jews. Scholars of Islamic history claim that this tolerant attitude was preserved in most countries until the second half of the thirteenth century. Only then, after the "local Christians" had collaborated with the Mongol tribes, did the attitude towards them change. E. Sivan writes: "De l'avis général des spécialistes, le changement décisif dans la position des minorités confessionnelles dans le Proche-Orient confessionnelles dans le Proche-Orient islamique au Moyen Age doit être rattaché à l'invasion mongole de 1258–1260."[38]

It should be remembered that the same scholars who claim that the "local

---

[35] Sivan, 1967a, 120–121.
[36] Smail, 1956, 51. It should be noted, however, that Smail was cautious enough to write that "the anonymous Syrian was able to preserve an outlook which by comparison is neutral."
[37] See, for example, Nicholson, 1973, 7–9. Nicholson's book is full of inaccuracies, but it would appear that his description of the conquest of Edessa is closer to the truth than that of Smail.
[38] Sivan, 1967a, 117.

Christians" had no reason to collaborate with the Franks maintain that the same communities collaborated with the Mongol tribes which invaded the Levant in the second half of the thirteenth century. These scholars, therefore, fail to explain why the Christians should have had no cause to collaborate with their European co-religionists while they found cause to collaborate in particular with the Mongols. If the attitude of Islam towards them was the reason for their loyalty towards their Muslim rulers, what did they gain by collaborating with the Mongol "barbarians" against their Muslim "benefactors"?

I do not intend to indulge in a detailed discussion about any alleged "act of treason" committed by one Syrian Christian or another. It appears to me that "acts of treason" committed by individuals or groups cannot serve as a yardstick for relations between populations and whole cultures. Moreover, the intercultural relations between Eastern Christianity, Western Christianity, Turkish or Arab Islam, cannot be explained only by economical or political interests of the various sects.

The relations between the Franks and the different Christian communities were too complex to be described in simplistic terms such as "collaboration" or "treason." Moreover, "acts of treason" existed in the ranks of the Franks, the Muslims, and the Turkish tribes as well.[39]

In the course of 200 years of Frankish rule these relations had their ups and downs, their hopes and disappointments, were affected by persecution and attempts at reconciliation, and were most certainly subject to mutual

---

[39] For Joscelyn's collaboration with the Turks against Bohemond, see William of Tyre, 13, 22, 614–615. For the intentions of Alice of Antioch to place the city under Zanki's rule, see William of Tyre, 13, 27, 623–624. For Hugo's collaboration with the Ascalonites against Fulco of Anjou, see William of Tyre, 14, 16, 653. For the presumed reasons for the failure of the Second Crusade, see William of Tyre, 17, 5, 766. For the betrayal of the defenders of Cavea de Tyrun, and for the hanging of the commander, who was the only one who had not defected to the Turkish camp, see William of Tyre, 19, 11, 878–879. For the hanging of twelve of the Templars of the Cave Castle, see William of Tyre, 19, 11, 879. For the betrayal of the commander of Baniyas, together with a canon named Roger, see William of Tyre, 19, 10, 877. For the suspects of treason during the Frankish and Greek siege on Damietta, see William of Tyre, 20, 15, 930. For the fear that Bohemond could collaborate with the Turks because of the interdict inflicted on him for marrying a second wife, see William of Tyre, 22, 6, 1012–1013. For acts of treason during the surrender of the cave castle in the Gilead, see William of Tyre, 22, 16 (15), 1028–1029. For a messenger to the Turks, who was formerly suspected to be their collaborator ("qui suspectus habebatur quod alia vice in legatione simili contra Christi populum maliciose fuisset versatus") but was sent to them again because of his mastering of the (Turkish?) language, see William of Tyre, 16, 12, 731–732. For acts of "treason" which were directed against the Turks: a Turkish "Satrap" of Armenian origin from Tantass, who proposed delivering to the Franks both Bostra and Sarhad, see William of Tyre, 16, 8, 724. For a Turkish soldier who asked the Franks to take Bosra, thus rescuing the Frankish army, see William of Tyre, 16, 12, 732. These few examples were taken from one source only – William of Tyre. It would be impossible, within the limits of this book, to cite all the incidents concerning treason of Franks, Turks, Saracens, and local Christians.

influences. "Eastern Christiandom" and "Frankish conquerors" should be regarded as heterogeneous, complex units which maintained complex and ambivalent relations between them. All such relations have enabled scholars to find evidence of completely different, and even contradictory, theories, which, in my opinion, is what occurred in the case of both the exponents of the old model and those of the new model. The Eastern Christian chronicles are full of fascinating and variegated expressions testifying to the complexity of the relations and the intensivity of the cultural and political metamorphoses, but they have not yet received the comprehensive and comparative research which would reveal this variability.

In the network of relations between the Christian communities and the Turks too there were different and even contradictory emotions. The descriptions of the Syrian chroniclers were undoubtedly influenced by hundreds of years of Arab–Muslim rule which was relatively tolerant and by the fact that the local Christians were totally dependent on their Muslim rulers; but they were also influenced by decades of Turkish rule which can hardly be described as tolerant. In many cases, therefore, they concentrated on the substance of events and not on the strict normative set-up.

The extent of Arabization of the local Christian population
The assumption that the local Christian population was almost totally Arabized is based on various texts which state that the "Syrian" inhabitants of Palestine used Arabic as their main spoken language and continued to use Syriac for liturgical purposes.[40]

The sources distinguish between "Saracens," Turks, and the various Christian communities. It is important to note that many of the legal sources refer to most of the Christian inhabitants of the country as "Suriani." The prevalent assumption, based on well-founded historical evidence, regards these inhabitants as Orthodox Christians subject to the religious hegemony of the Greek Orthodox Church, who used Arabic as their spoken language and Greek or Syriac for liturgical purposes. It would appear that this assumption is correct insofar as the decisive majority of local Christians is concerned, but the repeated use of the name Surianus and the fact that we have evidence (albeit scant) of local Syrians who spoke Syriac perhaps justifies a further examination of the assumption regarding the extent of Arabization. Apparently, even though most of the Syrian inhabitants of the Levant spoke Arabic already in the twelfth century, nevertheless the Syrian culture did not

---

[40] Cahen, 1971; Cahen, 1972; Riley-Smith, 1977; Bar-Asher, 1976. For the fact that the Syrians used Arabic script for everyday purposes and Greek for sacred writings, see Thomas, "Tractat," 145–146.

disappear completely from day-to-day use not only in Northern Syria but also in the border areas of Palestine, where the Syrian dialect still existed.[41]

It is perhaps important to note that even at the end of the Byzantine period, after about 1,000 years of Greek dominance during which Greek was the main written language and the principle medium of communication with the governing bodies, the local inhabitants continued to use the Syrian dialect. Although the transfer from one Semitic language (Syriac or Hebrew) to another (Arabic) is easier than a transfer between Syriac and Greek, nevertheless the parallel existence for 1,000 years of a superior and official language side by side with a popular language, of which the written evidence is very scarce, is bound to raise some reservations about the depth of absorption of Arabic amongst all the classes and in all regions already during the period of Frankish conquest.[42]

The enemies of the Franks

The exponents of the existing model tend to present the different Muslim communities as a more or less uniform group, with the main difference being the difference between Sunnis and Shi'ites. The esoteric groups such as the Assassins and the Druzes, as well as the Beduin nomads, are deemed to be exceptions. In many studies, no attempt has been made to distinguish between Turks who formed the bulk of the "enemies of the Frankish Kingdom" and the other ethnic groups, despite the decisive role played by the Turkicization process in the ethnic and cultural metamorphosis of the Levant in this period.

This comparative failure to recognize the importance of the Turkish ethnic factor cannot be ascribed to the paucity of relevant documents. In innumerable instances, beginning from Fulcher's description of the Council in Clermont and thenceforth, the Latin chronicles describe the enemies of the Franks as "Turks." It was the Turks and their allies, the Kurds, who defeated the Crusader Kingdom in the battle of Hattin, and it was the

---

[41] See Bar-Asher, 1976. According to Benjamin of Tudela the inhabitants of Southern Sinai spoke the language of the "translation" ("Targum"), i.e. Aramaic. "On the top of the mountain is a large convent belonging to the great monks called Syrians. At the foot of the mountain is a large town called Tur-Sinai; the inhabitants speak the language of the Targum [i.e. Syriac]." Benjamin of Tudela, 77, Hebrew text, 107. Hamilton attributes the fact that Benjamin uses the word "Syrian" in order to describe the monks and inhabitants of Mt. Sinai to the influence of the Franks who used this concept, see Hamilton, 1980, 140.

[42] In an article rich with quotations Korolevskij shows that the inhabitants of Palestine during the Byzantine period were never fluent in Greek, see Charon (=Korolevskij), 1908, 82–91. Korolevskij also wrote a book on this subject, but the first volume, which was supposed to deal also with the Arabization of the Syrians, was never published, although the author himself announced its coming publication and even published one of its chapters.

Mamluks, who were also of Turkish origin, who finally defeated the Franks.[43]

Is it possible to assume that the Turkish tribes, and even their leaders, already completed, in the eleventh century their own Arabization process? Even though the Arabic language became, through the medium of the Muslim holy scriptures, the most widespread language amongst the Islamic peoples, nevertheless it is difficult to imagine that the standard of education and the degree of Islamization of the Turkish tribes had already attained such a degree in the twelfth century. The Turks had control, till the second half of the eleventh century, in regions such as Persia and the Jazira, where Arabic was not spoken, and it is difficult to present them as being connected by "ties of culture and language" to the Eastern Christians.

Moreover, some experts of Turkish history note that the Turkish conquest brought in its wake changes whose importance cannot be exaggerated: according to Speros Vryonis Jr., for example, the Turkish infiltration into Asia Minor and the Jazira was accompanied by enforced Islamization, destruction of churches, expulsion of whole communities, etc. These drastic measures were in part the cause of the comparatively rapid Islamization of Asia Minor.[44] Cahen, on the other hand, adopts a completely opposite view: the Turks, he maintains, perpetuated the tolerant attitude towards the local Christians and the change in the attitude of the Muslims towards the Christians took place later, during the thirteenth century, due to political reasons, such as the Christians' collaboration with the Mongols.[45]

The stereotyping of "Eastern Christians" on the one hand, and "Muslim enemies of the Franks" on the other hand, arises, according to Prawer, from the attitude of the Franks themselves.

[43] Prawer, 1985b, 62: "Within the frontiers of the Latin states there were virtually no Turks or nomadic Turcomans. Only the beduins, called 'Arabs' in Moslem sources, stood out as a separate group."

[44] Vryonis, 1971, 286: "The destructive character of the Turkish conquest and settlement, which contributed so greatly to the violent dislocation of Byzantine society, was largely (though not exclusively) due to the nomadic Turkmen tribes. Entering Anatolia as unruly conquerors inspired by djihad and their instinct for plunder, and settling upon the land in compact groups, they were long a bane to the settled Christian populations." The following is a translation made by him of one of the fourteenth century documents: "The cities they rased to the ground, pillaged the religious sanctuaries, broke open the graves, and filled all with blood and corpses. They outraged the souls of the inhabitants, forcing them to deny God and giving to them their own [i.e. the Turks'] defiled mysteries. They [the Turks] abused their [Christians'] souls, alas, with wanton outrage! Denuding them of all property and their freedom, they left the [Christians as] weak images of slaves, exploiting the remaining strength of the wretched ones for their own prosperity." Demetrius Cydones, PG, 154, 964–968.

[45] "To a mind accustomed to the totalitarian mental categories of the twentieth century it is somewhat difficult to conceive how, in Asia Minor in the twelfth and thirteenth centuries, the convictions and behaviour of Ghazis could co-exist with a religious tolerance superior to anything found elsewhere in Islam." Cahen, 1968, 203. Cf. also Mayer, 1988, 5–6.

"Despite the efforts of some modern historians to distinguish different policies followed by the Crusaders respecting natives who were Christians and those who were not, in law – as distinguished from practice – no such difference existed."[46]

Even if this is correct and the Franks did treat each local community equally, this does not justify the historiographic approach common to all modern scholars. It would appear that the inclination to generalize with respect to the Eastern cultural and ethnic world is a result no less, and perhaps even more, of the scholars' opinion about the place and importance of that cultural and ethnic world. Further indications of this opinion can be found in studies dealing with the "non-Frankish" population.

In an article summing up the main points of his approach to the local population, Prawer uses the term "minorities" in order to describe the Christian and Muslim communities in the Levant in the twelfth and thirteenth centuries. Uncharacteristically, he ignores the clear etymological roots of the word "minority" and bases his theory only on the definition of the word given by Arnold Rose in the *International Encyclopaedia of Social Sciences*:

a group of people – differentiated from others in the same society by race, nationality, religion, or language who both think of themselves as a differentiated group and are thought of by the others as a differentiated group with negative connotations. Further, they are relatively lacking in power and hence are subjected to certain exclusions, discriminations, and other differential treatment.[47]

It is difficult to accept this definition when the reference is to nations subject to a regime of conquest, which is in essence discriminatory. Would every nation subjugated by a discriminating conqueror be deemed a "minority"? It is doubtful whether the above definition can be applied to medieval times, when "exclusions, discriminations and other differential treatment" were daily routine.

For our purposes, what is more important is the approach of the scholar and his conception of the society of the times – a conception which is reflected in the terminology which he choses. The very presentation of the local Christians and Muslims, who undoubtedly constituted a majority of the population, as "minorities" results from placing the Frankish rulers at the centre of society and relegating the locals with their different culture to the sidelines. If there is a "minority" then there must, perforce, be a "majority", and this majority cannot be anything but the Frankish class, considered by the exponents of the existing paradigm to be the social nucleus, with the rest of the population on the social periphery.

[46] Prawer, 1985b, 59.   [47] Rose, 1968, 365.

Some of the exponents of the existing model have given expression to ideas which do perhaps go deeper than the roots of the above approach. Smail, for example, has the following to say about the relations between the people of the Levant and the Franks: "throughout the century there were many signs of the mutual antipathy which could exist between Levantines and western Europeans."[48]

However, the approach which places the Franks at the center and relegates the rest of the population to the periphery reflects the main attitude of the existing model. It is true that the social periphery of the Crusader lordships is not presented as one unit: this periphery consists of a small Christian community, divided into sub-communities with marginal differences between them, and a larger Muslim community which is also divided into sub-communities. There are ethnic and religious groups (such as the Jews, the Samaritans, the Beduin and the esoteric Muslim groups) whose political conduct differs from that of the rest, but these groups are regarded as the periphery of the periphery. This social "periphery" tended, according to the proponents of the existing model, to collaborate with one another against the Franks.

I shall try to show that the widely accepted argument that the "local Christians" were indifferent to the Frankish conquest and that they even tended to collaborate with the Muslims is less convincing than the opposite argument advocated by the previous model. However, the other claim of the previous model stating that the Muslim inhabitants of the Latin states were also eager to collaborate with the Franks was justly rejected by the present model. Clearly, the complex social and cultural system created by the Franks and the "local Christians" cannot be described in oversimplified terms like "collaboration" or "treason." This set of relations was full of nuances and was highly changeable, but it owed its very existence to the participation of all its components. I shall try to show, also, that the Turks were considered to be, to a great extent, the common enemy of both the Franks and their Christian subjects.

The assumption that the Franks were a small minority in comparison with the local population

The present model assumes that the Franks constituted a small minority of the total population, a fact which contributed to the atmosphere of insecurity which prevailed among the Frankish settlers. In this context, the numbers

---

[48] Smail, 1956, 50. Smail, however, referred to the Frankish settlers in the Levant as a "minority." Smail, 1973, 61.

produced by Prawer and Benvenisti are somewhat surprising. Both these scholars maintain that in Palestine alone there were beween 100,000 to 140,000 Franks, constituting 15–25% of the total population. If these figures are creditable, then they refute the argument that the Franks were only a small minority whose very existence was in danger. It is difficult, in my opinion, to accept both that the Franks were compelled to enclose themselves in fortresses because of their small number and that they constituted almost 25% of the total population![49] I must point out, however, that the value of the demographic studies dealing with the Crusades is very limited. Not only do we not have any information about the size of the Latin population, but all other demographic factors are also unknown to us. We do not know the size of the whole population, what their age and sex distribution was, how many children a fertile mother might produce, the average life expectancy, the average marriage age, the death rate amongst children, the rate of death from illnesses and plagues, and other demographic details. Furthermore, the figures, of dubious veracity, given for the inhabitants of the large cities, include an unknown number of local Christians. The questionable measure of the size of the population of the large cities is based for the most part on descriptions of war and siege during which the rural population in the vicinity were also concentrated in the cities. The numbers given in contemporary historical sources are often grossly exaggerated and do not distinguish between the Franks and the local Christians. In such circumstances a real demographic study becomes only wishful thinking. Therefore, one has to regard the demographic conclusions of Prawer, Benvenisti, and Russell as estimates not based on any real demographic data.

I do not intend to rely on any other inaccurate material or to propose a new speculative estimate of the number of Franks who lived in the Levant. However, I will try to show that even if the Frankish population was much smaller than present-day scholars opine, this was not sufficient cause for them to build fortresses and to refrain from settling in the agricultural settlements.

Frankish fortresses

An additional difficulty arises from the tendency of the existing model to find the main reason for the "process of urbanization" and the "process of fortification" in the shaky state of security which prevailed in the Levant in the period of the Crusades. Even if one accepts the assumption that life in cities and other collective settlements was safer than in isolated estates, it is

[49] Prawer, 1975, I, 568–576; Benvenisti, 1970, 26–28; Russell, 1985.

difficult to regard the security conditions as the only, or main, reason for so farreaching a social process, and to accept the contention that these conditions were unique to the Frankish East. The process of Frankish "urbanization" and "fortification" must be compared to the process of transferral to collective, fortified settlements which was widespread in Europe from the tenth century on. It is now commonly accepted that the intensive process of fortification which accompanied the settlement in the tenth to twelfth centuries was not a result of any external or internal threat. An appreciable number of new fortresses were erected as kernels for new settlements, and many others were built near temporary markets and regional economic centers. Toubert, in his study of Latium, called the process "incastellamento," and this expression, widely accepted since then, will also be used in this study.[50] The proponents of the existing model followed the explanations which were popular in the 1950s and which tend to distinguish between the construction of fortresses, ostensibly because of security conditions and for strategic reasons, and the construction of new settlements, allegedly in view of the improved security and economic conditions.[51] This general approach was rejected already in the seventies. Fortresses were built anywhere in eleventh- and twelfth-century Europe and not only in "insecure regions." And although the construction of many fortresses was justified by contemporary chroniclers as being necessary for "security reasons," generally no factual basis for this justification can be found.[52]

The fortress, it is now commonly argued, was designed to be more of a power symbol and a nucleus for a new settlement rather than an answer to acute security requirements. The construction of new settlements as well as the construction of fortresses are considered to be the result of an improvement in the security and economic situation and not of its deterioration. They were both a result of social pressures arising from economic prosperity. The prosperity created a growing social class of small "entrepeneurs" who sought to exploit this economic progress. The claim that some of the Franks who settled in the Levant belonged to this new social class of petty

---

[50] The pioneer research of P. Toubert on medieval Latium opened the way to new conceptions concerning Mediterranean settlement during the same period. See Toubert, 1973, ch. 4, 303–447. For settlement in other Mediterranean regions, see Bonnassie, 1975–1976; Bonnassie, 1991; Bourin-Derruau, 1987; Magnou-Nortier, 1974; Coursente, 1980; Higounet, 1980; Poteur, 1988, and many others.

[51] Smail, 1951; Prawer, 1956; Prawer, 1958. It should be noted, however, that both Prawer and Smail stated very clearly that castles were built not only for security reasons but they saw their role as centers of administration and economic development as secondary to their military role. See Smail, 1956, 60–61; Prawer, 1980c.

[52] See chapter 1, n. 12.

"entrepreneurs" – a class which sought to change its economic and social fate – is not inconceivable.[53]

Many of the new European settlements were constructed at the initiative of the landowners who vested potential settlers with plots of land, houses, the status of free farmers, and physical protection. The farmers for their part considerably increased the income from the land, which till then had lain fallow and thereby earned the rights which they had been granted. The addition of settlers' dwellings is what gave the village its initial pattern of a rural burgus. Many of the new settlements which were surrounded by walls were called "castella" or "castra."[54]

According to this approach, no simple distinction can be drawn between a "fortress" and an "agricultural settlement," as the fortress was very often the kingpin of the agricultural settlement which developed around it, and the agricultural settlement was usually the raison d'être for the construction of a fortress. The study of medieval settlement cannot rely, therefore, on cataloguing types of settlement as "agricultural settlements" and "urban" or "fortified" ones – terminology which, for the most part, is too rigid and takes no account of the fact that most of the medieval settlements had more than one defined function.[55]

At the basis of this assertion is the conception that types of settlement are, first and foremost, the spatial manifestations of social structure. One cannot, in my opinion, fix boundaries between, and separate artificially, the social structure and its spatial elements. The exponents of the existing model argued that the security aspect was the main consideration behind Frankish settlement and fortification. This approach ignores the social background and the geographical legacy which the Franks brought with them from their countries of origin, and, at the same time, it ignores the close economic and social relations which the Franks created with the autochthonous Christian population. It is difficult, in my opinion, to accept that patterns of behavior which were so entrenched in European society of the twelfth century would have disappeared from the consciences of the Frankish immigrants after their arrival in the Levant; and one must perforce assume that at least some of the Frankish fortresses were built in order to provide a basis for rural settlement.

[53] "Aujourd'hui, sous les éclairages conjugués de l'archéologie castrale dans l'Europe du Nord-Ouest, et de l'incastellamento méditerranéen, une position médiane paraît atteinte: le château est un des éléments premiers de la vie du groupe, mais son rôle semble plus social, voire économique, que politique ou militaire." Fossier, 1989, 197. "In fact, it takes little time to dismiss the simplistic political or military explanation. As a nucleating point for men, the castle appears nowadays to constitute a determining factor" Chapelot & Fossier, 1985, 129.
[54] See Toubert, 1973, I, xxii–xxiii and 321ff; Settia, 1979, 361–430; Bourin-Derruau, 1987, I.
[55] Cf. Smail, 1956, 60–61.

I shall attempt, therefore, to show that many of the fortresses erected in the Frankish Kingdom of Jerusalem were erected and planned from the beginning as settlement kernels.

Scarcity of archeological research

The basic assumption according to which the Franks never really settled in rural areas could have been either justified or refuted with the aid of archeological tools. But since no comprehensive survey of Frankish sites was ever conducted, the assumption is based, *argumentum ex silentio*, on the scarcity of documents which explicitly mention such settlement. However, the pioneering archeological fieldwork carried out by Clermont-Ganneau, Rey, Conder, Bagatti, Benvenisti, and Pringle, and by the staff of the Department of Antiquities in the time of the British Mandate, has provided evidence that Frankish rural buildings did exist and allows for the hypothesis that the number of structures erected in the countryside was larger than hitherto assumed.[56]

Most of the findings were included in the "Crusader Palestine: Map and Index," prepared by Prawer and Benvenisti.[57] These two authors also prepared a list, as an addendum to the map, which included the current identities of 830 place names mentioned in medieval sources (700 of which appear within the framework of the present study). It is interesting to note that the map includes also 178 Frankish archeological sites. Seventeen of these sites are described by Prawer and Benvenisti as towns: eleven of them as fortified and six as "unfortified" towns. Seventy-two other sites are divided into sixty-four "small fortresses" and eight "big castles." Another seventy sites are described simply as Crusader ruins without any additional details. The remaining nineteen sites are described as monasteries, churches, or holy places. The "Crusader archeological sites," which compose about one quarter of the Frankish sites, appear only on the map and not in the addendum. It is obvious that these ruins were not fortresses (or else they would have been included amongst the "small fortresses") or towns. Prawer and Benvenisti did not make a complete list of them since the Latin names of most of them remain unknown.

Two scholars, Benvenisti and Pringle, tried to assess the importance of

---

[56] Abel, 1926; 1928; Bagatti, 1947; 1979; Benevisti, 1970; Benvenisti, 1982; Clermont-Ganneau, 1888, I, 308–311, 334–336, 336–337, 351–392; Clermont-Ganneau, 1898, II, 91–92, 95–97; Clermont-Ganneau, 1900, III, 141–142; Clermont-Ganneau, 1903, V, 70–79; Conder, 1881; Frankel, 1988; Pringle, 1983; Pringle, 1985; Pringle, 1989; Rey, 1877; Rey, 1883.

[57] Prawer & Benvenisti, 1970.

these "Crusader archeological sites." Benvenisti concluded that the names of at least eleven of them indicate that they were used for the purpose of raising cattle: in other words, for agricultural purposes. In his book *The Crusaders in the Holy Land*, Benvenisti devotes a whole chapter to "manor houses" and "farm houses" and comes to the conclusion that many of the small sites were manor houses. Benvenisti was also the first to perceive how many of these houses there were and the lack of uniformity in their geographic dispersion: "There is hardly a large village in the regions of Jerusalem, Ramallah or central Samaria without isolated remains of Crusader structures."[58]

In an article dealing with Frankish fortresses of the first generation, Pringle summed up the main points of his theory concerning these small sites. He relies on the basic assumptions of the existing model in deciding that the Frankish landlords hardly ever lived on their lands. Consequently, he does not separate the discussion of Frankish fortifications from the discussion of rural sites:

the Franks were always in a minority in Palestine; thus for security as well as for social reasons, they tended to congregate in the urban centres, rather than settle on the land . . . Even where a fief was related to lands, it was not necessary for the fief holder to reside on them. Rents would simply be levied in kind from the villagers at harvest time; and even this operation was often done by native Christian or Muslim estate officials (in some cases the village headman) on behalf of the owner or tenant.[59]

Some of the small "fortresses" of the twelfth century, as well as some of the other "Crusader archeological sites," were used, in his opinion, as residences of native officials, while some of the buildings which Benvenisti thought were manor houses (such as, for example, those at Kh. Ikbala and Kh. Tanur) were used, in his opinion, for ecclesiastical purposes. Nevertheless, Pringle agrees that some of these establishments "may well have had feudal owners or tenants and have been the Crusader equivalent of the maisons fortes – something between a house and a castle – found in the west." On the other hand, he claims that the physical remains of other sites do not allow for establishing their functions as the closed courtyards which were characteristic of them were also characterisic of the larger fortresses. "Courtyard buildings such as these are often referred to as 'manor houses', and are sometimes held to indicate the existence in the twelfth century of a class of non-feudal landowner, a sort of yeoman-burgess. This notion is hard to accept."[60]

Pringle does not explain the purpose of the seventy unfortified buildings

[58] Benvenisti, 1970, 233. [59] Pringle, 1989, 19. [60] Pringle, 1989, 20.

referred to by Prawer and Benvenisti (of which there were even more, as I shall later maintain), and he does not refer to the fact that they constituted at least 25% of all the recognized Frankish sites.

No one disputes Pringle's suggestion according to which the Franks used the services of the local inhabitants for the purpose of managing some of the rural estates, but is it feasible to assume that the Franks erected, at considerable expense, tens of stone buildings in order to provide accommodation for the local officials whom they employed in isolated agricultural districts? Is this assumption really substantiated in the written sources? Can one ignore clear indications of agricultural pursuits (such as terracing, irrigation canals, and installations including oil presses and grindstones for milling flour) in these sites and describe them as "ecclesiastical sites" only because remains of apses of churches were found in a few of them? And, in more general terms, was there a difference between medieval ecclesiastical and secular agricultural settlements? In any event, Pringle's explanations refer only to a very limited number of the seventy or more known sites.

Prawer himself underestimates the importance of these sites. In his important article "Colonization Activities in the Latin Kingdom," he deals only with Frankish villages which are mentioned explicitly in the written documents and ignores all the archeological sites. At a later stage, I shall attempt to show that even from these few documents which have already been used, much additional information can be gleaned about the existence of Frankish villages, estates, and manor houses. This additional information, in my opinion, completely changes the picture.

The model proposed in the present study

I shall try to prove that within the boundaries of the Latin Kingdom there was an intensive Frankish settlement which resembled, in many aspects, the settlement types which existed in southern Europe during the same period. The Frankish settlement included rural burgi, fortified and unfortified villages, manor houses, seigniorial strongholds, flour mills, roads, and other geographical characteristics of a medieval settled area. I shall try to show also that this settlement existed only in the regions which were occupied by a local Christian majority, or in sparsely populated agricultural areas. I shall try to show, also, that in the regions of the Latin Kingdom where there was a Muslim majority, there was no Frankish settlement. This pattern of settlement reflects, I believe, a social and ideological situation: the Franks, whose raison d'être for coming to the Levant was the liberation of the Eastern Christian communities from the Turkish yoke, perpetuated this original policy and established Christian, political entities in those same areas in which there was an appreciable minority, or even a majority of local Christians. These political entities were led by the Frankish minority and by classes of local Christians (Armenians, Greeks, and, on rare occasions, also Syrians) which could be called the aristocracy. The result was not, of course, the creation of a homogeneous society, as differences of status between the Franks and the Eastern Christians were preserved in the Levant just as the differences in status between the aristocracy and the lower classes were preserved in contemporary Europe.

The Franco-local Christian social structure existed also in the areas of Frankish settlement of the Kingdom. The Frankish settlers behaved like all immigrant societies and preferred to settle in an Orthodox Christian environment which gave them comparative social security. They settled near to the local Christian villages, married local Christian women, and very often used the same churches. The Franks were, in my opinion, a kind of "center" only in the political structure of their own political entities, but constituted a secondary factor in the long-term cultural and social processes which shaped the character of the areas over which they ruled.

The creation of Christian states was one stage, although important and perhaps crucial, in the process of Islamization and Turkicization of the Levantine world. The establishment of Frankish states was both the result of these processes – since the Crusaders were called upon to go to the Levant in order to rescue the Eastern Christians from the Turkish yoke – and the reason for the exacerbation of the eastern Christians' position and the entrenchment of the Turkish infiltration.

In the early stages of the Franco-Turkish conflict, the Crusaders succeeded, prima facie, in their mission: they exploited the power vacuum which had enabled Turkish infiltration into the Levant; they liberated the Christians from the Turkish yoke; they pushed the Turks out of part of the Christian–inhabited areas and even succeeded in reestablishing Christian rule in them. In the process they succeeded in establishing a political, social, and settlement system, based on the local Christian population.

Further along in the course of the conflict, the Turks succeeded in gradually uniting the whole of the Islamic world under their control and in transforming the conflict into a Franco-Islamic one, and to no small extent, a Christian–Muslim one. In later stages of this conflict, after the Turks had succeeded in bringing about the failure of the Frankish regime, the process of Islamization of the Eastern Christians was expedited as was the political and cultural influence of the Turks. The Crusaders' failure to protect their settlements resulted, therefore, not only in the failure to reestablish Christian hegemony in the Levant but also in the dramatic deterioration in the local Christians' status.

According to this model the failure of the Frankish regime was inevitable from the beginning: the Franks had no hope of coping with the inexhaustible reserves of steppe nomads who poured into the Levant during the whole of the twelfth century; neither could they counter the political processes that brought the Turks to the seat of government in all the focal points of power in the Muslim Levant. The failure of Frankish settlement did not follow, therefore, from any kind of political process, but from a demographic, ethnic, and cultural process, which eventually led to the take-over of the whole Levant by the nomadic offspring of the steppes. The change in the attitude of Islam towards the local Christian population can also be explained, perhaps, by means of this model. This change, around 1260, does not flow only from the Christians' collaboration with the Mongols, which perhaps was only an excuse for it, but rather from the final seizure of power by the Turks (the Mamluks) over Syria and Egypt and the standards which they brought with them.

I do not purport to examine, within the modest framework of this work, all the elements of the model I have presented here. An examination of this nature would overstep the limits of this present study. I shall concentrate, therefore, in the course of this study, on three main fields.

(1) I shall try to produce proof of the existence of Frankish settlements in several regions of the Frankish Kingdom of Jerusalem and to show the complexity of this settlement and its resemblance to, and difference from, contemporary settlement in Europe.

(2) I shall try to show that the network of relations that existed between the Frankish community and the local Christian community is not identical with that favored by some of the proponents of the existing model.

(3) I shall try to pinpoint fields of research which have not been properly studied and which could provide us with new information about the process of Islamization of the population of Palestine.

PART TWO

THE "CASTRUM," THE BURGUS,
AND THE VILLAGE

CHAPTER THREE

CASTELLUM REGIS

Mi'ilya is a Christian village in the heart of Western Galilee ten kilometers northeast of Acre. In the heart of the present village are the remains of a Crusader fortress with which students of the period are familiar.[1] The ancient kernel of the village, however, is to be found on the northwestern side of the Frankish fortress, on the flat area where several Byzantine and pre-Crusader churches were discovered.

Mi'ilya (Mhalia) or Castellum Regis is mentioned for the first time in a document which was issued in 1160. In this document, the management rights (*custodia et drogomanagium*) of the place and of several villages within its neighborhood were transferred to one Johannes of Haifa. "Balduinus . . . . Latinorum rex . . . dono Iohanni de Caypha, filio Gambre, et heredibus suis in perpetuum custodiam et drogomanachgium omnium pertinenciarum cuiusdam castelli mei, quod Mhalia nuncupatur, tam earum videlicet, que nunc habitantur, quam earum, que per dei graciam in futurum habitabuntur."[2]

The property transferred to Johannes' management was divided into two groups: one consisting of villages which were "inhabited at the time" and the other consisting of places which Baldwin III hoped, and possibly even expected, would be inhabited in the future. The king gives, in detail, the names of the villages which were inhabited at the time, but we do not know where the additional settlement was to take place. The document is not explicit on this point and the expectations expressed in it may be theoretical rather than concrete in nature. We do not even know if the additional settlers were expected to be Franks or local inhabitants. However, from the fact

---

[1] For a fuller version of this chapter, see Ellenblum, 1996. For the fief, the castle, and the neighborhood of Castellum Regis, see Frankel, 1988, 249–272; Mayer, 1980, 171–216; Mas-Latrie, 1878, 107–120; Mas-Latrie, 1882, 647–652; La Monte, 1938, 301–320; Barag, 1979, 197–217; Riley-Smith, 1973, 54.   [2] Strehlke, no. 2, 1160, 2–3 (Röhricht, *Regesta*, no. 341).

that the king relies on "the help of the Lord," we may conclude that he was not thinking of Muslim settlement within his domain but of the settlement of local Christians or Franks.[3]

Actions taken to attract settlers to European settlements of this period are well known. Landowners who sought to better the exploit of their property offered a variety of rights to settlers who sought to improve their own conditions of living. These new settlers enjoyed the rights of ownership over land and over other production measures. Examples of such attraction for estate owners and potential settlers was the order of the day in eleventh- and twelfth-century Europe and existed also in Palestine. The best-known instances of this arrangement were in Bethgibelin, Rama, Buria, Casale Humberti de Pace, and Magna Mahomeria, all thoroughly researched by Prawer.[4] Were similar transactions made in the Castellum Regis neighborhood, with the intention of attracting Christian or Frankish settlers?

An affirmative answer can be found in detail in document no. 128 in the archives of the Teutonic Order, edited by Strehlke in 1869.[5] This document, issued in Acre in 1243,[6] lists the immovable property bought by the Teutonic Order to date. The first part of the document lists twenty-one transactions which were concluded between the Order and Frankish villagers in ostensibly unknown places in Galilee. The rest of the extensive list, refers to property in Acre, Tyre, and other well-known places. However, a detailed study of the first twenty-one transactions reveals that they were all located in the same place.

- The vineyard of Iacobus Tripolitanus is mentioned in transaction no. 1 together with the neighboring vineyard of Dominus Boonecasa.
- This vineyard is mentioned again in transaction no. 11 together with another neighboring vineyard, that of the son of Marinus de Iader.
- Their neighbor, Dominus Boonecasa, is mentioned again in transaction no. 21 together with one of the beneficiaries of his will, Dominus Andrea.
- The same Dominus Andrea owned, according to transaction no. 2, a vineyard which was situated near the land of Domina de Amerun.

[3] Cf. Holy Sepulcher, no. 158, 1171, 308–309, which deals with local Christian villages near Lydda. Holy Sepulcher, no. 16, July 13, 1146, 63, and Holy Sepulcher, no. 52, 1160, 140 (Robertus de Git), include indications of the existence of Frankish settlement in one of these villages (Castrum Git). A recent archeological excavation reveals that the Frankish archeological site known as Kh. al-Burj (grid reference 152/145), is built on the site of the biblical city Gat-Gittaiym which might be identified as the medieval "Castrum Git."   [4] Prawer, 1980c.
[5] Strehlke, no. 128, 1243, 121–122 (Röhricht, Regesta, no. 510).
[6] Mayer, 1975, 71–73.

- The same Domina de Amerun owned another piece of land which was situated near the "new vineyard of.Bernardus Dives."
- Bernardus Dives is mentioned in transaction no. 6 as the owner of another vineyard and his descendants are mentioned in transaction no. 17 as the co-owners of the mill.

From such examples one can see that the document is a kind of jigsaw puzzle which, when completed, enables us to reconstruct a previously unnoticed Frankish village. Like many of its European counterparts, this village consisted of a castle and an adjoining rural burgus. Thirty-seven names of Frankish petty landlords and farmers who lived there are mentioned in addition to the location of fields, vineyards, gardens, a mill, and several establishments such as the church, the old curia, the *domus leprosorum*, etc. The identity of this village can be deduced from the first few words of the document, which are "Aput Castellum Regis." Strehlke, who edited the document, attributed those three words only to the first transaction and not to the remaining twenty. Consequently he did not regard them as a rubric for all twenty-one transactions, which are interconnected.

The first transaction which begins with "Aput Castellum Regis" deals undoubtedly with property which is located in, or very close to, Castellum Regis. There is a reference here to the purchase of two vineyards which were located opposite (contra) the road leading to Bucael. Bucael of the Frankish period is Buq'aiya, known today as Peqi'in, the neighboring village of Castellum Regis to the southeast.

The fact that Dominus Boonecasa, one of the owners of the vineyards, also lived in Castellum Regis is confirmed in another document issued in 1257, which describes him as a bourgeois from Castrum Regis. This document affirms that the Order bought all of Boonecasa's (or Benencasa's) property after his death.[7] However, I think it is superfluous to discuss all the transactions mentioned in the document and to show, again and again, that they all refer to the same village. Instead, I will try to summarize the information we can glean from some of the main facts contained in the descriptions of the transactions.

The network of roads (see figs. 1 and 2)

The aforementioned document enables us to reconstruct the network of roads, at least some of which were built by the Franks, connecting Castellum

---

[7] Strehlke, no. 112, 1257, 92: "Item petebamus dictos magistrum et fratres condempnari ad solutionem quadraginta bisantiorum annuatim pro faciendo annuali Benencase, burgensis Castri Regis."

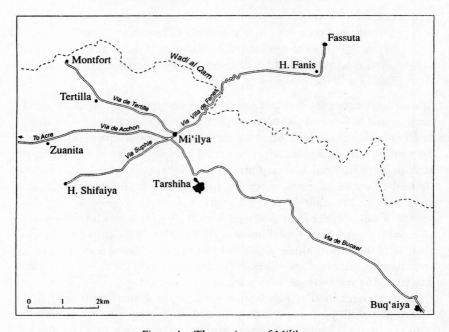

Figure 1   The environs of Mi'ilya

Regis with the neighboring villages. For example, both vineyards mentioned
in transaction no. 1 are opposite (contra) the road leading to Bucael. Another
road is mentioned in transaction no. 2 which deals with a parcel of land
that was located alongside the road leading to Tertilla. Tertilla, or Terfilla, is
identified as being two kilometers away from Mi'ilya and the road connecting the two sites is well known, ending at the Teutonic castle of Montfort.[8]
A third road, which is the main road leading from Castellum Regis to Acre,
is mentioned in transaction no. 5.

Transaction no. 6 refers to a fourth road which is described as "via villa
de Fenes." Fenes is undoubtedly Hirbat Fanis, four kilometers northeast of
Mi'ilya.[9] The road which connects Castellum Regis and H. Fanis was discovered and surveyed during my field work. It is very similar to the aforementioned road leading from Mi'ilya to Tertilla and Montfort. Part of it
was well built and part of it was cut out of the rock. We can date this road
quite accurately to the Crusader period because it cuts through a Byzantine
wine press and a burial cave which was converted in the early Muslim

---

[8] Frankel, 1988, 269–270; Friedman & Peled, 1987, 121–122.
[9] Grid reference 178/271.

period into a cistern. Transaction no. 12 refers to a fifth road which connected Mi'ilya with the neighboring village of Suphie which is H. Shifaiya, the ruins of which are found three kilometers southwest of Castellum Regis.[10]

The existence of a network of rural roads which started from Castellum Regis, and the fact that at least two of these roads, the one leading to Tertilla and Montfort and the other leading to H. Fanis, were constructed by the Franks, testify to efforts which were invested by them in the "regional planning" of this rural part of their domain.

The fortification of a Frankish village

Document no. 128 provides information also about the fortifications surrounding the village. In transaction no 3 the Teutonic Order acquired from Odo de Furhun a certain fortification on his property. The author of the document did not know exactly how to identify this fortification and called it "propugnaculum, quod alio modo appellatur barbacana."[11] This part of the fortification was adjacent to another part of the barbican belonging to Guido de Renay. It is difficult to know from the document alone what is meant by this "propugnaculum" or "barbacana," but it is not feasible that it refers to the castle of Mi'ilya for which the Teutonic Order had already paid an enormous sum and the sale of which had already been confirmed by the king of Jerusalem, the German emperor and the pope.[12]

In a survey I conducted at Mi'ilya I could establish that the whole village was surrounded by a wall of eight to ten meters high, part of which was con

[10] About Suphie and Castellum Regis, see Strehlke, no. 11, 1179, 11–12 (Röhricht, *Regesta*, no. 587). Baldwin IV confirms the purchase of the villages, Suphie amd Suhmata, from Petronilla, the vicecomitissa of Acre, for the sum of 4,500 bezants. Petronilla had houses in "regis Castello novo" which were sold together with the said villages and their "pertinentiae." From the fact that the owner of the villages sold "houses" in Castellum Regis and did not mention "houses" in Suhmata and Suphie, one can conclude that in the two latter villages there was no Frankish settlement, and it can be assumed that the Frankish settlement in Castellum Regis took place before 1179.

[11] For "aliud" better read: "aliter" or "alio modo." Prawer, 1985a, 3, referring to what he himself characterized as "a rather dubious Arabic or Persian etymology," stated that a barbican is "a kind of tower or fortification defending a particular point like a gate or a bridge." But according to Bloch and Von Warburg (to whom he himself made reference) "[a] Barbecane – Au moyen âge, designe surtout un ouvrage extérieur percé de meurtrières." O. Bloch & H. von Warburg, *Dictionnaire étimologique de la langue française*, Paris (1964), s.v. barbecane; cf. J. F. Niermeyer, *Mediae Latinitatis Lexicon Minus*, Leyden (1976), 85: "barbacana, ouvrage avancé en dehors du rempart." Du-Cange, C. Du Fresne, *Glossarium Mediae et Infimae Latinitatis*, repr., Graz (1953), 568: "Barbacana: Propugnaculum exterius, quo oppidum aut castrum, praesertim vero eorum portae aut muri muniuntur: unde Antemurale, promurale, et murus exterior."

[12] For the juridical difficulties and for these confirmations, see Mayer, 1980, 189–199.

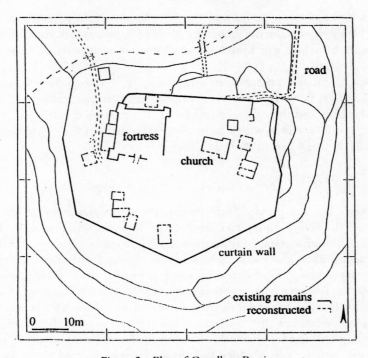

Figure 2   Plan of Castellum Regis

structed and part of which was hewn out of the natural rock. This wall might be the fortification mentioned in the text (see fig. 2 and plate 1).[13]

Village establishments and communal buildings

Even though no public buildings were sold in these transactions, there are several public establishments which are mentioned en passant. The wife of Wernerius de Paris, for example, sold a house which was located next to the "old curia." The existence of a curia in this village teaches us about the legal status of the villagers and their rights. It is also interesting to note that there was an old curia, which testifies to the existence of a new one, or at least to the destruction of the old one. In any case, the existence of an old curia con-

[13] For a "barbacana" used as a part of the fortification of a town, see Strehlke, no. 28, 1193, 24–25; Hospital, no. 972, Jan. 5, 1195, 617. For a "barbacana" situated between the two walls of a town, see Strehlke, no. 50, Aug. 1217, 41; no. 70, Apr. 1229, 55; no. 113, Nov. 1257, 95. Cf. also Röhricht, *Regesta*, no. 746, 1198, 199; Strehlke, no. 113, Nov. 1, 1257, 95–96.

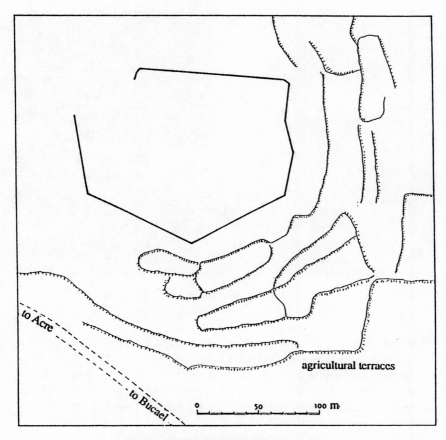

Figure 3   Plan of the fields of Castellum Regis

firms the assumption that the Frankish settlement of Mi'ilya was in existence for quite some time.[14]

Similarly, in transaction no. 2, there is a reference to the "domus" of the archbishop of Nazareth. This "domus" was not the only ecclesiastical "domus" in the village. The bishop of Acre also had such an establishment which is mentioned in another document issued in 1257.[15] In this latter

[14] Pringle is of the opinion that the new curia might have been the new castle of Montfort, which was built at the same time. See Pringle, 1986b. See also Hubatch, 1966. For the dating of the document to the very beginning of the thirteenth century, before the construction of Montfort, see Ellenblum, 1996, 115–119.

[15] Strehlke, no. 112, 1257, 91–92: "Item petebamus restitui ad possessionem vel quasi iuris per-cipiendi decimas in domo episcopali, que est in Castro Regis, fructuum et proventuum ex

Plate 1   Castellum Regis

document, reference is made to tithes in kind payable to the bishop of Acre "in domo episcopali, que est in Castro Regis." Transaction 12 indicates how this church property was managed, as it refers to Henricus who was the bishop's dispensator. Henricus was most probably the representative of the bishop in Castellum Regis and it was he who managed the collection of the tithes in the bishop's "domus."

There was also a church in the village, as mentioned in transaction no. 12. The plot of land purchased in this transaction is described as being next to the church of Mary Magdalene. This is the one and only reference to a church in the village and most probably it was the only one built there. The survey I conducted revealed that the church was on the same site as the present church in Mi'ilya.

Finally, from transaction no. 13 we can learn that there was a leper house in the village, a fact which is perhaps indicative of the prevalence of leprosy in the Frankish East.

omnibus pertinenciis dicti Castri Regis sitis in diocesi Acconensi; item et fetuum et fructuum, animalium et avium, que omnia dicebamus dictos magistrum et fratres solvere debere in domo predicta, ad quorum omnium vecturam usque ad locum predictum petebamus dictos magistrum et fratres condempnari debere."

The reconstruction of the field system

The text enables us to learn about the distribution of the fields of Castellum Regis and to reconstruct their location. In transaction no. 6, the Teutonic Order bought from Domina Dulcia a vineyard which was situated between the vineyard of the bishop and the vineyard of an anonymous Balistarius. In transaction no. 8, the Order bought another vineyard from the daughter of Hugo Merlin. This vineyard was situated between the aforementioned vineyard of the Balistarius and the vineyard of Petrus de Schalum. If we combine the two transactions, we can reconstruct a row of five vineyards: that of the bishop, that of Dulcia, that of the Balistarius, that of the daughter of Hugo Merlin, and the vineyard of Petrus de Schalum.

the vineyard of the bishop	the vineyard of the Balistarius	the vineyard of Domina Dulcia Hugo Merlin	the vineyard of the daughter of	the vineyard of Petrus de Schalum

Another example of field distribution can be deduced from transaction no. 3 that refers to a parcel of land which was bought from the wife of Odo de Furhun. This parcel of land was adjacent to the land of another Frankish settler by the name of Guido de Renay and is situated "in terra alba." The term "in the white soil" is quite vague, but, fortunately, as the land of Guido de Renay is mentioned again in transaction no. 5, it can be accurately located. This parcel of land is described as bordering on the lands of a "villa which is called Sivenete" and as being located above the road leading to Acre. Sivenete is undoubtedly the ruins of Zuanita which are three and a half kilometers west of Mi'ilya.[16] It is even possible to locate this field with greater accuracy if we take note of the geological hint that the lands of Odo de Furhun and Guido de Renay were in the "terra alba." "Terra alba" in this region can only be white soil which is created by the erosion of cretacious rocks of the Senonian age. On the road connecting Mi'ilya and Zuanita, there are only a few hundred meters where such rocks exist. There is no need to be an expert pedologist in order to recognize the difference between terra alba and the terra rosa which coats the rest of the area. The difference is obvious to any farmer, and it was obvious also to the Frankish villagers of the twelfth and thirteenth centuries who specialized in growing grapes.

A third example can be deduced from transactions nos. 6 and 8: in the

---

[16] Kh. Zuanita is a very extensive ruin of the Byzantine period. Grid reference 169/268. See Avi-Yonah, 1934.

former, a plot of land which was sold by Dulcia and which is above the "red" vineyard of Bernardus Dives is described. In the latter, a plot bought from the daughter of Hugo Merlin and which was also above the "red" vineyard of Bernardus Dives is described. Thus, one can reconstruct an additional part of the fields of Mi'ilya.

Dulcia's plot of land according to transaction no. 6	The daughter of Hugo Merlin's plot of land according to transaction no. 8
	The vineyard of Bernardus Dives according to transactions nos. 6 and 8	

It would appear that plots of land belonging to Dulcia and the daughter of Hugo Merlin were next to each other. Their vineyards, too, were not far apart, and only the vineyards of Odo de Furhun and the Balistarius separated them. The plots of land of Guido de Renay and that of the wife of Odo de Furhun were also next to each other as were the fortifications belonging to them. Can one assume that the connection between the plots of land and the houses of the various farmers was coincidental? In my opinion, the answer is no. Contemporary European settlement in new villages and towns was generally pre-planned and encouraged by the owners of the plots. It is feasible to assume, therefore, that the allocation of land in the new settlements of Palestine was also conducted in an organized and planned manner.

The layout of the village and the adjoining fields

From an analysis of Strehlke no. 128 and the conclusions to be drawn from my field study, it would appear that the rural burgus established at Mi'ilya was surrounded by a fortification consisting both of dwellings and a "propugnaculum sive barbecan." A stretch of land, empty of buildings, separated the houses from the fortifications. This stretch of land, which almost certainly contained the "gardens," varied from a width of fifteen meters at its narrowest part to a width of thirty meters at its widest part.

Within the village and its environments we succeeded in identifying the remains of seventeen dwellings which had been occupied by Frankish settlers. It would appear that a good many of the stone houses of the "modern" village (the reference is to stone houses built apparently during the Ottoman period) were constructed on Crusader foundations. This accounts for the fact that part of the external structure of the Crusader buildings was preserved as were parts of the Crusader buildings themselves. In the basement of building no. 1, for example, a barrel-vault dating to the Crusader period was completely preserved. Building no. 2 even retained the function for which it was used in Crusader times: then, as now, it was used as an oil press. In the building we discovered a stone which was part of the press whose posts were made of iron. This type of press was used only during the Crusader period.

Seven of the houses discovered were attached to each other and of the same height. Apparently, other structures of the same height were erected, creating a chain around the whole village. The two chains – that of the "gardens" and that of the houses – strengthen the theory that the village was built according to a preconceived plan. Only one building was found outside the fortifications. It was constructed where the road leading to Montfort began and it can be assumed that it was a leper house built, according to custom, outside the walls of the village.

One house, larger than the others built in the chain of houses, faced south. The builders of the modern house, constructed on the ruins of this Crusader building, found a Byzantine stone which had been remasoned during the Crusader period, and on the back of which a large cross inside a circle had been chiseled. The size of the house, its preferential position, and the large Frankish cross on one of its stones testify, perhaps, to its having belonged to some ecclesiastical institution. It was not, of course, the church of the village, as this was at the upper end of the village, near the fortification; it was also certainly not the leper house which, as stated above, was outside the boundaries of the village itself. One can safely assume that this house belonged to the bishop of Acre and was used as the center for collecting the tithes from the whole area.

On the same site where the church of the Frankish village existed, modeled on the Latin cross (with a transept), there is now a modern church, built in the nineteenth century. Fortunately, we managed to examine the church at exactly the same time that the villagers were busy destroying the remains of the original transept as they considered it a superfluous obstruction to the church's perfection.[17]

Even though according to the document there were more than thirty houses belonging to the residents of the village, we did not succeed in tracing more than seventeen of them. Remains of the others were apparently destroyed by the present villagers in the course of construction. From air photographs taken by the British in January 1945, it is apparent that there were many buildings in the center of the village which have been destroyed

[17] Transepts are very unusual in Crusader churches except in the church of Jacob's Well, the cathedral of Tyre, in al-Nabi Samwil, and possibly Caymont.

in the meantime. At the foot of the village, to the north, a large reservoir was discovered. It had apparently been used to provide water for cattle.

The planning of the agricultural plots (see fig. 3)

From an analysis of the alignment of the agricultural plots around the fortress it would appear that both the fortress and the wall surrounding it, as well as the agricultural fields, belonged to the same architectural-agricultural complex. The outlines of the agricultural terraces fit in with the alignment of the wall even in places where parts of the wall form an angle not necessarily required for topographical reasons. This fact proves, in my opinion, that the terraces, and not only the fortress and the adjacent burgus, were constructed during the Frankish regime. If the Franks had inherited the agricultural infrastructure and had not created a new infrastructure for themselves, we could not have expected to find such perfect compatibility between the Frankish wall and the fields. If this conclusion is correct, then it follows that the Franks established a new settlement which did not infringe on the agricultural rights or trespass on the fields of the local inhabitants.

The above conclusion is bolstered by the fact that the Frankish village of Mi'ilya was not established on the same site as the earlier Byzantine village but rather on a hill to the southeast of the earlier village. The church ruins and other remains found at the Byzantine site attest to the village that existed there and not on the nearby hill. Settling near the Byzantine village and not on it, the Franks created a new settlement network for themselves, which consisted of a new field system, and new terraces and overlapped to a minimal extent the fields and terraces of the earlier Byzantine village. Is it only a coincidence that the Frankish village of Mi'ilya was constructed near the earlier village and not on it? In the course of this work, I shall try to prove that the answer is in the negative. The Franks constructed their settlements in the neighborhood of local Christian sites but not on the exact same spot, and in many instances, they repartitioned the agricultural areas and created new agricultural networks.

Extension of Frankish settlement to neighboring villages (see fig. 1)

Another piece of information extractable from the document concerns the question of whether Frankish settlement was restricted to Castellum Regis only, or whether it existed also in the neighboring villages. In transaction no. 5, there is a description of the property bought from the wife of Wernerius de Paris. One parcel of land is described as being close to the spring of the "villa of Terschia" and near the property of the Holy Sepulcher. Terschia is the village of Tarshiha which is situated one kilometer away from Mi'ilya. Perhaps the cultivated lands of Castellum Regis extended all the way to Tarshiha and very probably there was a Frankish settlement in Tarshiha as well. This conclusion is strengthened by another document issued by the Frankish king in 1217, in which other Frankish property in Tarshiha is mentioned.[18] It should be noted that the property in Tarshiha was donated to the German Hospital already in 1217. It should also be noted that Tarshiha was included among the villages which were "inhabited" already in 1160.

Document no. 128 in Strehlke's edition of the archives of the German Order show that Castellum Regis was not only a fortress. The document describes an agricultural settlement which was established on an elevation and was surrounded by a wall. It provides details about its institutions and the names and occupations of its inhabitants. It is possible, therefore, to assume that in the case of "Castellum Regis" the word "castellum" should be interpreted in accordance with the current meaning in contemporary Europe – that is, a fortified rural settlement surrounded by a wall.

[18] Strehlke, no. 49, 1217, 41.

CHAPTER FOUR

EVIDENCE ABOUT THE EXISTENCE OF
FRANKISH SETTLEMENTS

Detailed documents such as the one dealing with Mi'ilya are very rare, and it is difficult, therefore, to depend only on direct evidence of this nature in order to reconstruct the network of Frankish settlement. There are, however, many less detailed descriptions from which one can learn about the character and dispersal of Frankish settlements.

Direct historical evidence

This type of evidence includes explicit references to Frankish settlers, rights vested in settlers, fields planted and worked by them, or houses built by the settlers themselves in non-urban areas. Such evidence, unambiguous and irrefutable in nature, was used by Prawer and Pringle in their study of settlements in places like Darom, Bethgibelin, Gaza, Blanchegarde, Magna Mahomeria, Parva Mahomeria, Calansue, Caco, Le Grand Gerin, Palmaria, Casale Imbert, and Buria.[1] In the course of my study, I shall attempt to show that there is other such direct evidence which has not yet been utilized.

Secondly, the vesting of parochial rights testifies to the existence of a Christian community. There would be no point in granting baptism and burial rights in an area in which all the residents are Muslims, and the only Christians are the Frankish lords who arrive only for the harvest or the vintage. Parochial rights are granted only in a Christian environment. From the very fact that such rights were granted to a Latin ecclesiastical institution in any particular village, we can learn that either a Latin Christian community, or a local Christian community subject to the Latin church, existed

---

[1] See Prawer, 1980c; Pringle, 1983; Pringle, 1985; Pringle, 1986a. Pringle attached little importance to rural settlement and ascribed most of the Crusader buildings with which he dealt to security considerations. See, for example, Pringle, 1986a, 7, 12.

there. The existence of such rights was of assistance in identifying the Frankish settlements in Sinjil, in "Terra Emaus," in the five villages near Lydda, in St. George next to Tiberias, in Legio, Ta'nakh, and others.[2]

Indirect historical evidence

Indirect historical evidence includes the identification of a Frankish settler with the name of a village. For example: a document issued in 1168 mentions a man by the name of Gaufridus de Qualquelia. Qualquelia is undoubtedly the village of Qalqiliyya (grid reference 146–7/177). One can assume that Gaufridus lived, and perhaps was born, in Qalqiliyya.[3] It is important to note that Gaufridus was not the owner of the village, since the owner of the village in the late 1160s was a certain Bartholomeus and not Gaufridus.[4] Another Frankish settler who was associated and even identified with the above mentioned place, although he was not its owner, was Hugo de Calcalia who is mentioned in 1181 as a member of the Hospital.[5] The combination of this evidence might indicate, in my opinion, the existence of a Frankish community in Qalqiliyya.

In some cases, one can even identify the house in which a Frankish settler, associated with the place, lived. In the village of Jifna, in which Raimundus de Jafenia lived, a Frankish building was discovered which, probably, served as his place of residence.[6] Examples of this nature are common, and there is no call to enumerate them all at this stage. It would appear that in Frankish estates in the East, as well as in many well-known instances in contemporary Europe, a person's identification with the name of a village testified to his origins, or to his place of permanent residence, or to the existence of a Frankish settlement in the place. It is not feasible that a Frank would be called after a place in which there was no Frankish settlement and all its inhabitants were locals. This conclusion is self-evident when the reference is to settlers who lived in well-known Frankish settlements (such as Petrus de Mahomeria

---

[2] See Hamilton, 1980, 90, n. 5. For the parochial rights of the church in Sinjil, see Holy Sepulcher, no. 159, Oct. 17, 1175, 310–311. For the parochial rights in Bermenayn, Capharuth, Git, Kephrescylta et Porfylia, see Holy Sepulcher, no. 158, 1171, 308–309. For the parochial rights in "Terra Emaus," see Holy Sepulcher, 107, 1141, 226–227, and Hospital, nos. 139 and 140, 1141, 113–115. For the parochial rights in St. George next to Tiberias, see Delaborde, no. 15. Hospital, no. 603, 4, 1126, 40; Kohler, no. 2, 1109, 113–114; Delaborde, no. 40, 1178, 87–88.

[3] Hospital, no. 398, 1168, 272 (Röhricht, *Regesta*, no. 448).

[4] Holy Sepulcher, no. 146, Mar. 2, 1168, 285: "in Calcalia, domum et terram quas Fed., frater Sancti Sepulcri, vobis dedit, et Bartholomeus, ejusdem ville dominus, donum ratum habuit, adjungens vobis unam carrucatam terre." [5] Hospital, no. 603, 1181, 412.

[6] Hospital, no. 625, Feb. 6, 1182, 424. Warren & Conder, 1882–1884, III, 437–8; Kochavi, 1972, 174; Benvenisti, 1982, 147.

or Paganus de Calenzun); but it can be assumed that it is also correct regarding villages in which Frankish settlement has as yet not been recognized.[7]

Villages identified with the names of their owners

An outstanding example of this linking of village and owner is the village of Akhziv, which was called "the village of Humbertus de Pace." It would appear that Humbertus received substantial rights in the village already at the beginning of the twelfth century, and was, perhaps, the first to settle there. Akhziv's identification with Humbertus continued for many decades after his death. The place continued to be called Casale Imbert during the entire twelfth century and until the second half of the thirteenth century.[8] In the course of this book, we shall see that there were many other examples of this kind.

Villages referred to only, or mainly, by their Latin name

It is difficult to distinguish between villages like Akhziv in which there was Frankish settlement and villages which belonged to a certain Frankish owner who did not establish his residence there. It would seem that this distinction could be facilitated by separating villages referred to by their local names only from those with Latin names or with the names of their owners. In my opinion, it can be assumed that in a substantial number of cases in which villages were given purely Latin names, there was Frankish settlement, or an attempt at Frankish settlement. Furthermore, in cases where Latin names are mentioned together with local names, such as Miʿilya, also called Castellum Regis, and Coquet (a French adaptation of the Arabic name Kuwaykat), or Coket, also called Belvoir or Bellum videre, one can find evidence of Frankish settlement. The local names, or the Latin or French corruptions of these names, are used mainly in early documents. In later documents, written after Latin settlement had taken root and become established, the local names gradually lost their importance until they disappeared completely from the Latin documents.[9]

---

[7] I would like to thank Prof. Jean Richard for the useful discussion we had on this subject.

[8] See Röhricht Regesta, no. 101, 1123; no. 240, 1146; no. 281, 1153; no. 733, 1197; no. 1175, 1249; no. 1208, 1253; no. 1250, 1256; no. 1307, 1261. The place is mentioned as Casal Imbert in Les Gestes des Chiprois, 207. In 1130 there was still need for explanation that Casale Huberti de Pazi is the place known as Siph, Röhricht, Regesta, no. 134, 1130.

[9] The local name "Mhalia" of Castellum Regis is used only in the first document in which the place is mentioned: Strehlke, no. 2, 1160, 2–3 (Röhricht, Regesta, no. 341). Belvoir too is described for the first time as the casal of Coquet which borders the territory of Gibul to the

The Frankish nature of the settlement is all the more obvious in the case of villages which had only Latin names. These were often the names of the Frankish lords. In the Latin documents one can find names like: Casale Amalrici, Casale de Ansquetino, Casale de Bacheler, Casale de Gaufrido Agule, Casale de Gerardo Bostgher, Casale de Porcel, Casale Galteri de Bulion, Casale Gaufridi de Portu, Casale Guillelmi de Balma, Casale Petri de Podio Laurentii, Casale Roardi, Casale Roberti, Casale Rogerii de Chastellion.

Other names identified the village with its ecclesiastical owner, as in the case of the villages of Casale Templi Domini, Casale Sancti Sepulcri, Casale Sancti Georgii, Casale Patriarchae, Casale Latinae, Casale Infirmorum, Casale Episcopi. In such cases it is not possible to establish with any certainty that the reference is to Frankish settlements, although we do have evidence of the existence of Frankish institutions in villages bearing such names too. There are some villages with descriptive Latin names, the names of their lords being difficult to find. Examples of these are: Casale Rubeum, Casale Novum (!), Casale Melius, Casale Feniculi, Casale Bubalorum (de Buflis), Casale de la Fauconnerie, Casale Balneorum, etc. Here, too, although we have written proof of the existence of Frankish settlements in places like Casale Feniculi, Casale Bublorum and even though it could be assumed that in Casale Novum too there was Frankish settlement, it cannot be established with any certainty that the reference is to new Frankish villages.

The borders of villages and agricultural plots

The subject of borders is too broad to be thoroughly treated here. We shall deal, therefore, with only the main points relevant at this stage. We shall discuss the subject more extensively within another framework.

In the Latin sources, one can find tens of accurate descriptions of borders of plots belonging to Franks. One can learn from these documents how the plots were marked, who was responsible for their demarcation, how legal measures were applied in case of disputes, who were the arbitrators in cases

north, Holy Sepulcher, no. 138, 1165, 270 (Röhricht, *Regesta*, no, 420). Three years later, after the huge castle of Belvoir was constructed, a French name (Belvear) and a Latin name (Bellum videre) were added to the Latinized Arabic name Coquet. Hospital, no. 398, 1168, 271–272. After the construction of the fortress, the new French name was initially not recognized and the first document in which the fortress is mentioned identifies it still by its old French-Arabic name "Castellum Coquet alias Belvear nuncupatum." In other words, it was the French-Arabic name which was the more common up to the time when the document was issued, the name Belvear having not yet been entrenched. Twelve years later the king granted the Hospital 100 Beduin tents "apud Bellum videre," and he no longer used the old name. From then onwards the place was called only by its Latin name.

of disputes between lay owners, and who were the arbitrators in disputes between ecclesiastical bodies. One can also completely reconstruct the judicial proceedings: the statements of the parties, the swearing-in of witnesses, the kinds of witnesses considered acceptable, etc. Before presenting some of this evidence, I shall note some general principles characteristic of all the documents.

(1) The documents do not mention the local farmers who could presumably have been the main interested parties. However, on the other hand, we do have detailed information about the personal and direct involvement of Frankish nobility of the highest order in all proceedings concerning the demarcation and division of land.

(2) All the judicial proceedings were conducted before Frankish judges or arbitrators. There is not even one example of an application to a local "rays" for a solution to a land problem. According to the accepted model, the Franks, who purportedly lived in the large cities, were almost completely cut off from their landed estates and were interested only in the harvest and vintage.[10] The person responsible for collecting the harvest, according to this model, was the local rays, who was presumably also in charge of dividing the burden amongst the occupants of the village. Disputes over land, if there were any, were supposed, therefore, to be settled by the rays. But it is difficult to explain why land disputes were brought before the Frankish judicial instances, why the Franks served as arbitrators, and why noblemen of the highest order were personally involved in the marking of boundaries, unless one agrees that the Franks were actively involved in the country life and that the property there was held by burgess tenure.

(3) The distribution of these descriptions is also of interest. Most of the detailed and accurate descriptions of plot and village borders deal with areas in which, according to a field study, there was intensive Frankish settlement. There is no evidence of the demarcation of land and no detailed descriptions of agricultural plots in other areas. Can one ascribe this solely to chance and to differential preservation of the documents? The answer, in my opinion, is in the negative. I think that in Palestine, as in contemporary Europe, marking and quarreling about borders is indicative of new settlement. The demarcation of borders in the manner and to the extent which will be described later would have been superfluous and void of any economic and practical logic if the previous land set-up had remained intact after

---

[10] For the duties and rights of the rays, see Riley-Smith, 1972, 9–15. "The rural population lived in village communities, in each of which disputes were settled and decisions on matters of common concern were taken in a village court presided over by one of the . . . community . . . the rays." Smail, 1973, 40.

the Frankish conquest and if the local inhabitants, who had worked those same lands under the Muslim regime, had continued to cultivate them under the Frankish regime. The intensive interest which the Franks showed in their landed property does not testify to physical severance from it, but rather to close, daily ties with it. It would appear, therefore, that where the Franks invested toil and effort in demarcating plots of land there was Frankish settlement.

Obviously it is possible that there were disputes over land whose ownership had been recognized for many generations. However, such disputes would have had the nature of violent altercations between local farmers. In such event, the disputes would not have been decided in the Frankish judicial proceedings but would have been treated as disputes between local farmers, which came within the jurisdiction of the local rays, unless criminal law was applicable.

A clear hint at the direct connection in Palestine, as in Europe, between new settlement and the demarcation of land boundaries can be found in the document describing the sale by Aimery, king of Jerusalem and Cyprus, of the village of al-Bassa in Western Galilee and of the *gastina* Missop (today near Kibbutz Mezzuva) to the Teutonic Order. One can learn from the document about the direct involvement of the marshal of the Kingdom in the marking of land and about the connection between the marking of land which was previously the ruined site (*gastina*) of Missop and the new settlement on the site.

Notum sit . . . quod ego Aymericus . . . vendidi et dedi . . . vobis, fratribus hospitalis . . . Alemannorum . . . quoddam casale in territorio Ackon situm, quod vocatur Lebassa, cum omnibus suis pertinenciis et unam gastinam cum omni territorio suo, que vocatur Missop, *que illa die erat gastina* [my emphasis]. Quod casale predictum cum omnibus suis pertinenciis et gastinam prenominatam, sicut superius divisum est, libere et imperpetuum habeatis et teneatis, sicut Iohannes marescalcus meus et homines mei precepto meo eiusdem predicti casalis et dicte gastine terram diviserunt et terminos posuerunt.[11]

I do not intend to claim that wherever there was a demarcation of borders or a land dispute, there were Frankish farmers who worked the land themselves. Very often, the affairs of the landed property were managed from "maisons fortes" in the heart of the village or built on heights outside the village. In such cases, it was the local farmers who worked the land while their Frankish masters kept a close watch over them. Sometimes, local Christians were employed as supervisors. But in general most of the

[11] Strehlke, no. 38, Oct. 1200, 31.

references to the demarcation of field boundaries are in connection with places in which there was Frankish settlement.

In order to understand the deep interest which the Frankish nobility and bourgeoisie had in the boundaries of their lands, I shall give a few examples.

(1) In a document issued in 1145, Galterius, the lord of Caesarea, describes the division of land performed by his father and himself. Galterius was present, according to the document, at the demarcation of the boundaries by means of stone crosses:

sicuti idem pater meus divisit territorium a casale Sancte Marie Vallis Josaphat et casale Sancti Petri Cesaree et casale de la Forest et casale Sabarim et casale Sancti Johannis Sebaste et a meo casali quod nuncupatur de Bufles, *et sicuti ego presentia mea signavi et designari feci in quibusdam locis per cruces in rupibus factas, in quibusdam autem in petris in terram fixis* [my emphasis].[12]

(2) In a confirmation of the property of the Chapter of the Church of the Holy Sepulcher, issued ten years later by Baldwin III, the stone signs which were still visible in the same area are mentioned: "medietatem casalis Fiesce, nunc casale Sancti Sepulcri nuncupati, quam . . . Eustachius Granerius, . . . ecclesie Sancti Sepulcri donavit, et totam terram illam quam Galterius, predicti Eustachii filius, circa idem casale canonicis Sancti Sepulcri, ultra flumen habendam usque ad *terminatos designatos qui usque in hodiernum diem apparent,* [my emphasis] dedit, sepedictis canonicis confirmo."[13]

(3) Amalric, when he was still the count of Jaffa and Ascalon, was also involved, through the medium of his "men," in the demarcation of boundaries of plots on his lands. In a document issued in 1160, there is a description of the donation of a village near Ascalon together with sixteen "carrucae" of land: "dono . . . casale quoddam quod vocatur Geladia, cum sexdecim carrucatis terre, juxta quod *per homines meos fuit eis tradita, divisa, terminis et metis designata, determinata.* [my emphasis]"[14]

(4) In that same document Amalric confirms that four "carrucae" were divided and their boundaries demarcated: "Confirmo . . . meis IIIIor carrucatas terre que est super flumen ante Joppen, sicut divisa est et terminis metata"

Land disputes between Frankish burgesses or knights

An example of a legal arbitration which terminated a land dispute between the prior of the Holy Sepulcher and the abbey of St. Mary of Josaphat, con-

---

[12] Holy Sepulcher, no. 59, 1144, 151.   [13] Holy Sepulcher, no. 42, July 13, 1155, 117.
[14] Holy Sepulcher, no. 49, Nov. 30, 1160, 133.

cerning the boundary between the lands of both ecclesiastic bodies, can be found in a document issued in 1162. The land involved was next to the fortress called Castrum Feniculi, in the lordship of Caesarea. The document is framed as an arbitration agreement appointing the archbishop of Caesarea as arbitrator. Present at the proceedings were also the abbot of St. Mary Josaphat and the prior of the Holy Sepulcher. They all arrived at the disputed land on the appointed day. Reliable persons from Caesarea who were well acquainted with the boundaries of both portions of land served as witnesses, and with the aid of their testimony the boundaries were demarcated. The boundary marks testify to the close acquaintance which the owners of the land had with the relevant plots of land. The parties also had expert knowledge of such details as the existence of carob trees, a botanical characteristic of the coastal area of Palestine.

Qui terram a palmo usque ad carrobletum, a carrobleto usque ad cannetum, a canneto usque ad flumariam recta linea et concorditer perambulaverunt. Postea vero nos ex gratia et ex bona voluntate et ut de cetero eterna pax inter ecclesias nostras permaneret, terram que a canneto in ultra, que quasi lingua est, eis concessimus, ita ut a canneto per transversum ad flumariam, divisa stabilis et firma fieret.[15]

The arbitrators were sometimes bourgeois inhabitants of the nearest Frankish city. There is even evidence that some of the arbitrators served in that role several times, and it is possible that this was their permanent function in the Frankish judicial system. In a document of the year 1185, Balian of Ibelin was asked by Jean, abbot of St. Mary Josaphat, to distinguish between the land situated in the hills of Aschar and those of Aschar ('Askar). Balian, the seignior of the area, appointed Bernardus Pelliparius, Guido Raitz, and Guido de Aschar, swore them in, and asked them to fix the boundaries and mark them: "terram . . . ipsam dividendo, certas metas et bunnas interposuerunt et cruces infixerunt . . . ut autem jam prefate terrae divisio rata permaneat et a nullo deinceps possit perturbari, hoc privilegium exinde fieri jussi et sigillo meo [et] testibus subscriptis corroborari praecepi."[16]

We find the following description of the legal practice in accordance with which land boundaries were demarcated in the area of Mahomeria: The dispute was between Arnaldus, the prior of the Holy Sepulcher, and Robertus de Retest. Both claimed (and the contents of their declarations are given) that they knew where the boundaries and the boundary marks of their

---

[15] Holy Sepulcher, no. 57, 1162, 149. Carob trees are unknown in Europe, where the Latin form of the Hebrew or Arabic word "haroub"- Carobbletum – was used.
[16] Kohler, no. 46, 1185, 155.

lands were. The court could not decide between them and transferred the proceedings (as in the Caesarean case) to the disputed area. The credible witness this time was an old Muslim – one of Robertus' men – who knew where the boundaries were. Robertus warned the man to tell the truth and to point out the real, true boundaries. He did so, and the case was decided on the strength of his testimony. Here too, the dispute centered on land which was close to a place where there was Frankish settlement; however, from the wording of the document, it is apparent that in some cases the local farmers continued to work the fields. [17]

In places where apparently there was no Frankish settlement, but there was nevertheless a land dispute, there are much more general descriptions of villages and their boundaries. For example, there is a document describing the donation of two villages, Gebul and Helkar, in which there was apparently no Frankish settlement, to the Church of the Holy Sepulcher: "Hujus autem terre longitudo a montanis per planum usque ad Jordanem elongatur, latitudo vero a divisione Bethsan et Tyberiadis usque ad cavam que est proxima casali quod dicitur Huxenia extenditur, et docet et dirigit rectitudinis lineam ad predicta montana flumenque prefatum."[18]

We can continue to find numerous such descriptions. In certain areas, such as that of Caesarea or the environs of Acre in the thirteenth century, one can rely on these descriptions in order to reconstruct an appreciable part of the land system in the whole area.

Frankel, who dealt with Frankish settlement in Western Galilee, and identified such marking stones, thought, at first, that the demarcation of boundaries was not common during the Frankish regime. "Since no similar Crusader boundary stones have been published in this country, the use of inscribed stones to demarcate land holdings was certainly not a common practice."[19] In a later article, he became aware of the large number of documents describing demarcation marks in the area of his studies, and wrote

---

[17] Holy Sepulcher, no. 121, 1158–1159, 247: "Item notum fieri volumus . . . quod prior Arnaldus et domnus Robertus de Retest, apud Mahumeriam quadam die pariter se convientes, dixerunt ad invicem: 'eamus et videamus metas et divisas agrorum nostrorum et terre nostre.' Placuit igitur ambobus. Egressi sunt ut viderent et peragrarent terrarum fines et metas. Elegerunt autem quendam Sarracenum antiquum, Pedem tortum nomine, qui preiret. Ipse enim sciebat terrarum divisias et terminos. Precepit autem ei domnus Robertus, cujus homo rusticus ille erat, ut veritatem diceret et per certos et justos terrarum terminos eos duceret, minando ei pedem bonum facere incidi si mentiretur et si aliquando a via recta deviaret. Preivit igitur rusticus ille et demonstrationem quam eis ostendit et sicut ivit utrique placuit." Among the witnesses there were "Petrus Judeus et Johannes, interpres."   [18] Holy Sepulcher, no. 62, 1132, 156.

[19] Frankel, 1980, 200. It is perhaps worthwhile to note that the border stones which Frankel identified are not the first stones to be found in Palestine. See Rotschild, 1949, 65.

that they make it possible to draw a map of land holdings in the area of Acre.[20] It can be assumed that a more comprehensive study of the land holdings around Acre, Nablus, al-Bira, Caco, and Caesarea may reveal the existence of boundary stones.

[20] Frankel, 1988, 261.

CHAPTER FIVE

THE RIGHTS AND DUTIES OF THE FRANKISH SETTLERS IN CASALE IMBERT AND NOVA VILLA

In the previous chapter, I tried to show that one can rely on other details contained in documents in order to decide whether the reference is to a rural "castrum" in the European sense, a term which indicates a more complex pattern of settlement, or to a fortress plain and simple. If, for example, it can be shown that at the foot of a Frankish fortress there was a church, one can assume that there was a "burgus" there of a Christian community. A typical example is found in a confirmation issued by Pope Honorius II in 1128 for the property of the Chapter of the Church of the Holy Sepulcher. The pope confirms the Chapter's ownership of the "castellum" and of the Church of St. Lazarus, of the "castrum" and of the church of Mahomeria, and of the "castrum" and the church of "Castrum Feniculi" in the neighborhood of Caesarea. In two of the places – the castrum of Mahomeria and Castrum Feniculi – the reference is undoubtedly to parochial churches which served the settlers who lived there. In the third place, Bethania, the reference is perhaps to the Frankish church constructed over the tomb of St. Lazarus, although it is quite possible that this church too served parochial needs. "In episcopatu Jerosolimitano videlicet ecclesiam Beati Lazari cum castello et omnibus pertinentiis suis, castrum Maome cum ecclesia et omnibus pertinentiis suis; in episcopatu Cesaree Palestine, castrum Feniculi cum ecclesia et omnibus pertinentiis suis."[1]

In the following chapters I shall try to show that such types of settlement were much more common than it is usual to assume. In addition, I shall try to show that if one combines all the fragmented evidence dealing with each settlement one can reconstruct the mechanism of the settlement process, the physical layout of some of the villages, and even the outlines of their social profile. However, scholarly attempts to distinguish between "settlements"

---

[1] Holy Sepulcher, no. 6, Sept. 4, 1128, 41.

and "fortresses" may be frustrated by the paucity of written sources and the sorry state of archeological research.

Frankish agricultural settlement of the "castrum" type existed, amongst other places, in Casale Imbert, which is Akhziv, and in Magna Mahomeria, north of Jerusalem. Settlement in these two places was studied previously, in particular by J. Prawer and D. Pringle. I decided to concentrate on these sites not because I differ, in certain details, with the conclusions of my predecessors, but because of their fundamental importance for the understanding of Frankish settlement.[2]

Casale Imbert

A document of the year 1123 hints at the existence of a Frankish settlement in Casale Imbert. The document confirms that an olive grove was given by Letardus, the viscount of Acre, to the abbey of St. Mary Josaphat. The olive grove was near the Casale Humberti de Pace. It is interesting to note that a village was named, already in the 1120s, after its Frankish landlord.[3]

During the first half of the twelfth century, the abbey of St. Mary Josaphat expanded its estate in the village. Although the monastery weighed the desirability of exchanging this property for land in the district of Tyre in 1146, and even signed a tentative agreement with the king to do so,[4] the agreement was eventually revoked and the monastery even expanded its estate. The fact that the transaction with the king did not materialize can be gathered from two confirmations issued by Baldwin III and the pope several years later. Both documents confirm that the monastery had managed, in the meantime, to acquire (or construct) a "house" (domus), described as being "below the village," and to acquire (or cultivate) a garden in addition to the olive grove which was already in its possession in 1123.[5]

As is the case in other documents, these confirmations do not elucidate what exactly is meant by the word "domus." The precise meaning can be gathered only from the context or from a comparison with textual and archeological parallels. In a study of the construction of Frankish institutions in Castellum Regis, I showed that several ecclesiastical establishments (such

---

[2] See Prawer, 1980c, 140–142; Benvenisti, 1970, 221–223; Warren & Conder 1882–1884, I, 155; Röhricht, 1887, 213 n. 6; Rey, 1877, 39; Pringle 1985.

[3] Delaborde, no. 12, 1123, 37 (Röhricht, *Regesta*, no. 101); Kohler, no. 17, Oct. 19, 1125, 125–127.   [4] Delaborde, no. 26, 1146, 60–61.

[5] Delaborde, no. 28, Mar. 11, 1154, 64: "In territorio Acon, . . . quatuor carurcarum terre olivarumque ad eas pertinentium apud casale Huberti de Paceo," Delaborde, no. 29, 1154, 69: "In casali vero Huberti de Pazi quod Siph vocatur, Letardus vicecomes dedit quatuor carrucas terre et olivetum et, infra casale, unam domum, et extra, [h]ortum unum." Cf. Prawer, 1980c, 140–142.

as those of the bishop of Acre and the archbishop of Nazareth, and the leper
house) had "houses" in the village from which they managed their agricultural estates. It can be assumed, therefore, that here too the agricultural
estates were similarly managed, and that the "houses" referred to in the documents were the local administrative centers of the ecclesiastical bodies. A
"house" of this nature, belonging to the Church of the Holy Sepulcher, was
excavated at Kh. Rushmiya near Haifa.

Between 1146, when the tentative agreement between the king and the
monastery was signed, and 1154, when both the king and the pope issued
confirmations of the monastery's property, the Frankish settlement in Casale
Humberti de Pace completely changed its status. Instead of a small village,
"below" which was a modest ecclesiastical settlement, it became a settlement
of free farmers. It is quite possible that advance information about the forth-
coming change led the monastery to change its mind about swapping the
land in Casale Imbert for land near Tyre. Contact with the new settlers was
maintained by Girardus de Valentia, apparently the viscount of Acre, who
acted probably as the agent of the king ("ego Baldwinus . . . dona sive conventiones, quas Girardus de Valentia Latinis in casali Humberti de Paci ab
eodem locatis iussu meo habuit laudo et concedo"). The charter of rights
was issued by the king in 1153.[6]

Seven years after rights were vested in the farmers of Casale Imbert, the
king gave Johannes of Haifa rights in several villages near Castellum Regis,
in the hope that the villages which had till then not been "settled" would be
populated. It is difficult to establish with any certainty whether Johannes of
Haifa was given the same authority as Girardus de Valentia and whether
Johannes did in fact undertake to try and expand Frankish settlement in the
villages under his management.[7] However, as the vesting of rights in
Johannes took place a short time after the king vested rights in free farmers
in the same royal domain, it can be assumed that he hoped that Johannes
would achieve in Castellum Regis the same success as Girardus de Valentia
had achieved in Casale Imbert.

---

[6] Strehlke, no. 1, Feb. 26, 1153, 1: "Notum sit omnibus . . . quod ego Balduwinus . . . dona sive
conventiones, quas Girardus de Valentia Latinis in casali Huberti de Paci ab eodem locatis iussu
meo habuit, laudo et concedo. Que dona sive conventiones hee sunt: predictus namque Girardus
memorati casalis incolis, quos ibidem posuit, domos dedit, ipsis etiam et eorum heredibus quiete,
libere et sine omni calumpnia vel impedimento habendas et iure perpetuo possidendas."

[7] Riley-Smith differs between the functions of the "locator" and the "custodia and drogomanagium" which were excercised by Johannes of Haifa in Castellum Regis. See Riley-Smith, 1973,
49, 53–54; Prawer, 1980c, 141. However, the existence of a dispensator of the bishop of Acre in
Castellum Regis (an office which, according to Riley-Smith, is identical with the office of the
locator) testifies to the fact that the exact functions of some of these offices are not yet clear
enough.

The rights vested in the settlers

Baldwin III vested the new Latin settlers (through Girardus de Valentia) with long-term leases on houses and exempted them from annual rent. The long-term leases extending over generations became actual only upon sale of the houses – when the seller had to pay one bezant into the royal treasury – or if they were sub-let. Each of the new settlers received a plot of arable land. In return for all this property the settlers had to pay the king one seventh of all their crops ("fructus terre"), 25% of the fruits in the vineyards and orchards, and 40% of the produce from the communal olive grove.

Two elements require explanation: the comparatively high payment imposed on the olive groves, and the reference to an olive grove owned jointly by all the farmers. The olive groves were spread throughout the territory of the village, "between the two stream and beyond them." As there are several fast-flowing streams in Western Galilee it is difficult to decide whether the reference is to the brooks of Keziv and Bezet to the north, or to the Keziv and Gaʿton to the south. Whatever the southern (or northern) border of the relevant olive grove may be, the reference is obviously to a broad expanse of land planted with olive trees. There is no doubt that the trees were planted neither by the new settlers nor by their Frankish predecessors who had established the original settlement. Apparently, the king received so high a payment on the olive groves because they were long established and well developed, while the farmers received 60% of the proceeds from the groves in return for caring for them and processing the oil from the olives.

The king retained some of his seigniorial banum rights: the farmers were required to give him one fifteenth of the bread baked in the oven constructed for them in the village. The banal payments were even higher for the people who had no rights in the village but paid the king in kind for the bread baked for them. The king's seigniorial rights included also 10% of the proceeds from the bath-house (the cost of a bath was one denier), payments for the use of the mill, and payments for the right of measurement, "pro mensuratione," which were one dinar for each bezant of agricultural produce.

The king granted the settlers other economic rights: he exempted them from payment of taxes on all movable products, such as bread, wine, meat, and agricultural produce, which they sold in the market in Acre, and allowed them to use the mill in the neighboring village of Fierge without additional payment. One can conclude from this last fact that in Umm al Faraj (Fierge) there was also a Latin settlement, though it was apparently more limited in nature and possessed fewer rights.

A Frankish "castrum"

The Frankish village of Casale Imbert was either surrounded by fortifications or had a castle in which the castellan of the king lived. 'Imad al-Din al-Isfahani, Ibn Jubayr, and Abu Shama describe the place as a fortress which was captured in 1187 by Salah al-Din.[8] It is difficult to rely on these descriptions to establish if the entire village was fortified, or if it was a settlement of the nature of "fortress and rural burgus." It is important to note that although the place was fortified (or contained some sort of fortification), it was called "casale," a word generally used to describe a village. Baratier, who worked in Provence, noted a similar lack of clarity in Latin documents in which castrum and villa are used alternatively for the same villages.[9]

In Casale Imbert, there was also a seigniorial presence, which can be gathered from the fact that the place served not only as the habitation of a Frankish rural community, but also as the center of a seigniorial estate to which many settlements belonged, at least in the thirteenth century.[10]

It should be noted that the fortifications in the place are not mentioned in the Latin sources and a large part of the village was completely destroyed in the 1950s and 1960s. All that remains of the village today are a few massive vaults in the northern part of the village and some architectural details preserved in the courtyard of the private local museum. The details include, amongst other things, the remains of several churches: a Byzantine church (at least one), a post-Byzantine church, and a Crusader church. The assumption that the place was a "castrum" is based also on the resemblance between the process of settlement in Casale Imbert and that in Castellum Regis. In both places the settlement processes were initiated by the king and in both cases the Latin settlement spread out from the castrum into the neighboring villages. In the case of Castellum Regis, the neighboring villages were Tarshiha and Terfilla; in the case of Casale Imbert, the neighboring village was Umm al Faraj.

Nova Villa, next to Magna Mahomeria

There is no doubt that the settlement known as Nova Villa was neither a castrum nor a fortified village. The document in which this settlement is

---

[8] 'Imad al-Din al-Isfahani, 111, line 3; 35, line 8; 187, line 14; 324, line 6; Abu Shama, Raudatayn, II, 87, line 35; 88, line 34; 142, lines 10–11; 183, line 4; 184, lines 1–2; Ibn Jubayr, 319: "On our way [from Acre to Tyre] we passed by a great fortress called al-Zab which dominates the continuous villages and farms."   [9] Baratier, 1971, 237.
[10] Strehlke, no. 105, 1253, 84–85.

described refers to only three Frankish settlers, as well as to other future settlers ("aliisque venientibus ad manendum infra casale nostrum de Ramathes"), and it details the rights and duties of these present and future inhabitants.[11] The document indicates clearly that it is based on the "custom of Mahomeria." Unfortunately, we have no other evidence regarding the "custom of Mahomeria" itself and we cannot know with any certainty what rights the Church of the Holy Sepulcher conferred on its occupants in order to attract them to the place. The only information we have comes from this indirect source. It can be assumed that the "custom of Mahomeria" was similar to that of Nova Villa with respect to details not specified in the document.[12]

The rights of the settlers

Each one of the settlers would receive free of charge:

(1)   A plot of land for building purposes.
(2)   A plot of land for planting gardens and trees. These plots, it is noted, are not of equal size; two settlers received one carruca each while a third received two carrucas.
(3)   The right to use the flour mill, the oven, and other banal facilities according to the "custom of Mahomeria." "Furnum vero et molendinum et alias consuetudines secundum Mahumerie usum illis predictis et aliis venientibus ad manendum concedimus."
(4)   Two of the inhabitants received the right to cultivate the vineyard at Ramathes belonging to the Church of the Holy Sepulcher in order to work it properly.

The duties of the settlers

In return for the above rights, the settlers had to give the Church of the Holy Sepulcher the following:

(1)   The tithes due to the archbishop of Jerusalem.
(2)   One quarter of the annual production of grain and vegetables.
(3)   One fifth of the fruit of the vineyards and of the olive groves to be planted in the village.

---

[11] Holy Sepulcher, no. 126, Mar. 25, 1160, 252–253.
[12] According to Pringle, Nova Villa and Ramathes/al-Ram were the same place, and the courtyard building in al-Ram is to be identified as the "voltas nostras de Noua Villa." Cf. Pringle, 1983.

(4)   One quarter of the olives in the old olive groves planted by Willelmus
       Beritensis and given to two of the settlers to cultivate, in addition to
       the tithes.

(5)   The new settlers had to transfer all the produce and the tithes owing
       to the Church to the local vault belonging to the Church ("ad voltas
       nostras de Nova Villa adportabunt"). This last instruction deserves
       further study. It is apparent from the mechanism for collecting tithes
       in the Galilee that Franks constructed "houses," such as the bishop's
       "house" at Castellum Regis, in which the tithes were stored.[13] There
       apparently was such a "house" in Nova Villa, even though this village
       was not far from Mahomeria in which there was almost certainly a
       similar "house," nor from Ramathes in which there was also a regional
       center of the Church of the Holy Sepulcher which could certainly
       have stored the tithes.[14] The Church built vaults in Nova Villa in which
       to store the tithes owed to it, and which could, possibly, have served as
       a basis for new settlement. There is no doubt that "houses" of this kind
       existed also in Parva Mahomeria, in which the building used as a
       "house" was actually discovered, and in Bayt Surik, in which the
       Frankish vault can still be identified. The multiplicity of administra-
       tion centers belonging to the Church of the Holy Sepulcher in a
       limited geographical area testifies to the great density of Frankish
       settlement in this region, since only the Latins were obliged to pay
       tithes to the Latin church (even though the burden of the tithes fell
       undoubtedly on the local farmers).[15]

There is room for comparing the articles of the custom of Mahomeria and
the parallel articles of Casale Imbert. In order to facilitate such a comparison, the respective duties are shown in table 1.

The fact that the Church of the Holy Sepulcher also received tithes provided it with a considerable income, amounting to from 30% to 35% of the
annual crop yield, as opposed to the king's income in Casale Imbert which
ranged from approximately 15% of the grain crop to 40% of the yield from
the old olive groves.

The rights which the king granted to the settlers of Casale Imbert
exceeded those granted by the Church of the Holy Sepulcher to its settlers:
the settlers in Galilee received houses and not only "land on which to construct houses" which the settlers of Nova Villa received. The payments for
grain crops were lower in Casale Imbert, but the payments for grapes and

[13] Strehlke, no. 112, 1257, 91–94. Cf. Hamilton, 1980, 150–159. For further discussion, see chapter
    11.   [14] Pringle, 1983.   [15] Hamilton, 1980, 145ff.

Table 1 *Rights and duties of the settlers*

	Casale Imbert	Nova Villa
	Rights	
	Houses in long-term leases	Plots of land for building houses
	Payments	
Crop yield	15%	25%
Orchards	25%	25%
Vineyard	25%	20%
Old vineyard		50%
Olive grove	40% (old olive grove)	20–25%

olives, particularly the latter, were much higher there than in Nova Villa, and probably also in Magna Mahomeria.

The text does not specify the banal rights of the Church of the Holy Sepulcher at Nova Villa. The settlers in Casale Imbert received exemption from taxes on the sale of their movable products and they also received free use of the flour mill.

Several different customs of settlement were studied by Prawer back in 1951.[16] Prawer argued that preferential rights were granted to the settlers of frontier settlements. This was the reason, in his opinion, why preferential rights were granted to the settlers of Bethgibelin.

However, the differences between the customs of Casale Imbert and of Nova Villa cannot be ascribed to the difference between "frontier settlements" and "hinterland settlements," and it is difficult also to find an explanation for them only in security considerations. It is difficult, therefore, to see how these differences could be ascribed to some central authority for "encouraging emigration to border areas," as Prawer sought to do.

If there is any room for finding some resemblance between the above rights and modern life, then it would be correct to explain these rights as a byproduct of the encouragement of petty enterprise: the landlord attracted entrepreneurs by granting rights and means of production and his income was in direct proportion to their success in raising crops. The success of a new settlement was dependent on how attractive the rights and the locality were. The landowners competed with one another in granting rights in order to increase the desirability of settlement on their lands. It could be expected, therefore, that in places where it was more difficult to engage in agriculture because the land was less fertile or because of inferior security conditions the landowners would grant better conditions than in places

[16] Prawer, 1980c.

which were more amenable for, and more sought after by, the settlers. Bethgibelin would appear, prima facie, to be a less attractive place than Magna Mahomeria or Casale Imbert.

In the light of all this, how can the superior rights granted to the settlers at Casale Imbert be explained? Can it be concluded that the region of Mahomeria was considered more suitable for settlement purposes than that of Casale Imbert? It is difficult to find a definitive answer to these questions, but it would appear that settlement in Mahomeria began earlier and was more intensive than that in the Western Galilee and that its success testifies to the greater attraction of this region. The Church of the Holy Sepulcher could, therefore, demand from the new settlers a little more than the king could demand from the settlers in his Galilean domain and still expect to attract them.

CHAPTER SIX

THE SETTLERS: PLACES OF ORIGIN AND OCCUPATIONS

The Frankish village of Magna Mahomeria

The casale of Bira in which the castrum of Magna Mahomeria was later built is mentioned for the first time as one of the twenty-one villages (casalia) which Duke Godfrey granted to the Church of the Holy Sepulcher.[1]

A Frankish "castrum" is mentioned there for the first time in a confirmation issued by Pope Honorius II in 1128 for the property of the Chapter of the Church of the Holy Sepulcher.[2] Only four years earlier the place was called "Birrum" and was described by Fulcher of Chartres as no more than a small village (viculus) with a tower recently built in it.[3]

It is interesting to note that already in 1128 the place was called by its Frankish name. The current use of the Latin name testifies to the existence of Latin settlement. Local villages retained their original or Latinized names till the Latin settlement had taken root and only in later documents were they called only by the Latin names. It is also interesting to note that when the local name of Mahomeria reappears, it is the Syriac form "Byrra" or "Bira" which reappears and not the Arabic form al-Bira. This phenomenon is in no way unique to Mahomeria. The same applies to the local Christian village of Effraon and the village Afarbala, both called in Arabic al-Taiyba, to Hadesse, called in Arabic Kh. 'Adasa, to Beitiumen, called Baytuniya in Arabic, to Turcarme, called Tulkarim in Arabic, to Ramathes, and many others. The use of Syriac names in the twelfth century testifies, in my

---

[1] Holy Sepulcher, no. 26, 1114, 87.

[2] ". . . castrum Maome cum ecclesia et omnibus pertinentiis suis . . ." Holy Sepulcher, no. 6, Sept. 4, 1128, 41.

[3] . ". . . prope Hierusalem viculum quendam, Birrum nominatum, [the Ascalonites] vastaverun . . . mulierculae enim et infantes in turri quadam tempore nostro illic aedificata se intromiserunt, et sic salvati sunt." . . Fulcher of Chartres, 731–732; William of Tyre, 13, 12, 595, 600.

opinion, to the continuity of the Syriac traditions in some regions of Palestine, a fact which will be dealt with in the last part of this book.[4]

From another document, issued only one year after, in 1129, one can learn about the agricultural nature of the castrum of Mahomeria. The document describes the acquisition of a vineyard and of a plot of land, situated in "a bend in the road at the exit of Mahomeria in the direction of Jerusalem," from Petrus de Sancto Gauter, his wife Audeartz, his son Andreas and his daughter Petronilla: "vineam quandam cum terra adjacenti circumsepta que venientibus Jherosolimis in egressu Mahumerie prominet in sinistrali conva-lle . . . precio CXL bizant(iorum)."[5]

Most of the later documents refer to the castrum of Mahomeria as an agri-cultural settlement for all intents and purposes. Its inhabitants did, it is true, participate in the wars conducted by the Franks, as did all the inhabitants of the Kingdom, and in one of the battles "sixty-five light armed youths" of the village were even killed. However, most of the documents deal with the agricultural property of the local residents.[6]

From the fact that the agricultural settlement of Mahomeria was estab-lished as a "castrum" at such an early period one can learn about the origi-nal objectives of the settlers. No doubt the Chapter of the Holy Sepulcher had no intention of establishing there a "military outpost." It would appear that soon after they received the land from Godfrey of Bouillon they began to establish a rural burgus which, twenty-five years later, had become an agricultural fortified settlement. The "turris" which is mentioned by Fulcher of Chartres, might have served as a kernel for this new castral settlement. It would appear that in the case of Mahomeria, as in that of "Castellum Regis," the word "castrum" should be interpreted as meaning a fortified agricultural settlement.

The inhabitants of the Frankish castra: places of origin

It is difficult to reconstruct the social, geographic, and economic background of the settlers of the Frankish castra. It is also difficult to hope for a success-ful reconstruction of the social profile of a "Frankish settler" in a society where it is almost impossible to reconstruct the basic biographies of some of

---

[4] In no document does there appear the addition of "al" to the name "Bira," as one would expect if the name were Arabic. The name was transliterated into Latin from its Syriac form. Cf. Abel, 1926; Pringle, 1985; for Ramathes, see Pringle, 1983, 161 n. 110. No attempt has been made so far to establish the percentage of Arabic names and that of Syriac and Hebrew names in the Latin cartularies and for that reason no attempt has been made to study the spatial distribution of the Syriac names.   [5] Holy Sepulcher, no. 66, 1129, 162.
[6] William of Tyre, 20, 20, 938–939.

the principal magnates. However, despite all the disadvantages and difficulties arising from dependence on partial information, an attempt can at least be made to extract as much as possible from the existing documents. Two documents which contain complete lists of the settlers in two of the Frankish castra, that of Magna Mahomeria and that of Bethgibelin, might facilitate this reconstruction.

The list of the settlers of Mahomeria was issued in 1156 and it includes more than 130 names. To these it is possible to add names which are mentioned in other documents issued during the same decade.[7] Altogether, we have 150 names of settlers who lived in Mahomeria or its environs in the 1150s and 1160s. The settlers included in the list can be examined in accordance with two criteria: according to the places of their origin and according to their occupations.

Places of origin in Europe

The place of origin of seventy-four of the settlers is known. Forty-four of them came from the West and thirty from various places in the Latin East. Of those who came from Europe:

- at least four came from Burgundy (and another one from Sens)
- four from Poitiers
- four from Lombardy
- three from Ile de France ("Francigena") and one from Paris itself
- three from Bourges
- three from Provence
- two from Gascony
- two from Catalonia
- two from Auvergne
- two from Tournai
- one from Bagniolet (apparently in France)
- one from Barleta
- one from Linedan(?)
- two from Pissot(?)
- one from St. Galterius
- one from Thorso(?)
- one from Venetia
- one from Tuschet(?)
- one from St. Auben (apparently in France).

[7] Holy Sepulcher, no. 117, Feb. 11, 1156, 237–239. Only names of heads of families were taken into account.

Of the forty-four settlers whose places of origin can be identified, 80% came from areas which are today part of France. Only seven of the forty-four came to Mahomeria from places which are today in Italy. Another two came from Catalonia. Only two of the settlers came from northern France (Tournai). There is also ' no mention of settlers whose origins were in Germany or England or other places in northern Europe.

The largest group of settlers, about eighteen, came to Mahomeria from central France (four from Ile de France, five from Burgundy, four from Poitiers, three from Bourges, and two from Auvergne). Five came from the south of France (three from Provence, two from Gascony); and two came from Catalonia. From the areas which are today part of Italy came seven settlers (four from Lombardy, one from Venetia, one from Tuscany(?) and one from Barleta). I was unable to identify the places of origin of the remaining ten people.

It is worthwhile to compare this list with the shorter list of settlers in the castrum of Bethgibelin.[8]

- two from Auvergne
- two from Gascony
- two from Poitiers
- one from Lesmeses(?)
- one from Lombardy
- one from Malasis
- two from Milac(?)
- one from Bordeaux
- one from Burgundy
- one from Carcason
- two from Catalonia
- one from Corozana(?)
- two from Corseniana in Tuscany.

Of the nineteen places of origin mentioned in this list, only fourteen are identifiable (about 74%).

In Bethgibelin, as in Magna Mahomeria, there were no settlers from northern France or from Flanders, not even from Ile de France. If it is possible to draw any conclusions from this list, then it may be concluded that the settlers in Bethgibelin came from more southern and western areas than the settlers in Mahomeria. The biggest group of settlers came from southern France and northern Spain: two from Gascony, one from Bordeaux, one

---

[8] Hospital, no. 399, 1168, 272–273.

from Carcason, and two from Catalonia. Central France was represented in Bethgibelin by two settlers who originated from Auvergne, one from Burgundy, and two from Poitiers. Three settlers came from Italy, two apparently from Tuscany, and one from Lombardy.

It is difficult to rely on these lists and reach any positive conclusions from them about the places of origin of the Frankish settlers. Only a more comprehensive study of the names of the Frankish settlers in the Latin Kingdom might provide a more solid basis for such conclusions. It would appear, however, that the fact that there was not even one settler in either Mahomeria or Bethgibelin who came from northern France is not incidental nor insignificant. This fact is inconsistent, for example, with the common assumption that many of the Frankish settlers came precisely from northern France. This assumption was based on the regions from which the participants of the First Crusade originated. In this context, the manner in which Prawer summed up the list of the settlers of Mahomeria merits additional attention: "Their origins may be traced to *every country and province which participated in the Crusades*, but chiefly to France and southern Europe [my emphasis]."[9]

Prawer ignored the fact that the places of origin of all of the settlers were in southern Europe and in the Mediterranean countries and that there was not even one who came from northern France, Lorraine, or other regions whose inhabitants had played a central role in the first two Crusades. The sweeping statement that the origin of the settlers "may be traced to every country and province which participated in the Crusades" betrays a personal viewpoint more important and interesting than the inaccuracies behind it. Prawer was of the opinion, with the concurrence of other scholars, that the demographic structure of the Frankish Kingdom was fashioned, to a considerable extent, by the composition and consequences of the First Crusade. True to his conception that the Frankish Kingdom was the "Crusader Kingdom," he assumed that the heterogeneous society of Mahomeria came from the same geographical surroundings as the Crusaders.

Prawer's point of view appears, prima facie, to be feasible. It is reasonable to assume that the Crusades brought together people from different ethnic backgrounds who settled together in the same places. However, from other studies which dealt with the social composition of the contemporary European castra, it would appear that in some of them too there was a heterogeneous society which originated from various and distant places. As the places of origin of the inhabitants of the European castra were as

---

[9] Prawer, 1980c, 127.

variegated as that of the inhabitants of the new Levantine castra, the Crusades cannot be the sole explanatory basis for this variety. Monique Bourin-Derruau summed up her conclusions concerning the origins of the settlers of the castra of Bas Languedoc as follows: "most of the names . . . testify to a distant place of origin. Amongst the settlers in the castra of Languedoc there were many who came from Balaguer (near Lerida), from Esperou, Gascony and Catalonia, and there were some who were complete strangers."[10] Languedoc was not the only place which attracted settlers from afar. In the port town of La Rochelle, which is in northwest France, a list of the inhabitants dating from 1224 has been preserved. From this list it can be seen that an appreciable number of settlers arrived from other regions of France (mainly from Flanders, Normandy, and Britanny), but others came from Italy (Lombardy and Genoa), from Spain (for example Saragossa and Pamplona), and from England (Norwich, Southampton, and London). It appears that the percentage of settlers from the rural areas nearer to the castrum (or to the city) increased as the urban society developed. Thus, at the beginning of the fourteenth century, 60% of the inhabitants of Reims came from the castra and the villages situated up to thirty kilometers away. An additional 10% came from the Ardennes and only 30% came from more distant areas in France and beyond. A similar pattern is noticeable in the town of Metz whose inhabitants at the end of the fourteenth century were mostly from Lorraine.[11] A heterogenous composition and distant places of origin are, therefore, not characteristic only of the inhabitants of the Frankish castra of the Levant. The heterogeneous composition is characteristic of many castra in Europe of the same period and can be seen to be characteristic of medieval settlements in general.

The similarity between settlement in the Levant and that of contemporary Europe is apparent also in the immigration pattern. In the Frankish castra, as in the European ones, heterogeneous societies, consisting of settlers who had arrived from distant places, were created. The immigrants who came from afar lived together with those who came from nearer areas. The inhabitants of the new castra were no longer obliged to live close to their birth places. They moved freely throughout the whole of Europe in search of a better place to settle down. Marc Bloch, who compared these migrations to a "Brownian movement," maintained that it was expressed everywhere: in every village and in every castrum. Enterprising settlers traveled far afield in their search for places of residence which would give them better social status and better economic conditions.

[10] Bourin-Derruau, 1987, 255–256.
[11] Le-Goff, 1980, 197; Perrin, 1924, 463–509 Cf. also Desportes, 1966.

Was the Levant included in these mass migrations? Did some of the Franks who settled in the Levant arrive there initially not as "Crusaders" but as potential settlers? Is it possible to assume that at least part of the people who settled in the Levant were cut from the same cloth as the settlers who reached Languedoc, Gascony, Catalonia, Sicily, or any other region of medieval colonization? If so, then only a highly developed sense of adventure brought them to seal their fate in the Levant. It is possible that some of the settlers were warriors who finally settled in the East after participating in the Crusades or after concluding their pilgrimage. It can also be presumed that some of them sought to combine the materially beneficial (the receiving of economic privileges) with the demands of soul and honor (which were attached, at least in the first half of the twelfth century, to the participation in the Crusades). On the other hand, it can also be assumed that many chose to settle in the Levant, almost by chance, rather than choosing one of the other possibilities open to them. If so, then the settlement in the Kingdom of Jerusalem was part of that "Brownian movement" referred to by Marc Bloch.

It would appear that the approach to this problem depends on the historiographic viewpoint of the scholar. Those who regarded the Frankish settlement as an integral part of the Crusades examined the colonization activities from the perspective of the conquest. According to them, the settlers in the Levant were mainly "Crusaders" who decided to stay in the East after the accomplishment of their Crusader vows. These scholars claim that the number of Frankish settlers was negligible as the majority of the participants in the First and Second Crusades returned to their countries of origin.

In contrast, practically no attempt has been made to look upon the Frankish settlement of the Levant as a process separate from the military occupation, despite the abundance of evidence concerning the arrival of many potential immigrants each year and despite the general familiarity with Fulcher of Chartres' description of European settlement as being unconnected with any military occupation. This alternative concept, which is advocated here, regards the whole process of Frankish settlement as a conquest of a new frontier: the Crusades established the borderlines for Frankish settlement, but it was the settlers, following in the Crusaders' footsteps, who changed the frontier into a settled area.

The Franks who chose to settle in the Holy Land were, in my opinion, a part of a much wider social and cultural process. It is doubtful whether in the minds of the Lombards or Burgundians there was any great difference between settlement in Languedoc and Catalonia or the Frankish East. Settlement in the East was, perhaps, somewhat more dangerous and more distant (if one compares the sea journey with crossing the Alps or the Pyrenees), but it also had many inducements. In any event, the new settlers who arrived in the East brought with them geographical concepts which were current in their countries of origin. At least some of these concepts, it may be assumed, were introduced into their new homeland.

Prawer looked for, and found, the "Crusades" in almost every manifestation of Frankish life. As the Crusades were regarded as a unique phenomenon influencing every aspect of life, the Frankish settlement was also deemed to be special: a "Crusader" settlement. Prawer saw the Frankish settlers as "fighting farmers" and regarded their settlement activities as "essential acts for the fortification of the frontier." His declaration that the settlers came "from every country and province which participated in the Crusades" is another manifestation of this general approach.

The rulers of the Frankish states were certainly aware of the need to protect the frontiers, but it is doubtful whether this provided sufficient inducement for attracting settlers from the West. These settlers were almost certainly attracted by the special charm of settlement in the Holy Land, but they were also attracted, as we learn from Fulcher of Chartres, by the tremendous opportunities available in this new area of settlement. The attraction of the Levant declined gradually in the course of the twelfth century when it transpired that settlement in the Levant was fraught with objective problems resulting from the aridity of the country and the difficulty of working the land. Potential alternatives in southern France, Sicily, and Spain were more exciting and more attainable. From the few available documents dealing with settlers who had tried to settle in the Frankish East, we can learn about the objective problems connected with such settlement: difficulties of daily life, difficulties of working the land, the need to contend with a technology unknown to many of the settlers of storing water and bringing it from a source to the fields, the frequent droughts, and locust plagues. All these difficulties made settlement in the East a poor competitor with the European alternatives.[12]

Places of origin in the Latin East

Some of the settlers of the Frankish castra arrived from other Frankish villages in the Levant. Eight came from Frankish villages in Samaria, three from Jaffa, three from Jerusalem, and one from Jenin (Le Grand Gerin). Only one settler arrived in Mahomeria from a comparatively distant region of the Latin

---

[12] See for example Holy Sepulcher, no. 121, 1158–1159, 246–247: "terram . . . dedit michi prior Giraldus, cum uxore mea que prius desponsata fuerat Umberto, qui, quoniam terram predictam secundum statutum morem colere non poterat, et terram et villam deserverat."

Kingdom – from the Frankish castrum in Baniyas. A similar pattern can be traced in the list of the settlers of Bethgibelin. Here, too, most of the settlers whose origins were in the Kingdom of Jerusalem came from other nearby settlements: two from Rames (Ramla), one from St. Abraham (Hebron), and only one from Edessa.

Bourin-Derruau, in commenting on the places of origin of the settlers of the castra of Languedoc, says: "Paradoxically, the origins of those who came from nearby places were the neighbouring castra and not the smaller villages (villae)." Bourin-Derruau goes on to ask: "Where does one find settlers whose origins were in the villae?" And she replies: "In the villae themselves and not in the castra." She does not deal with the social significance of this finding.[13] Can one conclude from it that the patterns of migration were not vertical and did not include transfer from small settlements (manor houses, villae) to large castra? Such a conclusion seems to me to be too farreaching. It is difficult to envisage a lateral migration from one castrum to another without there being a migration from small communities to larger ones. In any case, even if it is difficult to understand the social significance of these migrations, it is not difficult to discern the similarity which existed, insofar as the lists of places of origin are concerned, between Mahomeria and the contemporary castra in Languedoc: in Samaria, too, the settlers tended to migrate between nearby castra in the same geographical region. The interregional migration was comparatively limited, and vertical migration – from tiny villages and manor houses to castra – is not discernible in the lists of settlers.

The list of local castra in which the Frankish settlers originated is of great importance, since it testifies to the existence of Frankish settlements which are not sufficiently recognized. For example: Hugo de Sancto Helya came to Mahomeria from the nearby castrum of St. Elye; Bernardus de Monte Gaudii and Gauterius Dominicus de Monte Gaudii came from a Frankish settlement which was adjacent to the church of Mons Gaudii (al-Nabi Samwil); Otgerius de Casali Sancti Egidii and Willelmus de Casali Sancti Egidii came from the nearby village of Sinjil; Willelmus de Casali Sancta Marie came from the village of 'Abud; Petrus de Sancto Lazaro also came from a nearby castrum – that of St Lazarus in Bethany; Rainaldus Sicher and Robertus de Neapoli came to Mahomeria from the district of Nablus, one from Nablus itself and the other from the nearby village of Aschar where there was a village belonging to St. Mary Josaphat; Andreas de Valle Cursus was apparently the only settler who came to Mahomeria from a small place,

[13] Bourin-Derruau, 1987, 256.

perhaps a manor house (there are many small Frankish constructions in Wadi Haramiyya which is apparently Vallis Cursus and its environs, but to the best of my knowledge there was no castrum or other large Frankish settlement there); Petrus de Ramathes (Ramatha) came to Mahomeria from a large sister settlement of Mahomeria – Ramathes, identified by Pringle as the Arab village of al-Ram. Finally, Rampnulfus, frater Petri Joppensis and Arnulphus Jopensis came to Mahomeria from Jaffa, while Bernardus gener Bernardi de Gerin came most probably also from Jenin.

The places of origin of two settlers, Humbertus de Josaphat and Bernardus de Josaphat, are not sufficiently clear. In the precincts of St. Mary Josaphat itself, east of Jerusalem, there was an extensive Frankish settlement and the whole area was within the seigniorial domain of the abbey. As my book does not deal with the urban area of Jerusalem and its nearest environs, I shall not discuss this semi-urban settlement here.

Lists of occupations of the Frankish settlers

The list of occupations of the settlers of Mahomeria testifies to a high standard of expertise. The most common occupations were those associated with building and carpentry: there were no less than five builders ("cementarius" or "machon") and three carpenters ("carpentarius") among the settlers. Second place was taken by the agricultural occupations. Here the expertise is more obvious: of the five men engaged in agriculture two were vegetable gardeners ("cortiliarius" and "ortalis"), two were expert at caring for vineyards ("plantavigna" and "pastinace"), and one apparently at the cultivating of grain ("frumentinus"). There was also one man who raised, or drove, camels ("camelarius"), one who raised goats ("caprellus"), and one who raised pigs ("porcarius"). Amongst other well-known occupations were those connected with metalworks: there were no less than five blacksmiths and one silversmith. There were also several occupations which were typical of any village life: among the villagers there were two butchers, one baker, one watchman, one servant, and one valet.

The list of occupations in Bethgibelin was shorter and included one carpenter and one shoemaker, the only one in this trade in both settlements. This list is perfectly consistent with what one would expect to find in a central rural settlement.

As I previously compared the onomastic lists of Magna Mahomeria and Bethgibelin with the villagers' places of origin included in Borin-Derruau's study on Bas–Languedoc, I shall now compare the list of occupations with the same study. In Bas-Languedoc the two leading occupations, prior to 1150, were shoemaking and weaving. These occupations retained their leading position in the thirteenth and fourteenth centuries. Other textile occupations were extremely rare. In the young castra of Languedoc there was, before 1150, not a single tailor, and other textile occupations do not appear even later. The metal occupations are mentioned, but they become common only after 1150, "when the economic and social success of the blacksmiths was obvious in all the villages." Other common occupations included the operators of the ovens and flour mills. Agriculture also appears in the list of occupations but not prominently, and expertise is mentioned only in connection with the cultivation of vineyards. For our purposes, it is important to examine also what is missing from this list of occupations. Borin-Derruau says that "in the list of names there is no mention of persons who worked with wood . . . there is not a single carpenter . . . there are very few references to masons . . . no butchers, no bakers: these occupations appear too late amongst the rural activities to have made any mark in the list of occupations."[14] And as in our case, too, there are no merchants in the list of occupations.

The discrepancy between this list and ours is surprising: occupations which were most common in Languedoc are practically non-existent in our lists (there is only one shoemaker in Bethgibelin, and one in Mi'ilya in the thirteenth century), while the occupations which do not appear at all in Languedoc, such as masonry and carpentry, and others which were extremely uncommon, such as metalwork, were the most common in our lists. I find it difficult to explain this phenomenon. There is no doubt that the number of builders, carpenters, and blacksmiths in the countries of Europe was no less than in the Frankish Levant, and accorded with the requirements of the former countries no less than with the requirements of the latter. Perhaps the paucity of names of such craftsmen testifies more than anything to the social structure and status of these crafts rather than to the absence of persons engaged in them. This partial explanation is based in the special requirements of the Frankish Levant – requirements which vested the builders, carpenters, and metalworkers with a unique status, and were undoubtedly connected with the frenetic building and military activities. The carpenters, builders, and blacksmiths were engaged also in the preparation of instruments of siege, the digging of channels under enemy fortifications, the preparation of armour and arms, the shoeing of horses, etc. The

[14] Bourin-Derruau, 1987, 257–258.

military operations provided a living for a great number of carpenters, black-smiths, and builders, who, because of the nature of the work, had to be loyal to the Frankish regime. They could, therefore, have been only Franks or local Christians. However, it would appear that the number of local Christian masons, blacksmiths, and carpenters was small. It is important to remember that the Levant was never rich in timber and iron. The use of wood in building was minimal and remained so up to modern times. Building was done in stone, but apparently at the end of the eleventh century not many local Christian building craftsmen remained. The prohibition against the building of new churches and the restoration of old ones was instrumental in preventing the local Christians from acquiring any expertise in monumental building.[15]

The early Christian building tradition could be better preserved in the countries of the north: in Armenia, Antioch, and the Jazira. But it can be assumed that the number of building craftsmen who remained in Syria and Palestine was not sufficient and could not provide for the variegated needs of the Frankish settlers. The fact that most of the buildings which were con-structed were used for religious and military purposes added to the problem of a shortage of artisans. There was no alternative, therefore, but to use Frankish expertise and the services of the Armenian and Syrian masons.

It can, therefore, be assumed that the building occupations which were prestigious and sought-after even in the West would be all the more pre-stigious and sought-after in the Levant. It can also be assumed that the build-ing craftsmen, the blacksmiths, and the carpenters received higher wages for their services and preferred life in the East to the rat race in the West. The social status of the building craftsmen in the East preceded by a generation their status in the West, although there, too, their status was enhanced because of the increased demand for their services. This fact caused the bishop of Le-Mans to forbid a monk by the name of Jean, who was a mason ("cementarius") in the monastery of the Holy Trinity in Vendôme to return to his monastery, despite the fact that the head of his monastery threatened to excommunicate him if he failed to return. In the end, the monk went on a pilgrimage to the Frankish East and remained there. By so doing he dis-obeyed the abbot of his monastery once again.[16]

The specialized nature of the Frankish economy may also provide the explanation for the existence of Frankish experts in vine cultivation, veg-etable gardening, and in pig breeding. Finally, a different kind of expertise

---

[15] Cf. Ellenblum, 1992. For a local Christian "cimentarius" by the name of Elias, see Holy Sepulcher, no. 43, July 25, 1150, 120.   [16] Mortet & Deschamps, 292–294.

characterized the Franks who were engaged in occupations wholly or mainly endemic to the East, and were more in demand because of the local climatic and agricultural conditions, such as camel breeding or goat-herding. Frankish experts in these occupations filled the place of the locals, particularly the Muslims, and were certainly preferred by their fellow-Franks.

CHAPTER SEVEN

THE GEOGRAPHIC LAYOUT OF A FRANKISH VILLAGE: THE EXAMPLE OF PARVA MAHOMERIA

The Frankish settlement of Parva Mahomeria (al-Qubaiyba) is not mentioned in the Latin documents of the first half of the twelfth century. There is also no hint of its existence in the detailed lists of property belonging to the Church of the Holy Sepulcher, such as that confirmed in 1114 by Baldwin I,[1] or the later list confirmed by Pope Celestine II.[2]

The first hint of the existence of a Frankish settlement in Parva Mahomeria is found in a document issued in 1159 which describes a donation of the *gastina* of Bethanam to the Order of St. Lazarus. Bethanam is the village of Bayt 'Anan, west of al-Qubaiyba.[3] It seems that the *gastina* of Bayt 'Anan was not a desolate place, but it seems also that it was not a village. Bethanam is described as being in the part of Mahomeria belonging to a certain Geraudus called Rex, and the plot which was given to the Order reaches the plot owned by another landlord Brother Angerannus. The plot referred to extends from the road till the "cava [cave?, winery?] on the other side."[4]

Geraudus Rex lived in Parva Mahomeria itself since on the list of witnesses he is mentioned as "Geraudus Rex de Mahomeriola." It may be

---

[1] Holy Sepulcher, no. 26, 1114, 87–88.

[2] Holy Sepulcher, no. 12, 1144, 56. The conclusion that this list is later than the previous one is based not only on the later date but also on the fact that Birra, the most important village of the Holy Sepulcher in this region, is already referred to as "Mahomeria" and on the fact that it is mentioned first in the list of twenty-one villages. Some of the later lists repeat the earlier list. Cf. for example Holy Sepulcher, no. 42, July 13, 1155, 116.

[3] AOL, IIB, no. 16, 1159, 135: "Ego Milisendis. dono et concedo quamdam gastina, Bethanam nomine, que est de divisione Mahomerie Geraudi cognomine Regi, ut dominus Rohardus Jerosolimitanus metas ibi constituit, usque ad divisionem fratris Angeranni; ab hac enim divisione, sicut via protenditur usque ad cavam que est in opposita parte. Ad hoc autem hec nostra fit elemosina quod quendam leprosum super numerum aliorum pro salute anime mee et parentum meorum in domo sua cunctis diebus sustenient."

[4] For the Frankish main road to Jerusalem which passed near to Bayt 'Anan see Ellenblum, 1987, 203–218.

assumed that his neighbor, Brother Angerranus, also lived in the same village of (Parva) Mahomeria.

The officials who dealt with this transaction are also worthy of our attention: the viscount of Jerusalem was in charge of the demarcation of the land, and Queen Melisend granted the land without mentioning any rights to it except her own. Surprisingly enough, the Church of the Holy Sepulcher, which was going to be the owner of Parva Mahomeria is not mentioned at all and none of its own people appear even as witnesses. It would appear that at least part of Parva Mahomeria still remained in the hands of the royal household, and that the queen could grant plots of land to whomsoever she pleased.

Five years later, in 1164, Parva Mahomeria is mentioned already in the list of property belonging to the Church of the Holy Sepulcher which was confirmed by Amalric, count of Jaffa and Ascalon. The place is mentioned as the "villa" of Parva Mahomeria, established in the territory of Bayt Surik. The name "Birra" – which is the Syrian name for Magna Mahomeria – is mentioned here, after a long lapse of time during which only the Latin name "Mahomeria" appeared in the written sources. It would seem that the return of the Syrian name was meant to serve as an explanation for the appearance of a new Mahomeria – the "little" one. "Birra, que a modernis Mahomeria major noncupatur . . . Betsurieh, in cujus territorio fundata est villa que dicitur Parva Mahomeria."[5]

The reference to Parva Mahomeria as "the villa established in the territory of Bayt Surik" hints, perhaps, at the fact that Mahomeria was established not very much earlier and was not yet a large and well-known settlement.

In a later confirmation of Amalric (then already king of Jerusalem) three settlements of equal status appear: Magna Mahomeria, Parva Mahomeria, and Betsurie. All three are referred to as "villa" and in all three there were, apparently, Frankish churches with parochial rights and Frankish settlers. The document hints also at plans to establish additional Frankish settlements: "viginti et unum casalia que dux Godefridus cum pertinentiis suis ecclesie vestre dedit; villas etiam, quas edificastis, ut Magnam Mahomariam et Parvam et Bethsuri, et alias omnes , quas edificaturi estis, ubi Latini habitabunt, cum ecclesiis et omni integritate justicie et juris parrochialis."[6]

The later confirmations of Alexander III, and of Celestine III, repeat, almost literally the confirmation of King Amalric I.[7]

The Jewish traveler Benjamin of Tudela regarded the place as a Frankish village:

[5] Holy Sepulcher, no. 135, July 16, 1164, 262–263.
[6] Holy Sepulcher, no. 150, 1169, 295.
[7] Holy Sepulcher, no. 151, Sept. 9, 1170; Holy Sepulcher, no. 170, Feb. 13, 1196, 325.

From there it is three parasangs to Mahomerie-la-petite, which is Gibeah of Saul where there are no Jews, and this is Gibeah of Benjamin. Thence three parasangs to Beit Nuba, which is Nob, the city of priests. In the middle of the way are the two crags of Jonathan, the name of the one being Bozez, and the name of the other Seneh. Two Jewish dyers dwell there. Thence it is three parasangs to Rames or Ramleh.[8]

The plan of the village

The Frankish village in al-Qubaiyba is one of the only Frankish settlements which has been excavated archeologically and can, therefore, be almost completely reconstructed. It is true that part of the excavations were undertaken before the development of modern archeological methods, but as the site consists of a single level and was uninhabited thereafter, one can rely on the results for the reconstruction of the plan of the village.[9]

During World War II the Italian archeologist, Bellarmino Bagatti, undertook an additional excavation – the fourth in number – in the precincts of the Franciscan monastery of al-Qubaiyba. In addition to this archeological work he surveyed the neighborhood of the village and succeeded in discovering additional Frankish rural sites. Bagatti prepared a detailed map of the Frankish village which was based on his own excavations and the work of his predecessors (fig. 4).[10]

Bagatti's map includes 100 Frankish dwellings both in the village itself and its close vicinity. It would appear, however, that the real number of Frankish dwellings did not exceed the number of 50. The difference beween Bagatti's estimate and mine results from the exaggerated confidence which Bagatti had in the excavations of his predecessors. In the excavations conducted during the nineteenth century the central Frankish building, situated in the center of the village, was discovered and later replaced by a missionary school for the local children. It is reasonable to assume that the central building, which was more than fifty meters long and thirty meters wide, was used by the Church of the Holy Sepulcher for administrative, storage, and security purposes. Within the building there was also a small chapel which was almost certainly used by the administrative staff of the Church of the Holy Sepulcher. The nineteenth century's excavations revealed the foundations of several walls under the central building. Bagatti assumed that they were

---

[8] Benjamin of Tudela, 28.

[9] Other villages were discovered and excavated after this work was completed. One Frankish village was discovered north of Jerusalem and another near al-Tira south of Haifa. The plans of these villages are very similiar to the plan of Parva Mahomeria. Unfortunately the publication of the villages is not completed yet.

[10] The results of the excavations and the survey were published by Bagatti, 1947.

detail of the village core   מפת הכפר

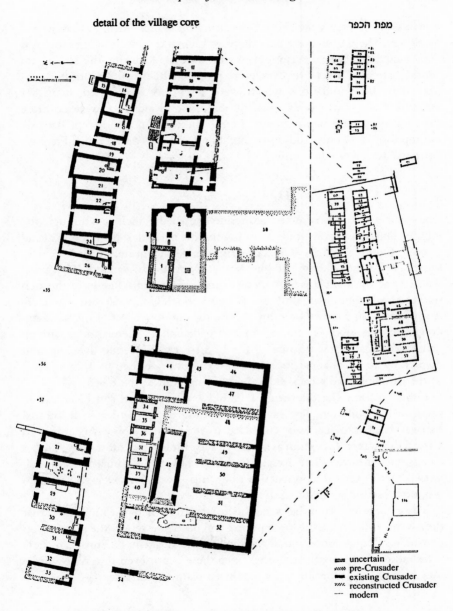

uncertain
pre-Crusader
existing Crusader
reconstructed Crusader
modern

Figure 4   Archeological remains of Parva Mahomeria (al–Qubaiyba)

remains of an earlier period of construction which included additional dwellings. These walls were later destroyed when the missionary school was constructed and their descriptions, which were made during the nineteenth century, are not sufficiently detailed to justify such an assumption. It is possible that the foundations which were discovered belong to an earlier Frankish phase, but it is also possible that these foundations were no more than retaining walls or basements. I tend, therefore, not to accept Bagatti's assumption of twenty additional buildings and to consider the Frankish "domus" as one building only.

The Frankish dwellings

The houses were constructed alongside the road which led through the village. The houses constitute a continuous line parallel to the main road and in every building there is at least one right angle. According to Bagatti, who remeasured the buildings, all the houses were barrel-vaulted. The usual diameter of the vault was 5.48 meters and the maximum height of the arch (radius plus height of the wall) was 6 meters. Such high vaults are characteristic of Frankish construction throughout the country. Most of the buildings consist of one central room, 5.5 meters wide and 15 meters long, with an exit to the main street. Some of the houses constitute one dwelling unit divided by an internal partition, the two parts were united by a door. Most of the dwellings had a back exit which opened out to the fields.

Other features characteristic of Frankish construction can be found in some of the buildings. For example, in house no. 3 there was an internal stairway built into the wall which led to the second storey. According to Bagatti this was an exception as he was of the opinion that most of the houses were single-storeyed. The average width of the walls – which was as much as two meters for the constructive side walls – was, however, sufficient to support a second storey in all the buildings.

The great resemblance between the houses strengthens the impression that they were built during the same period and possibly even by the same group of builders. Bagatti notes, quite rightly, that the village has a European character rather than a local Arab one, since there is not even one Arab village which was built according to an organized planning scheme.

The economic basis of the village: the oil industry

In thirteen of the twenty-nine houses, which were excavated in the precincts of the Franciscan monastery, small basins and hollows were found next to the exits. Basins and hollows were generally found together in the same building and it is conceivable that they had a common use. Bagatti suggested that the basins and hollows were used for the purpose of selling oil. It would appear that the occupation of an appreciable number of the Frankish farmers was the cultivation of olives and the production and sale of oil.

The important role of the olive plantations is apparent also from the comparatively large number of oil presses and oil press rollers which were found in the site. The oil presses are similar to those discovered at Miʻilya. Two of the oil press rollers were excavated within Frankish dwellings, and can therefore be accurately dated. As the village was uninhabited between the end of the twelfth century and the beginning of the nineteenth century it can be assumed that the other rollers and the millstones found at the site were also used by the Frankish settlers. Within the precincts of the monastery, eight such stones were found, and other stones were found in the village itself. The large number of oil presses, and the still larger number of basins used for the production of oil, testify to the important role played by the oil industry.

Archeological evidence of the custom of Parva Mahomeria

One can learn about the difference between the rights vested in the settlers and the rights which remained as "banum" with the Church of the Holy Sepulcher from the difference between the many vestiges of oil production and the scarce evidence for the milling of flour or for baking. No less than ten installations for the production of oil were discovered, but only one mill-stone and one oven.

The reason for this is apparently that in Parva Mahomeria, as in many other places, the mill remained in the hands of the banal authorities which took great care to ensure that the milling was done in one place only. Grain could have been stored and sold, but flour was intended for domestic use only and no accumulation of flour was possible.

The sale of flour was not part of the settlers' economy, and it had no pecuniary value unless it was a monopoly. Only if the flour was ground in one central flour mill which served the needs of all the inhabitants of the village could the process have been profitable. In Europe, too, the milling of flour was a banal monopoly which remained in the hands of the owner of the rights to the village.

On the other hand, the production of oil was a commercial right vested in the settlers, since olives could not be stored, and the saleable product was oil. For this reason there existed a comparatively large number of oil presses and places for selling oil in the village. The Church of the Holy Sepulcher undoubtedly encouraged the settlers to produce as large a quantity of oil as possible since, if the rules in this settlement were comparable to the rules of the nearby Nova Villa, it could claim almost half of its proceeds.

The use of the oven was similar to the use of the flour mill. Here too the banal authorities who reserved the right of the use of the oven, and made a considerable profit from it, were interested in having only one oven. Therefore only one oven was discovered amongst the houses of the village. The oven was constructed together with the house in which it was found. It seems that the oven was intended from the beginning to be used by the whole village. An additional hint at the central role of the oven can be found in the fact that it was constructed in the center of the village, opposite the northern exit of the church.

The geographical layout of the Frankish settlement in Parva Mahomeria was of an organized village, unlike the layout in the Arab villages. The village was established as a typical wayside village. All the houses faced the main highway which led to Jerusalem, but in contradistinction to the usual geographical approach this was not a village which developed gradually. On the contrary, it was well planned in advance. In its center there were the three main institutions which constituted the heart of the settlement.

(1) The church, which had parochial rights and which served the Frankish settlers in the village itself and in the manor houses and hamlets of its environs: in Bayt ʿAnan, in Kh. al-ʿAjab, in Kh. al-Masaka, in Kh. al-Burayj, and in Biddu we discovered remains of Frankish constructions.[11]

(2) The "domus" of the Church of the Holy Sepulcher. As the banal authorities of Parva Mahomeria was the Chapter of the Church of the Holy Sepulcher, a small chapel was erected inside this "domus." The building was sufficiently large to allow for the inclusion of storerooms for the storage of the produce to which the Church of the Holy Sepulcher was entitled both by virtue of its seigniorial rights and as tithes.

(3) The oven and the flour mill, which were built opposite the church in the center of the village, and were used by the inhabitants of the village against payment (of an unknown amount) to the Church of the Holy Sepulcher.

The well-planned appearance of the Frankish settlement of Parva Mahomeria was not fortuitous or unique. All the Frankish villages with whose format we are familiar, were well-planned. The fact that there was central planning could be deduced both from the general appearance of the

---

[11] For the Frankish sites in Biddu, Kh. al-Burayj and Kh. al-Masaka, see Ellenblum, 1987. For the Frankish site in Kh. al-ʿAjab, see Bagatti, 1947, 196–197.

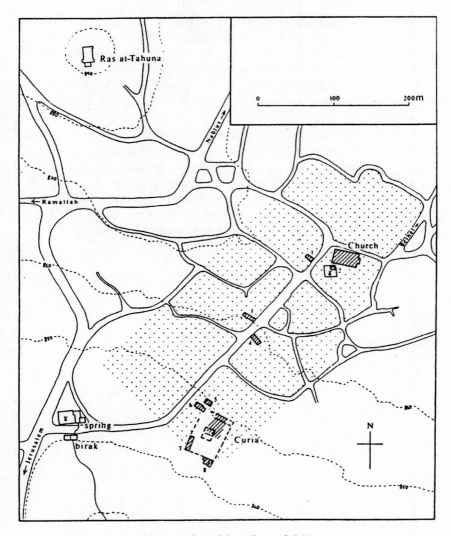

Figure 5   Plan of the village of al-Bira

villages and also from the institutions which they contained. The use of a central oven, and even of a central flour mill, did not accord with the usual structure of a Middle East village, where each house had its own oven ("tabun") for its own domestic use. Central ovens existed in the large cities of the Middle East but not in the villages.

Another fact which emerged from a study of the Frankish villages of

Mi'ilya, the two Mahomerias and others (such as al-Burj and Mons Gaudii) where archeological excavations were conducted, is that the Franks did not evict the local villagers from their homes. Most of the Frankish villages were established in places which had been abandoned before the arrival of the Franks or in places which were outside the boundaries of the previous villages. The new villages were planned in advance like their counterparts in contemporary Europe.

Pringle claimed that the orderly plan of the Arab village of al-Bira was also the result of the Frankish planning (see fig. 5), and there was apparently a similar plan for Casale Imbert. Castellum Regis was also a planned village. The houses were constructed in concentric circles: in the center was the "curia," the church, and probably the oven and the flour mill. The same observation is probably valid also for the Frankish castrum of Caymont which was constructed, like Mi'ilya, in a circular form.

CHAPTER EIGHT

THE NEIGHBORHOOD OF A FRANKISH CASTRUM: THE FIELDS AND THE ROLE PLAYED BY THE CASTELLAN

Agricultural estates and Frankish settlement near Caiphas

I pointed out above that many of the Frankish castra were essentially fortified agricultural settlements which were established near central fortresses which were used as administrative centers by the landlords. In this type of "castrum" which was well known in contemporaneous Europe the agricultural plots were not always adjacent to the walls of the central fortress and in many cases the Frankish farmers cultivated their fields at a comparatively great distance from its walls. The inhabitants of Castellum Regis cultivated fields in Tarshiha and apparently also in Tertilla, while those of Casale Imbert cultivated land in the neighboring villages as well.

The question arises as to how the Frankish settlers could have cared for agricultural land which was not close to the walls of the castra. Did they construct permanent buildings for the purpose of administering these lands? Did the castellan have to provide the infrastructure? Was he obliged, amongst other things, to see to the maintenance of the roads and paths connecting the agricultural fields? Did he have to ensure a supply of water to the desert areas, and a supply of lime for building purposes? There is evidence enough to confirm that the answers to all these questions are in the affirmative. In this chapter I shall present some evidence pertaining to one castrum – that of Caiphas (Haifa).[1]

Caiphas is regarded by many scholars as a Frankish city, built on the site of an early Muslim one. The Latin documents describe it as a large Frankish castrum, or at least as a small town with a well-developed agricultural periphery rather than a "city."

---

[1] For the history of Haifa, see Dowling, 1914, 184–191; Prausnitz, 1972; Prausnitz, 1974; Prausnitz, 1975; El-Ad, 1980, 191–207; Graboïs, 1978, 147–159; Ben-Zeev, 1986; Rotschild, 1934; Kopp, 1929; Bagatti, 1958–1962; Friedman, 1971; Friedman, 1979.

The earlier settlement of the eleventh century was not a large one and apparently not even an old one. Nassir -i-Khosrau, who was the first to make mention of Haifa, actually describes it as a village. Its importance increased, apparently, during the second half of the eleventh century as witness the gathering of the Palestine Academy there in 1082, and the descriptive information about the Crusader conquest. But it would appear that the change was not dramatic. Amikam El-Ad, who studied the Arabic texts and the Genizah documents dealing with Haifa, points out that although it was in fact surrounded by a wall during the second half of the eleventh century it was still a small town which had been established only a few decades previously. To the best of our knowledge Haifa was denuded of its autochtonous population (both Jewish and Muslim) during its conquest by the Crusaders and the subsequent slaughter of its inhabitants.[2]

It would appear that during the Frankish period, too, there was not a particularly large settlement in Caiphas. The earlier sources such as the writings of Petrus Tudebodus and of the anonymous author of the Gesta Francorum, desribe it as a "castrum." Theodericus describes the place, in 1172, as partially destroyed, while Oliverus calls it "oppidum." The author of Itinerarium Peregrinorum et Gesta Regis Ricardi also uses the term "oppidum" to describe this settlement.[3]

The Arabic sources, too, indicate that the place resembled a Frankish castrum rather than a town. So do the sources from the end of the thirteenth century. From Arabic descriptions of the agreement between the Franks and Sultan Qalawun, signed in 1283, it would appear that the place was indeed surrounded by a wall, but was not necessarily a large settlement. Al-Qalqashandi describes it as a fortress with an adjacent "large enclosed courtyard" (or slum area) surrounded by vineyards and fruit orchards belonging to it. Apparently al-Qalqashandi was referring to the Frankish burgus adjacent to the fortress.[4]

William of Tyre, on the other hand, describes Caiphas as a city already during the First Crusade.[5] Although, to be true, he describes it on one occasion simply as a "place," but in most of his references he uses the word

[2] Medieval Haifa is mentioned for the first time by Nassir-i-Khosrau in 1047, see Sefer Nameh, 18 (persian text), 60 (translation). Cf. El-Ad, 1980, 192. A Jewish community flourished there at the end of the eleventh century. Cf. Graboïs, 1978, and El-Ad, 1980. For the conquest of the city by the Franks, see Albert of Aachen, 519–523; Translatio Sancti Nicolai, cap. XLI–XLIII, 276–278; Baudry of Dol, 111. Cf. also Graboïs, 1978, 153–155.

[3] Petrus Tudebodus, 133; Gesta Francorum, 87; Theodericus, xliii, 51; Oliverus, 90–91; Gesta Regis Ricardi, Liber IV, cap. II, 252.   [4] Al-Qalqashandi, XIV, 55, lines 12–16; El-Ad, 1980, 203.

[5] William of Tyre, 9, 13, 437–438; "Concessit . . . Caypham, que alio nomine dicitur Porfiria, urbem maritimam cum suis pertinentiis predicto domino Tancredo." Cf. William of Tyre, 9, 10, 464.

"civitas."[6] William was of the opinion, that the castrum of Caiphas was near to the Byzantine bishopric city of Porphiria, and he called it New Porphiria. This was evidently the reason why he considered it to be a city. Both William of Tyre, and other Latin chroniclers who were influenced by ecclesiastical sources, such as Thietmar, described bishopric settlements as "cities" without any connection with their true urban status.[7]

Caiphas is referred to as a castrum in a document, issued in 1115, in which Baldwin IV of Jerusalem approves the property of the abbey of Josaphat. The king approves, inter alia, the property given to the monastery in the castrum of Caiphas and its outskirts by Tancred.[8]

Several other ecclesiastical bodies had property in the region of Caiphas. These included the abbey of St. Mary Josaphat[9] and the Chapter of the Church of the Holy Sepulcher. One can learn, from the documents describing this property, about the size of the agricultural terrain possessed by those bodies, and one can learn also that the manor houses managed by those same ecclesiastical bodies were in the confines of the castrum of Caiphas.

In 1164 Rogerius of Caifa and his brother Johannes granted the Holy Sepulcher six carrucas of land on both sides of the "River of Caifa," near to the springs. "Notum sit omnibus, . . . quod ego Rogerius de Caifa et Johannes, frater meus, dedimus canonicis Sanctissimi Sepulcri sex carrucatas terre ita determinatas, tres videlicet citra flumen de Cayfa prope fontanas, et tres ultra fines sitas supra ripas, quantum sex paria boum laborare et excolere poterint per omnes sationes, scilicet tres ad seminandum et alias tres ad garantandum."[10]

There is no doubt that the only river which fits the description "flumen de Cayfa" is the Kishon River.[11] One can learn from this document that the agricultural terrain of the Church of the Holy Sepulcher was on both sides

---

[6] William of Tyre, 10, 6, 461: "Inde oram sectantes maritimam, transeuntes Sydonem, Tyrum et Ptolomaidam usque ad locum, cui nomen Cayphas, pervenerunt."

[7] William of Tyre 13, 2, 587–588: "Urbes autem, que infra hanc provinciam continentur, sunt hee: ab austro novissima Porfiria, que alio nomine dicitur Heffa, vulgari vero appellatione dicitur Cayphas." Thietmar also refers to the place as a "civitas": Thietmar, ch. viii, l. 5–6: "In pede montis Carmeli sita est quedam ciuitas, que uocatur Cayphas." Thietmar, ch. viii, l. 13–14: "Super hanc ciuitatem, scilicet Caypham, in procliuo montis Carmeli est spelunca Helye et Elizei prophetarum." Cf. William of Tyre, 14, 11, 644; Philip of Savona, 77. The earlier descriptions do not give a clear indication of where the city of Porphiria was located. It seems that it was about six or seven miles south of Haifa. Cf. Antoninus of Placentia's itinerary in the English translation of J. Wilkinson, 79. For another opinion cf. Abel, 1938, 410.

[8] Delaborde, no. 6, 1115, 30: "Tancredus dedit ecclesie predicte . . . in castro nomine Cayphasi plateam ubi edificata est ecclesia et domos et furnum et molendinum et terras et arbores que sunt ante ipsum castrum."   [9] Delaborde, no. 28, Mar. 11, 1154, 64.

[10] Holy Sepulcher, no. 134, before July 1164, 261.

[11] The Latin sources tend to use the word "cavea" in order to describe a river-bed (both a dry and a full one), while the word "flumen" is used only for a river.

of the Kishon River. In other words it was some considerable distance from the city. This document can help us to reconstruct the size of the standard agricultural unit – the carruca. The text specifies categorically that the two plots of land consisted of three carrucas, each cultivated by six pairs of oxen. In other words, a carruca is an area which can be cultivated with one pair of oxen.[12]

Defining land according to the plowing ability of a pair of oxen was a common practice in medieval Europe as well as in the Eastern Mediterranean world ("faddan" in Arabic). This way of defining a plot of land, therefore, is not exclusive to our document. On the contrary, it is even difficult to find any other definition of a "carruca" in the Latin documents of the same period.

Rey and Prawer calculated the Frankish carruca in a different way. Their calculations were based on a note added at an unknown time, in an unknown place, by an unknown author to a late twelfth-century document. The note is based, according to its author, on the "Assizes of the said Kingdom."[13] According to their calculations, which are generally accepted, the size of the basic agricultural unit was more than thirty hectares. I was not able to find any other text from the twelfth century, or from any other period, which corroborates these calculations. The difficulty of accepting them is magnified by the fact that the terminology used, both in Europe and the Frankish Levant, for defining agricultural areas is taken from the kinds of plows used at the time: aratrum (a light symmetrical plow) which is also the area which can be plowed by a light, symmetrical plow tied to a pair of oxen.

The term carruca was used also to define the heavy asymmetrical plow, or, according to Du-Cange: "carruca, sequiioris aetatis Scriptoribus sumitur pro aratro." All the sources and all the definitions within my knowledge testify to the fact that in the Levant, as in Europe, the sizes of plots of land were defined according to the size of a standard area which a pair of oxen could plow.[14] It can be assumed that this standard unit was not significantly different from its European counterpart; and all the scholars agree

---

[12] For "pair" one might also read "team" but it is generally accepted that a "team" of oxen includes usually no more than a pair.

[13] Rey, 1883, 242–243; Rey, 1879, 157–186; Prawer, 1980d, 158–159.

[14] For example Holy Sepulcher, no. 28, 1125, 90: "(Dono et concedo . . . casale quoddam nomine Derina) . . . In conterminis vero ipsius casalis supradicti, circa montana, tantum terre quantum quatuor paria boum poterunt excolere de anno ad annum." Tafel-Thomas, II, 380: "et est tanta terra, que per unam diem potest laborari a duobus paribus bouum." Tafel-Thomas, II, 380: "que pecia terre potest laborari et est sufficiens duobus paribus bouum in Saraceno dictam peciam duarum carucarum per unam diem." For the aratrum as a unit for measurement, see Delaborde, no. 4, 1114, 27.

that the size of a European carruca was not more than three or four hectares.[15]

The idea that the "Crusader carruca" could have been more than ten times larger than the other medieval carrucas, or than the Arabic Faddan (as noted above Prawer and Rey estimated its size as thirty to thirty-five hectares) is not feasible, and is certainly not based on any sources save for the anonymous source mentioned above.

It can be assumed, and at a later stage I shall try to show that there is archeological proof of this, that the size of the Frankish carruca was similar to that of the parallel agricultural unit in Europe of the same period.

As already stated, the neighborhood of the castrum of Caiphas was dotted with agricultural estates, some of which belonged to ecclesiastical bodies. These estates were far away from the walls of the castrum of Caiphas as were the estates of the Order of St. John which owned houses and land in Caiphas and nearby Capharnaum. This property was granted to the Order already during the first decade of the Kingdom's existence and is mentioned in a confirmation given by Baldwin I of Hospital property in 1110. It appears that the reference is probably to an estate which stretched between the two places: "Paganus de Cayphas . . . (dedit) . . . terris ac domibus in Cayphas et in Capharnaum."[16] Capharnaum, near to Caiphas, is generally identified several kilometers south of Caiphas, so that this grant of land and houses indicates the extent of the territory of the castrum of Caiphas. From the landed property of the bishopric of Bethlehem, too, one can learn that the castrum consisted of additional terrain near Caiphas: in a document signed in 1227 the pope confirms a list of property belonging de jure to this bishopric throughout the country (some of the places mentioned in the document were not occupied by the Franks at the time). The pope confirmed the bishopric's ownership, inter alia, of a "house" in the territory of Caiphas, near the road to Acre. He also confirmed the bishop's ownership of two carrucas of land.[17] It would appear that both the "house" and the land belonging to the bishopric were beyond the confines of the castrum, as otherwise the

---

[15] Kosminskii, 1956, 214–217; Miller & Hatcher, 1978, 121–6; Langdon, 1982, 38. Examples which were taken from the Domesday Book: "In Kirby Beddon there are two sokmen & a half with 12 acres. Then and now they plough with 3 oxen." *Domesday Book*, II, fol. 143. The reference in the Domesday Book is in the singular for every pair of oxens. One acre is about 0.4 hectare which means that 4.8 hectares were plowed by three pairs of oxens, which is 1.3 hectares for each pair. "In Ashby there are two freemen . . . with nine acres. Now & then they plough with two oxen." *Domesday Book*, II, fol. 177b. Two pairs of oxens were enough to plough 3.5 hectares. Each pair plowed about 1.8 hectares. "In Plumstead is one Bordor, Godric's man, with nine acres of land. Now as then he ploughs with two oxen." *Domesday Book*, II, fol. 228b. Here too, each pair plowed 1.8 hectares.   [16] Hospital, no. 20, Sept. 28, 1110, 21.
[17] Röhricht, *Regesta*, no. 983, 1227.

house would not have been described in the document as being on the road to Acre. If the house had been within the castrum itself much clearer topographical details would have been provided.

A Templar fortress above Caiphas: another "domus" belonging to an ecclesiastical body was the "castrum" constructed by the Templars on the top of Mt. Carmel, in the area occupied today by the church of "Stella Maris." Elias Friedman, who examined the written evidence and the descriptions of the archeological remains that existed there in the past, provided proof that the fortress had in fact been built there and that next to it was the site of the Greek monastery of St. Margerite. The combination of fortress and monastery (which apparently preceded the Frankish period) perhaps provides the explanation for the use of the word "castrum" in order to describe the fortified building which the Templars constructed there.[18] The Templar castrum is mentioned only once by Theodericus: "in cuius etiam summo cacumine Templariorum extat castrum, quod procul navigantibus continentem facit esse cognoscibilem."[19] Thereafter it appears only in maps of the thirteenth century.

Only one of the Latin documents dealing with Caiphas refers to property within the castrum iself. All the rest refer only to its agricultural surroundings. In the neighborhood of the castrum there were settlers and institutions engaged in agriculture. Owners of large properties even built "houses" from which they administered their agricultural lands.

The castellan's responsibility for maintaining the field paths: the monastery of Mt. Tabor also had some modest property in Caiphas which was granted to it in 1250 by Garssie Alvarez, the lord of the castrum. As was customary in most of the documents describing grants of land, this document also enters into details of the landscape which were familiar only to contemporaries of the period. This document requires deciphering.

The plot granted to the monastery is described as being on the slopes of the Carmel beneath the old vineyard of "the house of St. Elijah of Carmel," in a place from which one climbs up to the edge of the vineyard of a certain Agis. The boundary of the plot stretches in a straight line to the cave of a "Templar brother" (the term "cave" is translated by Röhricht as "vallis" – a valley – but I think the word "cave" is preferable here, or perhaps "winery"). The other details identifying the boundary of the plot include, inter alia, a reference to a hewn-out path for those going up or down to "St. Margerite of Carmel." The path was evidently considered to be of great importance as, according to the document, it had to be kept open and free for use as it had

---

[18] Friedman, 1971, 295–348; Friedman, 1979, 90–91.   [19] Theodericus, xxxix, 43.

been in the past. The document provides other signs of identification for the path: it passes under a cistern and near to a reservoir ("berquil") next to the castrum's lime kiln ("nostre chaufor").[20]

Some of the landscape details can be identified: St. Margerite monastery is identified on the ridge, next to the modern lighthouse, on which the Stella Maris monastery is built today. Greek monks occupied the monastery and a pilgrim described it in the thirteenth century as being above "the hewn-out chapel of the prophet Elijah."[21]

The path, which is described in such detail, is still in use today. The path was studied by Friedman in another context.[22] A field study which I conducted supports the assumption that the present path was used also in the thirteenth century and is apparently the path referred to in our document. This conclusion is based also on the fact that this is the only possible path between Elijah's cave and the Stella Maris monastery, as well as on the fact that there are wine presses and reservoirs for collecting flood waters alongside it and, mainly, on the fact that it passes beneath a hewn-out cistern in the shape of a bell ("au chemin forchie de souz la cisterne qui monte a S. Marguerite dou Carme"). There are very few paths which can be described as being under a cistern and it is reasonable to conclude that the existing path is identical with the ancient one.

The discovery of the path is a geographic-historical curiosity which might, in itself, not have earned the attention it has received here. But the document does not only give us details of the alignment of a Frankish path. It also indicates how intensive the agricultural development of the Carmel slopes was. The joint existence of property belonging to the St. Margerite monastery, of a "house" belonging to St. Elijah, of agricultural property belonging to the Mt. Tabor monastery, of property belonging to a certain

[20] Chartes du Mont-Thabor, no. XXVI, May 5, 1250, Hospital, II, 913–914 (Röhricht, *Regesta*, no. 1189): "je Garssie Alvarez, sire de Cayphas, . . . don . . . à l'iglise de Monte Thabor la terre desus la vieille vingne de la maison de S. Helies dou Carme, si com l'on s'en monte jusques au chief de la vingne de Agis, et d'icelle vingne si com l'on s'en va dreit à la cave, que l'on dit la cave dou frere dou Temple, à main destre desouz, et de iqui dreit au chemin forchie de souz la cisterne qui monte à S. Marguerite dou Carme; lequel chemin deit demorer franc en montant et en descendant, ausi come davant; et de la veie forchée dreit au berquil pres de nostre chaufor à main destre."

[21] Michelant & Raynaud, 189: "A l'autre chef haut de cele montaigne, est une abbaye de Griffons, moignes ners, où seynte Margarete fist must de miracles, e sunt là de bons sentuaries. A la descendue de cele abbaye contre val est une chapele en la roche de seynt Helyes le prophete, où il fist must de miracles, e en la chapele est une bone fontaigne de ewe freide ke il trova e fist." Cf. Friedman, 1979, 86–91.

[22] Friedman does not mention this document but he does mention this road as a further proof for the location of the monastery on the top of Mt. Carmel. He argues that the ancient road was rebuilt by a certain hermit, named Giambattista, who lived there in the eighteenth century. Friedman, 1979, 87.

Agis(?), the use of cisterns and reservoirs on the slopes of the mountain, the existence of a castral lime kiln, and the scrupulous protection of the right of way on the paths connecting these properties on the part of the seignior of the castrum, all contribute to the creation of a picture of a well-organized and orderly Frankish castrum, whose surroundings were intensively cultivated.

An additional fact which emerges from the document is that the seigniors of the territory were responsible for ensuring the right of way on the roads and paths between the fields. This fact appears to me to be all-important. Responsibility for ensuring the right of way on paths which did not bring the castellan any revenue testify to the establishment of a well-developed system of rural administration controlled in detail by those responsible for it.

CHAPTER NINE

A CHURCH AS THE NUCLEUS OF A SETTLEMENT

The creation of new settlements was accompanied in the Latin Kingdom of Jerusalem, as in Europe, by the parallel establishment of a parochial framework, with the parish churches serving often as nuclei for the new settlements. The search for such parochial establishments is not easy, as the documentary evidence for the existence of rural churches is very scarce, and the publication of the only comprehensive archeological study of Frankish churches, that of D. Pringle, is not yet completed. Nevertheless, from the scant sources and the archaeological data which are available, it is possible to establish that the number of rural churches constructed by the Franks was much greater than would appear from an examination of previous studies. These rural churches served both the Franks who lived in the larger villages and those who lived in isolated estates in the vicinity of the villages. From other data it can be assumed that some of the churches were used also by the local Christian population.

Castellum Sancti Egidii

The Frankish village of Sinjil (Castellum Sancti Egidii, grid reference 175/160) is mentioned both in Latin and Arabic sources. In some of the Latin sources Sinjil is described as a "castrum" or "Castellum Sancti Egidii." Others refer to it only as a "casale" but it should be remembered that other Frankish fortified settlements, such as Casale Imbert, and Manueth are also referred to as "casale" in some of the Latin legal documents and as "castra" in others.[1] In the Arabic sources, too, the place is called "fortress" and 'Imad

---

[1] The place is mentioned as a "castrum" in the letters describing the fall of the Kingdom of Jerusalem in 1187. See Kedar, 1982, 119 and 122.

al-Din al-Isfahani includes it amongst the castles Salah al-Din conquered in 1187.[2]

The fact that the village was fortified emerges mainly from the written sources but it is strengthened also by an analysis of archeological remains: the Survey of Western Palestine mentions two towers, in one of which there was a Frankish church which was later converted into the village mosque, and the inspectors of the Department of Antiquities of Palestine referred to these same towers in their report of the village. To my regret, I was unable to examine these remains as during two visits to the village I was given a hostile reception by the local inhabitants (in April 1985 and at the beginning of October 1986). I was able, however, to make a brief visit to the village mosque which was originally a Frankish church. But I did not succeed in completing an inspection of the other Frankish sites.[3]

We do not know a good deal about the layout of the village and the rights of the Franks who lived there. Most of the documents dealing with Sinjil, a village which belonged to rear-vassals of the king and never passed into the hands of any ecclesiastical institution, have not been preserved. However, there is no doubt that it was a large Frankish village. One can learn about its size and importance from the fact that its seignior was bound to provide three knights for the army of the kingdom – only one less than the quota required from Castellum Regis.[4]

As the castrum of Sinjil was within the royal domain and as the seigniors owned it as rear-vassal of the viscount of Jerusalem, they required the authorization of the viscount for every land transaction which they conducted.[5]

The Frankish settlers of Sinjil

(I) Landed property belonging to the Hospital in the territory adjacent to Sinjil: the only evidence of the landed property which belonged to the Hospital of St. John in Sinjil can be found in a confirmation by King Baldwin IV for the land next to this village which was granted to the Hospital by

[2] 'Imad al-Din al-Isfahani, 111, line 5; 'Imad al-Din al-Isfahani, trans. Massé, 99; Abu Shama, ed. *RHC, HOr.*, IV, 303.

[3] According to Pringle, however, the tower at Sinjil was quite small, only about 10 meters E–W. In 1979 only the lower course of the S. wall survived, and since then a house has been built against it.   [4] Jean of Ibelin, I, 423.

[5] Hospital, no. 192, May 24, 1150, 149–150: "Notum sit . . . quod ego Rotbertus [sic] de casali S. Egidii, una cum uxore mea Odula, donavimus et concessimus (terram) . . . concessu Roardi ejusque uxoris domine Gille, de quibus nos istud feudum tenebamus et concessum, et confirmatione regis Fulconis et regine domine Melissendis et domini Willelmi patriarche." For Sinjil itself, see Holy Sepulcher, no. 160, Dec. 18, 1175, 312: "Notum sit . . . quod ego Balduinus, Dei gratia dominus casalis Sancti Egidii, una cum Stephania, conjuge mea, in presentia domni Roardi, castellani Jerusalem, soceri mei, et aliorum proborum virorum . . . assensum dedimus."

Robertus of Sinjil. Unfortunately, the document itself was not preserved and, consequently, it is impossible to identify the type of land referred to.[6]

(2) The burgesses of Sinjil: from the various documents in which Sinjil is mentioned it is possible to compile a list of names of Frankish burgesses who lived there, and who were engaged in agriculture. In one document, issued on October 30, 1186, only several months before the battle of Hattin, a piece of land was granted by a certain Adam Magnus, an inhabitant of Sinjil ("habitator casalis Sancti Egidii") to the Leper Order of St. Lazarus. Adam Magnus transferred wine which had been vinted from two of his vineyards and from a third vineyard which was owned by a certain Guillelmus Magnus, who might be his brother, and Robertus Evronis. In the description of the plots of land and their location there is another name which might be a name of another settler who lived in Sinjil emerges – or a name of a plot of land "Cahantaperdiz." Two other names of settlers in Sinjil can be deduced from the list of the witnesses to this document: Adam Juvenis and Hugo Scutifer. All these Frankish settlers are called "inhabitants of the village of Sinjil." One of them, Robertus Evronis, emigrated apparently from Hebron, which was also a Frankish castrum. It is important to note that Robertus Evronis was not given the Latin name of his castrum (as the owners of this estate generally were) but was named after the local and biblical name of the place – Hebron.[7]

This is not the only evidence of internal emigration in connection with the inhabitants of Sinjil. Two of its inhabitants emigrated to Magna Mahomeria: Guillelmus de Casale Sancti Egidii (no. 125 in the list of burgesses of Mahomeria) and Otgerius de Casale Sancti Egidii (no. 114 in the same list).

One can learn about other members of the seigniors' families from documents dealing with the transactions in connection with Emmaus in which other Franks who lived in Sinjil are mentioned.[8]

[6] Hospital, no. 498, 1176, 342.

[7] *AOL*, IIB, no. 31, Oct. 30, 1186, 148–149: "Notum sit omnibus . . . quod ego, Adam Magnus, habitator casalis Sancti Egidii, assensu et favore uxoris mee Florate, filiique mei Baldewini, concedo et trado . . . leprosis Sancti Lazari . . . de quadam vinea mea, scilicet de planta que est in quadam petia terre sub questu annuatim xxv litras vini, et de alia vinea quam habeo ad Terram Blancam xxv litras. Et, ut hoc donum meum sit firmum et stabile omni tempore, tali modo dispono ut quiscumque deinceps predictas vineas possidebit annuatim leprosis Sancti Lazari l litras vini persolvat; et, de quadam vinea, que est super terram de Chanteperditz, quam Guillelmus Magnus possidet, xxv litras vini quas dictus baronus concessit et tradidit eisdem leprosis; idem Willelmus Magnus et Robertus Evronis debent reddere et quisquis post eos eandem vineam possederit . . . Hujus vero rei testes sunt, de habitatoribus casalis Sancti Egidii: Gwillelmus Magnus; Adam Juvenis; Robertus Evronis; Hugo Scutifer."

[8] Hospital, no. 192, May 24, 1150, 149–150: two more inhabitants of the village "Pesellus de casali S. Egidii, et Dudo, ejus filius" are mentioned in addition to Rotbertus (*sic!*) and his wife Odula. Pesellus and his son are mentioned also in Hospital, no. 202, Feb. 5, 1151 or 1152, 155–157.

The parochial church of Sinjil

The only Frankish institution in Sinjil about which we have irrefutable evidence is the Frankish church which still exists. The remains were already studied during the last century by the surveyors of the Survey of Western Palestine who noted that the plan of the village's mosque is that of a Frankish church. The British archeologists also found "Crusader capitals" in the mosque.[9]

In 1145, Patriarch William of Jerusalem transferred the church and its parochial rights to the monastery of Mt. Tabor. The patriarch transferred the property and the contributions required for maintaining the church ("oblationes"), as well as half of the tithes of the villages of Turbasaim (most probably Turmus ʿAyya) and Dere (apparently Kh. al-Dayr), and all the tithes of the three vineyards belonging to the monastery of Mt. Tabor. The remaining half of the tithes was reserved for the Chapter of the Church of the Holy Sepulcher. This income was meant to be used for the ecclesiastical needs of the place.[10]

With this transfer of rights the patriarch terminated a dispute between the monastery of Mt. Tabor and the Chapter of the Church of the Holy Sepulcher. The document does not specify what the dispute was about and only establishes its determination. Hamilton is apparently right in his conclusion that until the settlement of the dispute it was the monastery of Mt. Tabor which was actually in possession of the church while the Chapter of the Holy Sepulcher collected all the tithes. The patriarch, as the head of the diocese, officially transferred the management of ecclesiastical matters to the monastery (which in fact already exercised this function) and sufficient tithes to enable them to maintain a parish of the size of Sinjil.[11]

The patriarch exempted the monastery from paying tithes on the three

[9] Warren & Conder, 1882–18884, II, 320.
[10] Holy Sepulcher, no. 24, Aug. 14, 1145, 84: "Willelmus, . . . patriarcha . . . controversiam de decimis casalis Sancti Egidii inter ecclesiam Sepulcri Domini [et ecclesiam Sancti Salvatoris que est in monte Thabor] . . . sedavimus. Nam ut inter easdem ecclesias pax conservetur eterna, ecclesiam prefati casalis Sancti Egidii cum oblationibus suis et suorum duorumque casalium, Turbasaim videlicet et Dere, decimarum mediatate vobis libere et absolute concedimus, ac ut trium vinearum vestrarum, quas nunc habetis, decima similiter, omni inquietatione sopita, juri vestro remaneat adicimus. Aliam vero decimarum partem, ecclesie Dominici Sepulcri canonicis reservamus. Ex his quidem, que ex nostra concessione possidetis, ecclesiam et clericos in ea Domino famulantes procurare debatis. Si que etiam unde decima reddi debuerit, postmodum acquirere poteritis, decime medietatem ecclesie Sepulcri Domini persolvetis. Sed et ne hec a memoria future deleantur posteritatis, cereum unius rotule in festivitate Jherusalem annuatim prefate Dominici Sepulcri ecclesie horum dabitis in recognitione."   [11] Hamilton, 1980, 147–148.

vineyards which it cultivated. It seems that the monastery, which was in possession of the church, had been obliged to pay tithes on its income to the Church of the Holy Sepulcher. The transfer of the tithes to the monastery was apparently intended to make amends for this. The patriarch nevertheless did not wish to exempt the vineyards altogether from paying tithes, as this would have complicated matters in the event that this landed property was sold to a body which was not entitled to such an exemption. Granting the monastery the right to the tithes was equal, from the point of view of income, to exempting them from the obligation to pay the tithes, while at the same time not prejudicing the rights of the patriarch.

The real parochial income of the monastery was, therefore, the ecclesiastical income from the village of Sinjil itself and tithes from the neighboring hamlets of Turmus ʿAyya and Kh. al- Dayr. The fact that the inhabitants of the neighboring hamlets were also included in the parish of Sinjil indicates that the area which the church served extended beyond the boundaries of the village. We do not know if other hamlets were included in the parish as the document deals only with the tithes of the two hamlets concerned and does not refer to the boundaries of the parish. One cannot learn anything from the document about other places whose incomes were undoubtedly divided between the same two ecclesiastical bodies. The document does not even refer to the tithes from Sinjil itself, apparently because the transfer of these tithes was taken for granted, as it was not feasible that a body which was entitled to parochial rights and tithes from the neighborhood would not receive tithes from the place where the church was situated. The only authorization for the levying of tithes on Sinjil can be found in another document signed several years later and from which it transpires that the tithes from Sinjil were also handed over to the monastery of Mt. Tabor. It follows, therefore, that the income from Sinjil and from the two neighboring hamlets was transferred wholly to the monastery and the remaining tithes from other neighboring hamlets was divided between the monastery and the Church of the Holy Sepulcher.

Thirty years later Garinus, the abbot of the monastery, waived the parochial rights to the place and returned them to the Chapter of the Church of the Holy Sepulcher. The transfer included the obligations and the rights. Garinus returned both the tithes from Sinjil and those from the two neighboring hamlets. The monastery was not able to retain the church because of the great distance between Sinjil and Mt. Tabor and the expense of maintaining the parochial church. At the same time the monastery sold the property which it had in Sinjil: the vineyards, houses, and chattels. It received 2,000 bezants for its property and wax and incense for Transfiguration Day.[12]

Two months after the liquidation of the ecclesiastical interests of the monastery in Sinjil and the sale of all its landed property, the secular owner of the village confirmed the validity of the sale, although there was no real need for such confirmation for the transfer of ecclesiastical obligations. From this confirmation, issued by Baldwin, the seignior of Sinjil, with the approval of Rohardus the castellan of Jerusalem, it can be seen that the monastery had, in addition to immovable property, exemptions from seigniorial obligations ("francicia et libertate qua abbates et monachi Montis Thabor temporibus predecessorum meorum et meo tenuisse").[13]

The scope of Sinjil parochial services

One of the two hamlets whose tithes were ceded to the Mt. Tabor monastery was the casale of Dere, or Kh. al-Dayr (grid reference 176/160) where I found a Frankish ruin. I did not examine the kernel of the second hamlet – Turmus 'Ayya.[14] Kh. al-Dayr is not the only Frankish estate which was discovered in the vicinity of Sinjil. Remains of Frankish buildings were discovered also in the following places: Kh. al-Burj, grid reference 173/161; Kh. Istuna (the manor house of Ancel Babinus?), grid reference 180/159; Kh. Shaykh al-'Auf, grid reference 175/161; Kh. Burj al-Lissana, grid reference 174/153. All these estates were found within a short distance (less than an hour's walk) from Sinjil. It is possible that other Frankish sites, up to two hours' walk away (taking into account the network of paths in the area) can be added to this list: a ruin with no name in the wadi near Kh. Shaykh

---

[12] Holy Sepulcher, no. 59, Oct. 17, 1175, 310–311: "Notum sit . . . quod ego Garinus, Montis Thabor abbas, . . . tali concordie convenimus quod ecclesiam nostram quam apud casale Sancti Egidii cum oblationibus suis et jure parrochiali aliorumque omnium ad eam pertinentium et cum medietate universarum decimarum ejusdem casalis et aliorum duorum, Turbasym videlicet et Dere quas ex concessione . . . W[illelmi] patriarche ab eisdem . . . tenebamus, remotione loci et magnitudine expensarum pregravati, . . . canonicis ejusdem ecclesie, de cujus jure procedebat, . . . reddidimus; vineas vero nostras, domos edificia et cetera mobilia nostra que tam laboris nostri exercitio quam precio conquisivimus, eisdem pro duobus M. bisanciis vendidimus."

[13] Holy Sepulcher, no. 160, Dec. 18, 1175, 312: " Notum sit omnibus . . . quod ego Balduinus, . . . dominus casalis Sancti Egidii, . . . assensum dedimus emptioni quam . . . canonici Dominici Sepulcri fecerunt de domibus, edifitiis et vineis cum omnibus pertinentiis suis que abbas et monachi Montis Thabor habebant, tam ex dono predecessorum meorum quam emptione vel conquisitione, in predicto casali, ut ea omnia libere et quiete teneant et possideant in perpetuum sine omni calumpnia, ea francicia et libertate qua abbates et monachi Montis Thabor temporibus predecessorum meorum et meo tenuisse noscuntur."

[14] Warren & Conder, 1882–1884, II, 331; Bagatti, 1979, 123; Rey, 1883, 382; Pringle, 1993, 196–197.

Qatrawani, grid reference 167/156; Kh. Tarfin, grid reference 170/155; the village of ʿAtara, grid reference 169/155.

Thus, within a short walking distance from Sinjil five to eight rural Frankish sites were found. It can be assumed that they were all within the parish of Sinjil and that the church served the needs of the inhabitants, while their landlords contributed tithes. Assembling this data one can conclude that the village of Sinjil must have been the central site of the whole area. It was fortified and contained a parochial church which served the Frankish settlers. A similar picture emerges from the documents dealing with the tithes and parochial rights of another settlement: Castellum Emmaus in Abu Ghosh.

The castellum at Emmaus

Robertus, the seignior of Saint Gille (i.e. Castellum Sancti Egidii), was also the owner of "Terra Emaus." For some unknown reason he decided to give a lease on this land to the Hospital of St. John in return for a high rent of 500 bezants a year. For the rights granted by the viscount of Jerusalem, the seigniorial lord of Robertus, the Order undertook to pay the generous additional sum of 250 bezants a year.[15] The documents do not go into detail about the reasons for such a high rental fee for the lease of the land.[16]

---

[15] Hospital, no. 139, Feb. 3, 1141, 113–114; no. 173, Feb. 1, 1147, 135–136; no. 192, May 24, 1150, 149–150.

[16] The sums paid for the lease of "Terra Emaus" were higher than the average: the village of Arthabec was sold in 1135 for 690 bezants including the sums paid to the overlords of the village and the seignior of Caesarea. Holy Sepulcher, no. 66, 1129, 129. The Chapter of Church of the Holy Sepulcher bought, in 1161, four villages, one *gastina*, and at least one manor house from the family of Iohannes Gothman for 1,400 byzantes: Holy Sepulcher, no. 87–88, Nov. 21, 1161 and Dec. 3, 1161, 199–203. Three villages in Central Samaria were considered equivalent of the annual payment of 150 bezants: Holy Sepulcher, no. 63, 1160–1162, 157–158. The Chapter of the Holy Sepulcher bought two villages, Kafarrus and Vetus Betor, for the sum of 480 bezants from the abbot of Mar-Saba: Holy Sepulcher, no. 133, 1163–1164, 260. 1,400 bezants were paid by the Hospital for the casale of Coquet (which later became the castle of Belvear), 1,000 bezants were paid for Loberium, and 1,300 bezants were paid for Losserin and Casale de Cherio: Hospital, no. 398, April, 1168, 271–272. The village of Caphaer was sold for 400 bezants: Hospital, no. 487, Nov. 29, 1175, 336; no. 488, 1175, 336; no. 489, 336. We do not know the exact ratio between the sums paid for a lease and those paid for the selling of land. We can get an idea about this ratio from the following transactions. An annual payment of 850 bezants and the service of one knight was paid for the lease of eight villages in Central Galilee: Strehlke, no. 4, Apr. 1168, 5–6. The global sum of 1,700 bezants was considered to be equivalent to the annual payment of 200 bezants: Hospital, no. 468, Dec. 13, 1174, 321. The annual payment of 1,000 bezants was considered equivalent to the lease of two villages, Araba and Sakhnin, and three *gastinas*, Derhenne, Mezera, and Misklin. 800 bezants were considered equivalent to the service of two knights: Strehlke, no. 7, July 3, 1174, 8. The annual sum of 230 bezants was paid by King Amalric I for Casale Amos near Nablus: Hospital, no. 454, 1174, 313. In several instances, higher sums were paid for the lease than the purchase a whole village. Hugo of Ibelin, for example, sold two villages for 3,000 bezants: Holy Sepulcher, no. 51, 1158, 137–138. The village of Hadedun was sold by Hugo of

The Hospital of St. John received the parochial rights of the land. The rights were transferred by the Patriarch William and by Petrus, the prior of the Holy Sepulcher. It is important to note that the same William and Petrus transferred the parochial rights of Sinjil to the monastery of Mt. Tabor four years later.[17] In Emmaus, as in Sinjil, the new parochial authorities undertook to pay the Chapter of the Holy Sepulcher half of the tithes collected in the parish. The other half was preserved for the maintenance of the churches and the chapels ("alia omnia . . . pro regimine suorum capellanorum et ecclesiarum retineant"). The patriarch allowed the Hospitalers to conduct sacramental ceremonies and to collect the usual ecclesiastical contributions.

There are two types of documents dealing with Emmaus: those dealing with the lease of "Terra Emaus" and those dealing with the parochial rights of the place and its environs. A comparison between the two types of documents — those issued by the seigniorial institutions and that issued by the patriarch — is interesting: the secular bodies were concerned only with "Terra Emaus" itself, whereas the patriarch refers also to other estates whose ownership was not transferred to the Hospitalers but remained in the hands of their landlords. It appears that the tithes from villages which were not leased by the Hospitalers were also transferred to them and that the Hospital received (half of) the tithes from the casalia of Huldre, Porcel, Gaufridus Agule, Ansquetinus, Bacheler, and Girardus Bostgher. All these sites receive no mention whatsoever in the deeds of the lease of "Terra Emaus."

From a comparison between the two types of documents one can learn

Caesarea to the Hospital for the sum of 2,000 bezants: Hospital, no. 350, 1166, 243. 3.000 bezants were paid for the "casale quod appellatur S. Marie, contiguum territorio Bellifortis, cum universis pertinentiis suis longe lateque sibi adjacentibus, excepta terra S. Marie de Bethleem infra territorium predicti casalis jacente." Hospital, no. 371, 1167, 254–255. Casale Moyen was sold by Iohanes of Arsuf to the Hospital for the sum of 3,000 bezants: Hospital, no. 497, 1176, 342. The village of Bethduras was sold for the enormous sum of 5,800 bezants by Johannes Arrabitus to Constance the daughter of Louis VI and she added another 250 bezants for the Scribanagium of the same place: Hospital, no. 495, 1176, 341; no. 516, 1177, 352.

17 Hospital, no. 140, 1141, 114–115: "ego Willelmus, . . . patriarcha, et Petrus, . . . Sepulcri prior . . . scriptum retinere studuimus quod fratres Hospitalis . . . , firmaverunt terram de Emaus cum suis casalibus et omnibus eorum pertinentiis; eo videlicet tenore ut canonicis Dominici Sepulcri medietatem decime de omnibus annonis . . . reddant, et fratres Hospitalis alia omnia, que inde provenire poterunt, pro regimine suorum capellanorum et ecclesiarum retineant; in quibus ecclesie oblationes, nuptias, purificationes, confessionem et visitationes infirmorum, baptisteria et cimiteria habeant; sed et de terra et de ceteris casalibus in ipsis montanis adjacentibus, scilicet de casale Huldre et de Porcel, et de Gaufrido Agulle, et de Anschetino, et de Bacheler, et de Girardo Bocher, que ipsi possident, vel de aliis que in eisdem montanis juste acquirent, similiter medietatem decime eisdem canonicis pacifice reddant. Si autem aliquod casale seu terram de eisdem quibuslibet Christianis vel Sarracenis ad firmam dederint fratres Hospitalis pro annona vel bisantiis, vel pro aliqua peccunia, similiter prefati canonici medietatem decime, veluti jam diximus, habeant . . . Roardus, de cujus feudo est ipsa terra; Robertus de casale S. Egidii."

about the existence of two parallel, non-overlapping administrative regulations: the secular one and the parochial one. The Hospital received a lease on certain property but it also received the parochial rights of neighboring villages and estates which were not included in the lease. It would appear that although the Order had great estates and although it received a very high rent, nevertheless this was not sufficient to maintain an independent parish.

It is also important to note that the other villages which had to pay tithes are not referred to by their local names but by the names of their Frankish landlords. A closer examination of the names shows that these Franks are familiar to us from other documents of the same period. They were all petty knights or burgesses who lived in the district of Jerusalem. Most of them, for example, were mentioned as witnesses in a document in which Baldwin II exempted the agricultural products from the vicinity of Jerusalem from taxation – and they apparently all had agricultural interests in the same area.[18] The only exception, presumably, was Huldre. Beyer, Benvenisti, and Pringle identified this village with Huldah (grid reference 140/136), which is about ten kilometers southwest of Emmaus, and consequently placed "Terra Emaus" in Emmaus, which is close to Huldah.[19] But even though we cannot prove that the "casale of Huldre" is not Huldah, it is difficult to accept this identification. The name "Huldah" does not appear in any other source from the same period, and there is no explanation why the name "Huldah" could have been changed to the name "Huldre." It seems more likely that this site, like the other sites in the same document, was named after its Frankish landlord. We might even assume that it was owned by one of the burgesses of Jerusalem called, alternatively, in different documents Holdredus, Oldereus, Holdreus, or Hildredus. Holdreus appears in many documents from the 1130s together with other burgesses and knights who owned villages in the same area.[20] If this interpretation is correct then the implication in our document is clearer: the parochial rights which were transferred to the Hospitalers were connected with the land leased to them and with isolated estates owned

---

[18] Five of them: Anschetinus, Goifridus Acus (most probably identical with Gaufridus Agulle), Porcellus, and Bachelerius witnessed the document in which King Baldwin II exempted the merchants of agricultural goods in the entrance to Jerusalem: Holy Sepulcher, no. 27, 1120, 89. Gaufridus Acus was the owner of a piece of land near the way which led to Bethlehem: Holy Sepulcher, no. 96, 1126–1130, 213–214. In Holy Sepulcher, no, 38, 1144, 109, he is described as a "baron." Anschetinus is possibly the viscount of Jerusalem between the years 1120 and 1135, or one of the king's burgesses who is mentioned in Holy Sepulcher, no. 51, 1158, 138. Gerardus Bocherius witnessed together with Porcellus a document in which a vineyard was given to Gaufridus Acu: Holy Sepulcher, no. 96, 1126–1130, 214. Bachelarius is mentioned again in 1138: Holy Sepulcher, no. 34, 1138, 100.

[19] See Pringle, 1993, 53; Beyer, 1942, 180 n. 5; Benvenisti, 1970, 349.

[20] In Holy Sepulcher, no. 103, Nov. 16, 1136, 223, Holdredus is mentioned as a Judex.

by the burgesses of Jerusalem and by petty knights who were obliged to pay tithes on their lands.

In the document describing the transfer of parochial responsibility there are additional details which are not absolutely clear. For example, it is not at all apparent to which "churches" (in the plural!) the patriarch could have referred. Could the tentative terminology have indicated the existence of plans to construct such churches, or were there actually churches in existence when the parochial rights were transferred?

There are other uncertainties connected with this document: it is clear that the reference is to villages near "Terra Emaus," but not within its confines. So why were only six villages mentioned? Were there no other villages in the neighborhood? Why were the villages referred to by the names of their Frankish seigniors? Did they not have local names? Was there not even one village in the vicinity of "Terra Emaus" with only a local name? But apparently it is the identification of Terra Emaus itself which presents a greater problem.

Where was "Terra Emaus"?

The Christian traditions place the biblical Emmaus, where Christ appeared to Cleopas and other disciples after his resurrection,[21] in three different places: the Arab village 'Imwas, built on the ruins of the Roman city of Nicopolis (hereinafter Emmaus-Nicopolis), Abu Ghosh and al-Qubaiyba. In all three places there are remains of Frankish churches and each of them could, therefore, have been "Emmaus" of the Frankish regime. The multiplicity of places in which biblical Emmaus is purported to have been is the result of the difference between the version of the scriptures, which located Emmaus about sixty furlongs from Jerusalem (7.5 miles), and the distance of Emmaus-Nicopolis from Jerusalem which is more than twenty miles away. This difference led to two Latin identifications of Emmaus, each of which was on one of the two important roads leading to Jerusalem, in addition to the traditional identification which located Emmaus in Nicopolis. The different versions and the multiplicity of traditions greatly occupied the Catholic scholars of the nineteenth century.[22]

From a careful scrutiny of the itineraries of Latin pilgrims it appears that the tradition identifying Emmaus as al-Qubaiyba did not exist in the twelfth century when there were only two existing traditions: one which placed

---

[21] Luke 24, 13: "Et ecce duo ex illis ibant ipsa die in castellum, quod erat in spatio stadiorum sexaginta ab Ierusalem nomine Emmaus."

[22] See for example: Mauss, 1892, 223–271; Vincent & Abel, 1932, 303–315; Vincent, 1931, 57–91.

Emmaus in Nicopolis and the other in Abu Ghosh. Travelers and Eastern pilgrims undoubtedly continued to identify Emmaus at ʿImwas. But the Latin traditions are less clear. The chroniclers of the First Crusade identified Emmaus as Emmaus-Nicopolis (i.e. ʿImwas), as apparently did later Eastern travelers like Iohannes Phocas.[23] It would appear, nevertheless, that the Frankish settlement in Abu Ghosh also started being called "Emmaus" or "Castellum Emmaus" in the second half of the twelfth century, and most of the Frankish sources refer to Abu Ghosh as "Castellum Emmaus." Belard of Ascoli, who was apparently the first to equate Abu Ghosh with Emmaus, already referred to "the village of Emmaus [Castellum Emmaus, which] is near to the house [of Zacharias, or ʿAyn Karim] by one large mile, and is the same distance from Jerusalem . . . In that village indeed, in the place in which Christ appeared to the two disciples, there is now a church."[24]

Theoderic, who went on a pilgrimage in 1172, during which he visited the monastery of the Holy Cross in the Valley of the Cross and passed via Modiʿin, "the city of the Maccabeans" (which is identified with Belmont), described Emmaus as follows: "near to these hills there is the castellum of Emaus . . . which the moderns call Fontenoit."[25] The proximity of "Emaus" Fontenoit to nearby Belmont gives credence to the assumption that the reference here is to Abu Ghosh. Corroboration for this identification can be found in a letter written by the Master of the Hospital, in 1168, to Bela III, the duke of Hungary. In this letter which refers to agricultural property near Jerusalem, "Castellum Emaus" is mentioned next to Aqua Bella, and it would appear that at that time Abu Ghosh was already identified with biblical Emmaus.[26] Other pilgrims who reached the place during the course of the twelfth century came there from Jerusalem and passed through ʿAyn Karim and Belmont, while pilgrims who reached Emmaus-Nicopolis arrived there via the highway from Lydda to Jerusalem which passed through Mons Gaudii.[27]

In later documents, too, in which mention is made of Castellum or of the village Emmaus, it is clear that the reference is to Abu Ghosh. For example, one of the Continuations of William of Tyre states that: "D'illeuc [from the Church of the Holy Cross in the Valley of the Cross] a ii lieues estoit Saint Jehan du Boiz, la ou Nostre Dame salua Elyzabeth; la fut saint Jehan Baptistre

[23] William of Tyre, 7, 24, 376; Albert of Aachen, 461; Iohannes Phochas, I, 556.
[24] Neumann dated this description to 1112 but Pringle suggested in a recent study that it was written later on, perhaps between 1112 and 1165. Neumann, 1881, 229; Pringle, 1993, 7.
[25] Theodericus, 43.
[26] Hospital, no. 309, 1163–1169, 222. The place was called Castellum Emmaus and it is stated there that it is not far from Jerusalem.
[27] Anonymus II, 8; Anonymus VII (c. 1160), 6; Anon. VIII (c. 1185), 5.

nez, et Zacharies ses peres. D'illeuc a une liue estoit li chastiaux d'Emauz ou
Nostre Sirez s'aparut a ses desciples le jour de Pasques."[28] Similar references
can be found in several other documents.[29]

One can conclude therefore that the Frankish settlement at Abu Ghosh
was called Castellum Emmaus, or Emaus Fontenoid, already in the middle
of the twelfth century. The assumption that the reference is to Abu Ghosh
is supported by the fact that in most of the places where there is some
mention of Emmaus Nicopolis, the two names are coupled together as
Emmaus-Nicopolis. This double-barreled name is so common in the Latin
documents and itineraries that the name "Nicopolis" is almost as familiar as
the biblical name "Emmaus." It is difficult to imagine that only the legal
documents dealing with the granting of the place to a Latin institution would
have omitted the name "Nicopolis" which was attached to the place in so
many different descriptions. The fact that Emmaus Abu Ghosh belonged at
later dates (1168 and 1172) to the Hospitalers also points to the conclusion
that the vague denomination "Terra Emaus" was meant to be Abu Ghosh
and not Emmaus-Nicopolis. Pringle and Abel, as already pointed out, based
their identification of "Terra Emaus" as Emmaus-Nicopolis mainly on the
unclear identification of the village of Huldre.[30]

Was there a Frankish "castellum" or "castrum" in Abu Ghosh?

In contradistinction to other cases, we cannot decide that the use of the term
"castellum" refers to a settlement of the nature of a castrum because the
name "Castellum Emmaus" is a biblical name. The Arab sources, too, completely ignore the place and it is difficult, therefore, to assume that it was fortified. However, there are certain other hints which allow for the assumption
that the Hospitalers tried to establish a larger settlement and maybe even succeeded in doing so. The first hint is to be found in the very existence of quite
a big church in the place.

The Frankish church at Abu Ghosh (Castellum Emmaus?)

Several studies have dealt with the architectural structure and the decora-
tive paintings of the church at Abu Ghosh. It would appear, in accordance

[28] Continuation de Guillaume de Tyr, ed. *RHC*, ch. 11, 512.
[29] Continuation de Guillaume de Tyr, ed. *RHC*, ch. 11, 504; *La citez de Jerusalem*, 442; Michelant
    & Raynaud, 99 and 229.
[30] Pringle, 1993, 53: "Be that as it may, the equation of Huldre with Khulda . . . serves to identify
    the Emmaus of the 1141 charters with 'Amwas rather than Abu Gosh."

with some of these studies, that the Franks built the church as a pilgrim center.[31]

At first glance, one could, perhaps, find three alternative explanations for the construction of this church: the church was to be (1) a chapel which served the regular community living there, (2) a church which was used as a pilgrimage center, or (3) a parochial church which served the Frankish settlers or the local Christian community.

· (1) It is difficult to imagine that so large a church served as the chapel of a monastery whose existence is unbeknown to us. It could perhaps be argued that the church served the Hospitalers in the neighborhood. But the center of the Order for the area was, apparently, in the nearby Belmont. It seems much more likely that if the Hospitalers had wished to construct a church for their own needs they would have done so in Belmont and not in Abu Ghosh.

(2) The possibility that it was a pilgrim church certainly appears reasonable, although the pilgrims' road to Jerusalem in the twelfth century bypassed Abu Ghosh. In an article dealing with the main road from Lydda to Jerusalem I maintained that almost all the travelers and armies that wended their way to Jerusalem in the twelfth and thirteenth centuries used the northern road which passed through Emmaus-Nicopolis, Bayt Nuba (Bethnoble), al-Qubaiyba (Parva Mahomeria), and al-Nabi Samwil (Mons Gaudii). The southern road which passed through Abu Ghosh was used during the early Muslim period, but almost went out of use during the twelfth century.[32]

There were, most certainly, pilgrims whose itineraries were not preserved, who also used the southern road. And it would appear, also, that "Castellum Emmaus – which the moderns call Fontenoit" took the place, in the eyes of several Latin pilgrims, of the sacred site in Emmaus-Nicopolis, which also served the local Christians. It can also be assumed that the identification of biblical Emmaus occupied the Franks, as it has occupied modern Christian research. But it is more difficult to assume that these reasons and considerations, per se, justified the construction of such a large church. It would be more reasonable to conclude that the church served both the pilgrims and the Latin inhabitants of the place and also, probably, the local Christians.

(3) The possibility that the church of Abu Ghosh was a parochial church for the use of the Frankish settlers and perhaps also for the local Christians rests on a comparison between it and the two churches, similar in size and in many architectural details, built in Parva Mahomeria and Bethgibelin. The

[31] For description of the church and for bibliography, cf. Pringle, 1993, 7–17; Kühnel, 1988, 149–180, figs. 119–122, pls. xxxviii–lxi; De Vaux & Stéve, 1950.

[32] Ellenblum, 1987, 203–218.

nearest parallel to Abu Ghosh both in size and design is St. Mary of the Germans in Jerusalem. However, I searched for parallels in the countryside and not inside the main city walls. There is no doubt that the former two churches served as parochial churches for the Latin communities living near them. It is possible, therefore, to assume that a similar church at Abu Ghosh also served the parochial needs of the Christian community living nearby, although it might also have served the itinerant pilgrims. This assumption is consistent with the parochial rights which were transferred to the Order of St. John and can also throw light on the Latin names of the neighboring hamlets: the six casalia whose local names were not preserved were, probably, Frankish estates. In the chapter dealing with agricultural farm houses I will argue that the number of such estates west of Jerusalem far exceeded the number of similar estates in other parts of the country. I believe that the local names do not appear because the estates established by the Franks did not have local names. The names which appear in the document are none other than the names of the Frankish owners of the estates.

These estates formed part of the same parish as the village of "Terra Emaus," and the Frankish church at Abu Ghosh, like its counterpart in Sinjil, was also a parochial center for these estates. Further affirmation of this assumption can be found in the fact that these casalia are mentioned only in the patriarch's authorization of the parochial rights of the Hospitalers, and they do not appear in any of the authorizations issued by the lay authorities, which refer only to the territory given to the Hospitalers.

It is perhaps worthwhile to reemphasise the importance of the role played by the parish churches as nuclei for new settlements in Mediterranean Europe. In many cases the parish churches were as important as the fortresses or the market in the process of absorption of the new population and for the purpose of attracting new settlers. The construction of a parish church per se may not have provided sufficient inducement for new settlers; however, when added to the economic advantages it played an important role.

It is difficult to maintain that the mere existence of a Frankish church served as a basis for future settlement. But there are several hints in support of the assumption that there was a serious attempt at Frankish settlement in Abu Ghosh. Amongst other things there are, east of the church, three buildings erected by the Franks, two of which are within the confines of the present-day Benedictine monastery while the third, which was identified by De-Vaux and Stève without any factual justification as a water reservoir, serves today as the Abu Ghosh village mosque. One two-storey building could have been used as a domicile for the Hospitaler baillif of Castellum Emmaus. There is also a large oven near the church which may have been

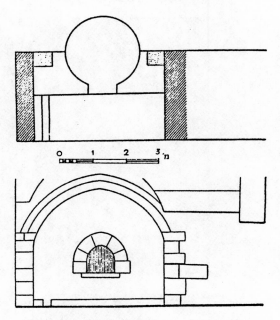

Figure 6   The Frankish oven in Abu Ghosh

used by the settlers. This oven was discovered by the inspectors of the Department of Antiquities of Palestine and its remains are visible to this day (see fig. 6). Also, the large number of crushing stones used in the oil industry are reminiscent of similar stones found in all other Frankish settlements in this region.

The archeological findings are too sparse to justify basing any conclusions as to the establishment of a large Frankish settlement on them. However, the heightened, quasi-fortified building of the village of Abu Ghosh would appear to resemble the typical construction of a medieval castrum (see plate 2). And I can find no other explanation for the existence of Frankish buildings and the large oven near the church, even though their presence may not provide decisive proof of the existence of a Frankish castrum prior to the Turcoman settlement of the sixteenth century.

To sum up, in Abu Ghosh a Frankish church, intended to serve the needs of the Hospitalers in the area and of the other Frankish settlers, was constructed. The church was the nucleus of the new settlement. In Abu Ghosh, as in Sinjil, the probable radius of the services provided by the parish church was larger than the administrative domain of the local landowners.

This farreaching geographical hypothesis raises additional problems. Did

Plate 2   Abu Ghosh, general view

the Franks establish a parochial network which was cut off from the local Christian population? It is customary to assume that the Latin clergy occupied the highest positions in the ecclesiastical hierarchy, and that the parochial set-up included the local followers of the Orthodox Church as well as the Latins. Can physical or spatial expression be given to these assumptions? Did the same churches serve both the Latins and the locals, or did the latter have their own churches? The answers to these questions are not simple and may not be decisive. It may be possible to rely on the fact that the parish church in Castellum Emmaus was not the only one of that kind and that in Galilee and other places too there is evidence of the existence of parish churches which served both the Frankish settlers and the local Christian population.

CHAPTER TEN

MIXED FRANKISH AND LOCAL CHRISTIAN SETTLEMENTS

An example of a joint Latin-Syrian parish: St. George above Tiberias

At the end of the 1170s a dispute broke out between the abbey of St. Mary Josaphat and the bishop of Tiberias over tithes and parochial rights. The dispute concerned also the church of St. George, which is described as "above Tiberias." This church was given by Bishop Bernard of Nazareth to the monks of St. Mary Josaphat already in 1109.[1] The arbitrators – the archbishop of Nazareth and the bishop of Acre – decided that the monks of St. George's should not admit parishioners of Tiberias who had been excommunicated or placed under an interdict by the bishop of Tiberias to the mass, nor should they baptize children of the Latin rite or enact marriages. In addition the arbitrators determined that the cemetery of the church should be reserved solely for the brethren, their servants, and Syrian Christians. "Nulli preter fratribus et servientibus suis et surianis sepulturam prestabit. Nulli Latinorum nisi surianis tantum in ea bapizari nulloque tempore in illa nuptias celebrari licebit."[2]

There can be no doubt, therefore, that the church of St. George, which came under the management of St. Mary Josaphat, gave burial services to, and probably also baptized and solemnized marriages for, Syrians and Latins alike.

The "Church of St. George" has still not been identified.[3] In excavations which were conducted on Mt. Berenice, which is above Tiberias, a church was discovered which, in accordance with the pottery found there, dated back to the end of the six century or the beginning of the seventh. The

---

[1] Delaborde, no. 14, 1126, 40; Kohler, no. 2, 1109, 113–114.
[2] Delaborde, no. 40, 1178, 87–88.
[3] Röhricht was of the opinion that this casale is identical with St. George de La Baena but Kohler assumed, quite rightly, that Dayr al-Asad which is St. George de La Baena is too far and never was within the confines of the diocese of Tiberias.

church continued to exist, and was even renovated during the 'Abbasid period and again in the twelfth century. It is possible, therefore, that the church on Mt. Berenice, which is in fact "above Tiberias," was none other than the church referred to in the documents.[4] It is perhaps important to note that the church was constructed at the southeastern edge of Byzantine Tiberias, very near to the walls of the city, but far from the medieval city of the twelfth century. This fact may be able to throw additional light on the nature of the dispute between St. Mary Josaphat and the bishop of Tiberias. The bishop must almost certainly have claimed that the confines of the city – and therefore the confines of the interdict – were those of the Byzantine period, while the abbey most probably argued that they were those of the medieval period. Incidentally, the arbitrators decided in favor of the bishop's claim which testifies to their geographic-historical approach to the early remains of the city. During recent archeological excavations (in 1993) a cemetery, which was adjacent to the north side of the church, was beginning to emerge.[5]

Wheresoever the casale might have been situated, there is no doubt that it contained a church and a cemetery which served both the Franks and the local Christian population. It is reasonable to assume that the same arrangement occurred in other villages – an assumption which is supported by historical and archeological evidence. While there is insufficient space here to provide all the evidence pointing to the existence of joint Frankish and local Eastern Christian communities, a few examples of the various types of joint existence will be examined.

A Frankish castrum in a local Christian village – Castrum Sancti Helie

The Frankish castrum which was established in al-Taiyba – Castrum Sancti Helie – is hardly mentioned in the Latin sources. The reason for this is that it was established within the royal domain and not much of its property was granted to ecclesiastical bodies. The fact that Frankish settlers lived there already in the 1150s can be extracted from a reference to a certain Hugo de Sancto Helye who is mentioned among the burgesses of Magna Mahomeria.[6] This settler must have lived in the castrum for an extended period in order to have earned the title "Hugo of St. Helya," and only later by the middle of the 1150s, went to live in Magna Mahomeria. Although it cannot be proved, it can be assumed, that Hugo, and perhaps other Frankish bourgesses, lived in this castrum already in the middle of the 1140s.

---

[4] Hirschfeld, 1993. Hirschfeld was not aware of the existence of this document when writing his article.   [5] Hirschfeld, 1993.   [6] Holy Sepulcher, no. 123, mid-twelfth century, 250.

The place is mentioned again in a transaction in which ownership of the "New Fortress" near Acre was transferred from King Baldwin IV to Joscelyn III, in 1182. The extended fiefdom in the Galilee granted to Joscelyn was in exchange, inter alia, for the castrum of St. Helia.[7] The place is mentioned yet again by Eracles when he describes the arrival in the Latin Kingdom, in 1185, of William III ("Boniface" according to Eracles), the grandfather of Baldwin V, king of Jerusalem. According to Eracles, the high-ranking knight came to the Orient in order to settle there, as endorsed by his giving all his property to his eldest son before crossing the sea. He was welcomed by the royal treasury with a gift of a "chastel" situated in the desert, on the other side of the river, near the place where Jesus fasted for forty days. The fortress, says Eracles, was seven miles from Jerusalem and thirteen miles from the Jordan, on top of a high hill, and was called "Saint Helyes," as it was said that Elias fasted there for forty days. Eracles says that the place was previously called Effra (or Effrain).

The castrum of St. Helya was undoubtedly within the royal domain as the king gave it away on two occasions without permission from anybody else: once to Joscelyn and the second time to his own grandfather. It is difficult to imagine that the king of Jerusalem owned two castra with the same name. There is, therefore, no doubt that Joscelyn received the castrum of St. Helie and then exchanged it later for extensive property in the Galilee.[8]

The Arab sources also describe the place as a Frankish fortress. 'Imad al-Din states expressly that there was a Crusader fortress there, and he includes it in the list of fortresses which were conquered by Saladin in 1187, while Yakut describes it as "a fortress in the vicinity of Jerusalem in Palestine."[9] In other sources, in which the fall of the Crusader Kingdom is described, the place is referred to as a "castrum." The place is mentioned also in the letter sent by Patriarch Eraclius to the Pope in 1187.[10]

---

[7] Strehlke, no. 14, Feb. 24, 1182, 13–14.

[8] Eracles, II, 14: "Et vos dirai d'un haut home de Lonbardie, qui avoit nom Boniface, qui estoit marquis de Mon Ferarre. Cil marquis estoit ayols dou roi Bauduin, qui enfes estoit, et peres fu de Guillaume Longue Espée, qui fu peres dou roi. Quant il oi dire que ses niez estoit rois de Jerusalem, si en fu moult liez et joianz, et vint et se croisa, et laissa sa terre a son ainz né fiz, et s'en vint Outre mer. Et quand il fu venuz en la terre d'Outre mer, li rois et li cuens de Triple et tuit li baron le recurent moult hautement, et furent moult liez de sa venue; lors vint li rois, si li dona un chastel, qui est ou desert, deca le flum, pres de la, ou Jhesu Crist jeuna la caranteine. Cist chasteaus est a vii milles de Jerusalem, et a treis milles dou flum Jordein, et siest en une haute montaigne, si l'apele l'en saint Helyes; et por ce l'apele l'en ainsi que l'en dist que ce est le lieu, ou Helyes jeuna xl jourz . . . et por ce que ce avint la, ou cist chasteauz siet, l'apelent cil dou pais saint elye, qui ancienement ot nom Effra."

[9] 'Imad al-Din al-Isfahani, 111, line 10, describes the place as a Frankish castle which was captured by Salah al-Din in 1187. Yaqut, III, 688, describes it as "a Castle in the neighborhood of Jerusalem in Filastin." [10] Kedar, 1982, 119, 122.

At the kernel of the village of al-Taiyba, at the top of the hill, there is a Frankish castle which was examined and described by Guérin, by Warren and Conder, by Bagatti, and lately also by Benvenisti (fig. 7).[11] The castle was surrounded by a spacious wall, the southern and eastern parts of which are now completely destroyed. Nevertheless, it is possible to establish that the wall surrounded an area much larger than that of the castle itself, and probably circumvented the whole of the built-up area on the hilltop. Guérin describes the place as follows:

This fortress was surrounded by a wall which enclosed a much larger area, and part of this wall is still standing . . . Beneath the fortress the village covers the spurs of the hill. Nearly all the houses are vaulted; some of them appear to be very old. In many places there are wells and reservoirs which were undoubtedly cut out of the foundation rock in ancient times, and which, together with the remains of the fortress, testify to the importance of the settlement at that time.

From surveys which I conducted there in 1985 and 1986 it became evident that amongst the buildings surrounding the castle there were houses with Frankish foundations. A description of such a house was given by Elihu Grant, who made a survey of the place in the 1920s; however, he apparently did not know that it was a building which had been constructed by the Franks.[12] The general impression which emerges is that of a small castle on a hilltop with a fortified suburb adjoining it. The territory occupied by the castrum of St. Helie was extensive and bordered on Magna Mahomeria. Proof of this can be found in a document, issued in September 1178, in which "the territory of the Castrum of St. Elias" is mentioned as near to Magna Mahomeria.[13]

The Frankish settlers and landlords changed the name of this castrum to a Latin one, as was the case with many other Frankish settlements. Until the advent of the Franks, the place was called Efrem or Effra, a name changed by the Franks to Castrum Sancti Helie, despite the fact that the original name was a Christian-Syrian one which had been in use for hundreds of years and had nothing Muslim or Arabic about it. It is perhaps important to note that here, as in Bira and many other places, the Syrian name continued to exist until the Frankish period and was exchanged for an Arabic name only much later. The connection of the Latin name to the aforementioned local tradition regarding Elijah having fasted at this site for forty days is self-evident. Indeed, "further south on the descent [from al-Taiyba]," says Guérin, "one

[11] Guérin, 1868–1869, III, 45–51; Warren & Conder, 1882–1884, II, 370–372; Bagatti, 1979, 31–36; Benvenisti, 1982, 147–151, figs. 19, 20, and 21.

[12] Grant, 1926, 186–195, pl. II, fig. 1, opposite 189; cf. also, Guérin, 1868–1869, III, 45.

[13] Röhricht, Regesta, no. 561, Sept. 8, 1178 (Paoli, I, no. 205, 247–248).

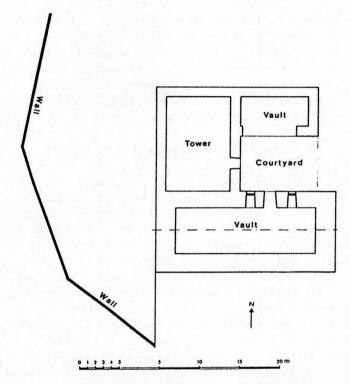

Figure 7   The Frankish castrum in al-Taiyba

can see . . . a famous cave, which both the Christians and Muslims call Mar
Elias. According to local tradition the prophet found shelter there on his way
to Jericho."[14] This tradition was perpetuated also in the name of the local
church.

The local inhabitants of al-Taiyba

The attitude towards local traditions is indicative of the relationship between
the local Christian communities and the Franks. But this is not the only evidence of that relationship. One can rely on several historical sources in order
to conclude that in the territory of Effra (which is the Castrum Sancti Helie)
there were local Christian inhabitants in the twelfth century. Effra was an
important Christian town already in the Byzantine period and is mentioned
twice in the *Onomastikon* of Eusebius: the first time under the name of Effra

[14] Guérin , 1868–1869, III, 46–47.

("which is in Benjamin and today there is the village of Ephraim 5 miles from Beth-El eastwards") and the second time under the name of Effron ("which is in [the land of] the tribal inheritance of Yehuda and today there is a large village, Ephraim, north of Jerusalem and about 20 miles from it").[15] The place is even mentioned in the Madaba map under the name of Efrem. From the descriptions ("5 miles from Beth-El" in the first case and "north of Jerusalem" in the second) it follows that the reference is to the same place in both cases.

In a Nestorian source, written in the ninth century, "Ephrem" is said to be "a large city situated 5 parasangs east of Beth-El." The author, Isho'dad, the Nestorian bishop of Hadatha, used the same expressions as Eusebius and it can be concluded, therefore, that the *Onomastikon* was in his possession. Even though his observations are not original it can be assumed that his testimony is reliable, since he referred only to Christian villages which were in existence at his time, for example Beth Phage. The fact that in this case he repeated Eusebius' descriptions does not derogate from the credibility of his claim that Christians lived in Effra in the ninth century.[16] One can rely on this source and conclude that there was a Christian community in Effra in the ninth century.

The Christian community continued to exist there in the post-Crusader period. According to the Ottoman tax census which was made in the sixteenth century a third of the population was still Christian. It is important to note the possibility that the census does not give a reliable picture of the number of Christians in the villages of Palestine and that the number of Christians in each and every village was apparently underestimated. There were villages in which the whole population was Christian at some later stage, whereas no reference whatsoever to a Christian community appeared in the census. In other places there is proof of the existence of many more Christians than appear in the census. Wherever there was a majority of Christians at the beginning of the twentieth century, the percentage of Christians in the sixteenth-century census was considerably smaller. The difference in numbers can come to 500%(!) in Galilee and to many tens of percentages in other parts of Palestine. It is not feasible that the Christian population of the Galilee could have increased forty times between the sixteenth and twentieth centuries and that of southern Samaria by many tens of percent. As this distortion is apparent in all the Christian villages of Palestine, it can be assumed that in al-Taiyba, too, the number of Christians was larger than the third registered in the tax census; in fact, in another

---

[15] Eusebius, *Onomastikon*, no. 100, 12; no. 418, 41.
[16] Bagatti, 1979, 32, and Isho'dad of Merv, I, 255.

census the total population (ninety-eight taxpayers) of al-Taiyba was registered as Christian.[17] In the nineteenth and twentieth centuries al-Taiyba was
still a purely Christian village without any Muslim residents. According to
Anthymus this was also the situation in 1838. At that time there were 200
Orthodox Christians living in the village.[18] In the census of 1922, too, the
large village (954 souls) appears as purely Christian, for the most part
Orthodox Christian, without a single Muslim inhabitant.

From all the historical evidence which I have collected it follows that the
Christian population at al-Taiyba remained in existence from the Byzantine
period until today. We have no information about the local population under
the Frankish and the Mamluk regimes, but it is difficult to imagine that a
village which was populated by Christians in the sixth and ninth centuries,
which had an appreciable Christian population during the Ottoman period,
and which was purely Christian in the first half of the nineteenth and the
first half of the twentieth centuries, was Muslim just in the twelfth century.

The church of al-Khadir

One can find support for the assumption that there was a local Christian
community in al-Taiyba in the twelfth century in the remains of the local
church of al-Khadir.[19] This church was originally a triapsidal Byzantine
church and was reconstructed in the twelfth century by Frankish builders.
As can be seen from the plan and from aerial and other photographs (fig. 8
and plate 3), the Frankish builders utilized the walls of the original church,
which was too large for their needs, and built a smaller church within its precincts. The church was in fact built by the Franks with the use of Frankish
technology, but it was apparently not intended for their exclusive use. This
assumption is based, first and foremost, on the fact that the rehabilitated
church was not built within the Frankish *castrum* but at the foot of a hill, at
some distance from the new fortifications. If the Franks had constructed a
church for the sole use of their burgesses, they would have constructed it
nearer to their own dwellings.

A similar analysis can be made of the considerations which prompted the
construction of the original Byzantine church on a low hill, far from the
fortress. From the location of the church (which was most certainly the
largest in the village, as it was triapsidal with an elaborate staircase leading to

---

[17] Lewis was the first and only scholar to pay attention to the absence of Christains from the entries
of several Christian villages, and he wrote: "A curious feature is the absence of any reference to
Christians in a number of places known in later times as Christian centres – such as Jafna, Rafidiya,
Zababida, Kafr Yasif, Mi'iliya, 'Ailabun, Bir'im, Ma'lul, Bir Zait, Ramallah, etc. Various explanations could be adduced." Lewis, 1954, 479; cf. 477.

[18] Anthymus, 1838, 490–495.   [19] Schneider, 1931a, plan opposite p. 15.

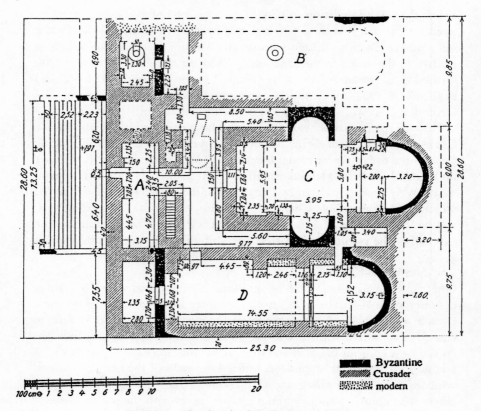

Figure 8   The church of al-Khadir in al-Taiyba

it) it can be deduced that the Byzantine village was either in close propinquity to it or extended beyond it. It is difficult to imagine that the early inhabitants of the village constructed so large and magnificent a church far away from their own dwellings.

During the early Muslim period the local population shrank and the church became too large for their needs and too far away. The Frankish renovated church could have served the local population (who probably lived nearer to it) and possibly also the Frankish settlers in the castrum. In any event, there are no traces of another Frankish church within the confines of the castrum or in any other place in the village. One should also note the connection between the name of the church (al-Khadir) and the name of the village (Castrum Sancti Helie). Both names have a close association with local saint traditions and both saints are considered manifestations of the

Plate 3 Al–Taiyba, church

prophet Elijah. It would appear that the Franks paid special attention to local holy traditions which even led to the choice of the Latin name for the village.

If the picture which I have presented here is correct, then we have an example of Frankish "incastellamento." The Franks, who established a new castrum next to the Christian settlement of Efrem, followed the same pattern they had adopted in many other places: the Frankish settlement was located on high ground, even though there was no vital need for this, the seignior's residence was placed at the top of the hill and near to it a small and fortified Frankish burgus was established, while the local Christian population continued to live at the foot of the hill. The chain of relations between the two communities was forged, in my opinion, by the fact that the old church was renovated by the Franks and that the name given to the new church (al-Khadir) was based on the same holy tradition from which the Latin name of the whole castrum was derived. The Frankish seigniors did not deprive the local Christians of their land or their status. They established their new settlement next to that of the local one and helped the local Christians to renovate their church.

This is not the only case where a Frankish castrum was established next to an existing local Christian settlement which had existed since the Byzantine period. In Miʿilya, too, a Byzantine church was discovered a few hundred meters away from where the Frankish castrum had been established. In many other places the Eastern Christian settlements continued to exist during the Frankish period. In the course of this book we shall see that in several Frankish castra there were local Christians who lived as castral inhabitants.

Frankish settlers in a Syrian village: the example of ʿAbud (grid reference 156/158)

Another example of the link between Frankish and local Christian settlements can be found in ʿAbud, which has been identified by Clermont-Ganneau as the Casale Sancte Marie.[20] The Casale Sancte Marie is mentioned in several Frankish documents. In one, dated 1167, there is a description of a sale of the casale, next to the territory of the village of Belfort, by the seignior of Mirabel to the Order of the Hospital. The latter paid 3,000 bezants for the casale and had to pay an additional annual fee of 200 bezants. The document refers to a plot of land which belonged to the church of St. Mary in Bethlehem and for that reason was not included in the deed of sale.[21]

In the list of the property which belonged to the church of Bethlehem, which was confirmed by Pope Gregory IX in 1227, the land belonging to the church of St. Mary is mentioned again. The document refers, inter alia, to eight carrucas of land which were in the Casale Sancte Marie. This church also owned the villages of Heberre, Bethmelchi, and Luban.[22]

---

[20] See Clermont-Ganneau, 1898, 166ff. Cf. also Riant, 1889, I, 144, no. 9 (1227); Hiestand, *Vorarbeiten*, III, 381, no. 190 (1227); Röhricht, *Regesta*, no. 518 (1174); *Les Archives*, 126–127; King, 1934, 29–30; Riley-Smith, 1967, 334; Pringle, 1993, 17–23.

[21] "Notum sit . . . omnibus, . . . quod ego Balduinus de Mirabel . . . casale quod appellatur S. Marie, contiguum territorio Bellifortis, cum universis pertinentiis suis longe lateque sibi adjacentibus, excepta terra S. Marie de Bethleem infra territorium predicti casalis jacente, tibi Giberte . . . Hospitalis . . . magister, . . . integre pro tribus millibus bisantiis, vendidi, concessi et tradidi." Hospital, no. 371, 1167, 254–255.

[22] Röhricht, *Regesta*, no. 983, 1227: "In casali Sancte Mariae, octo carrucatas terrae, casalia Bethmelchi, Heberre et Luban."

Seven years later the Hospitalers defrayed their annual debt (of 200 bezants) in exchange for a one-time payment of 1,700 bezants. All in all, the Order paid the sum of 4,700 bezants for the rights of this casale. It should be noted that a similar sum was paid for Cabor in Western Galilee – an estate with two Frankish manor houses (see chapter 15). As I claimed above, when a high price is paid for a village it is indicative of the presence of Franks in the village.[23]

The document of 1167 contains topographical descriptions which enable a reconstruction of the surroundings: it states that the Casale Sancte Marie was located next to the territory of Belfort and that the landed property of the church of Bethlehem was "below the territory of Casale Sancte Marie"; it gives the name of one of the witnesses to the document as Isaac de Naalein, who almost certainly must have been an inhabitant (either local Christian or Frank) of the neighboring village of Na'alin. Clermont-Ganneau succeeded in identifying some of the other villages mentioned in this document and incidentally confirmed the identity of 'Abud as the Casale Sancte Marie. According to him, Luban is the neighboring village of al-Luban, Heberre is Kh. al-Bira, and south of this ruined village there is another ruin, that of Kh. 'Ali Malkina, which might have been Bethmelchi.

Another village, Caphaer, which was also near to 'Abud, has still not been identified with any certainty, as it is difficult to rely on the name Caphaer ("village") in order to establish the village's exact identity. It is also difficult to accept Beyer's assumption that Caphaer is Kafr al-Dik. The connection between Caphaer and Casale Sancte Marie derives from a document in which the Master of the Hospital of St. John, Jobertus, undertakes to use the income from the Caphaer and Sancte Marie casalia for the purpose of providing white bread for the sick under the care of the Hospital in Jerusalem.[24] Although the location of Caphaer cannot be established with any certainty, we can establish that it was in the neighborhood of 'Abud and that it had Syrian occupants. This follows from the fact that in the deed of sale the whole village of Caphaer was sold, save for two carrucas owned by "the Syrian, Bufez." This punctiliousness concerning Bufez's rights is important for us as it indicates that the rights of the Syrian inhabitants were preserved.[25]

[23] For the sale of Casale Sancte Marie, see: Hospital, no. 468, Dec. 13, 1174, 321. For prices of casales in the twelfth century see chapter 7, n. 14.
[24] Hospital, no. 494, 1176, 339–340. The identification of Caphaer with Kafr al-Dik, was accepted by Prawer and Benvenisti and lately by Pringle. Prawer & Benvenisti, 1970; Pringle, 1993, 18.
[25] Hospital, no. 487, Nov. 29, 1175, 336.

Frankish settlers in 'Abud

We have several hints at Frankish settlement in Casale Sancte Marie ('Abud).
First of all in the list of burgesses in Mahomeria we find a certain Willelmus
de Casale Sancte Marie, who apparently lived in 'Abud before he went to
Mahomeria. We have no further written evidence about other Frankish
burgesses, but the assumption that there was Frankish settlement in the
village is further supported by the fact that the Franks called the place not by
its local name, but by its Latin name. I maintained above that in many local
Christian villages which had Frankish habitants, the local name was changed
to suit the language of the Latin landlords. Clermont-Ganneau produced the
same explanation for the source of the name "Casale Sancte Marie." He
thought the name was connected with the church in the village as "in 'Abud
one can still see a church in Frankish style dedicated to the Holy Virgin."
This is, therefore, an additional point of resemblance with the Castrum
Sancti Helie, whose Latin name was also taken from that of the most important church in the village, and apparently also with the church of St. George
above Tiberias. It can be concluded that names of villages which were occupied by local Christians were changed in several instances by the Franks to
the names of their patron saints.

The Latin sources do not hint at any fortification of 'Abud or at the
establishment of any castrum there. Neither do the Arabic sources depict the
place as a fortress. On the contrary, they describe it as an agricultural village
and Ibn al-Furat refers to its excellent waters.[26] In one of the documents
examined above there is a reference to the probably fortified neighboring
village of Belfort, which could be Dayr Abu Mash'al, built on one of the
high hills overlooking 'Abud. In this village there are impressive Byzantine
remains (apparently of a large Byzantine monastery) on part of which a
Frankish tower was erected.[27]

If, therefore, there was no Frankish castrum in 'Abud, and if, as I am
inclined to think following upon the survey I conducted in the village and
the previous surveys of Guérin, Bagatti, and Pringle, there were no fortifica-

---

[26] Yaqut, III, 585: "A tiny village in the region of Bayt al-Maqdis in Filastin." Ibn al-Furat, trans.
Lyons, VII, 10, line 12: "A village in the mountains with excellent water." Cf. al-Maqrizi, *Suluk*,
I, 612, lines 1–2; 613, line 4.

[27] Guérin, 1874–1875, II, 119: "A l'endroit culminant [of Dayr Abu Mash'al], je remarque, sur une
grande plate-forme, les traces d'une puissante construction, dont quelques assises inférieures exis-
tent encore et qui était bâtie avec de belles pierres de taille d'un magnifique appareil. Sous cette
plate-forme règne une immense citerne creusée dans le roc. Vers le sud se dresse un pan de mur
gigantesque fort épais, mais construit avec des pierres d'un bien moindre appareil que celles qui
constituent les assises inférieures dont je viens de parler." Guérin did not mention the marginally
drafted stones and the barrel-vault.

tions, then the Frankish burgesses who lived there obviously settled in an unfortified, local Christian village.[28]

The local inhabitants of 'Abud during the Frankish period

The Syrian sources leave practically no room for doubt about the Syrian identity of the population of 'Abud during the Frankish period. There was apparently a very important Christian community in 'Abud during the Byzantine period. And this community continued to exist in the second half of the eleventh century. In the walls of the church of St. Mary a unique inscription from this period was discovered. The inscription is written in the Palestinian Syriac dialect and its date was fixed by Milik as being the year 450 of the Hijrah – that is 1058. Milik had difficulty in reading the inscription and succeeded in reading only part of it to his own satisfaction. He was unable to decipher the Syrian date completely, but he succeeded in reading "almost certainly" the following words: "(the year) parallel to the year 450 of Beduin rule." On the basis of these words he fixed the date of the inscription at 1058.[29]

Moshe Bar-Asher criticized Milik's reading of the script in the following words: "Most of the text is illegible. The photograph and the stamp which the editor included indicate that it is difficult to decipher most of the inscription. Many of Milik's readings are based on far-fetched assumptions and guess-work."[30] But Bar-Asher does not disagree with Milik's dating of the inscription, and he, too, includes the inscription amongst the later Palestinian-Syriac sources. It would appear that only the words quoted above are fully accepted by both scholars. Pringle, who was unaware of Bar-Asher's reservations (which are contained in his doctoral thesis written in Hebrew) quoted Milik literally, without reference to Milik's own reservations about the reading of the inscription.

This inscription is not the only piece of evidence concerning the presence of a Syrian community in 'Abud during the eleventh to thirteenth century. 'Abud is considered to be the main territorial abode of Syriac literature in Palestine. Two of the few manuscripts in Palestinian–Syriac script from the eleventh to thirteenth century contain colophons which prove that they had been copied by monks originating from 'Abud. The earlier of these manuscripts was copied by "the monk Elias from 'Abud" in 1030, in the monastery of the Prophet Moses in the Madina (that is, the city) of Antioch. The copier returned at a later stage to his native-place where he built the

---

[28] Pringle, 1993, 18; Guérin, 1874–1875, II, 87–88; Schneider, 1933, 155–159; Bagatti, 1959–1960; Bagatti, 1979, 117–121.   [29] Milik, 1960, 197–204.
[30] Bar-Asher, 1976, source no. 148, 123.

monastery in Qauqab. Milik looked for and found this monastery about a kilometer and a half from 'Abud.[31] A later manuscript was copied by Mufarij Ibn Abu al-Hayr al-'Abudi in 1104, in the Sinai monastery.[32] Another Syrian monk, Sarur Ibn 'Abd al-Masih Ibn George Ibn Sa'id Ibn al-Hauk al-'Abudi, who originated from 'Abud, copied a Syriac manuscript in the thirteenth century, in Cairo.[33]

The Syrian population continued to exist in 'Abud in the Ottoman period. According to the sixteenth-century tax censuses, there was a Christian majority in the village: of the thirty-five residents who were registered in the census of 1553–7/961–4, there were nineteen Christians. I maintained previously that the numbers of Christians which appeared in the Ottoman tax censuses were distorted in favour of the Muslims. But despite this tendency, a Christian majority was registered in 'Abud.[34]

At the beginning of the nineteenth century, the entire population of 'Abud was Christian. In accordance with data available in 1838 there were 150 Orthodox Christians in 'Abud; and in accordance with the 1922 census, there were 335 Greek Orthodox Christians and 41 Latin Orthodox Christians.

The village is divided today into two parts: the northern, earlier one is exclusively Christian, while the southern part (whose inhabitants were not included in the census until 1948) is Muslim. The comparative age of the two sections can be gleaned from the oldest buildings which have been preserved: in Christian 'Abud, old churches with Byzantine foundations have been preserved on their original sites, while in Muslim 'Abud the oldest buildings are two splendid mausolea which were built during the Mamluk period. The division into two separate kernels is characteristic of most of the mixed villages in Palestine. But in 'Abud this division can also be dated: the earlier section continued to exist without interruption from the Byzantine period (or at least from the eleventh century when the Syriac inscription was made); while the "new" Muslim section was apparently established only in the thirteenth, or fourteenth, century.

The large church in 'Abud – the church of the Holy Virgin – was in existence already in the middle of the eleventh century. The aforementioned Syriac inscription is carved on a stone forming part of the springing of the S. aisle vaulting. No doubt, therefore, the stone bearing the inscription was not taken from an earlier building, and the inscription was intended to record

[31] Bar-Asher, 1976, source no. 85, 96; Milik, 1960, 201–204.
[32] Bar-Asher, 1976, source no. 87, 98; Milik, 1960, 202–203.
[33] Milik, 1960, 203; Pringle, 1993, 18; Lagrange, 1925, 499–504.
[34] Lewis, 1954, 478.

the date of the building of the vault in which it is set. This church was built in 1058 and was renovated again by Frankish builders who constructed the nave and reconstructed the N. aisle (see fig. 9). Clermont-Ganneau, who was the first to notice the Frankish improvements in the church, does not explain on what grounds he came to the conclusion that the church was probably a Frankish church. But he was the last scholar to examine the church before its internal walls were covered with plaster. The identifications of Clermont-Ganneau, who was the first to define the characteristics of Crusader construction methods in Palestine with any accuracy, are generally more correct and credible than those of his successors.[35] Pringle dated the later renovation of the church to 1058, relying on Milik's readings. It is important to note, however, that Milik's readings do not contain any reference to renovation, and there is no evidence that the church in its present form was renovated in the eleventh century. On the contrary, the style of the walls, windows, and portals verifies Clermont-Ganneau's assumption that the final appearance of the church was patterned by the Franks. It would appear that the Franks constructed the whole northern part of the church and changed two of the Byzantine pillars in the southern aisle into Frankish-style pillars. The difference between the northern and central sections of the church which were constructed, according to Clermont-Ganneau, by the Franks, and the southern aisle, constructed according to the Syriac inscription, in 1058, can be seen both in the different way of vaulting and the characteristic use of piers in the nave and N. aisle in contradistinction to the characteristic use of pillars in the S. aisle (see fig. 9.)

To sum up: 'Abud was a local village which was inhabited in the Middle Ages by an Orthodox Syrian Christian community. This community understood Syriac and used it at least until the middle of the eleventh century. The use of the Palestinian Syriac dialect in an inscription on the church, which was not intended only for scholars, testifies perhaps to the fact that the Palestinian Syriac language was still used at that time by the common people, at least within the confines of 'Abud. Certainly it is untenable to regard an inscription describing the renovation of a church to a liturgical process which required the use of the holy tongue. The monks and the well educated amongst the inhabitants of the village could write Syriac in the twelfth and thirteenth centuries, too, and they produced several copyists of Syriac manuscripts which were then distributed throughout the other Syrian centers in the Levant.

It can be gathered from the written sources that there was also a Frankish

---

[35] Clermont-Ganneau, 1899, 1–47.

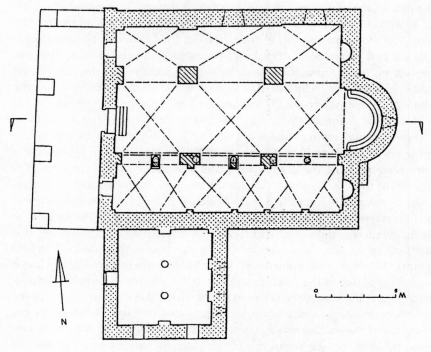

Figure 9   The church of St. Mary in 'Abud

settlement in the village of a size unknown to us. This settlement included
an ecclesiastical component (a large plot of land consisting of eight carrucas
belonging to the church of the Holy Virgin of Bethlehem) and a secular
component. There are no signs of fortification and no evidence that the
village had been fortified at any period of time. It would appear that the
Frankish burgesses lived within the local community and not separately from
it. In other words, this settlement cannot be equated with the examples of
castra discussed previously. The large church in the village – the church of
St. Mary – was built before the Frankish period and was renovated by the
Franks, as were the other two churches which were built during the same
time.

Frankish agricultural settlement in the 'Abud region

In the region next to 'Abud several Frankish castles and manor houses were
discovered. Those already referred to include Dayr Abu Mash'al, Baytilu,
Shabatin, Qibya, Dayr al-Mir, Kh. Tibnah. The church in 'Abud, which the

Franks renovated, like the churches in Sinjil, al-Taiyba, and Abu Ghosh, were built in the heart of the area in which there was Frankish settlement. We have no evidence about the parochial rights of the church but apparently this church too, like the others, served the local Syrian population, the Frankish settlers and the occupants of the castles, and the estates in the neighborhood.

Frankish private dwellings in local Christian villages: Jifna and Teqoʿa

Jifna al-Nasara (=Christian Jifna, Latin Jafenia) grid reference 170/152

Jifna al-Nasara is a Christian village, lying north of Jerusalem on the Nablus road. The remains of two Byzantine churches, which were discovered in the village, testify to the existence of a flourishing Christian community prior to the Muslim conquest.[36] The Christian community continued to exist in the Middle Ages and the village is still inhabited mainly by Christians.

The names of several Christian inhabitants of this village – Ibrahim and his brothers, the sons of Musa al-Jifnawi – appear in an inscription incised on a stone above the medieval gate of the monastery of St. George, in Wadi Qilt (Dayr al-Qilt, Choziba). The inscription refers to the completion of the restoration work which was carried out by the local Christian masons. Clermont-Ganneau, who was the first to publish this inscription, attributed it to the tenth century.[37] Schneider, however, suggested a different reading of this inscription and his reading was accepted recently by Pringle. Schneider and Pringle attributed this inscription to the year 1179.[38] Whatever the reading may be, without doubt there was still a Christian communitiy in Jifna in 950, and maybe even in the year 1179.

The Ottoman tax records present an intriguing picture: according to the data presented by Lewis and independently(?) also by Hütteroth and Abdulfattah, there were no native Christians living in this village in the sixteenth century. Toledano, who cited the same records, claims that the population of this village was still Christian in the sixteenth century. Toledano's version is more plausible as the population was still Christian at the beginning of the twentieth century and most of the inhabitants are still Christians even today.[39] It is certain that most of the inhabitants of

[36] Robinson & Smith, 1841, III, 77–78; Guérin, 1868–1869, III, 28–32; Warren & Conder, 1882–1884, III, 294, 323; Wilson, 1880, III, 104; Schneider, 1933, 158; Bagatti, 1979, 112–115; Benvenisti, 1970, 234, 238–240; Benvenisti, 1982, 147, figs. 16–18; Smail, 1973, 86; Kochavi, 1972, 174–175, no. 73; Pringle, 1993, 279–282.

[37] Clermont-Ganneau, 1899, II, 30–31; See also, Warren & Conder, 1882–1884, III, 196, fig. Lagrange, 1892, 442–443.   [38] Schneider, 1931b, 307–309; Pringle, 1993, 191.

[39] Lewis, 1954, 477, 479; Hütteroth & Abdulfattah, 1977, M142, 114; Toledano, 1979, 83–85.

"Christian Jifna" were local Christians in the twelfth century, as they are still today.

Apart from local Christians there was also a Frankish settlement in the village, as is attested to by the remains of the "maison forte" which was built in the lower part of the village.[40] In Jifna, like in many other sites in Palestine, the Franks built their settlement in the heart of the local Christian settlement.

A medieval church was also built in the village. Schneider prepared a plan of its apse, and other plans were prepared by Bagatti, by the 1968 survey, and recently also by Pringle.[41] The plan of the church reveals the same picture that we already described in al-Taiyba and ʿAbud. The church of Jifna was built before the Crusades and was reconstructed under Frankish occupation on a reduced scale. Here too, there was only one church for the local Christians and for the Frankish overlords.

Teqoʿa (Kh. al-Tuquʿ or Casal Techue), grid reference 170/115[42]

Another Frankish "maison forte" was built in the village of Tuquʿ, 9 kilometers to the south of Bethlehem. The local Christian population which still existed there at the beginning of the twelfth century were overjoyed at the conquest of the First Crusade and, together with the Christian inhabitants of Bethlehem, welcomed the Frankish conquerors.[43]

The local Christian population of the place is mentioned once more by Abbot Daniel who visited the place in 1108. According to him Teqoʿa was "a very big village" with a Saracen and Christian population. Daniel passed the night there and "was honored by the Christian inhabitants." The next morning he was accompanied by the armed headman of the village in order to visit the Christian holy places. The Mukhtar warned him against taking the direct road because of the "Saracen pagans who beat the Christians."[44] Beduin nomads who lived in the vicinity of Teqoʿa are mentioned also in a transaction in which the village was exchanged for the rights of the Church of the Holy Sepulcher in Bethany and for four more villages.[45]

[40] For a discussion of the Frankish isolated dwellings, see part III. For the manor house in Jifna, see Benvenisti, 1970, 234, 238–240; Benvenisti, 1982, 147, figs. 16–18; Kochavi, 1972, no. 73, 174–175; Bagatti, 1979, 112–113. Raimundus de Jafenia was most probably one of the owners of this "maison forte." Cf. Röhricht, *Regesta*, no. 613; Rey, 1883, 385–386; Johns, 1937; Prawer & Benvenisti, 1970.

[41] Schneider, 1933, 158–159, fig. 7; Bagatti, 1971, 251–255; Bagatti, 1979, 113–115, fig. 44, pl. 42–43; Kochavi, 1972, no. 73, 174–175; Pringle, 1993, 280–282, pl. cxciv and cxcv, illus. 81.

[42] Cf. Röhricht, 1887, 201; Röhricht, 1898, 219; Mayer, 1977, 375–382; Bagatti, 1983, 63–64; *IHC*, I, 31, pl. 11.

[43] William of Tyre, 8, 7, line 10, 394; cf. 1, 6, lines 39–41, 114: "Nec solum his qui in eadem urbe erant, sed etiam his qui in Bethleem et Thecua, ubi soli habitabant fideles."

[44] Raba, Russians, 53–54; Khitrowo, 49.

[45] Holy Sepulcher, no. 34, Feb 5, 1138, 99–100.

Another incident, which occurred in 1138, also testifies to the existence of a local Christian population in Teqoʿa. William of Tyre describes the flight of the inhabitants of this village because of a Muslim incursion. There was no reason for the local inhabitants to evacuate their dwellings unless they were either local Christians or Franks.[46] According to the Ottoman tax census of 1525/6 there was still a considerable Christian population in the village. Fifty-five out of the eighty-two families who lived there were Christian.[47]

The Frankish manor house was built on a rise at the edge of ancient tel of biblical and Byzantine Tuquʿ, facing the present-day Arab village. (plate 4).[48]

There was, therefore, a large local Christian settlement also in Teqoʿa, during the twelfth century, as well as a Frankish settlement. The settlement in Teqoʿa was exceptional because it had a mixed population of Muslims and local Christians already in the twelfth century. I attach great importance to the fact that in the region of Teqoʿa there were many nomads and lawless elements. In part IV I shall attempt to show that regions in which there were, already in the twelfth century, large concentrations of Muslims were regions which had, during the early Muslim period, gone through a process of nomadization followed by a process of sedentarization. The village of Teqoʿa had already, before the Frankish period, gone through a process of partial Islamization with the result that many of its inhabitants were Muslims.

Frankish castra with mixed Frankish–local Christian populations

Dayr al-Balah (Darom), (grid reference 088/092)[49]
William of Tyre describes how the fortress at Darom was constructed at the same time as he describes how it was attacked and besieged by Salah al-Din. According to him King Amalric I ordered the construction of a modest fortress on "scarcely more than a stone's throw of ground." The fortress was square with a tower at each of its corners. One of the towers was larger and more strongly fortified than the other three. The modest fortress had no moat and no barbican. It attracted settlers who established a burgus at its foot: "Here a few cultivators of the fields near by had united

---

[46] William of Tyre, 15, 6, 682.   [47] Toledano, 1979, 84.   [48] Bagatti, 1983, pl. 11.
[49] Cf. Warren & Conder, 1882–1884, III, 247–248; Musil, 1907, I, 302, 689; Guérin, 1868–1869, I, 223–226; Abel, 1940, 67–69; Burrows, 1932, 142–148; *IHC*, I, 87; Deschamps, 1934, 15, 19, 24, 44, 54 n. 1, 55 n. 4, 86–88; Deschamps, 1939, 14–15, 21, 236–237; Prawer, 1980c, 107–109; Pringle in Lawrence, 1988, 35–36; Pringle, 1993, 194–196.

Plate 4   Teqoʻa

with some traders and formed a little settlement. They built a suburb and a church not far from the castle and took up their abode there. It was a pleasant spot where conditions of life for people of the lower ranks were better than in cities."[50]

The process of establishing a burgus at the foot of a fortress was, at first glance, a routine one. We are familiar with a similar process all over

---

[50] "Convenerant autem aliqui ex locis finitimis agrorum cultores et negociationibus quidam operam dantes, edificaverant ibi suburbium et ecclesiam non longe a presidio, facti loci illius habitatores: erat enim locus commodus et ubi tenuiores homines facilius proficerent quam in urbibus." William of Tyre, 20, 19, 937; cf. William of Tyre, trans. Babcock & Krey, 373.

contemporaneous Europe and I dealt with it at great length in the chapter on Frankish *castra* in Palestine. William of Tyre notes who the inhabitants of the *burgus* of Darom were, but his observation is more than a little surprising. There is no doubt that the settlers in Darom were Christians, as they built a church and enjoyed the patronage and protection of the lords of the Frankish fortress . But it is difficult to imagine that they were Franks. William of Tyre speaks of settlers "of the lower ranks" who lived near to the fortress and were previously engaged in agriculture. According to his description, these people abandoned their previous homes and moved themselves and their church to the foot of the new fortress. The reference is, probably, to Christian farmers who lived near to the southwestern border of the Kingdom before the construction of the fortress — that is in the 1150s and 1160s — and not to new settlers. It is difficult to accept that these were Frankish settlers who had cultivated the land on the border of the Kingdom without the protection of a central fortress (although this assumption would add support to my theory that there was widespread Frankish rural settlement). It is more reasonable to assume that the farmers who lived in that region before the construction of the fortress were local Christians and not Frankish settlers. The farmers and the Eastern Christian traders linked their fate to that of the Franks and chose to settle in a more comfortable place which had been established by their masters, who were also their allies. If this assumption is correct, then it throws further light on the paternalistic nomenclature of William of Tyre: "tenuiores homines." According to William of Tyre's conception, the local Christian farmers belonged to the lower ranks of Levantine society, but they were an integral part of it. In other words: the Eastern society was composed of Franks and half-Franks, who belonged to the upper classes, and Eastern Christian farmers who belonged to the lower ranks of the same society.

The assumption that the region of Darom was populated also by Christians is strengthened by the confirmation issued by Pope Alexander III, in 1168, in which the direct jurisdiction of the patriarch of Jerusalem over Greek dioceses in which there were no longer any bishops was authorized. The region of Darom appears in the list of these dioceses. The Catholic Church inherited here, as in other places, the mantle of the Orthodox Church, and from William of Tyre's description it would appear that this was not an abstract or theoretical inheritance since in the regions referred to there were still large Eastern Christian communities. The confirmation of Alexander III, together with the description of William of Tyre, point to de facto cultural unity: the Latins occupied the higher echelons in the exclusive seigniorial hierarchy and enjoyed the rich income and the senior administrative positions, while the Eastern Christians, who constituted the majority of the population and of the castral burgi were "of the lower ranks."[51]

The place continued to be occupied by Eastern Christians after the Franks were driven out of Palestine. In the first Ottoman tax census, conducted in 1525–6/432, the place is described as a village with fifty-six (families of) Muslim taxpayers and eighty-seven (families of) Christian taxpayers.[52] In the next census, conducted in the middle of the sixteenth century, there were already 125 (families of) Christian taxpayers.[53]

The place apparently grew substantially during the twelfth century. In a description of Richard the Lionheart's travels the fortress is portrayed as surrounded by a wall with seventeen beautiful, strong towers, as opposed to the four towers referred to in William of Tyre's description. The fortress was protected at that time by a deep moat ("whose one side was paved with stones and the other with natural rock"), whereas William of Tyre states categorically that the fortress had no moat and barbican.[54] The place is mentioned also in other Latin and Arabic sources, which describe it as being on the border between Palestine and Egypt.[55]

The picture which emerges from these few sources is of a fortress which was not exceptional. Franks settled near to Eastern Christian communities in many other places, and Eastern Christians lived in many Frankish castra. In all these cases local Christian communities had either preceded the Frankish settlers, or had arrived after the Franks had already established themselves. In at least one case the Franks entrusted the protection and defense of a fortress to the local Christians, apparently because they constituted a majority of the population in the area. Shortage of space obviates the presentation of all the available evidence and in any case this is not the place in which to give an historical survey of each and every one of these fortresses. It is sufficient to present the sources relevant to this book, which show that at least some of the burgi established at the foot of Frankish fortresses were

---

[51] Holy Sepulcher, no. 142, Feb. 8, 1168, 276. Cf. Hamilton, 1980, 78; Mayer, 1977, 199–205; Hiestand, *Vorarbeiten*, III, 244–246, Pringle, 1993, 194–195.

[52] Lewis, 1954, 478.   [53] Hütteroth & Abdulfattah, 1977, 144.

[54] Ambroise, verses 9223–9229; *Gesta Regis Ricardi*, Liber V, cap. 39, 352–356. Cf. William of Tyre, 20, 19, 936–937: "castrum modice quantitatis, vix tantum spacium infra se continens quantum est iactus lapidis, forme quadre, quattuor turres habens angulares, quarum una grossior et munitior erat aliis, sed tamen absque vallo erat et sine antemurali."

[55] Al-Muqaddasi, 174 ("A castle on the caravan road from Gaza to Egypt"); al-Harawi, 33, line 5; Yaqut, II, 525 ("A castle which was destroyed by Salah al-Din in 584/1187"); 'Imad al-Din al-Isfahani, 111, line 5, 422 ("al-Darum, a castle on the Egyptian border"); Abu Shama, *Raudatayn*, II, 196; Abu Shama, *Dhayl*, 81, 195; al-Maqrizi, *Suluk*, I, 109, 134, 373. Cf. also Philip of Savona, 56; Jacques of Vitry, XL, 1070; *IHC*, III, 310–312.

populated also by local Christians, or that Frankish fortresses and burgi were constructed within the confines of local Christian villages. The few examples of these testify, in my opinion, to the rule.

Local Christian inhabitants in the castles of Transjordan: al-Karak (Crac, le Crac de Montreal)

The castle of Karak was built in 1142 by Payen the Butler.[56] Qalqashandi and Ibn Shaddad relate that this castle was built beause of the Beduin attacks against a Christian monastery and a local Christian settlement adjacent to it. The Christian inhabitants of the place begged the Franks to build the castle in order to protect them and their wish was fulfilled.[57] The description in the Arabic sources is confirmed in the chronicles of William of Tyre, who writes that during Salah al-Din's siege of the fortress, in 1171, "the inhabitants [of the burgus of Karak] were all Christians and therefore more reliance could be placed upon them."[58]

Later on, when William of Tyre describes the flight of the inhabitants of the surrounding areas into the besieged castle, he notes categorically that amongst them were "many Syrians, with their wives and children, who had come in from the surrounding country. The place was filled with them so that those who wished to pass back and forth could not do so freely on account of the dense crowds."[59] Something similar was said of the castle at Shaubac. Abu-'l-Fida', for example, describes the place as a town in which the majority of the inhabitants were local Christians.[60]

The two large castles in Transjordan were, therefore, built in the heart of the Syriac concentration – that is, of the local Christian population. These concentrations and the connection between them and the Franks provide the reason for the existence of the metropolitan see of Petra in the twelfth century, as well as for the fact that Baldwin II could, already in 1115, transfer Christians from Transjordan and settle them in Jerusalem.[61]

The mutual interdependence between the local Christians (who depended on the Franks for their personal security) and the Franks (because the local Christians constituted a majority of their subjects and provided them with most of the castral services) did not change the superior and contemptuous attitude of the Franks towards the local Christians. So that,

[56] William of Tyre, 15, 21, 703–704.
[57] Ibn al-Furat, trans. Lyons, 61, 50–51, the year 661; al-Qalqashandi, IV, 155.
[58] William of Tyre, 20, 27, 951.   [59] William of Tyre, 22, 29 (28), 1057.
[60] Abu-'l-Fida', *Taquim*, 247; Eracles, I, 500, the place "Cil dedenz estoient tuit crestien."
[61] William of Tyre, 11, 27, 535–536.

for example, during the siege of the Habis Jaldak fortress (Caua de Suet, al-Habis, grid reference 228/236) by Salah al-Din, William of Tyre notes that the commanders in charge were Syrians. In other words, the Syrians were not only passive subjects and providers of services to the Frankish overlords, but they also took an active part and even filled commanding positions on the battle-field. Furthermore, it is difficult to imagine that the ordinary fighters were Franks if the officers were Syrians, so that the defense of the fortress fell entirely upon the Syrian inhabitants of the territory. Nevertheless, this did not improve the image of the Syrians in the eyes of William of Tyre, who described them as "a race which is regarded by us as weak and effeminate" and who blames the loss of the fortress on the seigniorial lord of the area "who was responsible for placing men of such calibre in charge of so important a place."[62] William of Tyre therefore regarded the fact that the defense of the fortress was entrusted to "tenuiores homines" as so exceptional as to warrant severe criticism of one of the members of the important seigniorial families of the Kingdom, although he apparently did not criticize the fact that the Syrians had participated in the defense of the fortress. Evidently such participation was not exceptional but was, on the contrary, the accepted norm.

Local inhabitants in Bethgibelin

Another example of a Frankish–local Christian castrum can be found in Bethgibelin, where a Frankish castrum was established in 1136. This castrum was the center of an estate which included, amongst other things, two places known as Beithsur and the following places: Irnachar, Irrasin, Charroubete, Deirelcobebe, Meimes, Hale, Bothme, and Heltawahin. The king added the following villages from his own domain to the estate: Fectata, Sahalin, Zeita, and Courcoza. All the above property was transferred to the Order of St. John in 1136.[63]

The Frankish settlers received their settlement articles before 1170; and in the document granting these articles to them appear the names of Frankish burgenses who received these rights.[64] It is not clear from the documents whether there was also a non-Frankish population in Bethgibelin, and the impression one receives from them is that this was a completely new settle-

---

[62] William of Tyre, 22, 16 (15), 1029. For the history and archeology of the place, see Deschamps, 1933, 47–57; Deschamps, 1935, 285–291; Deschamps, 1939, 99–111; Nicolle, 1988; Tibble, 1989, 165; Pringle, 1993, 26.

[63] Bagatti, 1972; Guérin, 1868–1869, II, 357; Robinson & Smith, 1841, II, 357; Warren & Conder, 1882–1884, III, 270–271; Beyer, 1942, 207; Beyer, 1946–1951, 175–176; Hamilton, 1980, 182–183; Riley-Smith, 1967, 393, 437 n. 1; William of Tyre, 14, 22, 659–661; Hospital, no. 116, 1136, 97.   [64] Hospital, no. 399, 1168, 272–273.

ment. However, there had been a large Christian community in the place during the Byzantine period, but "it was abandoned by its inhabitants, who fell captive to the Arabs during the inter-tribal war which broke out in 796."[65] This did not lead to the complete destruction of the Christian settlement in Bethgibelin and the place was important enough in the ninth century to be the center of one of the thirteen *kuwar* (administrative districts) of Jund Filastin.[66] There is no reference in the Arabic sources either to the nature of the inhabitants of the district. We can conclude from the chronicles of Benjamin of Tudela that there were three (families of) Jews.[67] But we do not know whether these families lived in Bethgibelin before the arrival of the Franks or whether they settled in the Frankish burgus after its establishment. In any event it is clear that during the Frankish period there were also non-Frankish inhabitants of Bethgibelin.

The non-Frankish communities in Bethgibelin multiplied extensively in 1173. In a document of that year, many of the details of which are obscure, Jobert, the Master of the Hospital, granted the monastery of St. George to Meletus, the Syrian, the archbishop of the Syrian and Greek communities in Gaza and Bethgibelin. The grant was to expire with the death of the archbishop, who joined the Hospital Order as a confrater. It appears from the document that the Greeks and the Syrians had rights in Eluetropolis (i.e. Bethgibelin) and that the Franks recognized these rights. One can learn, furthermore, about the existence of the Greek monastery of St. George, which is not mentioned in any other source, and about the existence of an important non-Latin ecclesiastical establishment in the domain of the Kingdom of Jerusalem. These documents lead to the conclusion that there was a Greek or Syrian community in Bethgibelin. In other words: here, as in other places, there was a mixed Frankish–local Christian population.[68]

The "fortress and burgus" in Shafa-ʿAmru

The written sources allow for the assumption that there was a Frankish or local Christian burgus at the foot of the Templar fortress in Shafa-ʿAmru in Western Galilee. A pilgrims' guidebook from the thirteenth century describes the place as being formerly "a very beautiful and strong place." "Près d'El Phar est le Saffran, Saffran un liu où seint iake de Galice fu né, e unkore apert le liu en la roche, e soleit estre iadìs mult beau liu & fort."[69]

Another guidebook refers to the church dedicated to the saints James and John, who "were born there:" "en ce chemin [the road from Nazareth to

---

[65] Gil, 1992 (708), 474.   [66] Gil, 1992 (122), 111–112.   [67] Benjamin of Tudela, 42.
[68] Hospital, no. 443, 1173, 306–308; Pringle, 1993, 101; Hamilton, 1980, 182–183; Riley-Smith, 1967, 393, 435–437; Mayer, 1978, 188ff.   [69] Michelant & Raynaud, 198.

Acre] est Safran où il a d'Acre iij lieues, à laquele montaigne est l'yglise S. Iaque & S. Iohan, où il furent nés, & i apert encore la trace."[70]

A combination of both these pieces of evidence indicates that the place was both a fortress and a "place," apparently a burgus. The fact that there was also a church (which was not described as being within the fortress) leads to the conclusion that at least some of the inhabitants of the burgus were Christians. One cannot rely on these documents in order to decide whether the inhabitants of the burgus were Frankish settlers or local Christians who had lived there since time immemorial. It is nevertheless worthwhile to note two facts which testify apparently to the existence of a Christian community even after the Crusader period.

(1) Ricoldus de Monte Crucis called the place Castrum Zafetanum and said that Christians were still living there.[71]

(2) Till the beginning of the twentieth century there was a large Christian community in see Shafa-'Amru, and even today many Christians live there.[72] It is perhaps important to point out that the Christian community in Shafa-'Amru lives in the oldest part of the town. This phenomenon is common to many villages with mixed Muslim and Christian inhabitants, such as Kafr Kanna, 'Abud, Kafr Yasif, and others. In these villages one can find two ancient nuclei: the earlier one inhabited by Christians and the later one (which is also many hundreds of years old) inhabited by Muslims. As the phenomenon is not incidental or unique there may be room for theorizing that the Christian communities in the mixed villages preceded the Muslim communities which established new quarters separated from the existing Christian nuclei. This theory deserves a more in-depth examination.

The cases which were mentioned in this chapter do not include all the cases of Frankish–local Christian settlements. Another inventory can easily be put together including places such as al-Ram, Fahma, Bayt Jala, 'Ayn Karim, Sebaste, the Judean desert monasteries, and many other sites. The facts emerging from the analysis of all these cases will be discussed in detail in part IV: The Franks settled inside or in the immediate vicinity of local Christian villages. On the other hand, examples of mixed Frankish–Muslim villages are hardly to be found and it seems that such a phenomenon, if it existed at all, would have been very limited in scope.

---

[70] Michelant & Raynaud, 100.   [71] Ricoldus de Monte Crucis, 107.
[72] In 1922 there were 1,263 Christians (55% of the population), 623 Muslims (27%) and 402 Druzes (18%).

CHAPTER ELEVEN

FRANKISH SETTLEMENTS AND THE
COLLECTION OF TITHES

The limited number of Latin documents which deal with the rural areas does not allow for the complete reconstruction of the parochial system of the church in the rural areas, although we do have fragmented evidence of the existence of such a system (as I shall later show). All that can be shown is that the parochial churches served not only the Franks who lived in the villages but also those who lived in the "maisons fortes" and in the manor houses in their vicinity.

One component of this parochial system is very intriguing and is integral to the concerns of this book: the collection of tithes. From the various documents dealing with tithes and those dealing with disputes between the church and Frankish settlers, one can learn a great deal about Frankish settlement, the rural way of life, and the administration of the Frankish rural regions. In one document,[1] issued by the bishop of Acre, a dispute concerning church hegemony and the payment of tithes between the Master of the Teutonic Order and the bishop of Acre is described. The bishop details the demands presented to him by the Germans, his demands in return, and the compromise reached between them through arbitration. The names and status of the arbitrators are not mentioned in the document, which deals mainly with the extent of the exemptions granted and not granted to the Teutonic Order by the secular church.

In addition to ecclesiastical obedience, the bishop of Acre demanded that the Germans pay him the full measure of tithes "on the land, trees and vineyards in the diocese of Acre which the Master and brothers cultivated, and would cultivate, with the aid of their own money and labor." The bishop itemized his demand as follows: a tithe of all the agricultural products of the villages of Bassa and Massob, a tithe of all the agricultural products of the

---

[1] Strehlke, no. 112, 1257, 91–94 (Röhricht, *Regesta*, no. 1260).

145

villages of Cafriasim, Busenen, and Saphet, and a tithe from the village of Noye, which had been "stolen" from him earlier. The German Order was treated like an organization which was responsible for the settlement. The farmers had not lived on their land since time immemorial but had been settled there by the Order.[2]

The list of villages contained in the document appears somewhat puzzling. The Teutonic Order apparently occupied tens of villages within the diocese. So why were only a few of them mentioned? It should be remembered that the document in question was not an incidental one in which only a truncated picture of the status quo was given, as are most of the other documents on which we are forced to rely. The document details an agreement, in accordance with which a farreaching financial, legal, and apparently longstanding dispute between the bishop of Acre and the Teutonic Order was settled. It is difficult to imagine that there were other clauses of the agreement which were detailed in other documents; thus, it seems unlikely that there were other villages involved in the dispute between the two parties. Can one conclude from this that the Germans duly paid the tithes on all the other villages in their possession? In that case, why should they have omitted to do so precisely in the case of the villages mentioned in the document? Could there have been something common to them which lay behind this omission? Indeed, from other evidence available it would appear that in at least three of the villages referred to in the document there were Frankish settlers, and in at least two additional villages there apparently were local Christian inhabitants.

The village of Bassa

One can learn about Frankish settlement in Bassa from a document in which the transfer of the village and the neighboring *gastina* of Missop (H. Mezzuva, grid reference 164/276) to the German Order is described. In the document issued in 1200, King Aimery refers to "the *gastina* of Missop" as if it had been a "*gastina* [that is a ruin] *in the past*. [my emphasis]"[3] The fact

---

[2] "Item petebamus, quod dicti magister et fratres compellerent suos villanos et rusticos, quibus possessiones et terras suas sitas in diocesi Acconensi excolendas committunt, solvere integras decimas nobis et successoribus nostris . . . de illa portione fructuum quam habent et retinent dicti rustici et villani pro agricultura seu quacunque alia ratione." Strehlke, no. 112, 1257, 91 (Röhricht, *Regesta*, no. 1260).

[3] "Notum sit . . . quod ego Aymericus . . . vendidi et dedi . . . vobis, fratribus hospitalis . . . Alemannorum . . . quoddam casale in territorio Ackon situm, quod vocatur Lebassa, cum omnibus suis pertinenciis et unam gastinam cum omni territorio suo, que vocatur Missop, que illa die erat gastina. Quod casale predictum cum omnibus suis pertinenciis et gastinam prenominatam, sicut superius divisum est, libere et imperpetuum habeatis et teneatis, sicut Iohannes

that the grant was accompanied by a process of signposting the land suggests that there was a Frankish settlement in the place. In the course of a survey of the village, it was found that the partially preserved local church was founded on medieval foundations.[4] The inspectors of the Department of Antiquities have found amongst the ruins of the medieval villages of Bassa and Missop several capitals which were dated to the Crusader period and which are now in the Museum in Hanita. It is interesting to note that there was still a substantial Christian community in Bassa at the beginning of the twentieth century.

The village of Saphet

A settlement by the name of Saphet existed in the twelfth and thirteenth centuries in the territory of Acre. From the documents describing this settlement it is clear that it was not the town or the fortress of Safed, in Upper Galilee, but was some other settlement closer to Acre. In a document issued in 1208, a casale called Saphet "in territorio Accon" is mentioned. In 1208, Safed in Upper Galilee was still in Muslim hands and in any case was never in the territory of Acre.[5] Additional evidence of the fact that Saphet was in Western Galilee can be found in a document dated from 1220 which describes the village as being part of the fief of St. George. This document deals with a third of the fief and refers to Saphet together with Yrka, Yanuh, Kh. Cabara, Mazra'a, and Kh. Mabiliya. All the other sites were identified as being in the southwestern part of the Galilee.[6]

There are other documents which can identify Saphet more accurately. In a document from the year 1253, "Saphet [which is] in the plain of Acre" ("Saphet in planitie Acconis") appears once again;[7] and yet again in an itinerary of the second half of the thirteenth century. The author of this itinerary traveled from Nazareth to Acre and passed Shafa-'Amru on his way. After passing Shefar'am but before reaching Da'uq and Recordana he passed "German Saphet."[8] This description enables us to identify, with considerable

---

marescalcus meus et homines mei precepto meo eiusdem predicti casalis et dicte gastine terram diviserunt et terminos posuerunt." Strehlke, no. 38, 1220, 30–31 (Röhricht, *Regesta*, no. 776).

[4] Another small monastery in the neighborhood of Bassa was excavated by Cl. Dauphin. According to the published report (Dauphin, 1979) this monastic complex was fifth to eighth century.

[5] Strehlke, no. 43, 1208, 34–35.

[6] Strehlke, no. 53, 1200, 43 (Röhricht, *Regesta*, no. 934).

[7] Röhricht, *Regesta*, no. 1206, 1253.

[8] "En après del Saffran vent l'om en Acre, où il i a iij. liues. En quel chemin l'em trove Saphet des Alemauns, mès tut est abatu. Après hors de chemin à destre l'om vent à Doch. D'autre part à senestre a les molins de Doch. E utre un poi en là, l'om vent à Ricardane, e issi en Acre." Les chemins et les pelerinages de la Terre Sainte, texte B, in Michelant & Raynaud, 198.

confidence, "German Saphet" with the large village of Safad ʿAdi near the Shefarʿam crossroad. Amongst the ruins of this village, a great deal of medieval pottery was found. In a survey of the place I found a fragment of a Byzantine pillar made of marble, which originated in a Byzantine church.

From an examination of other documents, one can find further evidence of the existence of a Frankish settlement in Safad ʿAdi which was apparently inhabited by Frankish burgesses. In one of the documents a charitable grant of a house and three carrucas of "terra francesia" to the Teutonic Order is referred to: "Notum sit omnibus . . . quod ego comes Otto . . . dono et in perpetuam elemosinam concedo domui hospitalis Alamannorum Acchon tres carrucatas *terre francesias* aput casale, quod vocatur Saphet, *in territorio Accon situm et unam domum in eodem casali* [my emphasis]."[9]

Like many other rights which were granted in the Middle Ages, the expression "terra francesia" refers to land which belonged to "homines franci" and not to the rights of the land itself. From the fact that "homines franci" lived in Saphet one can conclude that there were free Frankish farmers there who were exempted from some of the seigniorial obligations. That Otto and his wife donated "a house" in the village adds verisimilitude to this interpretation.

One can learn that there were other burgesses (or noblemen) who owned property in the village from the fact that the German Order bought, in that very same village, "una wolta" from "domina Hensalme, soceri [sic] domini Menebof," and five additional carrucas for 1,300 bezants – a very large sum in comparison with the prices paid for land in Miʿilya.[10] Several years earlier, in 1231, a certain Castellana, "the wife of Arnulfus Aurifex and the daughter of Raimundus Barlerius," promised the Teutonic Order a house and two plots of land in Saphet from her inheritance.[11] Thus, it is clear that Frankish settlers lived in the village, that there was property there which belonged to two Frankish burgesses (Arnulfus Aurifex), and that there was land there which was exempted from part of the seigniorial obligations. Unfortunately, no other documents dealing with property and the Frankish settlers who probably lived in the village have been preserved. But even from the few details we have managed to glean, it can be concluded that there was a settlement of Frankish farmers, at least some of whom were freemen, which was later acquired by the Teutonic Order in the thirteenth century.

During the Byzantine period, there was a Christian community in Saphet (as indicated by the marble pillar found there) and during the Crusader

[9] Strehlke, no. 43, 1208, 34–35.
[10] Strehlke, no. 128, 1260, 124 (Röhricht, *Regesta*, no. 510).
[11] Strehlke, no. 75, 1231(?), 60 (Röhricht, *Regesta*, no. 1026).

period a Frankish settlement was created in the village. The settlement was later destroyed, apparently at the end of the Crusader period, or at the beginning of the Mamluk period, as it is not mentioned in the Ottoman tax censuses.

The settlement in Noye or Lanahia (Kibbutz 'Evron)

I shall discuss the settlement in Lanahia in chapter 13, which deals with the estate of the Camerarius Regis. In this settlement, too, there was a large Christian community during the Byzantine period and a triapsidal Byzantine church. Unfortunately, no evidence of the composition of the population of the other two villages mentioned in the document, Abu Sinan and Kafr Yasif, has been preserved. But the fact that there was a Christian community in both of them in the first half of the nineteenth century and at the beginning of the twentieth century supports the conclusion that they had communities of local Christians during an earlier period too.

Places not mentioned in the document

The bishop of Acre, careful as he was to demand that places like Bassa, Missop (H. Mezzuva), and Kafr Yasif pay tithes, does not mention the tithes from the most important places settled by the Germans, such as Montfort or Castellum Regis. The latter is in fact mentioned in the document but without any reference to tithes owed. The bishop deals only with tithes he claims were owing to him in the villages ("pertinentiae") of the Mi'ilya region and the transfer of these tithes to "his house" in Castellum Regis.[12] It is difficult to understand why there is no reference in the document to tithes from Castellum Regis and Montfort. Did the Germans pay tithes on their estates there or were they exempted from paying tithes on them? The document leaves this question unanswered. It seems that the payment of tithes by Castellum Regis and Montfort was not included amongst the matters in controversy between the two parties. It can, therefore, be concluded that the dispute over tithes did not apply to all the agricultural estates which "the Master and the brothers cultivated or would cultivate with their own money and labor," but only to those places specifically mentioned in the document.

The regions of Castellum Regis and Montfort were apparently regarded

[12] "Item petebamus restitui ad possessionem vel quasi iuris percipiendi decimas in domo episcopali, que est in Castro Regis, fructuum et proventuum ex omnibus pertinenciis dicti Castri Regis sitis in diocesi Acconensi." Strehlke, no. 112, 1257, 91–92 (Röhricht, *Regesta*, no. 1260).

as falling within the domain of the Order. Such "domains" of religious and military Orders enjoyed exemption from tithes from the middle of the twelfth century and onward. This exemption became an important economic asset for the Orders and monasteries which engaged in intensive agriculture and was considered to be one of the main causes for the success of Cistercian settlement in Europe. It would appear that the source of the controversy between the bishop and the Order lay in the exact definition of the area entitled to be exempted from tithes. The bishop apparently took issue with what the Order considered to be within its domain and consequently not taxable. He demanded what he considered to be his due, despite the fact that he knew, and even expressly stated, that the Order cultivated the lands itself and for its own use and at its own direct expense. The bishop did not dispute the Order's rights in Castellum Regis and Montfort, which he too regarded as coming within the Order's domain. But he did demand full payment from other places. The Order, on the other hand, demanded full exemption from payment of the tithes on all the lands which they cultivated themselves or for their own direct needs, even if they had not enjoyed this privilege previously. Furthermore, the Order demanded that the bishop recompense them for the tithes which had been unlawfully collected from them in the past.[13]

It would appear that the places for which the Germans paid "unlawful" tithes were those places referred to in the bishop's demands: Bassa, Massob, Lanahia, Cafriasim, Busenen, and Saphet. We do not know what the reason was for the conflicting demands of the bishop and the Order. A possible reason could have been that the exemption from tithes was not automatically granted upon acquisition of lands by an ecclesiastical body or upon their cultivation of certain lands. The acquisition of land by an ecclesiastical body did not exempt the body from paying tithes on the land if the land had previously been taxed. Indeed, the ecclesiastical bodies which acquired lands from commoners in the twelfth century invested large sums of money on settling the question of tithes on the lands, after investing similar large sums of money on acquiring and improving the lands.[14]

---

[13] "Ex adverso . . . petebant magister et fratres predicti . . . a nobis . . . sibi restitui et solvi viginti iiiior milia bisantiorum sarracenorum pro decimis, quas dicebant se solvisse ecclesie Acconensi indebite et ignoranter de terris et possessionibus, quas ipsi propriis laboribus et sumptibus excolebant, et de novalibus et nutrimentis animalium et virgultis tam in pecunia quam aliis rebus." Strehlke, no. 112, 1257, 92.

[14] For the process of "liquidation" of tithes, see Boyd, 1952, 139–140. Constable considers this process a kind of "sale of property." See Constable, 1964, 270–306. In addition, see there the resolutions of Lateran of 1215 which limited exemptions from tithes granted to the Cistercians to land which they possessed till 1215 and to "new" land to be developed by them in the future. Even before the Council of Lateran the Cistercians, the most important Order to conduct settle-

If my interpretation of the document is in fact correct, then in the territory owned by the Order there were apparently three kinds of landed property:

(1) The Order's domain, which was cultivated by the members of the Order and, therefore, was completely exempt from tithes. This included the village of Castellum Regis, which was purchased practically in toto by the Order before 1243 (as can be seen from Strehlke's document 128, discussed previously), Montfort, and others.

(2) Villages which belonged to the Teutonic Order and from which they enjoyed economic benefits which were liable for tithes.

(3) Settlements in which there were both members of the Order itself and others. The former regarded themselves as part of the Order's domain and thus exempt from tithes. But these settlements might previously have been occupied by local Christians or Franks who paid tithes on them. It is apparently these settlements which were the subject of the controversy between the bishop and the Order.

The arbitration agreement determined that there was a measure of justice in the Order's demands, as it was required to pay half of the tithes on all of its property – that is, on property which included the land which its members cultivated themselves and those which were cultivated by others for the Order's immediate needs. According to the agreement, all the land within the Order's domain were excluded from the bishop's demands, as were the seigniorial estates and rights granted them in the past, since these were exempted previously from the payment of tithes and would continue to be exempted in the future.[15] Full exemption from tithes was also given on fruit trees and on the mills which were within the Order's domain in River Keziv, "from the large spring and until the territory of Manueth."

It does not come within the scope of this study to establish which of the two parties acted in accordance with canon law and the customs of the time. From the fact that the arbitrators divided the tithes between the Order and the bishop one can learn that they found some justification in the Order's claims that the lands which were the subject of the dispute had been cultivated directly by members of the Order, or indirectly by way of pecuniary investment on their part. This interpretation is reinforced by the fact that in

---

ment, did not enjoy full exemption from tithes on all their property even though they were granted a general exemption during the reign of Innocentius II. This exemption was valid only insofar as tithes on the rearing of animals was concerned, and from 1200 there were exceptions even to this: Hoffman-Berman, 1986, 50–52; Constable, 1964, 241–245.

[15] ". . . salvis dricturis, que sunt tales: portagium herbarum ad areas, scribanagium, mensuragium, gardagium, scenequie, que libere levabuntur, item et dricture Ysembardi et Lamberti in casalibus, in quibus recipi consueverunt tempore huius compositionis." Strehlke, no. 112, 1257, 92.

the case of most of the places referred to in the document we have additional, independent evidence of the existence of Frankish settlement. The only places about which no such evidence exists are Abu Sinan and Kafr Yasif. I think one can rely on the document and assume that there was Frankish ecclesiastical settlement in the thirteenth century in these two places too.

I attach great importance also to the fact that in all the places referred to in the document it can be assumed that there was still a local Christian community in the thirteenth century, or that there were large Byzantine-Christian villages which continued uninterrupted into the thirteenth century. The importance of this fact will be explained during the last part of this book.

One can discover additional details about the rural way of life of the Franks in the document, including information regarding the transportation and the mode of payment for tithes and the boundaries of the Order's domain.

Transport

The bishop of Acre demanded that the Order transfer the tithes owing to him to his "house" in Castellum Regis. The document deals with such prosaic matters as who would be responsible for paying the farmers who carted the tithes. The cost of transport, according to the arbitration decision, was to be borne by the Teutonic Order while the bishop, at his goodwill, could give each of the farmers who carted the tithes one loaf of bread.[16]

Payment of the tithes – in cash or in kind?

It is clear from this description of how the transport costs were to be borne that the tithes were payable in kind and not in cash, otherwise there would have been no problem of transport. Furthermore, there were certain products, such as sugar cane and salt, which were of no interest to the bishop. Thus, if the Germans had decided to increase their production of sugar cane and salt, they would have to pay half the tithes to the bishop in the form of

---

[16] "Et ipsi [the master of the Teuthonic Order] et successores sui debent facere portari dictam quintam decimam de omnibus suis casalibus, que sunt ultra caveam [the Kziv Valley], suis sumptibus ad domum episcopalem in Castro Regis. Et nos episcopus, si placuerit nobis, dabimus unum panem cuilibet villano, qui dictam quintam decimam portabit." Strehlke, no. 112, 1257, 93.

wheat and barley, as if the land had been planted with grain and not with sugar cane.[17]

Hamilton was of the opinion that, in general, the tithes were collected in the form of cash and not in kind. He argued that by collecting cash the bishop's institutions would have avoided the complicated logistics and the heavy expense involved in collecting, storing, and selling agricultural produce.[18] But this document gives no hint whatsoever of the possibility of collecting the tithes in cash and it would appear that in the diocese of Acre the tithes were collected in kind only.

The boundary of the Teutonic Order's domain

The document defines the area in which the Teutonic Order could cultivate vegetables or plant trees without being obliged to pay even half of the tithes to the bishop: everything which the Order produced or would produce in River Keziv (save for vineyards), and all products ground in the mills there, would be exempt from tithes. The river was given an interesting legal definition: it stretched from the source ('En Keziv), called in the document "the garden of the large spring," apparently the large farm beneath Montfort which contained a mill, to the territory of Manueth. The width of the riverbed is defined as whatever a person standing on the ground of the river could see from the slopes.[19]

The method of collection of the tithes was both complicated and sophisticated. The fact that the tithes were in the form of agricultural produce demanded the establishment of complex logistical machinery with which to fix the amount of the tithes and their collection. These operations were carried out in the "houses" established by the secular, ecclesiastical authorities in central places. The "house" of the bishop of Acre in Mi'ilya is an example of such houses.

---

[17] "Etiam, si aliquo modo contingeret, quod dicti magister et fratres plantarent vel plantari facerent canamellas vel salinas facerent aut fieri facerent in aliquo casalium suorum et pertinentiis eorundem, ipsi et successores suis de tanta terra, quantam dicte canamelle et saline tenuerint vel occupaverint, dictam quintam decimam solvent, medietatem videlicet in frumento et medietatem in ordeo iuxta extimationem virorum bonorum, acsi dicte terre essent frumento vel ordeo seminante." Strehlke, no. 112, 1257, 93.

[18] Hamilton, 1980, 145–150. Cf. Smail, 1973, 85. It is questionable of course if one can generalize about practice in the diocese of Acre or in the whole Kingdom on the basis of one document.

[19] "De omnibus vero molendinis suis, ubicunque sunt et erunt, de iardinis quoque, de molendinis et arboribus tocius cavee in tantum, quantum cavea protenditur in longum ab ortu magni fontis usque ad territorium Manuetti et in latitudine tantum, quantum unus homo, qui esset in fundo cavee, super ripam aque posset videre in altum ex utraque parte, nihil debent nobis et successoribus nostris solvere nomine decimarum." Strehlke, no. 112, 1257, 93.

I showed earlier that a "house" was also the administrative center of an agricultural estate, and we can learn from our document about another aspect of Frankish agricultural management. It can be assumed that the bishops used to construct their "houses" in the centers of larger Frankish townships or villages in order to supervise from these houses, or granges, the processes of picking fruit, harvesting, and vintage. With the aid of our document (or with the aid of other similar documents) and the above assumption, one can reconstruct another aspect of the Frankish governmental set-up in the rural areas, since the tithes, and the centers from which they were collected, correspond with the regions in which there was well-developed Frankish agriculture. Any transfer of property to ecclesiastical bodies was expressed either in changes in the parallel ecclesiastical set-up or in legal disputes. These disputes provide a good source for dating the Frankish agricultural network. From the very existence of so complex and sophisticated a network in the Frankish Orient one can learn about the extent of Frankish settlement and about the well-developed nature of the Frankish ecclesiastical administration of the rural areas.

Two other documents, both issued by the pope at Lateran in 1238, provide us with additional details about the collection of tithes in the Frankish villages. These two documents deal with arbitrations intended to settle disputes concerning tithes between the bishop of Acre and the Hospitalers. One of the documents refers to half of the tithes on all the produce of Casale Album, half of the tithes on all the poultry reared in Cabor, and half of the tithes payable by Manueth. In all three of these settlements, according to the evidence provided by other, independent documents and by archeological surveys, there was Frankish settlement. The relevant document, therefore, supports my hypothesis concerning German property: that is, that disputes concerning tithes were not based on the principle of liability for payment per se, nor did they concern all the villages owned by the body litigating with the local bishop. On the contrary, they concerned only places in which there was Frankish settlement and where the litigating party could claim that the crops which were cultivated were for its own use. The two documents referred to above and the documents which we discussed previously are indeed similar in focus as is evidenced by the fact that the Hospitalers requested and were granted permission to retain an agreed-upon part of the tithes for which they were liable in order to pay for transport and other expenses.[20]

---

[20] "Preterea cum antedicti magister et fratres, pro vicesima de caragiis casalis ejusdem, quinque tantum bizantios exolvant eidem, et rationem illorum, qui recipiunt, ad majorem solutionem ei prestande vicesime teneantur secundum quantitatem receptorum, exhiberi sibi postulavit eandem." Hospital, no. 2199, May 10, 1238, II, 529.

Six days after the first document was issued, another document was signed in the papal curia. This document refers to the crops from villages called Beroet and Coket and the lands of Manueth where sugar cane, wheat, or barley were grown (the previous document mentioned only the vineyards of Manueth).[21] It would appear that the two former villages can also be added to the list of places in which there was Frankish settlement.

In this context it may be worthwhile to draw attention to the existence of other Frankish settlements which were apparently not of the fortress and burgus type and which were established in the centers of local villages.

Settlement in the village of La Hadia

Hints at the presence of Franks in another village in the royal domain near Acre can be found in documents dealing with Le Hodia, or La Hadia. This village has been identified as 'Ayadiya (grid reference 164/257) next to the road leading from Acre to Kafr Yasif. The place is mentioned in Mamluk sources as 'Ayadiya and sherds of Byzantine and medieval pottery were found in it.

In a document from the year 1178 the place is called "the village of Galterius Seagius."[22] This document deals with the grant of four carrucas of "terra francisia" from the casale of Galterius Seagius, called in Arabic "Lahadia," and of a house described as "of the bath," by Baldwin IV to a certain Balduinus de Cypro. The existence of "terra francisia" in La Hadia testifies to the presence of a Frankish settlement in the place, as exemption from part of the seigniorial duties was granted to persons and not to places. The fact that the village was named after a Frankish knight only strengthens this assumption.

In another document from the year 1255 there is evidence of the continuation of Frankish presence in the village. This document states that "a knight from Acre" by the name of Johannes Marraim transferred his estate near Acre, west of La Hadia, to the Order of the Hospital. From this document one can also learn that the village La Hadia was held in tenure by Rolandus Antelmus.[23]

In partial excavations conducted lately at the ruins of La Hadia, the

[21] Hospital, no. 2200, May 16, 1238, II, 531.
[22] Röhricht, *Regesta*, Add., 559a, 1178; "Inventaire," no. 125, 63.
[23] ". . . ab orienti est ei terra de la Hadia, quod tenet dominus Rolandus Antelmi; a meridie est ei terra domus militie Templi; ab occidenti est ei terra Johannis Coste; a borrea est ei via publica, que est ad pedem turonis, qui dicitur Saladini." Hospital, no. 2714, Feb. 11, 1255, II, 773.

remains of a massive Frankish building, apparently a manor house, were discovered.[24]

The proximity of La Hadia to Acre could raise the possibility that the owners of the land lived in Acre, although the distance between the two places is too great for commuting between Acre and the village. One can learn about this distance from the fact that between the village and Acre there was an additional estate – that of the commune of Genoa.[25]

Information about the size of Johannes Costa's estate can be gathered from the fact that his grandmother (?) who owned an estate in the region of Acre, owed one knight to the army of the first kingdom.[26]

In many villages – such as Mimas (Tel-ʿEmek), St. George above Tiberias, Saphet (Safad ʿAdi), La Hodia (ʿAyadiya), Bassa (Shelomi), ʿAbud, Qalqiliyya, and many others – there were, apparently, unfortified Frankish settlements. Most of the villages in which there was unfortified Frankish settlement had an additional common denominator: demographic, historical, and archeological evidence of the existence of a large Christian community during Byzantine times and a continuous Christian existence until the twelfth century. Several settlements were apparently inhabited by Christians during Byzantine times and later during the Frankish regime, too, but were later totally destroyed.

---

[24] N. Getzov, personal communication.
[25] Hospital, no. 2721, Mar. 19, 1255, II, 775 n. 1: Johannes Costa sold his landed property to the Hospital. The property is described as being close to the walls of Acre: "Ab orienti est ei terra ipsius domus, que fuit domini Johannis Marran; a meridie est ei terra domus Templi; ab occidente ei est terra comunis Janue; a septemtrione est ei via magna, qua itur ad Saphettum et S. Georgium."
[26] Jean of Ibelin, 425.

PART III

THE ISOLATED DWELLINGS

CHAPTER TWELVE

THE LIST OF JEAN OF IBELIN

The accepted reconstruction of the seigniorial hierarchy in the Latin Kingdom of Jerusalem is based on the lists drawn up by Jean of Ibelin in about 1265. One of these lists, according to its first paragraph, details the names of noblemen ("barons" and the other "gens dou reiaume de Jerusalem") who were obliged to contribute knights to the army of the Kingdom ("chief seignor dou dit reiaume") and the number of knights which each had to contribute. The list is attributed to the year 1187, on the eve of the battle of Hattin.[1]

The list was, it is true, drawn up at a comparatively later date and its author did not excel, in his other works, at accuracy and objectivity. But although it is difficult to determine to what extent the figures are accurate, it can be assumed that the relative numbers of the knights were realistic for three reasons.

(1) It would be difficult to explain why Jean of Ibelin tried so hard to provide an accurate list of owners of fiefs, who had all passed away at the time he wrote his book, and did not make a similar effort to give accurate numbers of knights each of the fief owners was obliged to contribute to the army.

(2) The sum total of knights who appear in Jean of Ibelin's list is consistent with what is known to us from other sources about the size of the army. A change in the number of knights any lord had to contribute would have forced Jean of Ibelin to falsify the whole list and it is doubtful whether he had any reasonable cause for doing so.

(3) Jean of Ibelin's list is also consistent with what is known to us from independent sources about the number of knights each of the fiefs was obliged to contribute to the army of the Kingdom. Many of the knights mentioned in it are known to us from other documents which were written

[1] Jean of Ibelin, ch. 271, 422–426.

at the end of the 1180s. Fiefs of knights who died a few years before the
battle of Hattin, or fiefs which were sold, together with their seigniorial
obligations, to ecclesiastical bodies, appear in the list under the names of the
heirs or under the names of the last lords. That is the reason for the somewhat surprising appearance of entries such as that of "the wife of Iohannes
Gothman" or "the fief of the sons of Robert de Pinquegni," which were sold
years before the battle of Hattin to ecclesiastical bodies. These cases are
sufficient, in my opinion, to give all the more credibility to the list.

Richard assumed, quite rightly, that at the time he wrote his book Jean of
Ibelin had a full and accurate list of knights of the Kingdom on the eve of
the battle of Hattin. He distinguished (following La Monte) between this
reliable document and other lists made by Jean of Ibelin which, according to
both these scholars, contained inaccuracies.[2]

If we are to rely on the amount of detail and accuracy in the lists, then the
list of fiefs of the royal domain is more accurate than that of the seigniorial
fiefs. This comparative accuracy testifies apparently to the sources which
were available to the author at the time he composed the document.

A careful examination of the list shows that it refers to the obligations of
the fiefs themselves and not necessarily to the obligations of specific owners.
Furthermore, a comparison of the list with the archeological findings shows
that in many of the larger fiefs, including those which were required to
provide only three, or even two, knights, there were "maisons fortes" which
served as administrative centers for their lords. If this proves to be true then
one can, on the basis of Jean of Ibelin's list, assess the number of seigniorial
centers which were established in the Kingdom of Jerusalem.

Unfortunately, the list generally contains only the names of the current
seigniorial lords and their knightly obligations and it does not specify the
exact location of the fief or the names of the villages which were included
in it. These details, which were not pertinent to the specific purpose for
which the list was made, are exactly those which are of importance for the
purpose of reconstructing the Frankish fiefs. In order to give archeological
and geographic content to the list, additional documents are required. In the
absence of such documents Jean of Ibelin's list will remain a vague list of
names some of which do not appear in any other sources.

Fortunately we do have several documents which supplement Jean of
Ibelin's list. These documents exist only in the cases in which fiefs were sold
to ecclesiastical bodies whose archives have been preserved. We can, for
example, reproduce the administrative structure of a substantial part of "the
fief of Joscelyn III" which, during the course of the thirteenth century, came

[2] La Monte, 1946, 207–208; Richard, 1954, 565–572.

into the possession of the Teutonic Order, whose archives have been preserved. Other documents which have been preserved enable us to reconstruct the geographical boundaries and the central location of other fiefs, and establish with comparative accuracy the location of the centers from which they were administered. If we did not have these additional documents, which are independent of Jean of Ibelin's list, these fiefs would have remained unlocated.

The fief of Iohannes Gothman

This Frankish knight, who was still alive in 1164,[3] participated in the Frankish raid on the Hauran in 1147. When it became evident that the raid was a failure and the Frankish army faced annihilation, it was suggested that the king should take flight on Gothman's horse which was considered the fastest in the Kingdom. The ownership of such a horse was undoubtedly a status symbol.[4] The fact that his daughter was married to Hugh of Caesarea, one of the most prominent knights of the realm, testifies further to Gothman's social status.[5]

Iohannes Gothman was taken prisoner in 1157 and his wife had to sell his property to the Chapter of the Holy Sepulcher, in order to raise the money required to ransom him.[6] The documents dealing with the sale contain the names of the four villages and one *gastina* which belonged to this property, the first of which is the village of Bethaatap undoubtedly the Arab village of Bayt 'Itab, fifteen kilometers to the west of Jerusalem. The other villages were: Culi, Derxerip, Derhassen, and Gastina Leonis. A very impressive Frankish "maison forte" is still to be seen in the ruined center of Bayt 'Itab and it is very probable that it was used by Iohannes Gothman as a residence when he stayed at his fief (see fig. 10).[7]

---

[3] Iohannes Gothman was witness to many charters, the first of which was issued in 1104. Röhricht considered the various "Gothmans" mentioned in the documents as being one person, but there exists a possibility of there being two different people. In the earlier documents "Gothman" appears with no first name, whereas in the later documents, dating from the year 1125 onwards, the first name Iohannes is always associated with the name Gothman. The relatively long period of time (appr. ten years) that elapsed between the two groups of documents, as well as Iohannes Gothman's participation in battle in the year 1157, support the assumption that there were two "Gothmans." If this were the same man, then Gothman should have been about seventy years old when taken prisoner.

[4] ". . . equum domini Iohannis Goman, qui omnes alios eiusdem exercitus equos celeritate et laboris pacientia longe superare dicebatur." William of Tyre, 16, 10, 729, lines 52–53.

[5] Röhricht, *Regesta*, no. 368, 1161.

[6] "Captus est inter ceteros . . . Iohannes Gomannus." William of Tyre, 18, 14, 831, line 16; Holy Sepulcher, no. 87, Nov. 21, 1161, 200; Holy Sepulcher, no. 88, Dec. 3, 1161, 201–202.

[7] See Clermont-Ganneau, 1899, II, 217; Bagatti, 1979, 128; Röhricht, 1887, 202; Robinson & Smith, 1841, 594; Warren & Conder, 1882–1884, vol. III, 83.

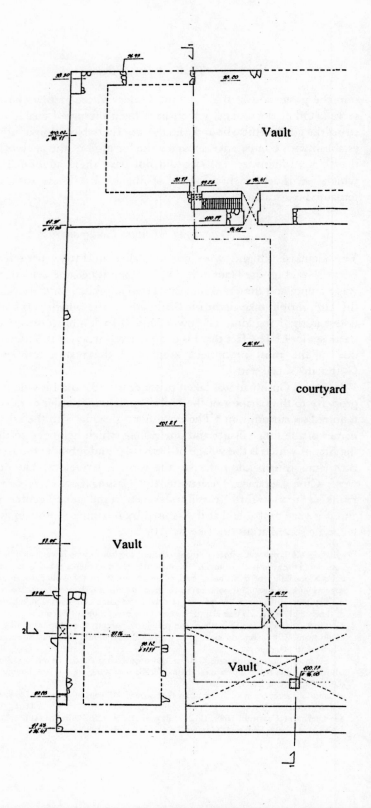

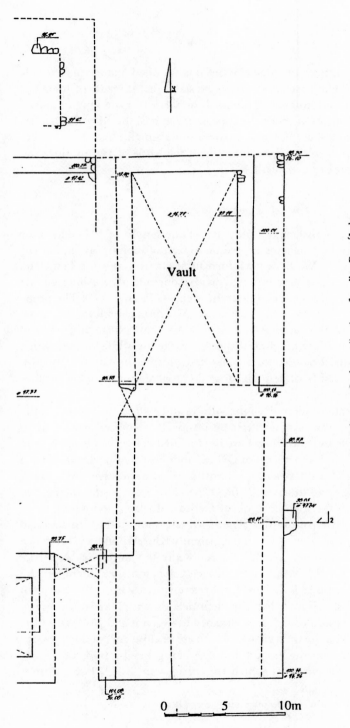

Figure 10   Iohannes Gothman "maison forte" at Bayt ʿItab

It is interesting also to note that this fief is mentioned many years after his death in Jean of Ibelin's list.[8] An entry there states that the wife of Iohannes Gothman owned four knights. If the list is only a list of the knights and of the fief owners' obligations, then the appearance in it of the wife of Iohannes Gothman is inexplicable. She was certainly not a knight, and she was certainly not the owner of this fief on the eve of the battle of Hattin, since she had sold it about thirty years earlier.

The fief of Lorens de Francleue

A similar example is that of the property of the family of Francoloco, or Francleue. Lorens de Francleue, according to Jean of Ibelin, was required to provide four knights. We have no information about Lorens de Francleue and the only Francolocos mentioned in the documents is Almericus de Francoloco, who witnessed documents between 1171 and 1175. The property of the family was sold before 1179 to the Mt. Zion church for unknown reasons.[9] Here, too, the name of Francleue is the name of the property and not only the name of the knight. Furthermore, the list of the villages which were owned by the Francolocos enables us to locate the family's "maison forte." The list consists of ten villages, all situated in the same region, northeast of Jerusalem.

Although we cannot identify all the villages and *gastinae* mentioned in the document, those villages which can be positively identified enable us to establish where the fief was and where the fortified center was erected. The first village in the list is the village of Gebea, undoubtedly the village of Jabʿa (grid reference 174/140) where the remains of an impressive three-storey Frankish building were discovered (fig. 11).[10] Three other sites mentioned in the list confirm the identification of Gebea with Jabʿa and define more clearly the boundaries of the fief: Aneth, which is apparently ʿAnata (grid reference 174/135); Amieth, which is apparently Kh. ʿAlamit (grid reference 176/136); and Farafronte, which is undoubtedly the spring in ʿAyn Fara (grid reference 178/137). Another village, Caphason, was identified by Prawer and Benvenisti as Kafr Sum (grid reference 158/126). But although there was a Frankish fief there too, the identification with Kafr Sum does not appear feasible, because of the great distance between it and Jabʿa. In all the documents of this nature only villages which are in close geographic proximity to one another are mentioned and one can generally find some geographic logic in the order in which the villages are listed. For example,

[8] Jean of Ibelin, 421.   [9] Röhrict, *Regesta*, no. 576, 1179.
[10] For the plan of the place, see Kochavi, 1972, no. 125, 183.

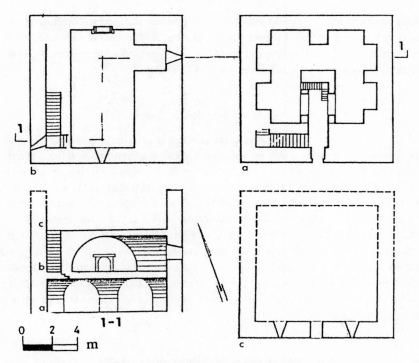

Figure 11   Plan and sections of the Frankish manor house in Jab'a

'Anata, Amieth, and the spring at 'Ayn Fara are on the road to Jerusalem in the direction of Wadi Fara. It is reasonable to assume, therefore, that Caphason was on the same road. It would appear that the reference is to Kh. al-Sum'a (grid reference 172/136). It is perhaps important to note that in 'Ayn Fara (which is Faraf[r]onte) a Frankish farm house was discovered.[11]

In this fief, too, the most important identification is that of the first village in the list which apparently served as the center of the whole fief.

The Frankish fief in Sinjil

Baudoyn de Saint Gille was required to provide three knights for the army of the Kingdom. The family established a settlement on their fief which was described in the Arabic sources and some of the Latin sources as a "fortress." The evidence concerning this settlement was discussed at length in chapter 9.

[11] See Bagatti, 1979, pl. 1, fig. 3.

There is practically no doubt that the center of the fief was in Sinjil, despite the non-existence of a complete list of villages. In the chapter dealing with the castrum of Sinjil I attempted to prove that here, too, there were several Frankish houses and manor houses around the center.

Castellum Regis

Even Castellum Regis, which is certainly not a knight, appears in the list which was presumably a list of knights. Castellum Regis was a fief which owed four knights. It was not the feudal property of any nobleman until it was awarded to Joscelyn III. It was part of the royal domain and it was administered from the Frankish castrum in Mi'ilya. That is apparently why the fief was called by the name of its central location and not by the name of its feudal owners. The "castellum" of Castellum Regis and the agricultural settlement which developed in it were dealt with in detail in an earlier chapter and do not require any further discussion. It is nevertheless important to note that Mi'ilya, which is the center of this fief and where the castle was built, is mentioned first in all the lists in which the villages of this semi-estate are detailed.

The Frankish fief of St. George de La Baena

The lordship of St. George de La Baena which included also the fiefs of Buq'aiya and al-Sajur and which was one of the largest in the territory of Acre, was administered apparently from the village of Dayr al-Asad (al-Ba'ina). One can learn about the comparative size of this fief from the fact that it was required to provide ten knights for the army of the Kingdom. A similar number of knights was demanded from the fief of the constable (which included the rich region of Turon), and a smaller number was required from the Frankish castra of Haifa and Scandalion.[12]

St. George de La Baena is described in the documents of the twelfth century as a part of the fief of Henricus Bubalus (or Henri le Bufle), who was the son of Guido de Miliaco (or Guy de Milli), a knight from Champagne known also as Guido Francigena (or Guy le Français). The fief was divided after his death among his three daughters.[13] In 1161 Philip de

---

[12] For the history of this estate, see Mayer, 1980; Frankel, 1988, 250–255, 264–265; Rey, 1878; Mas-Latrie, 1878; Pringle, 1993, 80–92.

[13] *Les Lignages d'Outremer*, 454; Philip of Novara, I, 542; Jean of Ibelin, ch. 271, I, 422; Mas-Latrie, 1878, 112–113.

Milli, who was then the head of the family, exchanged the family estate in the region of Nablus for land in Transjordan and Mt. Hebron.[14] The exchange included the services due from the fiefs of the rear vassals of the family. The document states that the exchange included the transfer of the services of Henricus Bubalus and Gaufridus Tortus to the king, who was to become the new seignior. Both Bubalus and Tortus had extensive estates in the Galilee: "Dedit eciam mihi Philippus iam tociens dictus feodum Henrici Bubali, fratris siquidem sui, eo quidem tenore, quo ipse Henricus de domino Philippo illud tenebat et servicium illi faciebat.

Dedit mihi preterea feodum Gaufridi Torti, ita videlicet quod, sicut Gaufridus Tortus illud prius a domino Philippo tenebat, sic deinceps illud ex me teneat mihique servicium faciat."

Therefore, the services due from the fief of Henricus Bubalus were transferred to the king in 1161, although he and his family continued to occupy it. Henry de Milli is called "a rich man" by Philip of Novara, which indicates that he belonged to the middle class, between the lower nobility and the barons, who were the owners of the large fiefs.[15]

It is difficult to establish when the family of Milli purchased (or received) their fiefs in the Galilee. It is also difficult to establish what the exact boundaries of these fiefs were. From the statements of Philip of Novara and the *Lignages d'Outremer* it would appear only that these fiefs extended over central Galilee and that their center was in St. George de La Baena i.e. Dayr al-Asad.[16]

After Bubalus' death the fief was divided among his three daughters. St. George de La Baena itself passed apparently to the eldest daughter, Helvis.[17] The fief was transferred gradually to Joscelyn III of Courtenay until 1182, when he received the absolute control of the place.[18]

The village was granted, while still under Muslim control, to the Pisans by Conrad of Montferrat.[19] The place was transferred once again to the

---

[14] Strehlke, no. 3, July 31, 1161, 3–4.   [15] Riley-Smith, 1973, 17.

[16] Philip of Novara wrote that Henry de Milli was the "Seigneur de Saint Jorge Labane et tout . . ." but the end of the sentence is missing. See *RHC, Lois*, I, 469–571, esp. 542. The *Lignages d'Outremer* tells us that he was the seignior of "Bouquiau et de tote la terre dou Saor." See *RHC, Lois*, II, 454. We can accept, therefore, Mas-Latrie's opinion that Henry's seigniorie included the whole of Beth-Hakerem Valley and the valley of Buq'aiya. Cf. Frankel, 1988, 250. Cf. also Hamilton, 1992.

[17] *Lignages d'Outremer*, 454; Jean of Ibelin, 422, 424–425. Philip of Novara says that each of Henricus Bubalus' daughters was obliged to contribute three knights to the army of the Kingdom and all of them together were obliged to pay the expenses of one more knight. See *RHC, Lois*, I, 542–3; Frankel, 1988, 253–254; Pringle, 1993, 80.

[18] Strehlkle, no. 12, 1179, 12 (Röhricht, *Regesta*, no. 588); Strehlke, no. 14, 1182, 14 (Röhricht, *Regesta*, no. 614).

[19] Müller, *Documenti*, no. 27, May 1188, 30 (Röhricht, *Regesta*, no. 674).

descendant of Henricus Bubalus and Joscelyn III of Courtenay and later on, between 1220 and 1249, the whole lordship came into the hands of the Teutonic Order.[20]

In the center of the combined village of al-Baʿina and Dayr al-Asad, which was most probably the administrative center of this fief, there is still a Frankish building which contains a large church, and which was identified by Pringle as a Carthusian abbey (fig. 12a). Another building which could have been a suitable domicile for the family of Henricus Bubalus was identified by us in al-Baʿina. This building might be the one referred to by ʿImad al-Din and Abu Shama who claimed that the village contained a Crusader fortress, which was captured by Salah al-Din in 1187 (fig. 12b).[21]

Evidence from the thirteenth century onwards indicates that the place was a monastery in St. George de La Baena. A French pilgrim text from about 1230 refers to a church of "moines grés" at St. George and a similar reference is made in two other texts.[22] One can learn about the religious character which was given to the place during the thirteenth century from the fact that both Burchard of Mt. Zion and Marino Sanudo identify it as the birth place of St. George. It would appear, therefore, that this was a major center for pilgrimage.[23]

Additional testimony in support of the hypothesis that there was an extensive Frankish settlement in the village can be found in a map dated by Röhricht to the first half of the thirteenth century (see fig. 13). The map is surprisingly, if only relatively, accurate. Even the topography is marked in a manner enabling identification of the hills and valleys.[24] The drawer of the map obviously never visited Samaria, as can be seen from the gross errors which he committed in connection with the geography of Samaria. For example, he makes Nablus and Sebaste one entity ("civitas Neapolis id est civitas Sebaste"); but his description of places which he did visit (he notes on the back of the map the walking distances between one place and another) are very reliable. Only three rural settlements in Western Upper Galilee appear on the map: Daʿuq, called "Casale Docke"; Kurdana, called "Recordane"; and "Seint George," which he thought to be a "civitas." This description was certainly not correct. There is no doubt that Dayr al-Asad was not a "civitas" in the thirteenth century, but there apparently was a Frankish settlement which was larger than the "fortress-monastery" discovered there.

[20] Strehlke, no. 53, 1220, 43–44; no. 58, 1226, 47; no. 100, 1249, 78–81.
[21] ʿImad al-Din al-Isfahani, 35, line 8; Abu Shama, *Raudatayn*, 87, line 3–5.
[22] Michelant & Raynaud, 102, 104, 188.
[23] Sanudo, ed. Bongars, 249; Burchardus de Monte Sion, ch. X, *IHC*, IV, 146.
[24] Röhricht, 1895, fig. 16.

The combined village of al-Ba'ina and Dayr al-Asad continued to exist during the Mamluk period. For example al-Qalqashandi describes Na'iba (the letters n and b, which are very similar in Arabic were exchanged by him, with the result that he calls the place Na'iba instead of Ba'ina) as a "village in the district of al-Sajur with a monastery."[25] Similar testimony can be found in a later source in which there was a large monastery in which the "mentally ill were treated."[26]

Pringle has lately published his findings concerning the fortified building in Dayr al-Asad. He makes no mention of the later sources which testify to the fact that the monastery continued to exist after the expulsion of the Franks from the country.[27] These sources can again tilt the balance in favor of the interpretation of Beyer who maintained that the "moines grés" referred to in one of the texts were Greek monks and not Latin monks, as the fact that the monastery continued to exist after the fall of the Frankish regime should be added to the persuasive textual arguments produced by Beyer.[28]

Hints at the existence of a larger settlement in the place, the fact that there was, apparently, a monastery with local monks there, the fact that the place served as an administrative center for the rich and important family of Henricus Bubalus, and the existence of a fortified house which served, apparently, as their domicile, would seem to indicate that a comprehensive examination of this village has yet to be undertaken.

The fief of Gaufridus Tortus

This fief was required to provide the services of six knights. In the documents describing the property of Joscelyn III, and in the documents describing the property of the Teutonic Order in the Galilee, only the villages in the eastern part of the fief are mentioned. Apparently only this part was transferred first to Joscelyn and later to the Teutonic Order, and, therefore, only this part is mentioned in the written documents. The whole estate was administered from the manor house of Gaufridus Tortus in Manueth. The eastern part of the fief was apparently administered from Fassuta, which is Bellum-videre, where the administrative representatives of Gaufridus were stationed: the dragoman and the scribe. As only the eastern part of the fief is mentioned in the written documents I shall deal only with this part. It is important to note that Fassuta, too, is mentioned for the first time in

[25] Al-Qalqashandi, IV, 153.   [26] Al-'Uthmani, 484.
[27] Cf. Foerster, 1969, 230–231; Pringle, 1993, 80–92.
[28] Beyer, 1945, 199.

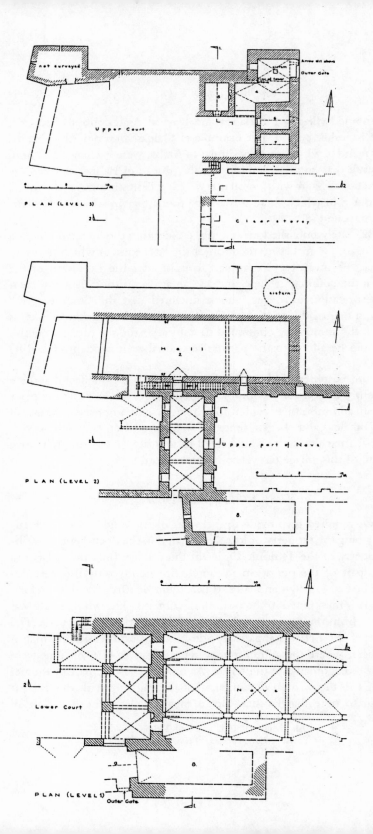

Figure 12a Dayr al-Asad, plan of the Frankish site

Plan

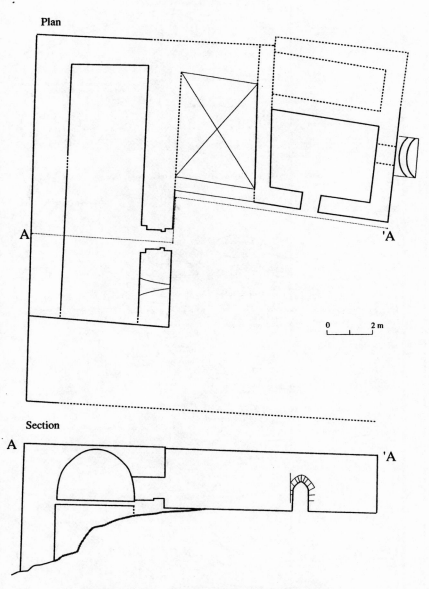

Section

Figure 12b   The Frankish manor house in al-Baʿina

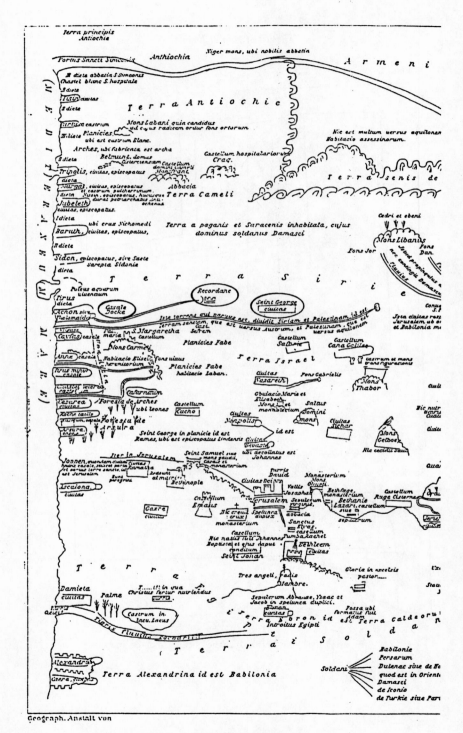

Figure 13   Map of thirteenth-century Palestine
Thirteenth-century villages of the Galilee mentioned in the text

z

16. Karte des Heiligen Landes
nach dem in Oxford befindlichen Original aus der 1ten Hälfte
des XIII. Jahrhunderts.

Monte

Mons Belinas

Fons
Farfar
fluuius
Abbana
fluuius

e mare
Ciuitas caput Sirie
Damascus

Simulacrum
Saldengra
Ista duo
flumina
absorbentur
...is

fluuius
ista
Jordanus
fit nunc
Dan

Hic nascetur
Antichristus
us Corozain

Bethsaida
tur in
Tiberie
Mare
Galilee
s Galilea

Mons
entana,
palme
Adrane
Mons
excelsus,
sius
temptacionis

ubi baptizatus est Dominus
ecclesia (Johannis) baptista
Terra Hus siue patria Job
et ubi ciuitas
Za. Zebee   Salmana.

r Loth
a satis
ons
Pisces inutiles

Sodoma
Comorra
Segor
Alia Mare
Alia
optimum
sal
alumen
ci. est intranabile

Penna super mare,
plena clauibu

lap

hie

Crag

Mount
Real

Terebinte ad.....ag........ post viduum .... mare
De mare
et sepultura marescalti

propinquior est Terra sancte genti Christiani
Iherusalem que est Terra Sanctam ege Mare, uu
media niciel (?) Ibcrilia est conterminin Orscient.
Sicilia,
Apulia,
Calabria,
Turcia,
Perria
quo ducatus (est?)
ad Alpes,
conterminum
habent eum Romanis
Patria apostri.
Wala conterminia
Venecia
Dalmacia

In Arabia est Tkamata
(ubi) grecia vicacii(?)palestrina
ibi. Et Dar (?)
media conternin

adra   id
armenia
est aern... ad.... est super Saracenos
Ep (?) XIX distat.

a patria conterminia prouincia

P...., ubi natus est siuecus Pasintho(?) et est, in....Armenia

super Tarsum (?)Anthiok et Yconium.

Wagner & Debes, Leipzig.

documents describing the eastern part of the fief and that it had a Latin name, like other places in which there was Frankish settlement. This fief, too, was known by the name of its former owner years after the rights were transferred to Joscelyn.

The list of Jean of Ibelin is therefore not, or at least is not only, a list of knights. It should rather be perceived as a list of the seigniorial fiefs of the Kingdom and it could be used to locate, by inference, their manor houses, because whenever the villages belonging to one fief are listed the first village contains the seat of the landlord.

The list reveals a connection between the administrative organization and Frankish settlement: in the centers of large Frankish sub-fiefs (those which were required to provide three or four knights for the army of the Kingdom) manor houses were erected. It cannot be proved at this stage that in the smaller fiefs too there were castles, but it would seem that this is true at least insofar as some of these fiefs are concerned. In order to provide a basis for this argument I shall now examine the structure of a small fief (in the fief of the Camerarius Regis), which was required to provide only two knights, and shall attempt to prove that in this fief too there were Frankish settlers and castles.

CHAPTER THIRTEEN

FRANKISH SETTLEMENT IN THE FIEF OF THE CAMERARIUS REGIS

.

The fief of the chamberlain was part of the royal domain, and was given to the camerarius by virtue of his office. As the office of camerarius could not be bequeathed, the fief passed from one camerarius to the next. For example, Casale Album, which was one of the villages of the fief, was called, in a document of 1149, "Casale Album camerarii"[1] and thirty years later it was still held by the king's camerarius, despite the fact that the holders of the office had changed several times.[2]

The heavy financial obligations contracted by one of the holders of the office at the end of the 1180s resulted in part of the fief's being sold to Joscelyn III.[3] From a confirmation of this sale given by Baldwin IV we can identify the names of the villages which were held by the camerarius as a part of his fief and which were sold in this transaction: Lanahia, Casale Album, Ancra, Clie, and Ambelie.[4]

We can learn about the size and importance of this sub-fief from the fact

---

[1] Hospital, no. 180, 1149, 140.

[2] Mas-Latrie provides us with a list of all the camerarii of the Kingdom. In 1152 it was Nicolaus (Holy Sepulcher, no. 36, 1152, 105), in 1156 it was Galvannus de Rochia, in 1171 it was Gerardus de Pogeio, who might have held the office in 1174, together with the office of marechal. Between 1175 and 1178 it was probably Aimery who was later on the king of Jerusalem and Cyprus. He was the camerarius of the king before he was appointed constable in 1179. In 1179 it was Iohannes who is mentioned in Strehlke, no. 10, April 2, 1179, 10–11. Mas-Latrie, 1882, 649–650; *Les familles d'Outremer*, 631.

[3] Mas-Latrie was of the opinion that Iohannes who is mentioned in Strehlke, no. 10, April 2, 1179, 10–11, is Johannes de Belesme or Jean de Belleyme, who is mentioned without an indication of his office in Hospital, no. 550, Nov. 17, 1178, 373. Mas-Latrie, 1882, 647. Johannes de Belesme was most probably the owner of a tiny Frankish castle near Jenin.

[4] Strehlke, no. 10, Apr. 2, 1179, 10–11: "Balduinus . . . , rex . . . concedo et confirmo tibi Ioscelino, . . . domos, quas Iohannes, camerarius meus in Accon habebat, et casalia subscripta, que in Acconensi territorio de feodo camerarie mee possidebat. videlicet: Lanahie, Casale Album, Ancre, Clie et Ambelie, que omnia cum pertinenciis eorum Iohannes predictus camerarius tibi pro solvendis debitis suis concedente uxore sua Isabella et Rohardo de Cabor et fratribus suis vendidit et pro quibus omnibus septem milia bisanciorum et quingentos eidem Iohanni dedisti."

that Joscelyn paid 7,500 bezants for it and undertook to provide two knights for the army of the king, which was half the number demanded from him in exchange for Castellum Regis.

In three of the villages mentioned in the document there was Frankish settlement: in Lanahia, identified as Yannuhiya (today Kibbutz 'Evron); in Casale Album (whose location is unknown); and in Ancra, identified as Arab 'Amqa (today Moshav 'Amqa).

A Frankish knight who lived in Lanahia (Kibbutz 'Evron)

Lanahia, called in some of the documents Lanoye, Noye, or Nohya, served as the center for sugar production and contained sugar mills.[5] One cannot conclude from this, of course, that it was the Franks who were engaged in the production of sugar. But the economic importance of the production of sugar in the Frankish Kingdom was such as to hint at direct Frankish involvement in Lanahia which undoubtedly played an important role in this industry.

In a document which was issued in 1180 and which deals with the lands of Palmaria near Tiberias, a Frankish knight by the name of Tibaldus de Lahahia (*sic!* and it was Röhricht who suggested correcting it to Lanahia) is mentioned. There is no doubt that the man was a knight, as he appears as such in the list of witnesses ("ex militibus"). I showed above that the very name "Tibaldus de Lanahia" could hint at the fact that the knight in question lived in Lanahia. As the place was an important economic center and as it appears at the head of the list of villagers of the fief, it can be assumed that there was a Frankish settlement there and that Tibaldus lived there.[6]

Frankish settlers in Casale Album

In the second village in the fief of the Camerarius Regis – Casale Album – there were Frankish settlers too. We can learn about a house and plot of land owned by Alelmus de Garrenflos from a document which was issued in 1179. The fact that the document mentions both the house and the plot of land hints at the possibility that the same Alelmus de Garrenflos lived in the village and cultivated his fields there.[7]

A document of the year 1200 deals with another house and a plot of land

---

[5] Hospital, no. 564, May 1, 1170, 383–384; Strehlke, no. 22, Oct. 21, 1186, 20.

[6] Chartes du Mont-Thabor, no. XIX, 1180, 908 (Röhricht, *regesta*, no. 594). Röhricht, *Regesta*, no. 594 n. 3, claimed that the place which is mentioned in the document is Lanahia.

[7] Röhricht, *Regesta*, no. 577, Apr. 1, 1179; *Les Archives*, 140–141.

of two carrucas in this village. This property was granted by William de Amandala, with the consent of his wife Agnes, the daughter of Joscelyn III, to one Joscelyn Ussier and his heirs.[8] Another hint of intensive Frankish presence in the place can be found in yet another document of the year 1200, which states that certain plots were marked with field-boundary marks.[9] One plot of land is described as stretching on the south from the lands of the Hospitalers and bounded on the north by a stream tangent to the lands of Casale Album where the field marks were to be found.

Additional evidence of a house, which had belonged to Frankish settlers, and of well-defined plots of land in Casale Album can be found in a document from the year 1245, in which two knights, the brothers Johannes and Symon de Treucis, transferred a house, three carrucas of land, and a barn to the Hospitalers, with the consent of their mother. Besides unambiguous evidence of the existence of houses which had belonged to Franks there is also a clear description of field boundaries.[10]

Franks who lived in the village of Ancra (identified with ʿAmqa in Western Galilee)

We have no direct evidence of Frankish settlement in Ancra since there is no description of a "house" in the village or its environs. But, nevertheless, there are a few documents which mention names of Franks which are connected with the name of the village. A man by the name of "Robertus de Ancora" appears twice in the lists of witnesses on documents from the year 1164.[11] In a document from the year 1208, in which half of "Casal Blanc cum pertinentiis" was granted to the Hospitalers by Beatrice (the daughter of Joscelyn III) and her husband, the name of Petrus de Ancra, appears in the

---

[8] Röhricht, *Regesta*, Add., no. 774a, 1200; "Inventaire," no. 188, 74.

[9] Strehlke, no. 39, 1200, 31 (Röhricht, *Regesta*, no. 777): "ego Guillelmus de la Mandelie concessione et voluntate domine Agnetis uxoris mee, . . . quondam comitis Iozelini filie, dono . . . et . . . concedo vobis fratribus hospitalis sancte Marie Alamannorum, . . . peciam terre que a meridie coheret terre hospitalis Sancti Iohannis et a parte septentrionis coheret rivulo, qui coniungitur terre casalis Albi, ubi mete sunt, qui eciam rivulus descendit usque ad divisionem vestri casalis de Cafersie, ubi iungitur mea terra casalis Albi terre Cafersye."

[10] Hospital, II, no. 2353, Apr. 3, 1245, 627–8: "et domum unam, quas habemus apud Casale Album, quod est situm in plano Accon, juxta viam que vadit apud Coquetum, casale Hospitalis. Prenominate vero terre sunt mete tales: a parte siquidem orientis coheret terre predicti casalis Coquet Hospitalis; in parte vero occidentis per longum continuatur terre domus Templi et terre S Thome; ex parte vero meridei adheret alteri terre Hospitalis nominati; ex parte autem boree jacet terra S. Samuelis in longum. Hanc itaque terram, et aream et domum prescriptas, cum omnibus juribus et pertinenciis nobis competentibus vel competituris, damus, concedimus et tradimus . . . Hospitalis, in . . . elemosinam."

[11] AOL, IIb, no. 21, 139; IIb, no. 23, 141.

list of witnesses.[12] Petrus de Ancra and Robertus de Ancora were not seigniorial lords of the place, as the place was part of "the fief of the Camerarius Regis" and not the private fief of some Frankish lord. One cannot even assume that these two Franks belonged to the same family. The reference is apparently to two men who lived, or were born, in Ancra. They might have had some feudal rights in the place, as the fief of the Camerarius Regis was obliged to provide two knights for the army. It can be assumed that Robertus de Ancora and Petrus de Ancra were two low-ranking knights or burghers who elected to live in Ancra.

Unfortunately, the remains of the villages of 'Amqa and Lanahia mentioned above cannot be examined and we do not know where Casale Album was. The British built a military camp on the ruins of Yannuhiya (Lanahia) and this was later replaced by Kibbutz 'Evron, while the village core of 'Amqa was completely destroyed at the end of the 1950s by Israeli authorities. It cannot be established, therefore, whether there were Frankish buildings in one, or all, of these villages. We managed to extricate from the ruins of 'Amqa some remnants of Byzantine churches (parts of pillars, Corinthian capitals, marble stones, etc.) which had not previously been discovered. But no traces have remained of the earlier buildings themselves.

But in spite of the destruction of all archeological evidence, resort can be had to written sources in order to establish that in at least three of the five villages of the fief there were Frankish settlers. We cannot decide what kind of rural institutions were built by the Franks in these villages. We can only assume that such institutions and buildings would not have been substantially different from others constructed by the Franks in other places. It can be taken for granted that the "maison forte" which might have served as the center of the fief was built in Lanahia and that in the other villages typical Frankish buildings were constructed.

[12] Hospital, II, no. 1313, Oct. 1, 1208, 94 (Röhricht, *Regesta*, no. 829).

CHAPTER FOURTEEN

FARM HOUSES AND MANOR HOUSES

In the chapter dealing with the immediate geographical surroundings of the large castrum of Caiphas, I referred to the existence of an isolated "domus" which was situated a few kilometers from the castrum itself. In the next two chapters I shall attempt to explain the function of such isolated estates and how it can be established whether they were built originally as centers of agricultural farms or as centers of larger estates.

Farm houses

In the very attempt to define the function of a site as a "manor house" or a "farm house" there are certain basic difficulties, as is the case with every functional definition. The economic, political, or military functions of an archeological site emanate from the conditions which prevailed during a certain period. Every change in conditions results in a change in the functions. Thus, a building which in certain circumstances served as a fortress could also serve as the center of an agricultural estate or a monastery, and a change in the political, social, or economic conditions could cause a monastery or manor house to be used as a fortress, a prison, or a center of an agricultural estate. The Cistercian houses scattered throughout Europe can serve as an example of this multiple function. Some of these establishments were converted, during the thirteenth century, into large settlements and even into *bastides*.[1]

The only definition on which one can, for the most part, safely rely is the typological one. However, as Pringle has already pointed out, it is very difficult to distinguish between Frankish maisons fortes and Frankish small castles since the architectural ground plans of these two types of buildings are similar.[2]

[1] Higounet, 1960; Higounet, 1980; Hoffman-Berman, 1986.   [2] Pringle, 1989, 20.

179

However, our definition of a Frankish construction as a farm house or a private agricultural estate is not based solely on the architecture of the main building but on the agricultural context. The assumption that many of the Frankish sites were farm houses is not based on the style of building and the architectural characteristics of an isolated site, but on an analysis of the geographic-agricultural context of each of the sites studied. Thus, the construction of a central building together with the establishment of an agricultural estate allows for defining the function of the whole system as a "farm house." If it can be proved that the construction of an isolated building was connected with the reorganization of the agricultural fields, the making of terraces, fencing and separation of different types of fields, the institution of a system of irrigation, or the creation of a network of rural roads, then the building can be deemed a "farm house." I shall not deal, therefore, with the typology of manor houses. The persons who established manor houses were probably influenced by the building traditions which they brought with them from their countries of origin, by their financial capacity, and by the topographical setting. An attempt to understand this set of considerations could provide the basis for an archeological study, whose results would certainly be interesting, but this would deviate from the primary framework of this book. The overall picture and not the architectural details is what testifies to the fact that the building being studied was a Frankish agricultural estate.

Most of these edifices were constructed in remote, out-of-the-way places, away from the main roads and in sites which do not possess any strategic value. However, such general geographical considerations are not enough as they are deterministic and difficult to substantiate. It is difficult, for example, to prove that a place which appears today to be remote and isolated and void of any strategic value was also so in the twelfth century; and it is certainly difficult to prove that a rural road was merely such at that time too. In other words, not every isolated building, however remote it might have been, was a "manor house" or "farm house."

The functional interpretation of buildings is all the more difficult in cases where the medieval geographic context is unrecognizably blurred, as in the case of buildings constructed by the Franks which today are in the heart of populated villages. In these cases, it is difficult to establish even whether the Frankish site was constructed from the beginning in the heart of a populated village, or whether the village developed around it at a later stage. It is nevertheless important to note that in many places, like Biddu, Belmont, Shabatin, Baytilu and Bayt 'Ur al-Fawka, in which Frankish buildings were identified, these buildings are at the heart of the ancient village core and were apparently the earliest buildings in the villages. It is also important to note that most of these rural constructions are impressive structures which were built at great cost. The following examples, I hope, will clarify this point.

The manor house at Kh. al-Lawza (grid reference 165/135)

The Frankish site of Kh. al-Lawza, was identified already in the nineteenth century. Conrad Schick was the first to publish its plan and Bellarmino Bagatti, who surveyed the place in the 1940s, also produced a plan.[3] The site is situated about four kilometers to the west of Jerusalem, in one of the confluents of Sorek valley, far from the main road to Jerusalem, above a rural road which probably connected it to the villages of Bayt Surik, Biddu, and to the Frankish monastic "burgus" of Mons Gaudii in one direction and to two other Frankish estates, that of Bet Telem (grid reference 166/134) and Qaluniyya (grid reference 165/134) in the opposite direction. Near the estate in Qaluniyya, the path joins the Roman road which leads to Jerusalem via Dayr Yasin, in which another Frankish rural estate was found.

Short, exploratory excavations at the site were conducted in April 1986, under the supervision of Dr. R. Rubin and the present author. The excavations brought to light several fragments of Romanesque columns and moulds and enabled us to reconstruct the plan of the site.[4]

The site is composed of a rectangular courtyard (approx. 29 × 40 meters) surrounded by several barrel-vaulted halls with a big water reservoir of 1,200 square meters close to its southeastern corner and a residential tower to the northwestern one. (see plan and section fig. 14; view plate 5 and reconstruction plate 6).

The site was not fortified and only part of it was walled in. A small aqueduct led water from a spring source into the reservoir which was used both for irrigation and for daily needs. Two networks of irrigation channels originated directly from the spring and from the reservoir. The construction of the place was associated with a complete reorganization of fields, with the establishment of an irrigation system and with the creation of a new network of paths which connected the main building with the fields. All these components correspond to one general plan and it is possible to assume that the maison forte and its dependencies were conceived as a whole. The context and not only the architectural details of the main building enabled us to define this as a Frankish rural estate.

On the eastern side of the wadi, facing the estate, there is a large area which today is planted with olive trees. It can be assumed that it was also

[3] For a fuller version of this chapter, see Ellenblum, Rubin, & Sollar, 1996. See also Bagatti, 1947, 232–233. The site was known already in the 1860s, see Guérin, 1868–1869, I, 257; Zschokke, 1865, 62–63; Schick, 1867, 127.   [4] Ellenblum, Rubin, & Solar, 1996.

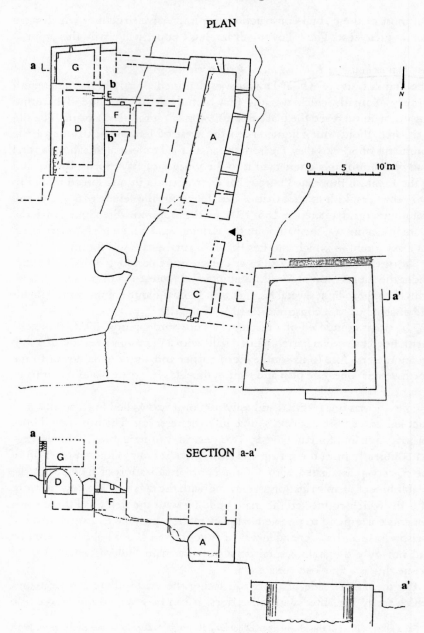

Figure 14   Kh. al-Lawza: plan and section

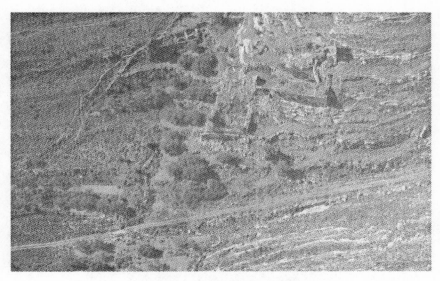

Plate 5   Kh. al-Lawza, general view

Plate 6   Reconstruction of the Frankish farm house in Kh. al-Lawza

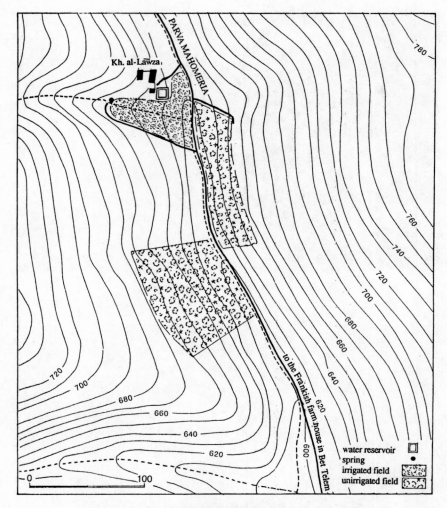

Figure 15   Plan of the agricultural areas at Kh. al-Lawza

planted with olive trees or grape vines during the Frankish period. Any other crop would have required the aid of irrigation (which was not possible) or a larger terrain (which was not available). Here too the terraces were fenced with a fence similar in appearance and size to that which enclosed the irrigated area. At the side of the fence there is a path containing cut-out steps. The path connects the terraces to the agricultural estate. There is no doubt that this plot of land, too, belonged to the agricultural estate itself (fig. 15).

Near the estate, on the southern side, there is a broad terraced area (about two hectares), which was also fenced in the same way as the other areas. It is possible that this area, too, was cultivated by the owners of the estate, resulting in an estate approximately 4.3 hectares in size, with the irrigated area about 0.8 hectare the unirrigated area about 1.5 hectares, near the farm house, and 2.0 hectares further afield. If the more distant area was not cultivated, then the cultivated area consisted of only 2.3 hectares. The size of the agricultural area is of great importance if we recall that according to the approach of Rey and Prawer the minimal cultivated area of a Frankish estate (a "carruca") was 35 hectares.[5] That means that the cultivated area of our estate was, according to my calculation, only one tenth of a carruca or even one twentieth of a carruca. As I indicated above, the size of a Frankish carruca was no more than 2.0 hectares of agricultural land. The estate, therefore, consisted of about one or two carrucas according to my calculation.[6]

The Frankish estate at Kh. Jariyut (grid reference 163/144)

Another Frankish "farm house," Kh. Jariyut, is situated in a deep valley which separates the village of Baytuniya and the village of 'Ayn 'Arik. Both Baytuniya (which appears in Latin Charters as Beitiumen) and 'Ayn 'Arik belonged in the twelfth century to the Chapter of the Church of the Holy Sepulcher, and in both of them we discovered Frankish rural sites. It is possible to assume that the Frankish site of Kh. Jariyut also belonged to the same establishment. The site consists of a massive barrel-vaulted tower, the remains of which can be easily discerned in plate 7, two dependent barrel-halled buildings, and a water reservoir, which was used for the irrigation of the fields. The main buildings, the water reservoir, and the irrigation system conform, here too, to the same general plan, and they were probably built together. In Kh. Jariyut, as in Kh. al-Lawza, the most important component was the irrigation system. It is clear, therefore, that in Kh. Jariyut, as in Kh. al-Lawza, the builder of the central building established an agricultural estate.

The site was also inhabited after the expulsion of the Franks, and a mihrab was cut in the southern wall. The existence of a mihrab indicates, of course, that the site was used as a mosque during a later period. From the setting of the mihrab and its irregular form it can be gathered that it was predated by the Frankish building. The Muslim occupants later converted the well-preserved Frankish hall into a mosque and placed the mihrab in it.

---

[5] See Rey, 1879; Prawer, 1980d, 158–159.   [6] Cf. chapter 8, pp. 97–99.

Plate 7   Kh. Jariyut

The Frankish estate at Kh. Salman (grid reference 162/141) (figs. 16 and 17)
A third Frankish estate, that of Kh. Salman, is located between the village of
Bayt Dukku and the village of al–Tira. This estate too was first discovered
and identified as a Frankish rural estate by Conrad Schick, who crossed Wadi
Salman when in search of the most convenient course for the railway line to
Jerusalem. The young Schick, who was most impressed by the beauty of the
spot, maintained that it was one of the most beautiful places in the whole
country.[7] Bagatti, who was unfamiliar with Schick's work, later rediscovered

---

[7] Schick, 1867.

A. Plan

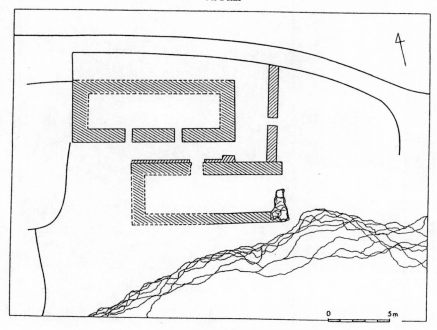

B. Elevation of the entrance gate

Figure 16   Plan of the farm house at Kh. Salman and elevation of the entrance gate

Figure 17   Reconstruction of the farm house at Kh. Salman

the place. He was also of the opinion that it was a Crusader estate and he even reproduced a plan of the place.[8] The writer of these lines cannot but accept the dating of his predecessors.

The neighboring villages of Bayt Dukku and al-Tira are mentioned in a confirmation of King Amalric in 1166 to the property of the Church of Templum Domini.[9] The king confirmed the donation by his mother at an earlier date of property which included. "duas gastinas terre nomine Heteyre et Beitdecoc, cum suis pertinentiis." Clermont-Ganneau was the first to identify Beitdecoc with Bayt Dukku and Heteyre with al-Tira north of it.[10] Since there is a reference to the pertinentiae of these two places, and since the very impressive farm house of Kh. Salman, which is located between them, is not mentioned in the document, we can conclude, although we cannot be sure, that it was built after the confirmation was issued, that is after the year 1166.

In Kh. Salman too the construction of the main agricultural system was completed together with the main edifice. The whole site was enclosed by a massive fence which had three gates: one faced Bayt Dukku, the other faced al-Tira, and the third gave access to the path leading to the water reser-

---

[8] Bagatti, 1947, 219–220.   [9] Chalandon, "Un diplome inédit."
[10] Chalandon, "Un diplome inédit."

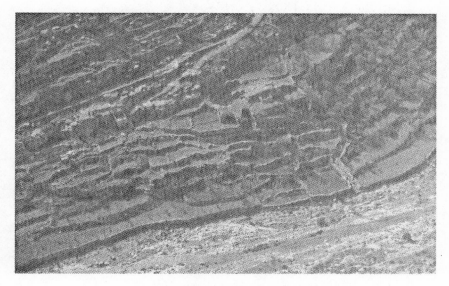

Plate 8   Kh. Salman, aerial view

voir. A very complicated irrigation system, which is still to be seen there, originated from the reservoir.

The central building itself was constructed on a rocky terrace about thirty meters above the bottom of Wadi Salman. This building included a two-storey barrel-vaulted northern construction of 26.9 meters and a second lower building which was used apparently for the farm equipment. The northern building was used apparently for dwelling purposes and extended over the corridor between the two buildings.

In the aerial photograph (plate 8), one can distinguish the irrigated fields which spread downwards from the farm house. The irrigated fields, like those at Kh. al-Lawza, are irregular, as they were intended to conform with the terrain and to exploit the flow of the water. The unirrigated fields and the olive groves extended over large areas in order to make full use of the topography and to save as much as possible the onerous task of constructing agricultural terraces.

The Frankish farm house at Kh. Burj Kafriya (grid reference 166/148)
(the "Tower of the Infidels" in Arabic, plate 9)
The Frankish agricultural estate at Kh. Burj Kafriya consists of a square building (30.5 × 25.1 square meters) built on the slope of a hill, about 30 meters above the valley. On the southern and western sides of the build-

Plate 9   Kh. Burj Kafriya

ing there were massive barrel-vaults. The external width of the southern vault reached 9.6 meters and the internal width 6 meters. The length of the western vault reached 14.5 meters, but its width could not be established. A modern building, constructed at the end of the first half of the nineteenth century, has made reconstruction of the plan of the house difficult.

Attached to the manor house, at its southwestern corner, a Frankish well-house was constructed. The well-house consisted of a pointed barrel-vault of 7 × 5 × 5 cubic meters. Part of the well-house was cut out of the rock and part was constructed. The water flowed into a square reservoir at whose corner there was a small opening from which a water channel led to the irrigated fields. Here too, as in other rural estates, the Franks succeeded in building an excellent installation for collecting, storing, and conducting water. Here too, as in all the other similar sites, an agricultural complex, of which the manor house was only one component, was created. It should be noted that the local inhabitants identify the place as the "Tower of the Infidel," which might testify also to its Frankish origin.

There is nothing surprising in the very existence of such rural estates or manor houses in the Frankish East. "Maisons fortes" existed in all parts of contemporary Europe and there is no reason why the Franks who settled the Latin Kingdom should have abandoned this very common way of habitation and of rural management.[11] The novelty lies more probably in the fact that the Franks succeeded, in a relatively short time, to master the technologies of irrigation with which they were not well acquainted in their countries of origin. Sophisticated water installations, like the channel networks running along the terraces, and the implements used for regulating and distributing water to the fields, might testify to the help which was given to the Franks by the local villagers.

The settlement of the Church of the Holy Sepulcher at Quruntal: the problem of water supply

The patriarch of Jerusalem owned immense tracts of land in Jericho, the income from which was estimated at 5,000 gold coins a year (this is, incidentally, one of the only pieces of evidence concerning the ownership of land by the patriarch himself, as distinct from the Chapter of the Church of the Holy Sepulcher). The Patriarch Arnulf gave the place as a wedding present to Eustache Grenier, on his marriage to Emma, the patriarch's cousin.[12]

In 1116, the Chapter asked Eustache to return the land which had been previously owned by "habitatores Sanctissime Quarantene," as well as the mill which used to receive water once a fortnight for twenty four hours.

ego Constantius, Sancte Quarantene servus, atque Willelmus obnixe rogavimus domnum Eustachium Granerium et uxorem ejus quatinus nobis terram redderent, quam quondam habitatores Sanctissime Quarantene possederant.

Quod facere, Deo inspirante, non recusaverunt. Reddiderunt autem nobis supradictam terram et unum molendinum in ipsa terra manentem per manum domni Arnulfi patriarche, ita ut in unoquoque XIIIIo die cum nocte aquam sine dilatione haberemus.[13]

Two important conclusions can be drawn from this document: (a) that agricultural settlement was conducted by the Church of the Holy Sepulcher already before 1116; and (b) that the Church and the owners of land understood, already then, that the right to the use of water, in desert conditions, was not less important, if not even more so, than the right to the land itself.

There is an additional hint in the document to the existence of Frankish settlement in the place: one of the witnesses to the document was Arnolfus,

---

[11] See, for example, Bur, 1980; Bur, 1981; Bur, 1986; Bur, 1987; Coursente, 1980; Noyé, 1980.
[12] William of Tyre, 11, 15, 519.   [13] Holy Sepulcher, no. 94, Apr. 8, 1124, 211–212.

the viscount of Jericho. From the very existence of a viscount it may be deduced that there were other Frankish citizens who had settled in the area, and this justified the introduction of the institution of a viscount.[14]

Immediately after the death of Eustache, the Church appealed to his widow and sons to double the amount of water allowed to the mill by letting the water flow for one whole day, once a week. Their request was granted.

Post obitum vero domni Eustachii, ego Constantius ceterique fratres, videntes penuriam aque, necessarium duximus deprecari domnam . Emam, uxorem supramemorati Eustachii, ut . . . nobis in unaquaqua ebdomada aquam accresceret. Illa vero, ut audivit inopiam nostram, pietate commota, concedentibus filiis suis Eustachio et Galterio, per manum viri sui domni Hugonis, principis Joppe, petitioni nostre assensum dedit, ita ut omni VIIo die, videlicet die sabbati, cum precedente nocte, dilatione procul posita, aquam jure perpetuo haberemus.[15]

The two grants of water testify to the importance of irrigation in the Frankish agricultural settlement in semi-arid zones, as well as to great technological skill. The local owners controlled the quantity of water granted to each and every body in the town. They could decide how much water each received and when. The amount of land owned by the Church of the Holy Sepulcher in Jericho can be deduced from these documents: the Church first received one fourteenth, and later one seventh, of the waters of one spring, most probably the spring of ʿAyn Diuc, as it is not feasible that the monastery or the town administrators could have succeeded in transferring some of the water from Wadi Qilt to the slope of the monastery of the Quruntal, as between Wadi Qilt and the monastery there is an impassable decline. It is important to note that in the aqueduct through which the water of ʿAyn Diuc still flows, there are clear signs of Frankish construction (or possibly restoration).

The settlement by the Church of the Holy Sepulcher continued to develop until, in 1134, it received the status of a separate priory, subject to the Chapter in Jerusalem.[16] Two years later, when a new altar was consecrated, the patriarch of Jerusalem granted them the tithes of Jericho.[17] The success of ecclesiastical settlement in Jericho derived apparently from the nature of the crops which were cultivated there: dates, bananas, sugar cane,

[14] Arnulfus the vicecomes is mentioned again in Holy Sepulcher, no. 131, 1161. It is not probable that the same Arnulfus was the vicecomes of a place like Jericho for so many years. For the office of the viscount, see Prawer, 1972, 497–498.
[15] Holy Sepulcher, no. 94, Apr. 8, 1124, 211–212.
[16] Holy Sepulcher, no. 21, 1134, 78.
[17] Holy Sepulcher, no. 22, 1136, 79; no. 142, Feb. 8, 1168, 276.

and indigo, used for dyeing material.[18] At the foot of the monastery, virtually on the rib of the mountain, the remains of Frankish buildings were discovered. Clermont-Ganneau notes that he found there Frankish capitals and a sugar mill.[19]

[18] Jacques of Vitry, ed. Bongars, I, 1075.
[19] Clermont-Ganneau, 1899, 16; Benvenisti, 1970, 357–358.

CHAPTER FIFTEEN

ADMINISTRATION OF RURAL ESTATES

In previous chapters I brought textual and archeological evidence of the existence of the maisons fortes, which served as administrative centers for agricultural estates. However, the documents and the archeological remains do not provide evidence of how the estates and the manor houses were administered, whether the Frankish masters lived in them permanently, and whether they received help from the local population. Furthermore, they do not provide answers to the question of whether the local population who participated in the administration of these estates was Christian or Muslim. Nonetheless, it is difficult to imagine that the Franks would have invested so great an effort in building maisons fortes if they had not intended to live permanently in them. Furthermore, from an examination of the agricultural remains discovered in the Frankish farm houses, as discussed in the previous chapter, it transpires that the Franks used agricultural and irrigation technologies developed in the Orient over a period of hundreds of years, and that it is reasonable to assume that they employed local labor in order to apply this technology, most of which was unknown in the Latin Occident.

This chapter is devoted to proving that the Franks did actually build their estates and manor houses for their own use, although their day-to-day administration was entrusted, apparently, to members of the local Christian community.

The Frankish maison forte in Kabul

During a survey which I conducted in Kabul (Cabor of the Frankish period), I discovered remains of a large barrel-vault and of fortifications from the Frankish period. The place is also mentioned in several documents, one of which lists the names of the lords of the place, describes how it was administered, and outlines the rights and obligations of the manager. This docu-

ment, issued in 1175, describes the transfer of the rights of the dragomanagium of the villages Turon, Cabor, and Coket from Juetta, the lady of
the place, and her grandson Rohardus to a certain Barutus, for the sum of
250 bezants only. One can learn from the document that the office of the
dragoman of the place was hereditary, with rights and obligations attached
to it, and that it was not a purely administrative function.[1]

The rights of the head dragoman

Each one of the inhabitants had to give to the dragoman one *modius* of
wheat and one *modius* of barley for each carruca of land which he cultivated; in addition two *manipuli* of wheat and two *manipuli* of barley were
payable on each carruca of land cultivated jointly by the "master" and the
farmers.[2]

The aforementioned document deals not only with different kinds of
produce, but deals also with different kinds of ownership. It would appear
that two different kinds of fields are mentioned: the carrucas of the farmers
("unusquisque villanorum . . . de singulis carrucatis terre sue") and the carrucas from which the common produce of the "master" and the farmers was
harvested ("unaquaque carruca, de communi domini et villanorum
annona").[3]

In Casale Imbert too, it will be recalled, there were two different kinds of

---

[1] Hospital, no. 480, June 26, 1175, 330–331: "Notum sit omnibus . . . quod ego Balduinus, . . .
concedo et confirmo tibi Barute et heredibus tuis drugomanagiam de his casalibus de Cabur et
de Turone et de Coket; quam drugomanagiam Juetta, avia Rohardi, et ipsius filius Petrus filiolus
tibi et heredibus tuis dederant; et nunc tandem ipse Rohardus, concessione uxoris sue Deline, tibi
et heredibus tuis in curia mea Accon concessit, et privilegio meo vobis confirmari impetravit; et
tu propter hoc ducentos et viginti quinque bisancios ei dedisti. Sunt autem hec illius drugo-
managie jura: videlicet quod unusquisque villanorum horum casalium, de singulis carrucatis terre
sue, dabit tibi unum modium frumenti, et unum ordei; . . . Preterea cum fueris in uno istorum
casalium, villani providebunt tibi et equitature tue victualia. Cum vero fueris extra casalia cum
domino tuo, ipse solummodo equitature tue dabit prebendam; et si perdideris eqitaturam tuam
in servitio domini tui, ipse tibi pro ea reddet quindecim bizancios. Insuper, quando dominus et
villani communiter acceperint de annona centum modios, tu postea accipies de communi sex
modios, et sic de paucioribus secundum proporcionem." Cf. Riley-Smith, 1973, 54.
[2] " . . . habebis etiam pro unaquaque carruca, de communi 'domini et villanorum annona, duos
manipulos frumenti, et duos ordei." Hospital, no. 480, June 26, 1175, 330.
[3] The common produce of the master and the villages is mentioned again in the same document:
"Insuper, quando dominus et villani communiter acceperint de annona centum modios, tu postea
accipies de communi sex modios, et sic de paucioribus secundum proporcionem." Riley-Smith
interpreted this text in the following words: "For every carrucate in a petty lordship near Acre
the dragoman received from the villein owning it a *modius* of wheat and a *modius* of barley, and
two *manipuli* of wheat and barley from the harvest piled up on the threshing floors before its division between the lord and the villagers. For every one hundred *modii* divided in this way, he could
take a further six, although of grain of the poorer quality." Riley-Smith, 1973, 55.

land ownership. There, too, there was land which could be possessed by individual settlers, and other land which was cultivated jointly by all the farmers and on which they had to pay the king 40% of their harvest.

The upkeep of the dragoman did not fall only on the farmers. The master also had to share the burden. The dragoman received, in addition to a fixed payment collected from the farmers, a fluctuating remuneration of 6% of the produce from the jointly owned land. In other words, part of his income was at the expense of the master. To this must be added the partial financing of the dragoman and his knights as follows: the villagers provided for his food ("victualia") and that of his men (or horses), as long as they were billeted there. When they left the village on the service of the lord ("cum domino tuo") the latter paid for the maintenance of the men (or the horses). The master was obliged to pay the dragoman for the loss of a horse while on his service. The document does not state who was obliged to maintain the dragoman himself, while he was on the master's service, and apparently the farmers were liable for this in all circumstances.

The duties of the office of dragoman

The dragoman had to accompany his master, as a rear-vassal, on all the missions on which he was in danger of losing some of his men (or horses). Apparently, the reference here is to the duty of auxilium. The document does not leave much doubt as to the physical presence of the heads of the dragomanagium in the relevant villages. "Preterea cum fueris in uno istorum casalium, villani providebunt tibi et equitature tue victualia. Cum vero fueris extra casalia cum domino tuo, ipse solummodo equitature tue dabit prebendam."

Riley-Smith interpreted this as meaning that "he [the dragoman] could requisition supplies for himself and his horse when travelling round the villages."[4] But this interpretation was apparently influenced by the assumption that the Frankish masters never settled on their lands and that they certainly never lived amongst their subjects. Other documents, also dealing with Kabul, provide a contrary picture – that the Frankish master (and not only the dragoman) lived in Kabul. For example, in a document issued in 1180, Rohardus, the grandson of Juetta, is mentioned again, this time as "Rohardus de Cabor." It is reasonable to assume that the village of Cabor was not bound up with the name of Rohardus by chance. Rohardus was, and remained, the seigniorial master of the terrain, even after the drago-

---

[4] Riley-Smith, 1973, 55.

managium rights were transferred, because in granting such rights the family did not waive its own seigniorial rights.[5]

In another document, also issued in 1180, another maison forte is mentioned as belonging to Rohardus. The document sums up a longstanding dispute between the Hospitalers and Rohardus concerning a plot of land between Beroeth and "the Hill of Rohardus de Cabor."[6] The "Hill of Rohardus" was still called "the Hill of Juetta" many years later, although the family of the masters of Kabul had already lost their rights to the place. A comparison of the two documents mentioned above shows that the "Hill of Juetta," which is none other than the "Hill of Rohardus," was Tel Kison, called "Toron." It would appear that it was Juetta who purchased the place and most probably built a residence to live in it. That is apparently the reason why a "hill" was connected with her name and not with that of Rohardus, even though the latter had given his name to the hill when he served as the seignior of the estate.[7]

There were, therefore, three villages in the dragomanagium: Kabul, Toron, and Coket. There was at least one maison forte in Kabul (the remains of which were discovered) and another (if my interpretation of the written documents is correct), in Tel Kison. It is not unlikely that in the village of Coket too (which is either the village of Kuwaykat or the village of Kaukab) there was a castle or Frankish tower. In Kuwaykat, M. Makhouly recorded in 1934 remains of a rounded barrel-vault, representing all that remained of the "old Khan." This barrel-vault could be medieval. Support of this assumption can be found in the fact that in all the documents this village is referred to by its French name of Coket and is never referred to by its Semitic local name. However, Kabul was apparently the center of the estate, as is hinted at by the fact that the seignior of the estate was called "Rohardus de Cabor" and one of his heirs was called "Girardus de Cabor," and by the additional fact that Cabor appears first on the list of villages of the estate.[8]

---

[5] Strehlke, no. 10, Apr. 2, 1179, 10–11 (Röhricht, *Regesta*, no. 579, 1180).

[6] Hospital, no. 579, Jan. 21, 1180, 392–393 (Röhricht, *Regesta*, no. 591): "Notum sit omnibus . . . quod ego Balduinus, . . . concedo et confirmo . . . domui Hospitalis Jerusalem . . . quandam terram, inter Beroet et tolonum Rohardi de Chabor sitam, quam ipse Rohardus injuste calumpnians in proprios usus reflectere nitebatur. Ad cujus divisionem et metas constituendas, quia controversiam, que longo tempore inter vos et ipsum Rohardum pro predicta terra ventilata fuerat, determinare, et pacem inter vos et ipsum reformare voluimus, misimus comitem Jocelinum."

[7] Röhricht, *Regesta*, no. 1210, 1253. The hill of Rohardus is named here after domina Joietta, even though it had already passed to the Order of Hospital of St. John and both Rohardus and his grandmother lived in the twelfth century and not in the thirteenth. The description of the hill enables us to identify it with Tel Kison.

[8] Evidence of the name of another seignior of the place is to be found in Strehlke, no. 43, 1208, 34–35 (Röhricht, *Regesta*, no. 668), where Girardus de Cabur who might have inherited the place from Rohardus is mentioned.

Additional, independent evidence of the existence of a Frankish tower in
Kabul appears on a map ascribed by Röhricht to the thirteenth century. The
village is described there as two towers joined by a wall.[9]

The question as to whether the manor house was inhabited by the seignior
or the dragoman is difficult to answer completely. The family of the masters
of Kabul had a house in Acre. Interestingly enough, the document refers to
the house in Acre as part of the "feodum of Cabor." In other words, there is
no reference here to a knight from Acre who also had an agricultural
feodum, but to the owner of an agricultural feodum who also had a house
in Acre.[10]

Rohardus apparently divided his time between his (two or may be even
three?) towers and his house in Acre. He entrusted the practical management
of the fief to his vassal Barutus, mentioned above, in his capacity as a rear-
vassal. The dragoman had to contribute one knight as remuneration for the
dragomanagium. This fact too is consistent with my assumption that Barutus
had to serve as an auxilium to his masters. It would appear that Barutus, too,
had to divide his time between the two (or three?) towers constructed in his
master's estate. This emerges from the document describing the award of the
dragomanagium which states, inter alia, that "when you are in one of these
casalia the farmers will provide you and your horses (or men) with your daily
sustenance."

Finally, the village of Kabul was, at the end of the twelfth century, part of
the royal domain, as can be gathered from the document mentioned above,
in which Guy de Lusignan, king of Jerusalem, granted the village of Kabul
to Joscelyn III, without the approval of Girardus de Cabor, who was at the
time the lord of the estate.

The Frankish tower at Manueth

Another tiny seigniorial estate which has many of the characteristics of
Cabor was situated in Kh. Manot – the Manueth of the Franks (plate 10).

[9] Röhricht, 1895, fig. 1. It can be argued that marking the place with a symbol in the form of
fortress is meaningless since most of the places which appear on the map look like fortresses and
that medieval and Renaissance cartographers habitually used conventional symbols of this sort.
But it should be noted that only a negligible minority of Frankish sites which were in existence
in Palestine at that time appear on the map and those that do appear had, apparently, some special
significance for the cartographer. It is also important to note that places like Casale Doc and Kabul
do not appear as they were Biblical sites or were of some special historical or religious importance. These facts turn the map into an historical document which, in addition to the tower discovered in Kabul, testify to the existence of a Frankish fortress in the place.

[10] Strehlke, no. 22, 1186, 20 (Röhricht, *Regesta*, no. 654): "Concedo . . . quoddam casale Cabor
nuncupatum . . . pro quo servicium unius militis mihi et meis heredibus facere teneris, et quandam
domum in Accon, que ad feudum de Chabor pertinet."

Plate 10 Manueth, general view

Manueth was inhabited even before the Frankish occupation.[11] The place
continued to be called a village (casale) in all the Latin documents, although
a Frankish fortified manor house (maison forte) was built there. For example,
Gaufridus (Goifredus) Tortus, the seignior of Manueth, undertook to grant
Garinus, the abbot of the monastery of Mt. Tabor, an annual sum of twelve
bezants from the income derived from sugar from "his casale Manueth."[12]
Thus the Frankish sources do not deal directly with the tower built there,

---

[11] Ibn 'Asakir, I, 395; Ibn Taghri Birdi, IV, 135.
[12] Chartes du Mont-Thabor, II, no. XIV, Sept., 1169, 905–906 (Röhricht, *Regesta*, no. 468).

and we learn of its existence only from the Arab sources which deal with "the fortresses conquered by Saladin," as well as from the archeological remains preserved there.[13]

The reference to the Frankish fortified village in Manueth as a "casale" is not unique. The well-developed Frankish settlement in Casale Imbert, which included both a fortress and a castrum, is called a casale in Frankish sources, as is the Frankish tower in Kabul. This indicates that the word "casale" had a more complex connotation in Frankish sources than it is customary to assume.

There was a great deal of similarity in the way the castles in Kabul and Manueth were administered. First of all, Gaufridus Tortus of Manueth, like the seigniors of Kabul, had a house in Acre from which his financial affairs were conducted. Evidence of this can be found in the document mentioned above, in accordance with which Gaufridus undertook to pay twelve bezants a year to the monastery of Mt. Tabor. The agreement between him and the monastery provides that the payment be made "in his house in Acre." Thus in Manueth, as in Kabul, it is impossible to establish incontrovertibly that the lord lived in his maison forte.

Certainly the castle in Manueth, like that in Kabul, was associated to a great extent with its seigniors although Gaufridus is not called "Gaufridus de Manueth" in any document. It is reasonable to assume that he used to spend most of his time in Acre since the gate of Acre which was near his house was called "the gate of Gofredus Tortus."[14]

From an analysis of the list of lords who had seigniorial rights in Manueth it transpires that there was a resemblance between the ways the maison forte in Manueth and the tower in Kabul were administered. In 1212, Jean of Brienne sold the casale of Manueth to the Hospitalers for 2,000 bezants, a comparatively small sum for a fortress but not for a casale.[15] As the full text of the document has not been preserved, we cannot know what property and what rights were sold by the king to the Hospital. But it is difficult to imagine that Jean of Brienne would have transferred full ownership of a Frankish tower and its land for so low a sum. We cannot know either whether the original text contained a reference to other rights owned by other seigniorial lords.

We can learn about the existence of other claimants to such rights from another authorization which was issued five years later, and in accordance

[13] 'Imad al-Din al-Isfahani, 35, line 8; Abu Shama, II, 87 (ed. *RHC* 301). For the archeological remains, see Benvenisti, 1982, 135; Warren & Conder, 1882–1884, I, 173.

[14] Strehlke, no. 70, 1229, 55–56: "porta, quae dicitur Gaufridi Torti."

[15] Hospital, II, no. 1383, Apr. 15, 1212, 141.

with which Beatrice, the daughter and heiress of Joscelyn III, waived the rights which she and her husband had in Manueth, of which she was apparently the owner at the time.[16] There were still other claimants to rights in this maison forte. In several documents issued during the thirteenth century, a legal dispute over rights in the place, conducted by "Nicholaus filius filie Sayt Scribe" is described. There is almost no doubt that his rights were inherited from his grandfather, who is mentioned in documents describing the rights which the grandson had in Manueth. As the dispute centered on the legality of the sale of rights and not on the rights themselves, we do not know what rights Nicholaus had in Manueth. One can gather from the documents that no one doubted that he had had rights in the place in the past.[17]

One can learn about the nature of the rights from another, earlier document, which refers to the rights of the grandfather, Seit. The document deals with the sale of the property of Gaufridus Tortus in the area of Fassuta. The sale of the land was conditioned on the reception of suitable compensation for the rights of the "scribania et dragomanagium" which were held by two men – Seit and Guilelmus – described as sergeants ("servientes") of Gaufridus Tortus.[18] The scribania and dragomanagium are described in the document as "feoda" and not as purely administrative functions. Gaufridus undertook to grant each of the two men a feodum in another place. The document does not indicate what alternative place is offered to each of them, but it can be assumed, with a great deal of certainty, that one of the places was Manueth. That, in my opinion, was the reason why Nicholaus mentioned the name of his grandfather and his status in the seigniorial hierarchy ("sayt scriba"). As Gaufridus did not sell all his property in Galilee, but only

---

[16] Hospital, II, no. 1526, Jan. 1217, 206–207: "Ego Johannes . . . rex decimus . . . , notum facio . . . quod nobilis mulier Beatrix, . . . Joceleni filia, in mea et mee curie presentia absolvit sanctam domum Hospitalis Iherusalem, . . . a petitione casalis quod vocatur Manueth, cum omnibus suis pertinenciis in perpetuum; et quicquid in eo haberet vel habere deberet ipsa, generalis procuratrix omnium bonorum a marito constituta, et liberam habens et generalem administrationem, dedit et diffinivit dicte domui, et magistro, et fratribus, ad omnes eorum voluntates faciendas in sempiternum."

[17] Hospital, II, no. 1996, Sept. 28, 1231, 424–425: Balian of Sidon, the Bailli of the Kingdom of Jerusalem, confirms that Nicholaus, the grandson of Seit, sold "feodum suum, quod habebat apud Manuetum" after presenting it properly in Acre, Tyre, and Caesarea, and after receiving 1,600 bezants for his fief. The legal process, which lasted "for a long time" ended when Nicholaus admitted on Dec. 5, 1251 that he had sold his fief properly. Hospital, II, no. 2756, Aug. 9, 1255, 792.

[18] Strehlke, no. 16, 1183, 15–16 (Röhricht, *Regesta*, no. 624): "Notum sit omnibus . . . quod ego Balduinus. . . . concedo et confirmo tibi Ioscelino, . . . hec subscripta casalia cum eorum pertinenciis et divisionibus, . . . tali tenore, quod feodos, quos Seit et Guillelmus iam dicti Gaufridi servientes in eisdem casalibus habebant, scribaniam scilicet et drugumanagium, in presencia mea quietos clamaverunt et idem Gaufridus Tortus alibi eis alios assignavit feodos."

the eastern parts of his estate, it can be assumed that Seit received the administration of Manueth as a "scribania."

From the litigation conducted by Nicholaus, Seit's heir, it can be seen that Manueth was a fief. Nicholaus announced the sale of the feodum which he had "apud Manuetum" in 1231. This triple announcement in the large cities of the Kingdom was part of the usual procedure in the sale of a landed feodum.[19] In other words, Nicholaus, as the heir of Seit, had inheritable rights, which he sold as any other landed feodum is sold. At the end of the legal dispute it transpired that his rights were sold legally and had ended up in possession of the Hospital.

In order to obtain control of Manueth, the Hospitalers had to acquire the rights, or obtain a waiver, from three classes of owners of rights in this feodum: (a) royalty, since rights were sold to them by Jean of Brienne, (b) the seigniorial lord, whose rights were granted to them by Beatrice, and (c) the sergeant, who managed the place on behalf of the seigniorial lord, and whose scribania rights were sold to them by Nicholaus.

A similar situation existed in Kabul. There, too, the royal house and the owner (Juetta and later Rohardus) had rights and there, too, rights were given to the sergeant who served as a dragoman. The difference between dragomanagium and scribania is not sufficiently clear, and I do not see any call to speculate about their nature. Nevertheless, we have already seen that the dragomanagium had to provide the service of one knight whereas the scribania was apparently a sergeant estate.[20]

The next question to be considered is whether Seit scriba was a Frankish settler or a local Christian. In the opinion of Riley-Smith who saw in the offices of the scriba and the dragoman the successors of the Muslim regime, "four or even five of the scribanies known to us were locals." In this context Riley-Smith assumes that Seit was none other than Sa'id and that people like Georgius of Betheri, the scriban of Bayt Daras, Adam of Arsur, and others were "local inhabitants."[21] Riley-Smith's assumption is not sufficiently clear, as he does not explain what he means by the concept of "local inhabitants." It is difficult, and sometimes even impossible, to rely only on a name in order to establish if a particular person was a Frank or a "local inhabitant." On the other hand, one can rely on certain names in order to establish the religion of the holder of the name. There is no doubt, for example, that Seit was a Christian, as his direct descendant and heir was called Nicholaus. There is

---

[19] Hospital, no. 1996, Sept. 28, 1231, 425. *Livre au roi*, ch. 45, 629. Cf. Mayer, 1980, 190.
[20] For the offices of the dragomanagium and the scribania, cf. Cahen, 1950–1951, 306–307; Smail, 1973, 82–84; Riley-Smith, 1972, 15–26; Riley-Smith, 1973, 53–61; Riley-Smith, 1977, 1–22.
[21] Riley-Smith, 1973, 57.

also no doubt that Georgius of Betheri and Adam of Arsur were Christians. This conclusion is bolstered by logic: even if one were to assume that Gaufridus Tortus did not live in the impressive tower which he built in Manueth, it would be difficult to assume that he entrusted the management and protection of a place described in Arabic sources as a "fortress" to a local Muslim.

I think that Riley-Smith's assumptions that Seit was none other than Sa'id and that "local inhabitants" were part and parcel of the Frankish feudal system are justifiable. But I think that it should be added that the evidence in our possession points to the fact that the "local inhabitants" referred to were actually local Christians who had sergeantries and were rear-vassals of the higher echelon of Frankish society.[22]

The settlement of Manueth was small and may even have disappeared for a time after the incursions of Baibars into Western Galilee. Testimony of this can be found in a document which states that, in the light of the bad state of the fortress of Montfort, Hugo Revel, the Master of the Hospital, allowed the Teutonic Order to cultivate the lands of the casale of Manueth for one year only, so that the Teutonic Order could not later claim rights of possession. One can learn from this document that the Hospital had already ceased to work the land in Manueth earlier on. This document strengthens my previous assumption that the inhabitants of the "casale" of Manueth were Franks or local Christians. I can see no other explanation for the fact that the inhabitants of Manueth abandoned it at the beginning of Baibars' incursions,

---

[22] It seems that most of the holders of the office of the rays were local Christians: the rays Bolos and his brother Guillaume were undoubtedly Christians: Röhricht, *Regesta*, no. 1272, 1259. The same is true for Iohannes raicius: Röhricht, *Regesta*, Add., no. 706, 1192; Escandar: Röhricht, *Regesta*, no. 389, 1163; and Guido raicius, Röhricht, *Regesta*, no. 567, 1178. The same Guido held half a *gastina* in tenure, near Nablus, and he was named the rays of Nablus: Röhricht, *Regesta*, no. 643, 1185. Morage raiz was the owner of a "domus" with a mill in Jerusalem: Röhricht, *Regesta*, no. 265, 1150. Georgius was a rays near Antioch: Röhricht, *Regesta*, no. 424, 1166. Another Georgius was a rays near Tripolis: Röhricht, *Regesta*, no. 519, 1174; in the same document two other local Christians were called "reguli": Guillelmus and Symon. For Georgius the rays of Margat, see Röhricht, *Regesta*, no. 521, 1174. The scribania of Bayt Daras was given to Georgius of Betheri: Röhricht, *Regesta*, nos. 545 and 546, 1177. Evidence of Muslims in the office of the rays is thus very limited. Besides the well-known testimony of Ibn Jubayr, there is only one document which refers to Muslims in this office: Röhricht, *Regesta*, no. 1237, 1255, which deals with the property of the Hospital in Eastern Galilee. Cf. Ibn Jubayr, 316–317. For the authenticity of Ibn Jubayr's description, cf. Cahen, 1934. The names which are mentioned there are Abet, Messor, Brahym, Bennor, and Asyae. The fact that there is only one such document which refers to Muslim ra'ises and so many documents which refer to local Christian rayses shows that Muslims rayses were the exception rather than the rule. The existence of five rayses in the same place of this marginal dry region might indicate that heads of Beduin tribes were referred to as rayses. It should be noted also that the court of the rays dealt especially with local Christians. See the discussion of Riley-Smith, 1972, 1–15; Riley-Smith, 1973, 47–49, 90–91; Prawer, 1985b, 103–104; Kedar, 1990, 164.

which obviously would not have affected Muslim farmers. On the other hand, it is important to remember that according to the evidence of Ibn 'Asakir there were also Muslim inhabitants in the village before the Frankish conquest. It would also appear that the settlement of Manueth succeeded in recovering from the wounds inflicted by Baibars, as eight years later land owned by Franks and bordering on the casale of Manueth was sold to the Hospitaler of the Hospital in Acre.[23]

It is difficult to draw farreaching conclusions on the strength of the few documents at our disposal. Nonetheless, it is possible to assume that the Frankish lords lived, at least part of the time, in the castles which they built in the heart of their rural estates and the Christian managers, in their capacity as dragomans lived on these estates permanently.

[23] See Hospital, III, no. 3400, July 10, 1270, 231; Ibn 'Asakir, see n. 11; Hospital, III, no. 3679, Oct. 16, 1278, 376.

CHAPTER SIXTEEN

SETTLEMENT ACTIVITIES OF THE MILITARY ORDERS: THE CASTLE AND FLOUR MILLS IN DAʿUQ (CASALE DOC) AND RECORDANA

The Franks built flour mills near the springs of Recordana (ʿEnot Afeq, grid reference 160/250) already in the middle of the twelfth century. The casale and flour mills are mentioned for the first time in 1154, in a confirmation of Baldwin III.[1]

The place was also used, particularly in the thirteenth century, as a meeting place for the Frankish armies before they set out to battle.[2] Such meeting places were usually established near to abundant springs and grazing meadows in the immediate vicinity of Frankish settlements or fortresses. Such were the meeting places in Qalansue, Safforie, and Tubania in the Jezreel Valley. At these meetings thousands of men and mounts would gather. The soldiers would be briefed on organizational arrangements in the camps, on the state of the grazing meadows and springs and on security measures to be taken by the first arrivals. Proximity to a Frankish settlement or fortress facilitated and expedited the efficient organization of these meetings which were perforce, because of their very nature, arranged at short notice.

Downstream, in Casale Doc (Daʿuq), about three kilometers northwest of Recordana, the Templar knights established another castle. From a survey of the impressive remains (see fig. 18 and plate 11) it would appear that the castle was large and fortified. The fact that the castle at Daʿuq is neither mentioned in Latin sources from the twelfth century nor in Arabic sources which describe the Muslim conquest of Salah al-Din indicates that it did not exist during the time of the First Kingdom and was built only after the battle of Hattin. It is worth recalling that the Arab sources refer to the castle of Gaufridus Tortus in Manueth, which was much smaller than the castle in

---

[1] Hospital, no. 225, July 7, 1154, 172 (Röhricht, *Regesta*, no. 293).
[2] Prawer, 1975, index.

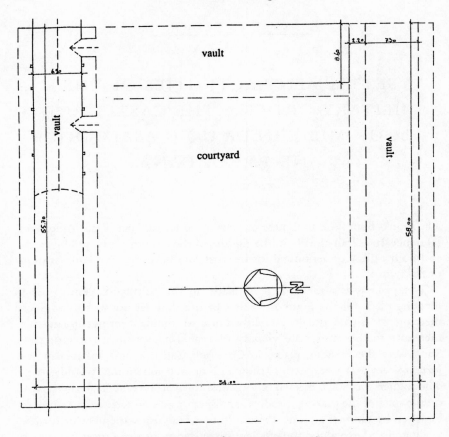

Figure 18   Kh. Daʿuq (Casale Doc): plan

Daʿuq, as a "fortress." If the castle in Daʿuq had already existed in 1187 it would, almost certainly, have earned some mention in the Latin or Arabic sources. The only time the castle is mentioned in twelfth century sources is the reference to "the bridge of Daʿuq " in a Muslim source describing the siege of Acre; and even there no hint of the existence of a castle is given.[3]

The assumption that the castle in Daʿuq was built only at the beginning of the thirteenth century is strengthened by documents which deal with a legal dispute between the Templars and the Hospitalers which concerned the River Naʿaman which flowed between both sites.

The mills in Daʿuq are mentioned for the first time in an agreement,

[3] Baha al-Din, ed. *RHC*, 200.

Plate 11   Kh. Daʿuq, view

drawn up between the Templar and Hospital Orders in 1201.[4] The agreement, whose complete text has not been preserved, deals with the use of the
water for irrigation purposes and for the operation of the mills of Recordana
and Daʿuq. The agreement of 1201 was the first in a long line of agreements
and mutual claims between both parties, during the first half of the thirteenth century. The agreement of 1201 was of vital importance and was certainly the first of this series, since without it the agricultural functions in both
places could not be implemented. The Hospitalers went later on to the
trouble of collecting all the documents connected with the dispute and these
documents were preserved in their archives, and it can be assumed, therefore, that there were no preliminary stages with which we are not familiar.
The fact that the first agreement between the two parties was concluded at
the beginning of the thirteenth century indicates, in my opinion, that the
"fortress" in Daʿuq was built only after the battle of Hattin. The Templars
then built a new dam for the use of their flour mills on the Naʿaman. The
consequent rise in the water level impaired the effective use of the mills built
by the Hospitalers upstream, and this led to the dispute between the two
Orders, which was not settled until 1262. It follows therefore, that the
Templar castle was not built before the thirteenth century, and it is reason-

[4] Hospital, II, no. 1144, Apr. 17, 1201, 7.

able to assume that their flour mills were built shortly thereafter so that they could reap the benefit from the waters of the river.

The first agreement between the two military Orders, drawn up in 1201, was revised in 1235. From the text of the new agreement it would appear that the Templars, whose mills were downstream, built a dam for the purpose of raising the level of the water and putting it to greater use. The small difference in height between Recordana and Da'uq led to the flooding of the Hospitalers' mill, which was based, according to the remains which have been preserved, on the stream technique and not on the dam technique which is based on raising the water and letting it fall at a certain point (the same technique was used in Recordana and elsewhere). This flooding prevented the Hospitalers' from using their mill effectively. The Templars' dam, and the consequent dispute, led also to denying the Hospitalers the right of free navigation on the river. Under the agreement the maximum height to which the level of the water could be raised was fixed by a sign placed within the purvey of the Hospitalers' mill. Any additional raising of the water level was subject to the Hospitalers' consent. There is an additional clause in the agreement dealing with the elevation of the banks of the river. The navigation rights of both parties were also laid down in the agreement, while the Hospitalers, for their part, undertook not to release the waters in their reservoir at one go. The disputes between the two Orders reached the courts time and again and testify to the intensive exploitation of the river for agricultural purposes.[5]

The archeological remains and the documents indicate that Frankish "maisons fortes" were built in both Recordana and Da'uq. The castle in Recordana was smaller than that in Da'uq, but both castles had similar functions: the representatives of the military Orders who lived in them were in charge of maintaining the valuable equipment and of cultivating the agricultural fields.

The mill at Recordana was occupied by Baibars in 669/1270, according

---

[5] See Röhricht, *Regesta*, no. 1062, 1235; Hospital, II, no. 2107, Apr. 10, 1235, 483 (Röhricht, *Regesta*, Add., no. 1061a, 1235); Hospital, II, no. 2117, July 25, 1235, 486–487 (Röhricht, *Regesta*, Add., no. 1062, 1235): "Noverint universi . . . quod, cum inter . . . domus milicie Templi . . . et domus Hospitalis . . ., super aqua et molendina fluminis Acconensis, quod descendit ex fonte Recordane, questio verteretur . . . tandem, . . . et concordiam devenerunt: videlicet quod . . . fratres Templi habeant potestatem retinendi aquam, que est supra molendina ipsorum, in tantum quod possit ascendere usque ad signaculum quod est factum in molendinis Hospitalis." Cf. also Hospital, nos. 3026, 3027, 3032, 1262. A document of the year 1250 describes Da'uq as a "place": "Item invenit extra civitatem Accon terras duas comunis . . . in plano, una quarum est sita loco ubi dicitur Dochum, terminis sexdecim terminata, et cui sunt confines soliti dessignati, et multi ex ipsis terminis sunt circumscripti hac litera: Ianua." AOL, IIB, no. 3, 224. Cf. Prawer, 1975, 152 and 454.

Plate 12   Somelaria, view

to Arab sources. But it was still included within the domain of the Crusader Kingdom of Acre in the treaty drawn up in 682/1283 with Qalawun. The fact that the income from it was later on devoted to the mausoleum of Qalawun in Cairo proves that the mills continued to operate after the Franks were expelled from Palestine.[6] It seems that the castle in Daʿuq was damaged by the Muslims but was not completely destroyed. The Muslim forces occupied it and damaged it badly already in 1253. But from the fact that the legal dispute over the castle continued until the 1260s, and from the further fact that the castle is referred to as a village within the Frankish domain in the agreement of 1283, it can be concluded that the mills of Daʿuq continued to function until the last days of the Kingdom.[7]

The Frankish manor house and the suburb in Somelaria Templi (Regba)

Another castle belonging to Templar knights was built in Somelaria Templi during the second half of the thirteenth century. Remains of this castle (plate 12) can be found amongst the ruins of the village Al-Saumariya which is on

[6] About Baibars who camped in the place after the conquest of Montfort, see al-Yunini, II, 453, line 6. Al-Yunini describes the place as "Kurdanah, a village next to Acre." Ibn Taghri Birdi, VII (c), 153, line 12. For the agreement of 1283, see al-Qalqashandi, XIV, 55, line 12; Barag, 1979, no. 28.   [7] Prawer, 1975, 454, n. 11; Barag, 1979, no. 27.

the Acre–Naharia road (near Moshav Regba, grid reference 159/264). We do not know what the agricultural basis of the Frankish castle at Somelaria was, but there is no doubt that it was part of the agricultural hinterland of nearby Acre.

Somelaria is mentioned twice in the written sources from the last days of the second Kingdom. One document, drawn up in the 1270s states that it was issued "In campis Acconis sub tentorio domus Templi juxta ejusdem casale Somelaria."[8]

In one of Pope Nicholaus IV's letters the church which was built there is mentioned: "Ecclesia S. Georgii de la Saumelaria." The fact that there was a church in Somelaria shows that there was a Frankish settlement next to the castle, or that there had been a local Christian settlement there before the castle was built.[9]

The above are only a few examples of castles which were built by the military Orders on agricultural land. It can be assumed that there were many other castles of the same kind and it is only reasonable to conclude that the castle which was discovered in Tell Hannaton or the manor house in Mazra'a in Western Galilee were also built by the military Orders. The fact that the archives of the Templar Order, which owned a great deal of land and property in Western Galilee (the large fortress in Shefar'am, for example), were not preserved prevents us from knowing more about these castles.

These few examples indicate that military Orders in Palestine also established settlements for agricultural purposes. In Casale Doc, Recordana, Bethgibelin, and many other places agriculture was the main pursuit.

---

[8] Röhricht, *Regesta*, no. 1413, July 1272. For a description of the site and a schematic plan, see Mayer, 1964.

[9] Röhricht, *Regesta*, no. 1413, July 1272, n. 1. Prawer (personal communication) suggested that the place was used for beasts of burden of the Templars (sauma, soma, etc.: burden of a beast of burden).

PART IV

THE SPATIAL DISTRIBUTION OF
FRANKISH SETTLEMENT

CHAPTER SEVENTEEN

THE BOUNDARIES OF FRANKISH SETTLEMENT IN WESTERN GALILEE AND SAMARIA

The map of Frankish settlement in the Latin Kingdom, as emerges from the documentary and field survey (Map 1 and appendix), is totally different from that presented by the proponents of the existing model. The Franks created developed castra, unfortified villages, centers of seigniorial estates, manor houses, farm houses, monasteries, abbeys, and many other types of settlement. They constructed new roads and saw to the maintenance of the existing ones. They instituted transport regulations for the rural roads and byways and took care to ensure free movement for the users thereof. They dealt with the marking and apportioning of fields, understood the importance of water in semi-arid zones, built flour mills and bridges, and learnt how to cultivate edible products, such as sugar cane, with which they had not been familiar in their countries of origin. I attach great importance also to the collection of tithes in kind and not only in coin – a fact which necessitated the construction of storerooms and a network of rural roads, and the acquisition of greater expertise concerning seasonal cultivation and the quality of crops. In short, this rural settlement was exploited by a comparatively well-developed system of rural adminstration.

The boundaries of Frankish settlement in Galilee

A careful examination of map 1 reveals the existence of regional differentiation in the spatial distribution of Frankish settlements. The Franks settled only in some of the regions while they refrained from settling in others. In the western part of Galilee, for example, there is a comparatively large number of Frankish rural sites, whereas in the eastern part of the same region, east of the imaginary line joining the villages of Fassuta and Tarshiha, there is not a single Frankish rural site (save for the large fortresses built in Safad and at Vadum Jacob in the 1160s and 1170s). There is also no evidence of the collection of tithes or of any other adminstrative activities on the part of the Frankish regime. Furthermore, there are very few Latin documents containing references to settlements east of this line. In contrast, in Western Galilee there was intensive settlement activity, the traces of which can be found in tens of documents and in tens of archeological sites.

The paucity of references to Eastern Galilee in Latin documents may be accidental. Zvi Razi, who was the first to notice this phenomenon, suggested two reasons for it. (1) Since the Safad fortress was in the hands of the Templars, it is possible that the whole region was under this Order's jurisdiction already in the twelfth century. The documents dealing with the region were destroyed, he assumes, together with the rest of their archives. (2) Alternatively, Razi suggests, the villages of Eastern Galilee were the private domain of the prince of the Galilee and not many transactions were conducted there. In the absence of such transactions, he claims, no documents dealing with transfer of ownership were signed, which provides at least one reason for the "silence of the sources." In other words, Razi sees no real difference between the distribution of the settlement in Eastern Galilee and that of the West.[1] He was aware of the difficulties inherent in both his explanations since he dealt at great length with the fact that the fortress of Safad was given to the Templars only in 1168, and the princes of the Galilee could have, had they wished, transferred land and castles to ecclesiastical bodies before then. Razi agrees that there is no explanation for the absence of any evidence concerning the region till that date. Razi also refrains from maintaining that the whole of Eastern Galilee was given to the Templars, together with Safad, already in 1168.[2]

---

[1] Razi, 1970, 234–235, n. 169.

[2] It would appear that Safad at the beginning of the twelfth century was no more than a "tower" erected already in the early Muslim period. Ibn Shaddad writes: "It [Safad] was at the beginning a hill (tel) and on the hill was á flourishing village beneath Burj al-Yatim. It was in the hands of the Muslims until the Franks captured it after they occupied Syria, in the year 495/1101–2. The Templars built it." He adds that "nothing is mentioned about it in the early Islamic history books." Ibn Shaddad, 146; Cf. Ibn al-Furat, trans. Lyons, I, 112; II, 88. Van-Berchem was aware of the fact that the fortress was not in the hands of the Templars at the beginning of the twelfth century. Ibn Shaddad, he said, who wrote his book at the end of the 1280s and was still under the influence of the slaughter of the Templars, thought that the place had been erected by them already at the beginning of the twelfth century. Van-Berchem, 1902, 413–415. The place is mentioned also in Röhricht, *Regesta*, no. 39, 1103, as Turon Saphet and not as a fortress. In the course of the twelfth century a burgus was apparently established beneath the "tower," as William of Tyre calls the place a "castrum" in 1157. William of Tyre, 18, 14, 830. In 1168 Amalric I bought the castrum of Safad from Fulco, the constable of Tiberias, and transferred it to the Templars (Röhricht, *Regesta*, No. 447, 1168), and during the same year the fortress of Safad, regarded as "the limit of the country," was reinforced, and was transferred to the Templars. The reinforcement resulted from the shaky security situation of the Kingdom, after the failure of the Crusade to Egypt and the capture of Baniyas and Château Neuf by Nur al-Din. Jacques de Vitry tells of the refortification, Jacques de Vitry, ed. Bongars, 1074 (chapter 48). Cf. also Yaqut, III, 399; al-ʿUmari, 134, and al-ʿUthmani, ed. B. Lewis, 1954, 480; Favreau-Lilie, 1980. I would like to thank R. Amitai for some of the references cited here.

The second explanation given by Razi also gives rise to difficulties. As discussed previously, many documents which deal explicitly with the royal domain were preserved, as were documents dealing with the seigniorial domains. It is difficult, therefore, to claim that only a few documents referring to the domain of the principality of the Galilee were preserved. Furthermore, the absence of any Frankish rural settlement in Eastern Galilee cannot be ascribed to a lack of general information and documentation. We are well acquainted with Eastern Upper Galilee, which has been studied archeologically time and again, without any site of possibly Frankish rural nature being discovered. The fact that in Eastern Galilee, east of Fassuta and Dayr al-Asad (St. George de La Baena), there is no sign of Crusader settlement indicates that the paucity of documents dealing with Eastern Galilee is not only due to differential preservation. It would appear that the "information line" based on Latin sources is congruent with the "eastern line of Frankish settlement." This similarity cannot be ascribed, in my opinion, to chance or to technical circumstances only.

Razi bases his two alternative explanations on an extract from the text which describes the enterprises of Bishop Benoît of Marseille in the Holy Land. According to this biography, Benoît was involved in the construction of the Templar fortress in Safad. The text was written after his second visit to Safad, between the years 1261–5. His biographer claims that during his second visit, apparently at the end of 1264, about 260 villages were counted within the district and jurisdiction of the fortress of Safad. "Habet etiam castrum Saphet sub dominio et districtu suo casalia, que in Gallico ville dicuntur, plusquam CCLX, in quibus manent plusquam X milia hominum cum arcubus et sagittis."[3]

The exact number (not "hundreds" and not "many villages," but "more than 260 villages") bolsters Benoît's reliability and provides an explanation for Razi's attempts to find technical reasons for the lack of references to this region. The fact that Benoît could receive this detail from the castellan of Safad, or even from the Master of the Temple, adds still further to his credibility. And yet this number seems surprising. At no time in history, not during the Byzantine period nor during later periods, were there so many populated sites in Eastern Galilee. During the Byzantine period the number of settlements in Eastern Galilee was 59, according to the results of a comprehensive archeological survey carried out there.[4] The number of settlements during the Frankish period was certainly less. Is it possible that the anonymous biographer of Benoît simply invented the figure of 260?

The solution lies, apparently, in Benoît's estimate of the function and

---

[3] *De constructione Castri Saphet*, 43, lines 258–260.
[4] M. Aviam, personal communication.

importance of Safad as the main, and perhaps the only, source of defense for the entire Galilee. Benoît, who regarded himself as the moving spirit behind the construction of the fortress, repeatedly describes the changes which occurred in the Galilee after its construction. The whole of the Galilee was, in his eyes, the property of the fortress whose construction he had so passionately advocated, even though there was no factual or legal justification for this opinion. The number 260 could, therefore, have referred to all the settlements in the whole of the Galilee.

Corroboration of this conclusion can be found, in my opinion, in the Turkish tax registers of the sixteenth century. According to these registers, no more than 287 villages were counted in the Sanjak of Safad (this maximum figure appears in the census for the year 1547–8).This figure includes all the villages in the Nahia of Jira (which today would be Eastern Galilee and part of Southern Lebanon), in the Nahia of Acre (which is Western Upper Galilee), Tiberias (which includes the whole of Lower Galilee), Tibnin, and Shakif Arnun. The number is slightly larger if we count the maximum figures in each census:[5]

In the Jira, in the census of 1525–6	56 villages
In the Nahia of Acre, in the census of 1555–6	62 villages
In the Nahia of Tiberias, in the census of 1547–8	55 villages
In the Nahia of Tibnin, in the census of 1547–8	81 villages
In the Nahia of Shakif, in the census of 1547–8	39 villages

The maximum total of villages in what is present-day Israeli and Lebanese Galilee (including the Lower Galilee and the valleys of Bethsan and Jezreel) did not exceed 293 villages, which were populated at least during part of the sixteenth century. The numbers in each census were lower, and even nearer to the figure of 260 mentioned in Benoît's treatise. The proximity between the number of villages according to Benoît and the number of populated villages in the Galilee at the end of the Mamluk period (at which time settlement in Eastern Galilee was flourishing) gives credence to my assumption that Benoît included all the villages of the Galilee in his figure of 260 and not only the villages at the foot of the fortress.

It can therefore be concluded that the region of Safad was not blessed with an exceptional burst of settlement during the Frankish period, as Razi assumed. The assessment in Benoît's biography of 260 villages in the whole of the Galilee (according to my interpretation) would appear to be credible. This explanation makes the second figure quoted by the unknown biogra-

[5] Rhode, 1987, 179–218.

pher also more credible. He maintained that in the whole of the Galilee (this too according to my interpretation) there were more than 10,000 fighting men ("armed with bows and arrows"). It is difficult to decide whether the reference here is to Frankish settlers or to local Christians who participated in the Frankish military organization. In any event, the text refers explicitly to the residents of the rural areas only and does not include the Franks who lived in Acre. If we rely on this source then we must conclude that in the rural areas of the Galilee there were at least 50,000 Christian inhabitants who had been absorbed into the Frankish network and protected it (in view of the fact that the reference is to 10,000 fighting men, the multiplication by five seems reasonable).

The state of security in Eastern Galilee in the twelfth and thirteenth centuries

From the Hebrew and Latin sources dealing with the eastern part of the Galilee, one can learn that it contained a mixed population of Jews and Muslims who were harassed by nomads and criminal elements. The only two detailed and explicit Latin descriptions of the population of Eastern Galilee refer to a wild and insecure locality ruled by bands of nomads and highwaymen. William of Tyre describes an event which occurred when the fortress of Vadum Jacob was under construction (at the end of 1178 and the beginning of 1179).[6] According to his description, the king succeeded in repelling a band of robbers who had terrorized the inhabitants of Eastern Galilee. The reference is to robbers from Bucael (modern Peqi'in). William also provides a description of the place: a place in Zebulun, at the top of a mountain, well irrigated and thickly planted with fruit trees. The robbers who had taken over the place are described as bold and daring fighters who joined forces with other fugitives from the law. They were engaged in highway robbery and subjugated all the inhabitants of the region. They carried on their activities for a long time without any interference and were hated by the local inhabitants, Christian and Muslim alike. Their domination of Eastern Galilee was cut short when the king attacked them suddenly and occupied the village, killing all those who remained there. Most of the robbers, according to William of Tyre, escaped and fled to Damascus from where they continued regular attacks against the Franks.[7] Eastern Galilee is described as a place which was not subject to Frankish law. The seigniorial government (if there was in fact such, since William of Tyre does not mention any seignior or representative of the king whose task it was to restore order to

[6] William of Tyre, 21, 25 (26), 997–998, lines 35–70.
[7] William of Tyre, 21, 25 (26), 997–998, lines 35–70.

the region) had not succeeded in subjugating the robbers, and it was left to the king to put an end to their reign of terror. There is no doubt that the reference is to robbers and lawless elements of the Muslim faith, as they were supported by Damascus.

In the description of the second journey of Benoît, eighty-five years later, a similar unruly state of affairs in Eastern Galilee is depicted, until the construction of the fortress of Safad in 1240–1. The region is described as being terrorized by nomads who robbed travelers up to the city of Acre itself. "Quantum autem necessarium et utile sit castrum Saphet toti terre christian-orum et infidelibus quantum nocivum, scire possunt per experientiam qui noverunt quod ante edificationem dicti castri Sarraceni, Biduini, Coramini et Turcomani faciebant insultus frequenter usque Accon et per terram aliam christianorum."[8]

The construction of the fortress improved the security situation both for travelers and for farmers between the Jordan and Acre, and in particular between Acre and Safad. "Sed edificato castro Saphet positum est repugnac-ulum et obstaculum ne ad nocendum publice transire audeant a flumine Iordanis usque Accon, nisi esset maxima multitudo, et ab Accon usque Saphet vadunt secure honerati saumarii et quadrige, et agricultura et terre colonia libere ab omnibus exercetur."[9]

According to this description, the robbers' activities affected all the inhab-itants of the region between Damascus and Acre. The construction of the fortress served as protection for the Frankish territory and as a base for the attacks which the Templars of Saphet launched against Damascus. "A flumine vero Iordanis usque Damascum remanet terra inculta et quasi vasta propter metum castri Saphet."[10]

From this fact, one can learn that the reference is not to "guerrilla units" organized by Ayyubid Damascus, as the invaders continued to attack and terrorize territory under Ayyubid rule.

The earlier description – that of William of Tyre – depicts a situation in which local lawless elements or the heads of nomadic tribes succeeded in establishing their own autonomous enclaves in the center of the Galilee over a long period of time and in completely ignoring the central Frankish govern-ment. It is possible that this description even includes the beginning of the Druze incursion into central Galilee and the Golan. It should be noted also that Benoît mentions as a source of insecurity the attacks by nomads such as the Turkomans, the Coramini (probably the Khwarizmians), and the Beduins.

---

[8] *De constructione Castri Saphet*, 42–43, lines 243–247.
[9] *De constructione Castri Saphet*, 43, lines 247–251.
[10] *De constructione Castri Saphet*, 43, lines 251–252.

What is unique about both these descriptions is that they refer to events which occurred at a comparatively late period. Similar descriptions of harassment on the part of nomads and highwaymen in other parts of the country appear in Latin sources.[11] However, these harassments were stopped already in the early years of the Frankish Kingdom. It would appear that Eastern Galilee did not come within the bounds of the territory whose inhabitants were secure.

The composition of the local population in Eastern Galilee

The text refers several times to the composition of the local population in Eastern Galilee. At first, it maintains that the encampment of the Templars, who built the fortress, was situated in a place where there were both a Muslim mosque and a Jewish synagogue; later, it claims that until the construction of the fortress the Christians were not able to pray freely to Jesus.[12] The description includes components which can be interpreted as polemical, making it difficult to accept it literally. The writer describes the construction of the fortress in Safad as though it were a victory for Christianity over the Muslim world. However, the mere fact that Benoît refers also to a Jewish synagogue next to a Muslim mosque indicates that he was aware of the religious practices of the inhabitants of Eastern Galilee and of the connection which existed then between Jewish and Muslim religious practices. Elhanan Reiner, who studied the medieval Jewish pilgrimage to Palestine, summed up the connection between Jewish and Muslim holy places in the Galilee as follows:

A good many of the Jewish holy places . . . were sacred to the non-Jewish population too . . . Furthermore, it would appear that most of the holy places mentioned in Jewish itineraries . . . were held by Muslims and the Jews participated only partly in their rites, just as the Muslims participated only partly in the rites of the holy places held by the Jews.[13]

The important role played by the nomads in Eastern Galilee need not surprise us. In the Golan, in Hawran and in the Jordan Valley tribes of nomads lived for many centuries side by side with the sedentary population. When the central government succeeded in restraining the nomads the sedentary communities and the nomadic ones balanced each other out. This happened, for example, during the Roman and Byzantine periods, when those regions were heavily populated and the sedentary population flourished, although there

---

[11] See Chapter 2, n. 18. See also William of Tyre, 14, 8, 639–640.
[12] *De constructione Castri Saphet*, 38, lines 125–6; 43–44. [13] Reiner, 1988, 252–3.

were also an appreciable number of nomads. When the central rule was weak, the strength of the nomads increased and the sedentary regions went through a process of nomadization. The decline in the power of the central government during the early Muslim period undoubtedly contributed to this process. The large centers of Hawran which were established from the beginning on the important crossroads continued to exist; however, the rural and agricultural settlements were abandoned and were not resettled, because of harassment by the nomads, until the second half of the nineteenth century.[14]

The process of prolonged nomadization can be seen, inter alia, in the rare state of preservation of Byzantine buildings in villages at the edge of Hawran and in the state of preservation of medieval fortresses constructed at the borders of the desert. This preservation of dwellings was possible, in my opinion, only in areas which, after their initial abandonment, ceased to be populated by sedentary communities almost until modern times. Permanent occupants are the ones who destroy early buildings by converting them into "quarries." Nomads, on the other hand, rarely damaged the stone houses which served them as temporary shelter.

It seems that the Franks refrained, as much as possible, from engaging in military confrontations with the nomadic tribes, who lived in the territory northeast of the Kingdom of Jerusalem. However, when such confrontations did occur, they happened in territory outside the boundaries of the Kingdom. Some of the tribes established good relations with the Frankish regime, and they were allowed to live in the peripheral regions of the Kingdom and their territorial control over such regions was officially recognized. We know, for example, about the existence of 100 tents of Beduin who lived near Belvoir.[15]

It is important to remember that the struggle between a central regime and nomadic tribes differs fundamentally from the struggle waged by a central government against a regular external enemy. In contradistinction to attacks by the regular armies, the nomadic threat is constant and prolonged. The nomads, as was their custom throughout history, waited for signs of weakness on the part of the central government before attacking settlements on the periphery. In addition, they did not require a complicated logistic set-up, and their sorties were immediate and damaging. In certain instances, nomadic tribes even succeeded in defeating regular Frankish armies, and in others the central regime in Damascus utilized the forces of nomadic tribes in order to attack the Frankish settlements.

[14] See, for example, Peters, 1979, 315–326; Sartre, 1982, 77–91; Lewis, 1987.
[15] Hospital, no. 582, Apr. 28, 1180, 395–396.

The immediate proximity of these nomads is the reason, in my opinion, why the Franks refrained from settling the Eastern Upper Galilee. The nomads were not capable of inflicting permanent defeat on the Franks; however, they were capable, in accordance with the testimony of William of Tyre and the biographer of Benoît, of causing a feeling of unrest and insecurity and of harassing the population in the permanent settlements. The danger in this region did not emanate, according to my assumption, from the regular armies of Damascus, as the Franks had displayed obvious military superiority until the middle of the 1160s, but it was impossible to remove the threat of the nomads by a one-time military operation. The occupation of the territory, or even the levying of taxes, could have been effective as long as there was a Frankish presence in the area. However, the Franks were incapable of ensuring their permanent presence in the territory east of the Jordan Valley. This was, I believe, the explanation also for the surprisingly great number of military operations which the Franks carried out in Hawran and the Golan during the first half of the twelfth century. Many of these operations were directed against the nomads and not against the central government of Damascus.[16] The Jews who lived in Eastern Galilee joined the nomads or other Muslim forces when possible.[17]

In order to support my theory, I shall give another example, this time from Samaria, of what was, in my opinion, another internal limit for Frankish settlement. I shall try to argue that there too the borderline of Frankish settlement can be tied to the processes of both nomadization of the territory and sedentarization of the Muslim nomads.

[16] The control of the nomadic tribes over the territory east of the Jordan Valley was recognized in the second agreement between the ruler of Damascus and the king of Jerusalem concerning the division of power in the Golan, in 1118. In the agreement two new areas, not mentioned in the first agreement, were defined: al-Jabaniya and al-Jarah. See Sibt Ibn al-Jauzi, ed. *RHC*, 541. In 1118 there was a battle of the Franks against the Beduin tribes of Banu-Halid and the Banu Rabi'a south of the Yarmuk. The Beduin succeeded in defeating a large Frankish army consisting of a cavalry of 200 and eventually surrendered to Baldwin II, to whom they undertook to pay 4,000 bezants, apparently also as compensation for the Crusaders' loss of life. Ibn al-Athir, ed. *RHC*, IV-1, 325–326; Albert of Aachen, 710–712. In 1121 Damascus constructed a fortress at Gerasa. A year later they set out to take control of the Golan and were supported by the local Beduins. See Fulcher of Chartres, 643–645; William of Tyre, 12, 15, 565–566; Ibn al-Athir, ed. *RHC*, IV-1, 344–345; Sibt Ibn al-Jauzi, ed. *RHC*, 562. See also Fulcher of Chartres, III, 50, 793–794, lines 1–15; William of Tyre, 13, 18, 608–609; Ibn al-Qalanisi, trans. Gibb, 289–290; Abu Shama, ed. *RHC*, IV, 57; William of Tyre, 21, 26 (27), 999; Hospital, no. 582, Apr. 28, 1180, 395–396.

[17] For a full discussion of this point, see Kedar, 1984a. Cf. *Gesta Regis Henrici secundi*, II, 93; Roger of Howden, III, 20.

CHAPTER EIGHTEEN

THE SPATIAL DISTRIBUTION OF FRANKISH SETTLEMENT NORTH OF JERUSALEM

Like similar settlements in other parts of Palestine, the network of Frankish settlement north of Jerusalem included developed castra and castella, various suburbs, administrative centers of seigniorial estates, parish churches, and dozens of farm houses. It would appear that settlement in the central hilly regions was more developed than that which can be reconstructed in Western Galilee. From a comparative study of the few settlement regulations which have been preserved it transpires that the rights granted to the settlers in the region of Parva Mahomeria were inferior to those granted to the settlers in Western Galilee. From this it can be assumed that it was not very difficult to attract settlers to this region. An expression to the density of population in this region was given in a text describing Salah al-Din's conquest. The text refers to the "castella et villulas Francorum" which were in the hill region. Another document, referred to above, testifies to the fact that in the region of Jerusalem there was no land for sale.[1]

Traces of well-developed Frankish rural settlement can be found also in the roads which they constructed. The road to Jerusalem, for example, was apparently built by the Franks themselves, and there is no evidence concerning the use that was made of it before the First Crusade (fig. 19). The Franks also took care of its maintenance and placed road accessories alongside it. The continuous maintenance of the roads testifies to the Frankish government's far-sighted attitude towards them. Building a road demands a great one-time effort; but the upkeep and maintenance of a road, on the other hand, requires the permanent investment of material and manpower which indicates that this was one of the duties of the seigniorial lord.

Centers of secondary economic activity, such as the sale of oil in Parva Mahomeria, were also developed in the region. Evidence can be found, in

---

[1] De expugnatione, 233; Hospital, no. 309, 1163–1169, 222.

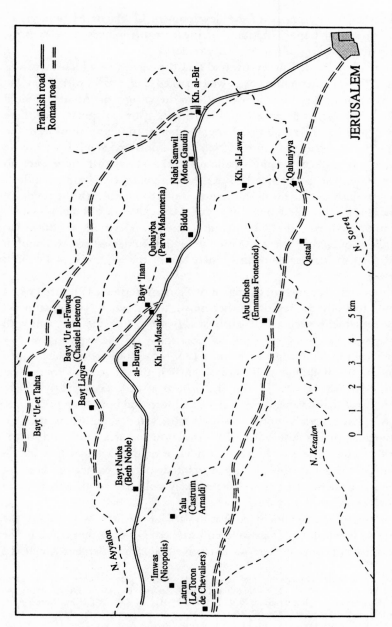

Figure 19 The Frankish road from Lydda to Jerusalem

the names of the burgesses, of the development in Magna Mahomeria of various agricultural specializations, in the care of animals, in carpentry, building, forgeing, and other necessary trades.

In the course of my survey I found that the region in which there was intensive Frankish settlement was well marked and was bordered on the north by an imaginary line, drawn between the villages of 'Abud and Sinjil and Kh. Istuna (grid reference 180/159). South of this imaginary line there was an area of dense Frankish settlement, whereas to the north of it, in the region of Central Samaria south of Nablus and north of Sinjil, I was unable to find any remains of Frankish buildings and it seems that there were no such settlements at all (see map 1). But the unequivocal conclusion that there was no Frankish settlement in this region is not based only on the results of my field study. I also failed to find any hint of the existence of Frankish settlements in the written sources. Nor could I find any references whatsoever to gifts of plots of land or houses, to the marking of landed estates, to Frankish names given to local settlements, which hint at the existence of Frankish settlement.

Written evidence for the existence of Frankish settlement returns when we come to study the region further north, near Nablus. The documents refer to settlements such as Aschar, Balata, Betheri, and Cafarcos, and with them appear archeological findings consisting of the remains of the Frankish ruin in Yanun (grid reference 183/173) southeast of Nablus, and remains of the buildings in Rafidiya, Junayd, the flour mill house near Nablus, Bayt Wazan, Kh. Shaykh Sha'al (near al-Nakura), Sabastiyya, Kh. Babriya near Sabastiyya which are all located west and northwest of Nablus. But, as I have already noted, there is no evidence, either written or archeological, of Frankish villages and castles in the area south and southwest of Nablus. There is, however, evidence of the fact that part of the tithes from villages in this area were granted to ecclesiastical bodies, but there is no evidence that they were actually collected or that there were parochial churches in the area.[2]

It can, therefore, be concluded that in parts of Samaria, as in parts of the Galilee, no Frankish buildings were constructed. On the other hand, in the southern part of Samaria there was intensive Frankish settlement which was

---

[2] The tithes of Burin, Caphastrum, Gul, and Gerable were given to the church of Mt. Zion. Röhricht, *Regesta*, no. 576, 1179. The tithes of Luban, Ruezun, Gerraa, and Derach were given to the Chapter of Templum Domini. *ROL*, 8, (1900–1901), 312–316 (Röhricht, *Regesta*, Add., no. 422a, 1166). The tithes of Gemail, Assir, and Beithbezim were given to the abbey of St. Mary Josaphat. Röhricht, *Regesta*, no. 101, 1123; Röhricht, *Regesta*, Add., no. 129a, 1129; *ROL*, 7, (1899), no. 17, 125–127. For Casale Esckas see Röhricht, *Regesta*, no. 1122, 1244. For the villages of Azatil, Eincheitem (Eiucheilem), and Eincanephis, see Beyer, 1940, 186 n. 13.

bordered by the Sinjil–ʿAbud imaginary line. Beyond this border not a single Frankish agricultural settlement was found.

The cultural border in Central Samaria

The two borders mentioned above – the Frankish settlement borders in the Galilee and Samaria – were not created in the Frankish period. Cultural borders existed in the same places during the Byzantine period, and perhaps even earlier.

One can learn about the Byzantine cultural borders from four of the maps in this book. In maps 2 and 3, I have attempted to reconstruct the spatial distribution of the three religions which existed in Palestine on the eve of the Arab conquest, that is, at the end of the sixth century. Map 2 shows the sites of sixth-century Jewish synagogues and Christian churches. The map was brought up to date on the basis of recent research and excavations which have not as yet been published.

Map 3 depicts the distribution of Samaritan sites. The map was prepared according to data collected by Conder and later revised by Ben-Zvi. These data, too, were brought up to date on the basis of new findings discovered in archeological excavations and studies conducted in recent years.[3]

The Samaritans rebelled again and again against the Christian Byzantine authorities. The last rebellion occurred about forty years before the Muslim conquest. The Byzantines suppressed the revolts with terrible bloodshed, leaving behind them a devastated country. The whole region of Samaria was almost totally deserted. For this reason I decided to show Samaritan settlement as it looked in the fifth century, and the beginning of the sixth century, rather than at the beginning of the Muslim conquest.[4]

Map 4 is a toponymic map illustrating the distribution of villages in Samaria with the name "Dayr" ("monastery" in Arabic).

Maps 2 and 3 show quite clearly that during the fifth and sixth century AD the country was divided between various religious groups, each dominating its own region. Different religious communities did not intermingle, at least not in the rural areas. Mixed communities existed only in the commercial centers, such as the episcopal cities of Caesarea Maritima, Scythopolis, Acre, and so on.

The Galilee was divided into a Western Christian region and an Eastern

---

[3] Conder, 1876, 182–197; Montgomery, 1907; Ben-Zvi, 1970, 63 (map A); 99 (map B); Mayer, 1956, 252–253; Safrai, 1977, 84–112; Barkay, 1987, 6–18.
[4] See Avi-Yonah, 1956; Avi-Yonah, 1973.

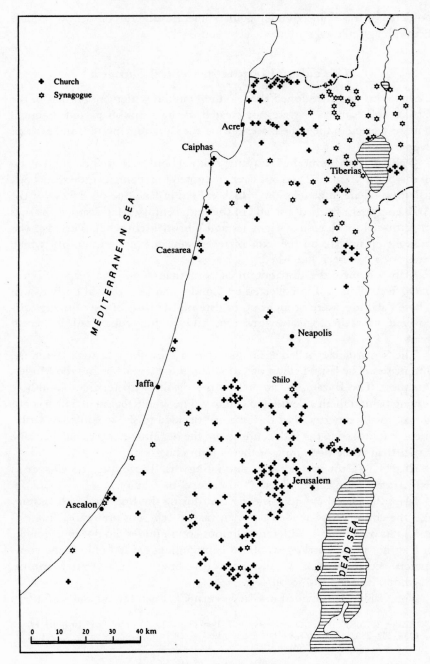

Map 2   Byzantine churches and synagogues in Palestine
The northern part of the map is based on information given by Mr. Mordechai Aviam
of the Israel Antiquities Authority. The southern part of the map is based mainly on
Ovadiah, 1976.

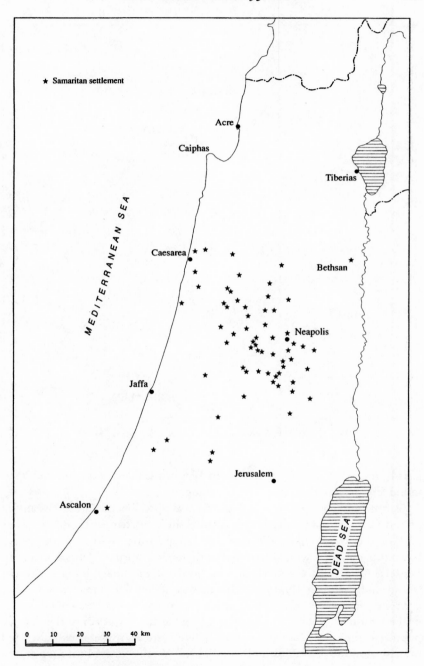

Map 3   Samaritan sites of the Byzantine period in Palestine

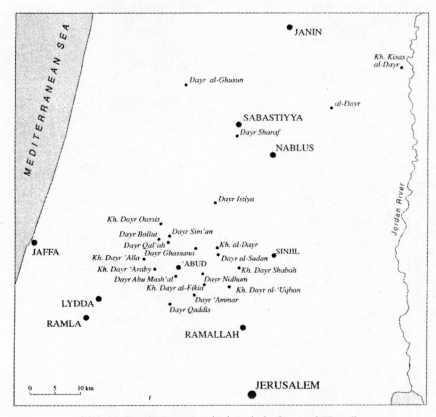

Map 4   Sites in Samaria which include the word "Dayr"

Jewish one. Map 2 shows it clearly: in Western Galilee only churches were found and in Eastern Galilee only synagogues.

As can be seen from map 1, Samaria was also divided in the Byzantine period by a cultural border which divided the Christian Orthodox population in the south, from the Samaritan population in the north. Many Byzantine churches were discovered in the region north of Jerusalem and in Western Galilee. In Central Samaria, north of the line joining Sinjil and 'Abud, not even one Byzantine church was discovered. There was another concentration of Byzantine churches, as can be seen on the map of churches, in the region of Nablus – Sabastiyya, as well as further north in the densely populated region of North Samaria. There were also several churches and monasteries east of Nablus, in the 'Aqraba – Yanun – Bayt Furiq region. In those parts of Samaria in which there were no churches there was a dense Samaritan population during Roman and Byzantine times. This population was hostile to the Christian inhabitants and to their Byzantine rulers. No churches were built in these areas because there were no Christian communities living there.

One can learn about the cultural border in Samaria also from map 4, which, as I have already noted, depicts the distribution of villages in whose names appears the Arabic word "Dayr" (monastery). It appears that most of the villages in Samaria, in whose names the presence of a Byzantine monastery was preserved, were on this line and south of it. There are practically no villages and ruins whose names begin with the word "Dayr" in the Central Samaritan region. It can be assumed that at least some of the monasteries were built on the interfaith boundary for missionary purposes amongst the Samaritans and in order to fix the territorial borders with them. This assumption is strengthened by a comparison with the functions performed by the monasteries near the interfaith borders in Europe in the early Middle Ages and later.

To the best of my knowledge there are practically no studies which deal with monasteries on the interreligion frontiers of Byzantine Palestine, or with other non-desert monasteries, and there are certainly no theoretical discussions of their functions. But the absence of research need not divert us, as from a glance at the spatial distribution of the word "Dayr" in Palestine one receives the impression that the number of villages within the inhabited part of the country which have preserved the existence of Byzantine monasteries in their names is much larger than the number of desert monasteries which have been studied over and over again. Furthermore, the archeological remains of some of these monasteries testify to the fact that the construction of many of them was the result of central planning by the provincial administration or even by the imperial government. I cannot believe that the vast expense involved in building monasteries of the nature of those in Dayr Qal'ah (see plate 13), Dayr Sam'an, or Dayr Abu Mash'al could have been borne without the financial and technical assistance of the central administration. These monasteries, in my opinion, are a fascinating and unexplored expression of the ethnic struggle between the Samaritan community and the Byzantine rulers during the fifth and sixth centuries.

The correlation between the Frankish borderline and the Byzantine borderline is clear: the Sinjil–'Abud line which was, during Byzantine times, the northern line of dispersion of the Christian community was also the northern borderline of Frankish settlement during the Frankish period.

Plate 13   Byzantine monastery of Dayr Qal'ah

The Galilee borderline in the Byzantine period

In the Galilee, during the Byzantine period, there was also a clear border-line, west of which only churches were constructed, and east of which only synagogues. According to the findings of Mordechai Aviam this line too was marked by Byzantine monasteries. Aviam maintains that the Byzantine monasteries in the Galilee were constructed mainly on the frontier which separated the Byzantine-Christian population from the Jewish one.[5]

[5] The Galilean borderline is investigated by Mr. M. Aviam of the Israeli Antiquities Authority. I would like to thank him for the archeological data which he provided me.

Although we have very little written information concerning the size and distribution of Christian settlement in the Galilee during the Byzantine period, we do have a great deal of information about the distribution of Jewish settlement during the same period and the historical sources which describe the Jewish activity in Galilee in the Roman and Byzantine periods confirm the existence of the Galilean frontier. On the basis of this information we know that Jewish settlement existed only in the eastern part of Upper Galilee.[6] This frontier continued to exist during the Frankish period when it became also the eastern border of rural Frankish settlement.

The fact that both in Samaria and the Galilee there were, during the Byzantine period, cultural frontiers which separated the distinctly Christian regions from the hostile cultural (Samaritan in Samaria and Jewish in Eastern Galilee) regions, and the fact that in the two areas these frontiers continued to exist in Frankish times, cannot, in my opinion, be coincidental. In order to prove that there was not a rare combination of chance here, one would have to show that the reasons which led to the existence of the cultural borderline during the Byzantine period continued to exist during the Frankish period. In other words: one would have to show that during the Frankish period, too, the division was a cultural one and not a deterministic, ecological one which influenced the nature of the settlement. And if it was a cultural one, one would have to find an explanation for the fact that despite the deep cultural changes which occurred in these regions between the sixth and the twelfth century, the frontiers continued to exist.

Cultural frontiers in the Latin Kingdom

Hans E. Mayer summed up the attitude of the Latin sources to the Muslim inhabitants of the Kingdom as follows: "If I am not mistaken, the Muslim inhabitants of the Latin Kingdom hardly ever appear in the Latin chronicles. 'Saracens' are very often mentioned, and almost invariably the term refers to the Muslims outside the Kingdom, to the enemy attacking, winning or losing battles." Mayer suggested two explanations for this strange phenomenon: "The Muslims living within the confines of the Latin Kingdom could safely be ignored (a) because normally they were not much of a problem, and (b) they hardly ever appear to have acted politically in the broadest sense of the word, either in helping or in damaging the interests of the ruling Latins."[7]

The two alternative explanations of Mayer are not consistent with the

---

[6] Klein, *Sefer Ha-yishuv*, map and index.   [7] Mayer, 1978, 175.

common model that the Franks refrained from settling in rural areas because they were afraid of the local Muslim population. Nevertheless we do have evidence from which it transpires that the relations between the Muslim inhabitants and the Frankish conquerors were not always untroubled. At least in two incidents the Frankish rulers maltreated the Muslim inhabitants, who retaliated with active resistance (in the case of the Muslims of Transjordan) or with passive resistance (in the form of flight, in the case of Samaria). One of these instances, echoes of which appear only in the Arabic sources, concerned the Muslim rural inhabitants of the region north of the Frankish settlement borderline in Samaria.[8]

Kedar, who studied the status of the Muslims under Frankish rule, suggested a new explanation for the distribution of Muslim and Christian settlements.[9] Kedar shows that even in the absence of a great deal of data we can identify the regions in which local inhabitants, Christian or Muslim, lived. We can establish, for example, that in the region of Nablus there was already in the twelfth century a Muslim majority, and that in the region of Jerusalem there was still a substantial minority, or even a majority, of local Christians. In other words, Kedar claims that regional manifestations of Islamization do not apply only to the large geographic units (such as Anatolia, North Syria, Egypt, etc.) and that non-uniform distribution of the Christian and Muslim populations can be discerned also in the small geographic units. With the aid of this regional approach Kedar succeeded in reconciling the apparent incompatibility between the statements of the Muslim scholar Ibn al-ʿArabi, who spent several years in Palestine and maintained that in approximately 1095 the country was still "theirs" (the Christians') as they "work its soil, nurture its monasteries and maintain its churches," and those of Ibn Jubayr and Usama Ibn al-Munkidh, from which it follows that the majority of inhabitants in the rural areas of Palestine were Muslim.[10] According to Kedar's approach both Ibn al-ʿArabi and Ibn Jubayr described a demographic reality: one referred to the Christian region near to Jerusalem and the other to the Muslim region near to Acre.

In the following pages I shall expand on the argument that I expounded above, in accordance with which the Franks settled in mixed Franco-local Christian villages, and I shall try to show that they settled mainly, and perhaps exclusively, in those regions in which there was a large local Christian population, and perhaps even a local Christian majority. The Franks did not

---

[8] For the rebellion of the Muslims in Transjordan, see William of Tyre, 16, 6, 721–722. For Samaria, see Drory, 1988, 93–112.   [9] Kedar, 1990a, 135–174.
[10] Regarding Ibn al-ʿArabi's comments, see Gil, 1992, [276], 171; Ibn al-ʿArabi, *Rihla*, 81. Cf. Kedar, 1990.

settle in regions in which there was a majority of non-Christian inhabitants. According to this claim the borderlines of Frankish settlement in Samaria and the Galilee were the eastern and northern borderlines of Christian settlement, both in the Byzantine and the Crusader periods. I shall also try to find an explanation for the fact that the regions which were populated during the Byzantine period by Samaritans or Jews went through a more rapid stage of Arabization and Islamization than the regions in Western Galilee and north of Jerusalem which were populated during the same period by local Christians.

This claim is consistent with the approach adopted by Mayer that the Franks hardly referred, in their written documents, to their Muslim subjects, and with Kedar's approach that the Muslims did not constitute a majority in all parts of the Kingdom. The Franks did not refer to the Muslim population because they did not settle among them. Or, in other words: the Franks settled only amongst their fellow-Christians.

CHAPTER NINETEEN

SPATIAL DISTRIBUTION OF CHRISTIAN AND MUSLIM SETTLEMENTS IN SAMARIA

In the absence of reliable statistics it is difficult to establish whether any particular region was populated by Christians or Muslims during the Middle Ages. One cannot, in general, rely on the accounts of the chronicles and on itineraries which were most probably influenced by ideological considerations and personal preferences, and no other data is available. Kedar's hypothesis that there was a large Christian community around Jerusalem during the Frankish period, and that in Samaria there was a Muslim population, is based both on the evidence of chroniclers and on other unconnected documents.[1]

In the following pages I shall bring evidence about the religion of specific inhabitants who lived in villages north of Jerusalem during the Frankish period. This list should provide corroboration of two additional claims: (a) that the border between the medieval Muslim and Christian communities passed through the Sinjil–'Abud line and was, therefore, identical with the northern border of Frankish settlement; and (b) that in the region of Nablus, where there were Christian communities during the same period, there were also Frankish settlements.

The list includes villages whose residents were, to the best of our knowledge, either Christians or Muslims, and references to isolated individuals in some of the villages. This fragmented evidence is of limited value per se, but existence of a Muslim or Christian community in a certain village can have regional significance if it can be shown that in neighboring villages there were similar communities. I added to the list of Christian villages those villages which had a substantial Christian population in the sixteenth century and in which there was still a semblance of Christianity in 1667 and 1838.[2] The list includes also villages in which the decisive majority of the population was Christian according to the British census of 1922.[3] The inclusion

[1] Kedar, 1990.   [2] Charon (=Korolerskij), 1911; Anthymus, 1838, 490–495.
[3] Cf. Barron, 1923.

234

of these villages is based on the assumption that if a village of the Byzantine period had a Christian majority at the beginning of the Ottoman period, in 1838 and at the beginning of the twentieth century, it is reasonable to assume that it contained Christian residents in the twelfth century too.

Evidence for the existence of Christian communities in the territory north of Jerusalem in the twelfth century

Calandia In 1151 the prior of the Holy Sepulcher granted a Syrian by the name of Nemes, his sons, and the children of his brother, Antonius, land and vineyards which they occupied "apud Calandriam," in return for one half of their harvest. The conditions attached to this grant were much more stringent than conditions attached to grants to free Frankish farmers.[4]

Another reference to the Christian inhabitants of Calandia is contained in a document in which Baldwin III waived the rights he had over Christian farmers in four villages: Ramathes, Aithara, Bethelegel, and Calandia. It appears from the document that the local farmers had the status of permanent serfs and were owned by the Church of the Holy Sepulcher.[5] The document details the names of the villagers in each of the villages. The names of the villagers who lived in Calandia leave no doubt that they were Oriental Christians. Names like Cosmas, Georgius, Samuel, Nichola, Hanna, Elias, Abraham, Solomon, Jacob, and Butrus (Arabized form of Petrus) can only be the names of Oriental Christians.

One can learn about the status of the Christians of Calandia from another document, issued two years later, in accordance with which Queen Melisend exchanged Syrian villagers whom she owned for shops and two money-changer counters in Jerusalem. In Melisend's list of villagers there are names which did not appear in the earlier document, while some names which were mentioned in the earlier document do not appear in her list.[6] One can conclude from this that Melisend's list refers to additional Syrian villagers. Neither document states categorically that all the inhabitants of Calandia

---

[4] Holy Sepulcher, no. 69, 1151, 166: "Unde ego Amalricus, . . . Sepulcri prior, . . . Nemes Syriano et filiis suis et filiis fratris sui Antonii, terras, vineas quas tenent apud Calandriam . . . concedimus, ea videlicet conditione ut singulis annis medietatem fructus terre, videlicet omnium annonarum et vinearum et arborum quas ipsi jam edificaverunt, vel in posterum edificabunt, (cum aliis redditibus quos prefate ecclesie debent . . .) fideliter reddant."

[5] Holy Sepulcher, no. 43, July 25, 1150, 120–121: "Ita dumtaxat quod Surianis de quibus agitur sive eorumdem heredibus ubicumque sint, vel ubicumque inveniantur, a dominio pretaxate ecclesie deinceps se substrahere, vel alicujus stimulatione sive tergiversatione, ad alium quemlibet dominium se convertere, nullatenus liceat, sed sicut antiquitus et a priscis temporibus ecclesie Dominici Sepulcri dinoscuntur, ita in perpetuum ipsi et ipsorum heredes eidem subjaceant."

[6] Holy Sepulcher, no. 36, 1152, 103–104.

were Christians, but one can conclude, from the large number of Christians mentioned in the documents and from the fact that no Muslim names appear in them, that all the inhabitants were in fact Christians. In Calandia, where at the beginning of the twentieth century there were only Muslims, there was a Christian community in the twelfth century.

Ramathes (al-Ram?)   The inhabitants of Ramathes, which Pringle identified with al-Ram were Christians.[7]

In the aforementioned grant of Baldwin III the names of the inhabitants of Ramathes are mentioned, and most of these are Christian names. Here too there were Arab names like Barachet, Hubeit, Yuset, Salem, Ubeit, Munsor, and Phara, but the owners of these names were closely related to people with purely Christian names. From this it can be concluded that they, too, were Christians who underwent a process of Arabization.

In the other document, that of Queen Melisend previously referred to, there appear the names of four additional local Christian farmers not mentioned in the list of Baldwin III. If Pringle's identification of Ramathes as al-Ram is correct, then the Church of the Holy Sepulcher apparently built a manor house, or castle, near to the Christian-Syriac village (the manor house was built at the edge of the village, a little distance away from the ruins of the Byzantine church found there).

Bethelegel (Kh. al-ʿAdasa, grid reference 172/137?) The village of Bethelegel was also a purely Christian village as can be seen from the document of Baldwin III. Clermont-Ganneau succeeded, with the aid of local traditions, to locate the casale of Bayt Lijja in Kh. al-ʿAdasa.[8] If this identification is correct (as I tend to think), then there is another document which deals with this village, but which failed to come to Clermont-Ganneau's attention.

This is a document, of the year 1161, in which a land dispute between the Holy Sepulcher settlers in Ramathes and the Jacobite church of St Mary Magdalene is described. The dispute concerned land near to Hadasa which belonged to the Jacobites. Hadasa is without any doubt Kh. al-ʿAdasa identified by Clermont-Ganneau also as Bayt Lijja (Bethelegel).[9]

The village of **Aithara**   This was either al-Tira, next to Ramallah (grid reference 168/145), or Kh. al-ʿAtara, opposite al-Ram (grid reference 172/140), or the more common, but less acceptable because of its distance, village of ʿAtara. (grid reference 169/156). Baldwin III's list contains names

---

[7] Pringle, 1993, 160–163.

[8] Clermont-Ganneau, 1898, 92. Nevertheless, Bethelegel might also be identified with Kh. al-Ijl (grid reference 169/148) and Haessa might be identified in Kh. Addasa (grid reference 170/139).

[9] Holy Sepulcher, no. 131, *c.* 1161, 258.

of villagers from this village which were typically Christian, and others which were Arabized, but there are no Muslim names.

The Syrian village of **Turcho**   Turcho, whose location is unknown to us, was another Syriac village in the territory of Jerusalem. This village was apparently destroyed at some later stage and the ruins were given an Arabic name which obviates its identification. The Syriac inhabitants of this village received an exemption from taxes on the raisins which they sold in Jerusalem, from King Amalric I.[10] It would appear, therefore, that Turcho was very near to Jerusalem, as otherwise its inhabitants would not have sold their agricultural products in that city.

Caphaer   Caphaer, in the region of ʿAbud, was another village with Syriac inhabitants. According to a document of the year 1175 Baldwin, the seignior of Rama, sold the Hospital the village of Caphaer, save for two carrucas of land which belonged to a Syriac by the name of Bufez.[11]

Belveer (Qastal grid reference 163/133[?])   A hint at the presence of a Syriac inhabitant in this village can be found in a document of the year 1173, in which the Hospital is said to have transferred a house and empty plot of land in the vicinity of Jerusalem – that is in "curtilum Belveer" – to one Arianus Jacobinus. The document does not state expressly that he was a Syriac, but the name "Arianus Jacobinus" implies that the reference was probably to a local Christian inhabitant of the village. Amongst the witnesses who signed the document was one Robertus, a relative of Radulphus, the dragoman. It was general practice for translators to act as witnesses on documents given to local inhabitants, and by their signatures they confirmed the credibility of the document or of the translation.[12]

Syriac ownership of property near to Jerusalem   In the city of Jerusalem itself there were many local Christian inhabitants. Some of them had remained from the period before the Frankish conquest and others were brought there by Baldwin I from Transjordan.[13] The size of the Jerusalem Syriac population is not relevant to our present discussion, which concerns the rural communities and not those who lived within the walls of cities. But the Syriac and Greek ownership of landed property outside the walls of Jerusalem does appear to me to be relevant to my subject-matter.

We can learn that a field in the area known as "The Field of Blood (Hakel-Dama)" belonged to Syrians since time immemorial from a document, issued

---

[10] Holy Sepulcher, no. 156, Mar. 14, 1171, 306; cf. Prawer, 1980a, 302 and 331.
[11] Hospital, no. 487, Nov. 29, 1175, 336; cf. Hospital, no. 114, Nov. 18, 1135, 96.
[12] Hospital, no. 450, Oct., 1173, 311–312 (Röhricht, *Regesta*, no. 501). On the tower that existed there when Guérin visited the place, see Guérin, 1868–1869, 170.
[13] Cf. William of Tyre, 11, 27, 535–536; Kohlberg & Kedar, 1988, 116; Prawer, 1980b, 92–93.

in 1143, in which Patriarch William of Jerusalem gave the Hospital Order the church in that same place.[14]

We can learn about Syrian ownership of vineyards on the way to Bethlehem from two documents, of 1150. It appears from these documents that the plot of land referred to in them was very large and extended over twelve carrucas. The Syriac owner received 1,050 bezants and one horse from the Order of St. Lazarus for his plot.[15]

About other plots of land which belonged to Eastern Christian institutions on the road leading to Bethlehem we can learn from another document of 1179. This document relates that Nicholas Manzur (who, according to his name, was also an Eastern Christian) sold to the Hospital Order land on the road leading to Bethlehem, south of land belonging to the Greek nuns and the monks of St. James (apparently Armenians).[16]

In another document we can learn about an Armenian monk by the name of Abraham who gave a well, which he had received from the Patriarch Garmundus for the benefit of the poor, to the Order of St. Lazar, with the proviso that after his death it would pass to the Leper Order.[17]

When Melisend sought to remove a flour mill which was operated at the gates of Jerusalem by the Leper Order, she gave them, in remuneration, five carrucas of land in the plain of Bethlehem on condition that the two farmers who were working the land, Georgius and Solomon, were not prejudiced.[18]

Settlements which were Christian at the beginning of the twentieth century and had a Christian population during the Ottoman period

Al-Taiyba   In this village a Frankish castrum and church were established within the existing local village (see chapter 14).

---

[14] Hospital, no. 150, 1143, 121–122: "notum facio quod ego ecclesiam quamdam, que in agro qui Acheldemach dicitur sita est, ubi peregrinorum sepeliuntur corpora, cum tota ejusdem agri terra, ab antiquis Surianis, nobis presentibus, divisa, Hospitali . . . concessi." "Hec itaque, quam prelibavimus, a Surianis facta divisio a fidelibus rata conservetur, nec aliqua inimici hominis sinistra vexatione de reliquo inquietetur."

[15] *AOL* IIB, no. 7, 1150, 128: "Ego itaque Baldewinus, . . . rex . . . concedo et confirmo, . . . emptionem xiij carrucarum vinee in planis Bethleem, quam emerunt fratres Sancti Lazari extra muros Jerusalem leprosi, scilicet magne pietatis viri, a Melengano, siro regulo, pro M et L bisancis et equo uno." *AOL*, IIB, no. 8, 1150, 129: the confirmation of Queen Melisend to the same act. The plot of land is defined without mentioning its superficy. The name of the "surianus" is transliterated differently: "Inter cetera . . . fatio vel laudo, venditionem leprosis de Sancto Lazaro, a Mozzageth suriano factam, laudavi et concessi et sigilli mei munimine confirmavi, quatuor videlicet pieces vinee in plano Bethleem, predicti vero Sancti Lazari fratres de suo proprio mille bisancios et concum cum equo uno presentie nostre largiti sunt."

[16] Hospital, no. 554, 1179, 376.   [17] *AOL*, IIB, no. 1, 1130–1145, 123.

[18] *AOL*, IIB, no. 10, 1151, 130: "quandam vineam que est in planis Bethleem quinque terre carruatas in se continentem, absque omni calumpnia . . . trado; tali vero conditione quod Georgius et Solomon, prefate vinee cultores, laborum suorum medietatem ex ea recipiant."

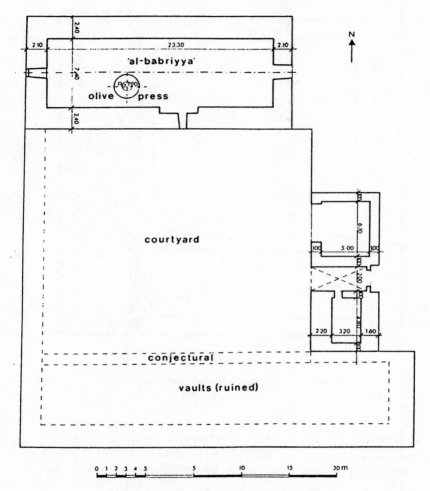

Figure 20   Plan of the manor house in Jifna

Jifna   A Frankish church was built within the existing local village (see chapter 10; cf. fig. 20, the manor house).

Bir Zayt   Near to this village there was a building which, apparently, served as the center for a large Frankish estate (see fig. 21).[19]

---

[19] According to Hütteroth & Abdulfattah, 1977, there were no Christians there in the sixteenth century. According to Toledano, who studied the same sources, the whole population of the village was Christian. See Toledano, 1979, 84. For the "maison forte" of Jifna, see Benvenisti, 1982, 147.

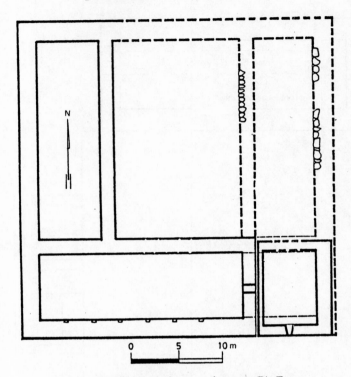

Figure 21   The Frankish manor house in Bir Zayt

Ramallah   This township had an overwhelming Christian majority as
late as 1922. There was a Frankish building at its center.[20]

ʿAyn ʿArik   In the course of my survey a Frankish building was found
there.[21]

ʿAbud   See chapter 10.

---

[20] In the census of 1922 there were 777 Christians and only 119 Muslim inhabitants in the village.
For the "maison forte." Cf. Abel, 1928, 50–51; Kochavi, 1972, 173–174; Pringle, 1986a, 20.
According to the Turkish tax survey 98% of the inhabitants of Ramalla were Christians and only
11% Muslims. A similar picture arises from the census of 1922: 96% of the population was
Christian and only 4% Muslim. See Barron, 1923. For the "maison forte" of Ramalla, see Grant,
1926.

[21] According to the Turkish tax survey 42% of the population was Christian and 58% was Muslim.
According to the census of 1922 56% of the inhabitants were Christians and 44% were Muslims.
See Barron, 1923. Like all the other villages with mixed Muslim-Christian population the village
core of ʿAyn ʿArik is divided into two. A Frankish ruin was found in the village during our survey.

Bethany   A Frankish ecclesiastical castrum attached to a monastery was established there and its church was renovated by the Franks.[22]

Ramun   In Antimus' list, of the year 1838, five Christians and a ruined church in the village are mentioned. Next to the village is a cave called "The Christian's Cave." In the course of my survey a Frankish building was discovered in the heart of the village.

ʿAyn Samiya   Guérin recalls an impressive building, built of stone with marginal dressing and resembling a fortress, which existed north of the village, above the spring. The land in the area was worked during Guérin's time and until today by men from Kafr Malic. Architectural remains of a church and a Greek inscription from the sixth century were found there. In 1838 there were ten Christian families consisting of fifty members living there, but without a church. At the beginning of the twentieth century the place was settled by Muslims only. In Kh. al-Samiya a Frankish building was discovered.[23]

Bayt Rima   Most of the inhabitants of the village are Christian to this day.[24]

Shuʿafat   Guérin discovered remains of a church called al-Kanisa, facing east. He thought it was a Frankish church. Abel, too, was of the opinion that it was a Frankish church established by the Order of our Lady of Mons Gaudii, relying for this opinion on a bull issued by Alexander III, in 1180. The tomb of Shaykh ʿAbd-allah was built on this church, which served according to Baldi the pilgrims who were on their way to Jerusalem. It would appear that Theodericus referred to this church when he said: "Two miles north of the Holy City there is a small church from which the Crusaders see this city for the first time, and in great ecstasy plant their crosses. They remove their shoes . . . Three miles away there is a large village called today Mahomeria." [25]

There is, therefore, cause for assuming that in the area of Jerusalem there were at least eighteen settlements in which there was a Christian population in the twelfth century. We have direct evidence of the existence of Christian villagers and other Christian inhabitants from Jerusalem itself, as well as from the territory to the north of it.

---

[22] For the Frankish community in Bethany, see Mayer, 1977, 372–402; Saller, 1957; Pringle, 1993, 122–137.

[23] For ʿAyn Samiya, see Abel, 1907, 275; Warren & Conder, 1882–1884, II, 394; *PEFQS*, 1907, 237–238; Guérin, 1874–1875, I, 210–213; Bagatti, 1979, 37–38.

[24] Lewis, 1954, 477.

[25] Guérin, 1868–1869, I, 390; Abel 1931, 143; Theodericus, xli, 44. Wilkinson's translation: Wilkinson, 310.

Twelfth-century evidence concerning the Muslim population near Jerusalem

Only three pieces of evidence concerning the region of Jerusalem provide a possible hint at the presence there of Muslim inhabitants.

First, a document of 1120, in which Baldwin II exempted the agricultural products at the entrance to Jerusalem from taxation, states that the exemption applied to the Muslim inhabitants too. It is difficult to learn from the different variants of this exemption what the comparative size of the various communities was. According to the version preserved in the archives of the Holy Sepulcher the exemption was granted both to the Saracens and the Christians, while according to the version of William of Tyre it was given first and foremost to the Latins and then "to Syriacs, Greeks, Armenians and everyone of every nation, even to the Saracens." The Saracens are placed by William of Tyre at the end of the list and apparently their role in supplying food for Jerusalem was smaller than that of other communities.[26]

Secondly, a reference to an old Saracen who was a witness in a dispute concerning land next to Mahomeria.[27]

Thirdly, the only local village south of the 'Abud–Sinjil line whose inhabitants had Muslim names is the village of Bayt Surik. In Bayt Surik one can find, amongst others, names such as Salman Ibn Mahdi, 'Abd al-Rahman, Salim, Hassan, Nasir, Muqaddam, Sulayman, Mahmud, Za'afar, Salem, etc. Any reservations with regard to an unequivocal conclusion that these were the names of Muslims flow from the absence of several very typical Muslim names such as Muhammad, 'Ali, and Ahmad. A comparison between the list of names in Bayt Surik and the list of names in the local villages both south and north of the 'Abud–Sinjil border line reveals the surprising absence of typical religious names, either Christian or Muslim.[28] In contemporary lists

---

[26] Holy Sepulcher, no. 27, 1120, 88–89: "Absolvo itaque ab omni exactione omnes qui per portas Jherusalem frumentum aut ordeum, fabas, lenticulas et cicer inferre voluerint, habeantque liberam facultatem ingrediendi et egrediendi, atque vendendi ubi et quibus voluerint, absque molestia tam Sarraceni quam Christiani." Cf. William of Tyre, 12, 15, 565: "Dedit etiam Surianis, Grecis, Armenis et harum cuiuslibet nationum hominibus, Sarracenis etiam nichilominus, liberam potestatem sine exactione aliqua inferendi in sanctam civitatem triticum, ordeum."

[27] Holy Sepulcher, no. 121, 1158–1159, 247.

[28] Holy Sepulcher, no. 36, 1152, 103–104: "ego Milesendis . . . ratum certumque fieri volo quod illam calumpniam, quam ecclesie Dominici Sepulcri ejusdemque loci canonicis quorumdam suggestione, super villanis de Bethsuric videlicet Selmen, filio Maadi, Habderahmen, Selim, Hasem, Nasen, Mekedem, Seleemen, Sade, Brahin, Kannet, Nasser, Ariz, Mahmut, Zafer, Demsis, Resselem, Tameh, Rosec, Sahe, Salem, filio Sade, et reliquis omnibus terraque ejusdem casalis feceram . . . libere et quiete dimitto; ita scilicet ut canonici, absque omni contradictione seu reclamatione mea vel alicujus heredum meorum, predictos villanos, super quibus calumpnia agitata fuerat, . . . libere et quiete . . . habeant, teneant et possideant, sicut a tempore illustrissimi ducis Godefridi liberius ac quietius habuisse, tenuisse et possedisse noscuntur."

of Muslims who lived in Central Samaria one can find typical Muslim names such as Abu Bakr, Ahmad, Muhammad, ʿAbd-alla, or ʿUbaydalla, or other forms of "servant of God" such as ʿAbd al-Wahid, etc. There are also other typical Muslim names such as ʿAli, ʿUmar, etc. All these names appear many times on the list of Samarian villagers, while practically no use is made of other Muslim names such as Hasan or Husain which appear on the list of villagers in Bayt Surik, although they too are regarded as typically Arabic-Muslim.[29] It could perhaps be argued that the original names were distorted by the author of the document or by one of the copiers, as they did not know Arabic. But the absence of such typical names like Ahmad, Mahmud, ʿAbd-alla, and ʿUmar cannot be ascribed to error only. From the fact that there is not even one name in the list which is asociated with a Christian saint it follows that there were no Christian inhabitants there.

According to the express testimony of a Latin source a Frankish settlement was established in Bayt Surik. If in fact there was a Muslim population in Bayt Surik in the twelfth century, then this is the only example of the construction of a Frankish settlement in a Muslim village.[30]

From the written sources we receive a hint of the certain presence of a Muslim farmer in one place only: Magna Mahomeria. It can be assumed that in Bayt Surik too there were Muslim inhabitants; and from the document of Baldwin II it can be concluded that there were perhaps other Muslim inhabitants. But this evidence is as nought in comparison with the unequivocal evidence of Christian inhabitants in nineteen other villages and townships.

Evidence of the presence of local inhabitants in Central Samaria

The picture which emerges from the written sources concerning the religion of the local inhabitants of Central Samaria is the complete opposite of that which we saw in the Jerusalem–Sinjil area. There is no evidence, neither historical nor archeological, of the existence of medieval Christian communities to the north of the borderline up to Nablus. All the available evidence seems to indicate that the whole region was populated by Muslims or Samaritans. I shall present all the evidence which I was able to find in order to substantiate this picture.

Evidence concerning the presence of local Muslim inhabitants
A twelfth-century religious mutiny of Muslim farmers against their Frankish landlord, seated at Mirabel, resulted in the migration of about one hundred

---

[29] On the personal names of villagers in Central Samaria, see Kedar and Alhajuj, 1990, 45–57.
[30] Holy Sepulcher, no. 150, 1169, 295.

and fifty Muslims from Central Samaria to Damascus. One of their descendants, Diya' al-Din who was born in 1173 and died in 1245, recalls these events and gives a detailed description of his parents' native villages all of which were located north of the cultural border.[31]

Moreover, Diya' al-Din refers to the existence of six rural mosques in these villages, and I myself discovered in this Muslim, formerly Samaritan region, a dedication inscription of a seventh, which was built five years after the battle of Hattin.

From this text one can deduce the presence of Muslims in the following villages.

Jama'in, grid reference 169/170.   In which there was a mosque during the Frankish period.[32]

Marda, grid reference 168/168.

Yasuf, grid reference 172/168.

Jit, grid reference 166/180.

Qira, grid reference 166/170.

Dayr Istia, grid reference 163/170.

Funduq, grid reference 163/177.   In this village a Hanbali scholar by the name of Ahmad Ibn 'Abd al-Daim al Maqaddasi al-Hanbali was born in the year H 575. He died there in the year H 668 (1270).[33]

Dayr 'Urif, grid reference 171/174.

As-Sawiya, grid reference 174/165.

The document mentions also Muslim villagers whose places of origin were as follows:

Hawara, grid reference 174/173.

Ramin, grid reference 164/187.

Kafr Saba, grid reference 144/176.

Burin, grid reference 173/176.   The founder of the family of Banu Ghawanima was born there in the year 1166. He entered Jerusalem in 1187.[34]

'Ajjul, grid reference 167/157.   An Arabic inscription from the twelfth century (apparently 1192) was found in the village mosque. It refers to the renovation of the mosque at the time. Here, too, as in Shilo and Jama'in this is another testimony for the existence of a mosque in a rural area of Palestine in the twelfth century.

[31] Diya' al-Din al-Maqdisi, Hijra. For a partial English translation, see Drory, 1988, 95–112. For earlier reference to these events, see Laoust, 1950; Sivan, 1967b; For a translation into Hebrew of unknown passages of this author, see Talmon-Heller, 1990, 27–63. For a discussion in English, see D. Talmon-Heller, 1994.   [32] Kedar, 1990.
[33] Drory, 1988; al-Yunini, II, 436, line 9.   [34] Drory, 1988, 102 nn. 56–58.

'**Aqraba**, grid reference 182/170. 'Aqraba was a Christian village during the Byzantine period. It appears from a Syriac text that there were two monasteries there: one called Mar Titus and the other Mar Stephan. The village went through a process of Islamization already in the early Muslim period and in the year 180 H/796–7 AD an Egyptian acquaintance of al-Shafa'i (one of the founders of the Shafa'i sect) by the name of Shihab al-Din Ahmad al-'Aqrabani was buried there.[35]

Al-Luban (Luban al-Sharqiya), grid reference 173/164. The qaddi, Muhammad Ibn 'Abd al-Wahid al-Makhzumi al-Lubanni was born here in approximately 593 H. He died in 658/1260 while serving as the qaddi of Ba'al-Beq. Although he was born after the termination of Frankish rule in this region, it can be assumed that his family did not take up residence in the village immediately after the Franks were chased out of the country, but arrived there earlier.[36]

Shilo, grid reference 177/163. Al-Harawi speaks of a mosque which existed in Shilo during his visit there in 1173. This is one of the only pieces of evidence concerning the existence of mosques in the Frankish Kingdom of Jerusalem.[37]

We have direct evidence, therefore, of about at least seventeen villages in which Muslims lived, and incontrovertible evidence about the existence of seven rural mosques. All this unequivocal evidence points to settlements in an area in which not one Frankish building was found. In other words: all the evidence testifies to the fact that the villages in this territory were Muslim or Samaritan, whereas almost all the evidence concerning the more southern territory, between Sinjil and 'Abud indicates that the villages in this territory were Christian.

Evidence of the presence of nomads and Muslim bandits in Samaria

Nomads In 1178, Amalric the viscount of Nablus sold the Hospitalers all the Beduin who lived in tents of the Benekarkas and other tribes, for the sum of 3,500 bezants. The viscount stated categorically that he was referring to "all his Beduin." "vendo domui . . . Hospitalis Jerusalem, . . . omnes Bedevinos meos, videlicet illos qui sunt de genere Benekarkas, et omnes alios qui habitant in tentoriis ubicunque fuerint, sive in regno sive extra regnum, cum omni familia eorum et cum omnibus heredibus eorum, et cum omnibus rebus eorum, . . . pro III millibus et D bisantiis."[38]

---

[35] Gil, 1992, (401), 290. In the village there is a construction inscription in Arabic from 817/1414.
[36] Al-Yunini, II, 74, lines 9–10.   [37] Al-Harawi, 24, lines 11–13.
[38] Hospital, no. 530, 1178, 363.

In his endorsement of this transaction Baldwin IV also sanctions the sale of the village of Seleth in the district of Nablus by the viscount of Nablus to the Hospital. The document contains full details of 103 "Beduin tents" (paternal homes) referred to in the previous transaction. King Baldwin links the sale of the nomads to the sale of Seleth, for both of which purchases the Hospital paid 5,500 bezants. In the viscount's document only 3,500 bezants are mentioned, from which one can conclude that the Hospital paid 2,000 bezants for the village of Seleth. From the fact that Beduin tribes appear together in the same transaction with the village of Seleth (undoubtedly Silat al-Dhahar, grid reference 167/191) allows for the conclusion that the nomadic territory of those same Beduin was close to this village.[39]

A Syriac inscription, discovered in the Church of the Holy Virgin, in 'Abud, states that renovation of the church was carried out at the end of the 450th year of "Beduin" rule. Milik is of the opinion that the reference may be to annoy the Muslim rulers. But he did not attempt to examine the possibility that the local Christian inhabitants regarded the Muslim occupation as equivalent to a nomadic incursion. And indeed, most of the Syriac writers of the time describe the Saracen rulers as Beduins.

Muslim bandits In an account of his visit to Samaria Usama Ibn al-Munkidh describes his encounters with the Frankish legal system. He relates how during his sojourn in Samaria he witnessed a duel between two men who, according to Hitti's translation, were Franks. The cause of the duel was that some thieves, apparently Muslims, had suddenly attacked one of the villages in the district of Nablus. One of the inhabitants of the village was accused of having been the thieves' guide when they attacked the village. He consequently fled from the village and the king ordered the arrest of his children. The villager appealed to the king, saying: "Let justice be done. I challenge the man who claimed that I was the person who led the robbers to the village, to a duel." The king then ordered the lord of the village to find a man to fight a duel with the villager. The seignior went to the village, where a blacksmith lived, and ordered the blacksmith to fight a duel with the accused villager. This story was followed by a description of the duel which was supervised by the viscount of Nablus.[40]

We can learn, from Usama's account, about the presence of Frankish agricultural settlers in the area of Nablus (as I shall maintain, in short, in the latter part of this chapter). There were also artisans amongst these settlers. The

---

[39] Hospital, no. 550, Nov. 17, 1178, 373. Cf. also Hospital, nos. 531 and 532.
[40] Usama, trans. Hitti, 167–168.

administration of the affairs of the Frankish burgesses who lived there was conducted by the viscount of Nablus, who, according to this account, managed not only the affairs of the town of Nablus and of its burgesses but also the affairs of the burgesses and artisans who lived in the villages nearby. For our purposes it is more important that there were Muslims who could attack the Frankish settlements. Apparently these Muslims were not permanent residents (as attacks by them would have resulted in retaliation against their villages) but persons whose places of residence were unknown. It is possible that they were nomads.

Theodericus' itinerary On his way from Jerusalem to Sychar (which is almost certainly the Frankish village of 'Askar, near Nablus) Theodericus passed a group of Saracens who were plowing a well-kept field with oxen and mules. "They let out a frightening scream, which is not unusual for them when they start working, but which filled us with fear. There are a great number of pagans in every town, village and field of that province. Because of the generosity of the King of Jerusalem, or of the Hospitalers or Templars, they work their fields there." It is difficult to know what Theodericus meant by "province." Was he referring to Samaria or the Jerusalem region? Or was the reference to the whole Kingdom of Jerusalem? That he was referring only to Central Samaria is hinted at in the fact that Theodericus did not indulge in similar descriptions of other regions of the Kingdom and it would appear that he did not meet with Muslim farmers in every place he visited.[41]

It is important to take note, in this connection, of the comparatively great number of Muslim attacks against places near to Nablus – attacks which, at least on one occasion, enjoyed the cooperation of the local inhabitants.[42]

An identical picture emerges from the various kinds of evidence: in the area south of Nablus there was a Muslim population. We have evidence of seventeen Muslim villages in which there were at least two mosques. We also have evidence of teaching of Muslim sages. From the general descriptions of pilgrims we learn that the region was densely populated by Muslims, and this information is strengthened by the fact that Muslim attacks, to the extent that there were any, were concentrated in the area of Nablus, where the attackers could hope for cooperation from the local inhabitants.

---

[41] Theodericus, xli, 44: "Per hanc viam nobis transeutibus multitudo Sarracenorum occurrit, qui omnes cum bubus et asinis incedentes magnum amenitatis campum sunt aggressi procindere, qui clamore horrisono, more eis non insolito, cum operis quippiam adoriuntur, intonantes terrorem non modicum nobis intulerunt." Wilkinson's translation: see Wilkinson, 310–311.

[42] See chapter 2, n. 13.

Local Christian settlements in the region of Nablus–Sabastiyya

In Nablus and north of it the Franks settled in regions which were inhabited by local Christians.

'**Askar** (Frankish Aschar)   In 'Askar there was a Frankish village, which belonged to the abbey of St. Mary Josaphat. In the Ottoman tax census of 1525–1526 fifteen Christian taxpayers were counted in the place out of a total of forty taxpayers.[43]

Rafidiya   Most of the population of Rafidiya was Christian in the year 1922. In 1838 there were 200 Greek believers, a priest, and a church. In the middle of the nineteenth century there were, according to Robinson, 400 Christian inhabitants. In 1922 there were 250 Christians of whom 40 were Protestants, who had almost certainly been converted during the second half of the nineteenth century. There are remains of a Frankish building in the village.[44]

Sebaste and environs   In Sabastiyya there was a Frankish see and a Frankish cathedral was built there. From the very fact that there was a bishopric see there, it can be concluded that it had Christian congregants in its diocese.[45] This assumption is buttressed by additional unconnected sources. (see plate 14)

The following is a list of villages and sites in the region of Sabastyyia which had Christian inhabitants, even at a later time.

Babriya next to Sebaste, grid reference 166/186.   A Frankish farm house was found in this place. We do not have any information about Christians who lived there in the twelfth century; but a Byzantine Greek inscription, which mentions the prophet Elijah, which was found at the site indicates that the place was populated by Christians already in the Byzantine period.[46]

Al-Nakura, grid reference 169/185.   There was a Christian population in the village which is still mentioned by Anthimus in 1667, but by then there was no church. In the outskirts of the village, not far from the Shaykh Sha'al tomb (grid reference 169/185) there are the remains of a large Frankish maison forte.

I'jansinyia, grid reference 170/186.   I'jansinyia still appears in the list of Greek parochial churches of 1667. In 1838 there were still sixty believers there, but there was no church.

---

[43] Lewis, 1954, 478.
[44] Guérin, 1874–1875, II, 182–183; Bagatti, 1979, 58–59; Robinson & Smith, 1841, 137.
[45] Sebaste was an ancient bishopric see, which, unlike many others, continued to exist in the Crusader period.   [46] Benvenisti, 1982, no. 5, 144.

Plate 14   Sebaste, aerial view

Nusf Jubayl, grid reference 170/186.   In 1838, 200 Christian believers were still counted in this village. There was also a priest and a church. Guérin speaks of no less than 300 Christians living there. In the 1922 census only 88 Christians were counted.

Bayt Imrin, grid reference 170/188.   In 1667 there was still a Greek Orthodox community in the village. In 1838 there were 50 Christians and a priest. In 1922 there were 515 Muslims and only 15 Christians in the village.

Barka, grid reference 169/189.   According to the Survey of Western Palestine there were still Christians living in this village in 1946, when they moved to Haifa because of Muslim pressure.[47]

---

[47] Warren & Conder, 1882–1884, II, 159; Bagatti, 1979, 71.

Sabastiyya itself (where Burchard of Mt. Zion was the guest of Greek monks) must, of course, be added to all the above places, as must **Fahma**, where a church of the Frankish period was discovered, **Zababida**, where the remains of a Frankish "bovaria" were discovered, and **Raba** (next to Zababida), where a Frankish chapel was discovered by the Survey of Western Palestine during the British survey, and others.[48]

From the above exhaustive study of villages in Samaria in which a Christian or Muslim population lived, the following conclusions can be drawn.

(1) In those regions which were populated by Christians during the Byzantine period there were still, during the twelfth century, local Christian communities. Many of the Byzantine settlements ceased to exist and it can be assumed that the size of the local Christian population decreased considerably, but the distribution of the local Christian settlement in the Crusader period remained similar to that during the Byzantine period and can even be described as the degenerate distribution of the Byzantine Christian settlement.

(2) There is evidence of Christian villages and of strictly Muslim villages, but there is no evidence of the existence of settlements with mixed populations in the twelfth century. In other words: the historical evidence indicates that there were two parallel networks – a Christian and a Muslim one. As the Christian distribution preceded the Muslim one it can be assumed (and I will try to prove it later on) that the Muslims created a new settlement system that does not continue the former one.

(3) The connection between Frankish settlement and local Christian settlement existed both at the territorial level and that of the individual village. Many of the local Christian settlements contained Frankish sites. This is particularly evident in villages on the periphery of Nablus. South of Nablus, in the region where mainly Muslims lived, there was no Frankish settlement or even manor house. In the villages northwest of Nablus, which were even further from the town than the Muslim settlements to the south, many Frankish sites were found. In my opinion there is no way of explaining the presence of a Frankish church in Fahma, or for the Frankish sites in Zababida, Junayd, al-Nakura, and Rafidiya other than the connection between the Christian inhabitants (who lived in those villages till early modern times) and the Frankish population. And by their very existence they add verisimilitude to my thesis that the Franks settled and built their

[48] Warren & Conder, 1882–1884, II, 243–244.

rural settlements in places and regions in which there was still a substantial local Christian population.

(4) These Christian settlements, together with the other Frankish sites, provide the explanation, in my opinion, for the bishopric see in Sabastiyya, as the very fact that there was a bishop there, means that there was a Christian diocese and Christian population. The establishment of a see could not have been the consequence only of the existence of a holy place or of the presence of monks.

To sum up: in the region north of Jerusalem in which there was a dense Christian population during the Byzantine period, there was still a Christian population, and perhaps even a Christian majority, in the twelfth century.

In Central Samaria, where Samaritans lived during the Byzantine period, there was a Muslim majority in the twelfth century. The Frankish settlers lived only in those areas in which there was a substantial Christian population.

It can be established, with a great deal of certainty, that the Frankish border of settlement was not fixed for deterministic, ecological reasons, but for cultural reasons. In short, the Franks very obviously preferred to live in regions in which there was a local Christian population and refrained from living amongst Muslims.

The information which we have is not complete, but if we join together all the sources we can receive a more comprehensive picture indicating a consistent model: the Franks settled in regions which were occupied by Eastern Christians, occasionally within the Christian villages themselves, and never settled in Muslim regions. Furthermore,, in all those places which it was possible to examine it is apparent that the Franks did not prejudice local ownership of the land but settled on the high ground beyond the local Christian villages.[49] They used the same churches (as in al-Taiyba, ʿAbud, and even in more central places such as the Church of the Holy Sepulcher and the Church of the Nativity in Bethlehem) and the Franks did not hesitate to settle as individuals within the local Christian communities. From everything stated above a clear picture can be gained of a migrant society settled far from its cultural origins. The Frankish migrants were not sufficiently confident in order to settle just anywhere. They preferred to settle near to the local Christians, with whom they could intermarry, from whom they could learn the secrets of eastern agriculture and in whose churches they could pray.

That is a typical model of a migrant society settled within a maternal

[49] For the return of two villages which were confiscated by the Franks from their Syrian owners, see Martin.

society prepared to absorb the newcomers more easily, and the Franks were no different in this from similar, later societies.[50]

This approach does not explain the regionality in the distribution of the Christian and Muslim settlements within the Latin Kingdom. Although this question does not really come within the scope of this book, which deals with Frankish settlement in Palestine, I shall try to answer it.

In the previous chapter, which dealt with the Eastern Galilee, I maintained categorically, and in this chapter I hinted, that in the regions in which there were no Franks and no local Christians there is evidence of the presence of Beduins. Did the fact that the Franks refrained from settling in certain parts of the country result from insecurity due to the presence of nomads, or did it result from the absence of local Christians in those parts of the country?

In the following chapter I shall argue that there was a connection between the existence of a nomadic population and the existence of Muslim villages. I shall try to show that those regions in which, already in the twelfth century, there was a considerable Muslim population are the very regions which underwent, already during the early Muslim period, a double process of nomadization and sedentarization, culminating in their transformation into Muslim regions.

[50] Guibert of Nogent, 258G, refers explicitly to the fear of the Franks from the local Muslim society. I would like to thank Prof. B. Z. Kedar for turning my attention to this reference.

CHAPTER TWENTY

DIFFERENTIAL GEOGRAPHICAL CHANGES
AND THE CULTURAL BORDERS OF
SAMARIA AND THE GALILEE

The decline and the geographical changes in the spatial distribution of the local Christian community between the Byzantine and the Frankish periods reflect also the process of Islamization of this community. This process is usually described as continuous and irreversible adaptations of the basic structures of the non-Muslim societies to conform with the cultural, ethnic, and economic changes which occurred in the Levant after the Arab-Muslim conquest. The process of Islamization can be described as a process of "longue durée" accelerated momentarily by political and social events.

Most of the scholars who dealt with the causes for the Islamization of "the Dhimmi" during the early Muslim period tended to ascribe it to the social and economic difficulties suffered by the Christian and Jewish communities. These scholars point to the high rate of special taxation, the direct assaults of Muslim mobs, the occupation restrictions, the general feeling of helplessness, and other economic and social causes as possible incentives for mass Islamization. Most of the scholars agree that until the beginning of the eleventh century there were not many cases of Islamization by coercion, as this was forbidden by Muslim religious law.[1]

Most scholars agree also that the direct and indirect motives, which brought Christians and Jews to convert to Islam during the early Muslim period, did not disappear and were even stronger during the later periods, when direct discrimination and deliberate persecution on the part of the Mamluk and Turkish rulers were added to the incentives for Islamization. In short, most scholars tend to assume that the process of Islamization was not completed during the later Muslim period, and particularly under the Mamluk regime, but that it continued to take place during these periods as well.[2] It can be assumed, therefore, that the comparative size of the Christian

---

[1] Cf. chapter 2, nn. 20, 23–25.   [2] Cf. chapter 2, n. 24.

community continued to decrease during the Mamluk and Ottoman periods and that the demographic–cultural change was, in general, irreversible.

The scholar whose subject is a process which began in the seventh century and has continued virtually to this day must contend with objective and contradictory problems. The importance of the process, its continuity, its geographic distribution, and its variegated aspects must serve as obstacles in the path of every scholar who attempts to discover the reasons for, and the pace and the implications of, the process particularly since the contemporary historical sources are so scanty. We have very little information concerning the size of the population and its ethnic content in any of the regions of Palestine, which are the subjects of this study, during the Middle Ages. The few references to the process of Islamization are contained in descriptive texts and in the impressions of chroniclers and pilgrims of their own social environment. Weaving these texts, which were written in various languages and in various places, into an integral whole is a Sisyphean task which it is doubtful will produce a clear and credible picture even if accomplished.

This book, which deals with a small strip of country and a limited period of time, does not presume to solve these problems. I shall nevertheless attempt to show that one of the models used for the purpose of explaining the process of Islamization is consistent with the facts which emerge from my work. I shall attempt to show also that one can apply geographic settlement principles in order to reinforce this model.

The regional and individual process of Islamization

Two of the important students of Islamization, Speros Vryonis Jr. and Nehemia Levtzion, distinguished between the process of Islamization of individuals, which is slow and continuous, and the Islamization and Arabization of a region, which could be much more rapid. In regions which were deserted by their inhabitants as a result of nomadic pressure, the process was rapid, because of the fact that the settlement vacuum was filled by the slowly sedentarized nomadic-Muslim tribes. Levtzion maintains that the occupation of a region by nomadic tribes was accompanied, insofar as the geographic conditions permitted, by the settlement of the conquerors or their relatives, which led to cultural and ethnic changes expressed in Arabization or Turkicization. The two scholars take care to emphasize that the rapid process of Islamization resulted from the sedentarization of the nomads and not from the conversion of the previous inhabitants.[3]

[3] Levtzion, 1979, 1–23.

A detailed example of this process was examined by Vryonis in Asia Minor. The first hundred years after the Turkish conquest (from the 1070s until the end of the twelfth century) were characterized, according to him, by the flight of the urban Christian population to the western coast and beyond the borders of Asia Minor. Following upon this flight, and perhaps because of it, the process of sedentarization of the Turkish tribes began, bringing with it the Turkicization and Islamization of the region. Vryonis apparently went too far in maintaining that it was nomadic pressure which led to the destruction of the cities of Asia Minor, as it would appear that these cities sank, and some were even reduced to ruins, earlier on, and that the penetration of nomadic population was, at least partially, the result of this decline and not only its cause, but the general model which he suggested for the region is very convincing.[4]

Brice's toponymical studies support Vryonis' theory. He found that the majority of the settlements, which had been Byzantine-Christian settlements before the Turkish invasion and remained on the same sites, retained their original names; but that all the new settlements (other than the Byzantine-Christian ones which continued to exist) had Turkish names. Brice also proved the opposite: that is, that most of the Byzantine ruined villages which were not reoccupied and remained abandoned have Greek-Byzantine names. Brice ascribes the big number of both Turkish and Byzantine names to the fact that the Byzantine-Christian rural settlements were abandoned but many of them were not resettled by the Turks who established new settlements instead. The desertion of the Byzantine-Christian villages led to the creation of two parallel systems: the semi-abandonded system of Byzantine-Christian origin and the new Turkish system.[5]

It is important to stress that although I accept the model of Vryonis, Brice, and others, and assume, like them, that desertion of a region and its resettlement by nomadic tribes, who underwent a process of sedentarization, was a more rapid process than individual Islamization, I accept also the approach of Levtzion and like him I do not think that rapid regional Islamization and slower individual Islamization contradict each other. On the contrary the two processes complement each other, and many regions which underwent a dual process of nomadization and sedentarization were Islamized rapidly, but the complete Islamization of the rural population occurred only at a later stage, after assimilation and intermarriage of the remaining population with the new one who controlled it politically. However, the conversion of individuals in a sedentarized rural population is a difficult and painful process,

[4] Vryonis, 1971.   [5] Brice, 1955.

linked to estrangement from previous lineage groups, from the community, from religious practices and from family relations. It is reasonable, therefore, to assume that the break-up of the sedentarized Christian communities occurred at a later stage, after the creation of strong and organized Muslim communities.

One of the great advantages of the combined approach of Levtzion and Vryonis is that it can be demonstrated not only by written sources. Although Vryonis wrote his book on the basis of mainly historical sources, Brice showed that the same conclusions could be confirmed by toponymical research. Unfortunately it is very difficult to base similar research connected with Palestine on toponymical sources. Such research can be conducted only in cases where the demographic-cultural change is expressed also in the different languages of the inhabitants, and where the names of new settlements reflect this change. The autochthonous population of Palestine used, for thousands of years, Semitic languages: Hebrew, Samaritan, Palestinian-Syriac, Jewish Aramaic, and Arabic. Almost all the place names in Palestine have Semitic roots and there are practically no place names with Greek or Turkish origin and very few with Latin origin. The similarity of the different Semitic languages and the ease with which a Syriac, Samaritan, Hebrew, or Arabic name can be identified with any of these languages makes it very difficult to analyze the historical meaning of place names. As the Islamization of Palestine was accompanied by the Arabization of the population and not its Turkicization, it is difficult to apply toponymical methods in examining it.

Another non-literary source which can be used in examining the development of such a system is that of archeological excavations and surveys. Archeology was almost completely unexploited in the Levant insofar as medieval settlement is concerned, but it can be seen to be very useful for the purpose of establishing whether a process of complete or partial nomadization or sedentarization occurred in any particular region.

According to the model which was presented above, there is a correlation between the processes of nomadization and sedentarization and the process of Islamization. The desertion of the former population because of nomadic pressure, and the resettlement of the deserted regions by the formerly nomadic population, accelerate the process of Islamization. I shall attempt to show that the opposite is valid as well and that the process of Islamization in the regions which did not undergo an earlier double process of nomadization and sedentarization was slower and occurred at a later stage than in those regions which did undergo these processes of nomadization, sedentarization, and consequently also a process of Islamization.

Table 2   *A comparison of the size of sites in Eastern and Western Galilee in the Byzantine period (fifth to sixth centuries AD)*

Superficies of the site	No. of sites in Eastern Galilee	No. of sites in Western Galilee
0–5 dunams[a]	2 (4%)[b]	35 [31%]
5–10 dunams	21 (36%)	56 (49%)
More than 10 dunams	32 (54%)	20 (17%)
Unknown	3 (5%)	4 (3%)
Total	58	115

[a] 1 dunam = 1,000 square meters. [b] Two Christian monasteries on the lake of Galilee.

This approach is based on the assumption that human geography is also a manifestation of the society and culture which created it. In other words: that the form and distribution of settlements give expression also to the cultural and social needs and not only to deterministic factors such as agricultural conditions and the economic potential of the land. The infiltration of a new population, or major cultural changes experienced by the existing population, are expressed in the parallel creation of a new geographical landscape, and vice versa: demographic and cultural continuity is expressed in continuity and in the preservation of previous forms of settlement and landscapes. I shall try to show that in Palestine, as in Asia Minor, nomads who undergo a process of sedentarization do not maintain the previous system of settlement even though there may be deterministic reasons for doing so.

Culture and geography: "Jewish" settlement and "Christian" settlement on both sides of the Galilee cultural border

Map 5 shows the sizes of Byzantine sites in the Galilee.[6] It testifies to the existence of a clear borderline dividing two groups of settlements: the group in Upper Eastern Galilee, which was mostly Jewish, and the group in Western Galilee, which was Christian. A comparison of the size of the villages on either side of the cultural border shows that religion was not the only difference between these two regions and that the average size of the Jewish villages was larger than that of the Christian ones (see table 2).

The superficies of 54% of the sites which existed in the Jewish region surpassed 10 dunams, which in Byzantine Palestine is considered to be a large

6 The map was prepared by the author together with Mr. M. Aviam as a part of a joint article dealing with the development of spatial distribution of villages in the Galilee between the sixth and the thirteenth century.

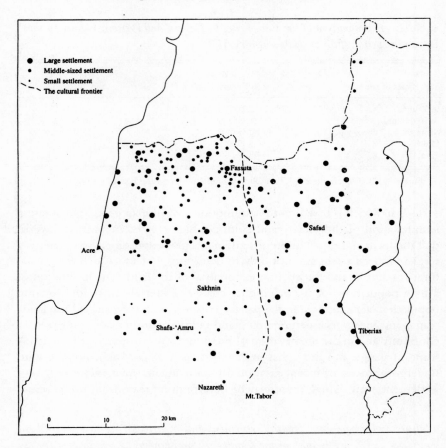

Map 5   Byzantine sites in the Galilee, by size. The map is based on data accumulated
in the course of a field study conducted by Mr. Mordechai Aviam of the Israel
Antiquities Authority.

village. Of them, 90% surpassed the medium size of seven dunams. There
were no isolated houses, tiny hamlets, or farm houses in this region. We can
conclude that all of the Jewish sites were relatively large.

The size of the sites in the Christian region is more variegated: the villages were surrounded by small hamlets, which can be regarded as farm
houses or small monasteries and these small–scale habitations constituted at
least 31% of the known sites. It should be remembered that in the East there
were no such sites. Only 17% of all the villages in the West were large in size
in comparison with three times that amount in the East. Of the Christian

villages, 49% were of medium size in comparison with only 36% in the Jewish part.

The differences between the settlement patterns in Eastern and Western Galilee are too material to be ascribed to chance. One can try to explain these differences in several possible ways: one can argue that the differences resulted from economic deterministic reasons or from a different pattern of agriculture; one can even argue that in Western Europe, too, the isolated settlement (the villa) was the most common form of rural settlement until the ninth century and that only in the ninth to twelfth centuries was there a recognizable transition to the concentrated village or township. The transition in Europe was bound up with a different system of agricultural work, with demographic growth, with the introduction of progressive agricultural technology, and with social and political changes. It can, perhaps, be argued that similar changes occurred in Eastern Galilee during the Byzantine period. But it seems to be unfeasible to rely on parallels so distant in time and space in order to explain settlement distribution in Palestine, particularly since there is no question here of desertion of estates and the establishment in their place of larger rural settlements, but rather of the creation of large and medium-size villages only. Likewise, the Jewish pattern of settlement cannot be interpreted on a deterministic basis since there is no significant economical, geological, or climatological difference between the Jewish and Christian regions. If the differences had resulted from deterministic economic or agricultural reasons, we could have expected to find a difference in the settlement scale between Lower Eastern Galilee, which is comparatively dry, and Upper Eastern Galilee, which is rich in water. But there is no such difference in the scale of the villages.

Another possible explanation for the differences in scale between Eastern and Western Galilee was propounded by David Amiran in another context.[7] He attributed the comparatively large size of settlements in the south of the country to security considerations, arguing that settlers who lived on the border of the desert tended to concentrate in comparatively larger settlements as a defence against nomads. But this explanation too is not suitable in our case, as it is difficult to imagine that the inhabitants of Eastern Galilee were compelled to concentrate in large settlements, already in Byzantine times, in order to defend themselves against nomads, who lived mainly in the desert areas, many tens of kilometers away. This explanation is inapplicable for the further reason that there was a high standard of general security during those times. In any event it is unfeasible to look for deterministic or

---

[7] Amiran, 1953, 192–209.

security reasons in order to explain the material difference in settlement distribution between contingent regions in Central Upper Galilee.

The differences between the settlement scales in Western and Eastern Galilee result, in my opinion, from cultural and historical reasons. There is no doubt that economic and security needs, as well as technological skills are very important, but they are not exclusive. The pattern of settlement and the spatial distribution are influenced also by values, traditions, communal relations, and forms of worship, and they are all expressed, in my opinion, in the differences between Eastern and Western Byzantine Galilee. That is the reason why settlement consisting of a multiplicity of isolated dwellings could not be characteristic of a geographical environ in which the majority of the inhabitants were Jewish.

Jews cannot live out of, or away from, bigger communities. Jews have to live within a short walking distance from synagogues, because walking outside one's village on Saturdays and Jewish holidays is forbidden. The Jewish laws forbid certain rituals in the absence of a "community" which is defined as ten male Jewish adults. The Jews need specialized butchers to slaughter their animals, they have to take a ritualistic bath in the Mikveh, which is essentially based on the collecting of rainfall, and so on. Communal institutions are an essential daily requirement for Jews. One can, of course, maintain a proper Jewish way of life in a small settlement, or even in an isolated house; but this imposes a heavy burden on anyone choosing to do so, and requires regular commuting to a larger community. For this reason it is difficult to find Jews living in isolated or remote places. The settlement distribution of Eastern Galilee, in which almost all the villages were large, is typically "Jewish," as this enabled the Jewish villagers to pursue their religious practices without having to resort to commuting.

For the Christian way of life there is no obvious advantage in living in a village over living in an isolated estate, as walking distance from a church is not restricted. Furthermore, some of the other services provided by the Christian religion to its followers are available in their own residences. The difference in the size of the Christian settlements evolves from reasons of economic necessity and not from reasons of faith or tradition. One can find in contingent regions settled by Christians during Byzantine times manor houses, monasteries, medium-sized villages and large villages, whereas in the Jewish regions there were practically only medium-sized and large villages.

However, the existence of isolated farm houses in sixth-century Palestine is not so obvious as it might have been in contemporaneous Europe. The establishment of an isolated farm meant an investment of enormous expenditure. The lack of timber and the necessity of using stone as a building material made the erection of the main buildings and the necessary dependencies extremely expensive. The construction of a complicated irrigation system which is a precondition for agriculture in the dry Mediterranean climate and the very costly terraces which were essential both for the irrigation system and for the preservation of the soil added enormous sums to the preliminary expenditure. The maintenance of these systems demanded manpower beyond the ability of any local family. Living in communities reduced the cost of construction of the infrastructure: the irrigation system was common to all as were the wine press, the oil press, and other necessary dependencies. Even the cost of the terraces was reduced because the responsibility for their maintenance was divided between the families.

The existence of farm houses testifies to the economic and social status of their owners: only wealthy farmers could afford their cost and only they could benefit from advantages such as utilizing minimal water sources which were not sufficient for the needs of a village, or living away from the local community with its conflicting interests.

During the Byzantine period, therefore, two types of small settlements were developed in Palestine: the estate, or the isolated farm house, in which the financial elite who were probably close to the Greek rulers, lived. In Galilee, on the border of Jewish settlement, and in Samaria, on the border of Samaritan settlement, there were also small monasteries which were also closely connected with the Greek administration.

It is difficult to distinguish, in archeological surveys, between "villas" and "monasteries," as the structural differences between them are very slight. They both had agricultural functions and in both cases there were very few central buildings. The only distinction between the estate and the monastery was the existence of a chapel, but locating monastery chapels archeologically is a very difficult process usually involving expensive excavations.

It would seem, therefore, that the archeological settlement map of Byzantine Galilee is more illustrative of the cultural and social background of the settlers than of the deterministic economic and security circumstances of the settlements themselves. The owners of estates and the occupants of monasteries were members of the Byzantine population or of the affluent communities with close ties to the Byzantine upper hierarchy .

Differences in the spatial distribution of the settlements on both sides of the cultural border in Samaria

In South Samaria, too, the political and religious differences can be defined archeologically. In a survey conducted by I. Finkelstein in this region 267

Byzantine sites were discovered – a record number for this region and for all periods. But the sites were not divided equally. Two-thirds of them (in which, from their size, more than 75% of the inhabitants must have lived) were discovered in the more southern part of the region, which was inhabited by Christians and which was south of the cultural border we are dealing with here, while only one third of the settlements and 25% of the inhabitants were in the northern Samaritan region of the same size. It would appear that this uneven distribution also has no deterministic explanation, as in earlier periods there was an opposite division of the sites: two-thirds of them were discovered in the northern region. At the end of the Byzantine period the number of settlements in the northern region was drastically reduced: of thirty-one Roman sites only six small ones and four doubtful ones remained (the archaeologist was not certain whether the latter four had even existed). In other words, in the course of the Byzantine period the "Samaritan region" was almost totally abandoned. The number of settlements was reduced by 66% to 80%, and the number of inhabitants was reduced by even more. Finkelstein assumes, quite rightly, that the reason for this can be found in historical events.[8]

Among the possible historical events was the devastation suffered by the Samaritans following upon their revolts against Christian-Byzantine rule. According to the Samaritan and Byzantine chronicles, which narrate the horrors of the suppressions, thousands of Samaritans were killed, many more were exiled, and a large part of the Samarian hill country became a no-man's land.

In the revolt of 529 almost 20,000 Samaritans were killed in one battle and others fled over the Jordan where they were captured by Christian nomadic tribes and sold into slavery. Their synagogues were destroyed and many of the survivors were forced to convert to Christianity. The last revolt of 556 was followed by massive expropriation of their property and a plague which decimated the population. According to the sources the number of Samaritans who were butchered was 100,000 or even 120,000. Many others were tortured and exiled. The persecution of the Samaritans continued even after the suppression of the revolts. According to one Samaritan source the slaughter of the Samaritans continued until the beginning of the seventh century. There is no doubt that the frequent revolts and the oppressive measures of the administration, which continued apparently until the Muslim conquest, were the cause of its ruin and the flight of its inhabitants.[9]

[8] Finkelstein, 1988–1989, 158–164.
[9] Cf. Crown, 1989, 55–81.

Arab settlement in Central Samaria during the early Muslim period:
archeological evidence

The devastation is evident from the archeological surveys too. The number of Samaritan villages which still existed in the fifth century AD is five to ten times larger than their number on the eve of the Arab conquest, two hundred years later. The large new settlements, which were established later in the early Muslim period and continued to exist during the Frankish period, were not established on the sites of the preexisting Samaritan villages. Hence, for example, no Byzantine pottery was found in places such as Salfit, Jama'in, Marda, Jit, 'Urif, al-Sawiya, Hawara, Burin, and many other places. I have chosen these villages from a long list of similar ones, because they are all mentioned in the documents of the twelfth and thirteenth centuries as being populated by Muslims.

From the data given above it can be concluded that the Muslim population of Central Samaria, during the early Muslim period, was not an autochthonous population which had converted to Christianity. They arrived there either by way of migration or as a result of a process of sedentarization of the nomads who had filled the vacuum created by the departing Samaritans at the end of the Byzantine period.

In the absence of sources and historical data it is difficult to decide which of the two processes – migration or sedentarization – was the more dominant. But there are several reasons for opting for sedentarization. I indicated above that during the Frankish period there were still nomadic tribes living in Central Samaria. Detailed descriptions of Beduin tribes are very rare in medieval Latin sources and the description of nomads in Central Samaria is, to the best of my knowledge, the only occasion on which the Latin sources mention the existence of nomads in the heart of the settled part of the country. The Frankish sources refer to the existence of nomadic tribes in places other than Central Samaria too; but in general these places are on the periphery of the Kingdom: in the Jordan Valley; near Belvoir; in "Terre de Sueth"; in the Hawran; in Eastern Upper Galilee; near Hebron; and in Transjordan. From the document in our possession it can be established that there were Beduin tribes, who had still not gone through a process of sedentarization, living in the heart of Samaria during the twelfth century. Abraham Poliak, who studied the process of Islamization of the Samaritans, was also of the opinion that the Islamization of Samaria followed upon the sedentarization of the Muslim nomads. According to him this process continued into the Ayyubid period when Beduin streamed into the country at the initiative of the rulers who exploited them for military purposes.[10] Poliak notes, in this context, another interesting fact: the Beduin tribes who settled in Samaria do not appear in the lists of Beduin tribes in Syria and Palestine of al-'Umari, al-Qalqashandi, and Ibn Khaldun. Apparently a mixture of Beduin and other nomads, who later went through a process of sedentarization, settled in Samaria.[11]

To sum up: in the only rural region in Palestine in which, according to all the written and archeological sources, the process of Islamization was completed already in the twelfth century, there occurred events consistent with the model propounded by Levtzion and Vryonis: the region was abandoned by its original sedentary population and the subsequent vacuum was apparently filled by nomads who, at a later stage, gradually became sedentarized.

Archeological evidence of nomadization and sedentarization in Central Samaria during the early Muslim period

The above assumption is strengthened by the comprehensive archeological surveys conducted in Central Samaria.[12] The archeologists who conducted these surveys divided the sites which they discovered into four categories, according to their sizes: small sites (no more than two dunams), small villages (approximately three to eight dunams), medium-sized villages (about ten dunams), and large villages (about twenty dunams) (see table 3). Because of the limitations of archeological surveys the archeologists could not distinguish between "Crusader sites" and "Mamluk sites," and all the sites are called "medieval sites."

The number of sites was drastically reduced – from 106 to 49 – during the early Muslim period. A statistic examination of the data shows a 50% reduction in the number of settlements, but a more meticulous examination reveals that a considerable number of larger villages continued to exist. In fact, 80% of the large Byzantine villages remained in existence in medieval times. On the other hand, 82% of the estates and monasteries, and more than 50% of the small villages, disappeared. Nor was the region resettled during the early Muslim period, only five new settlements having been established during that time. It can be concluded that the network of large settlements continued to exist, albeit in a deteriorated state, and that the construction of new settlements was marginal.

---

[10] Poliak, 1938, 56–57.   [11] Poliak, 1938, 56–57; al-Qalqashandi, IV, 203–215.
[12] I. Finkelstein was kind enough to allow me the use of the results of his survey, which were not published yet.

Table 3   *Archeological data concerning the "Christian region" south of the Sinjil–ʿAbud line (cf. maps 6 and 7)*

Sites occupied in the sixth century	Sites continuing to exist in the "Middle Ages"
47 farm houses and monasteries	9 (18%)
36 small villages	20 (20%)
18 medium–sized villages	16 (88%)
5 large villages	4 (80%)

Table 4   *Byzantine sites in Central Samaria which continued to exist in the Frankish period*

Byzantine sites	Byzantine sites which continued to exist in the Frankish period
30 sites	7 only (23%): 5 became small villages and 2 became medium-sized villages
25 small and medium-sized villages	17 only (68%): 6 became large villages and 11 remained small ones
2 big villages	These villages were deserted

Changes in the spatial distribution in the "Muslim region" north of the Sinjil–ʿAbud line ·

As I noted above, the region north of the Sinjil–ʿAbud line was almost totally abandoned during the late Byzantine period. The settlements which were established in this region during a later period created a new pattern of settlement. Table 4, based on comprehensive archeological surveys, illustrates the limited extent to which the new settlers used the old Byzantine sites for their own settlements.

The changes are all the more apparent upon examining the data concerning the new villages. Between the late Byzantine period and the Middle Ages thirty-nine new settlements were established in Central Samaria. Ten of these were large settlements and twenty-nine were medium-sized and small. No Byzantine pottery was found in any of them.

Only twenty-four, out of fifty-seven, of the sites which were settled in this region in the early Byzantine period (most of which were abandoned for an extended period in the sixth and seventh centuries) continued to exist during later periods. Some of them, as already noted, were reestablished at the time. In other words: out of sixty-two medieval settlements in the region

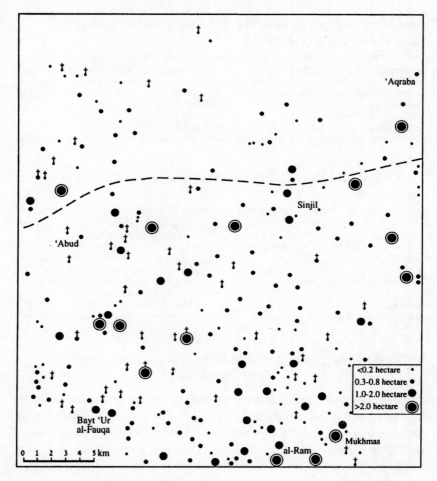

Map 6   Early Byzantine sites in Samaria, by size

thirty-nine did not exist at all during the Byzantine period and were established only later.

To sum up: in central Samaria, in the region north of the Sinjil–'Abud line, a new pattern of settlement was created during the early Muslim period. The creation of this system can be described according to the following stages.

(1)   During the first stage the region was abandoned by most of its sedentary inhabitants as a result of oppression by the Byzantine rulers.

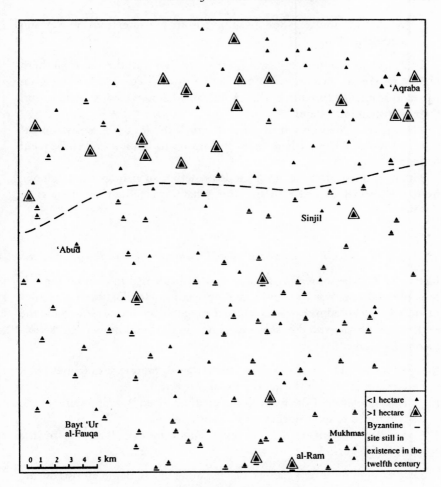

Map 7   Medieval sites in Samaria, by size

(2)   During the second stage nomadic tribes infiltrated into the region.

(3)   The nomadic tribes underwent a process of sedentarization during the
early Muslim period and established a new pattern of settlement completely different from the previous one. We know from independent
historical sources that the region itself went through a process of
Islamization during the early Muslim period and that at the beginning
of the twelfth century all the inhabitants were already Muslims. The
whole process, therefore, can be seen to have been one of Islamization

by way of nomadization (resulting from pressure from above) and sedentarization.

The opposite manifestation was no less important. In the more southern region, where the dual process of nomadization and sedentarization did not occur, many large Byzantine villages remained untouched, together with their Christian inhabitants.

The Franks settled only in regions in which the local Christian population had remained and where there was no nomadization and subsequent sedentarization.

The next question to be considered is whether an analogy can be drawn from this model in order to discover what occurred in other parts of Palestine.

Archeological evidence of nomadization and sedentarization in Eastern Galilee

In Eastern Galilee something similar to what happened in Central Samaria took place, although at a later period. From a comparison between the settlements which existed in Eastern Galilee during the Byzantine period and the settlements which existed in the same region in the Frankish period, the following facts emerge.

(1) At least eighteen of the thirty-two large Byzantine sites (about 50%) continued to exist during the Frankish period.
(2) At least eleven of the twenty-one medium-sized Byzantine sites (52%) continued to exist during the Frankish period.
(3) Smaller settlements did not exist either in the Byzantine or the Frankish periods.

According to these data Eastern Galilee suffered a settlement crisis during the early Muslim period, when half of the sites which were inhabited during the Byzantine period were abandoned. This crisis was less severe than that suffered by Central Samaria during an earlier period. Samaria was abandoned by two-thirds of its population and 80% of its sites fell into ruin. Other peripheral regions, such as the Beth Shean Valley, the southern plains, Gaza, and the Negev, suffered a similar fate. But these regions were not resettled later on. They went through a process of nomadization but did not go through a process of sedentarization.

The process of nomadization occurs normally when there is a weak central government which is unable to impose law and order on the nomadic tribes. As a result of this weakness, the rural population emigrates or goes through a process of nomadization and joins the nomadic tribes.[13] Central Samaria does not appear to fit into this scheme. The first stage in the process of nomadization – that of the flight of the sedentary population – did not occur because of the weakness of the central government but, on the contrary, because of the excessive power which it exercised over the native population. The flight from Samaria was a forced one, and it was this flight which enabled the nomadic tribes which, in any case, dominated the country politically and religiously, to infiltrate into the region. The fact that this process was unusual was the cause for its speedier termination in Central Samaria than in other regions. The process of sedentarization was also more rapid because the region lay between two veteran and well-established settlement centers which exercised government control – Nablus and Jerusalem.

Eastern Upper Galilee went through a partial process of nomadization and desertion. Pressure from the nomadic tribes, which was still considerable during the Frankish period, was certainly stronger during the early Muslim period. It can be assumed that the Jewish inhabitants of the region did not enjoy the protection of the central government during that period, which probably accounted for their flight. The "desert line," east of which there was practically no permanent settlement, passed, at the end of the early Muslim period, through the Hawran and perhaps even through the Golan and advanced, gradually, into Eastern Galilee. The process of nomadization was stopped and changed course when a large fortress was built in Safad. Bishop Benoît points out that the fortress restored, by its very existence, security and order to the whole region. It can be assumed that it was the restoration of law and order to the region which led to the beginning of sedentarization, as happened in every other region at the height of nomadization. The fact that the huge fortress continued to exist in the Mamluk period and even became one of the important centers of administration in Palestine, strengthened this process.

From a map of the sites in Eastern Galilee during the Mamluk period, and from a list of settlements which existed there at the beginning of the Ottoman period, it can be established that no less than twenty-five new settlements (from amongst the fifty-four sites) were built during the Mamluk period (see maps 8 and 9). Here, too, many of the new settlements were built on sites which had not existed during the Byzantine and Frankish periods. In other words: during the Mamluk period a new pattern of settlement was

---

[13] For general discussion of nomadization and sedentarization, see Lattimore, 1976; Lewis, 1987; Dakhshleiger, 1978, 361–369; Bunimovitz, 1994, 253–283. On the process of nomadization of Palestine in the early Muslim period, see, among others, Sharon, 1976; Fraenkel, 1979; Tsafrir, 1984; Shmueli, 1981, 94–95, 128–130; and also Amiran & Ben Arieh, 1963, 162–166.

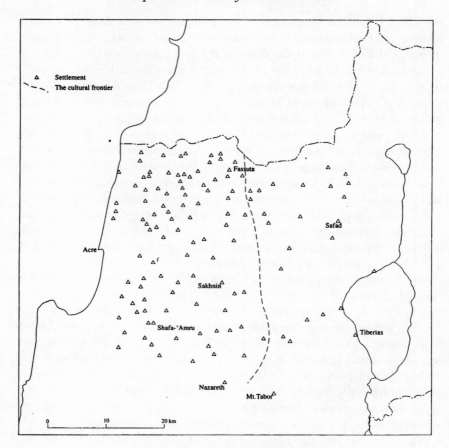

Map 8   Frankish sites in the Galilee

created in Eastern Galilee, reminiscent of the pattern of settlement which was created earlier in Central Samaria. The new settlements in Eastern Galilee, too, undoubtedly absorbed immigrants from regions where the process of sedentarization of the nomadic tribes had left its mark, until the construction of the fortress of Safad.

The development of regions which did not undergo nomadization and sedentarization: the example of Western Galilee

Western Galilee suffered a much milder process of desertion by its settled inhabitants, making it more reminiscent of the region between Jerusalem and Sinjil. Table 5 testifies to this.

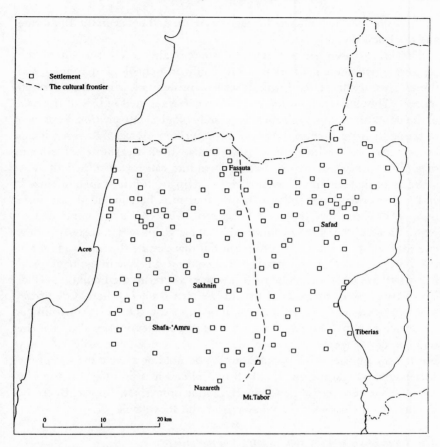

Map 9   Sixteenth-century sites in the Galilee. Based on Rhode, 1985.

Table 5   *Byzantine sites in Western Galilee which continued to exist in the Frankish period*

Byzantine sites	Byzantine sites which continued to exist in the Frankish period
34 hamlets (monasteries and farm houses)	5 (14%)
56 medium-sized villages	44 (85%)
20 large villages	15 (80%)
4 unknown size	4 (100%)

Ten large and medium-sized villages were created between the Byzantine and the Frankish periods.

The list is based on two types of sources: the reconstruction of the Byzantine settlement network is based mainly on archeological findings; and the reconstruction of the Frankish settlement network is based on written sources. The difference between the sources has resulted in bias of the data of the Frankish period, since there is no archeological information on sixteen of the settlements mentioned in the Latin written sources. However, it can be assumed that at least some of them had been Byzantine settlements originally.[14] I have, therefore, divided them into categories in the same way as the identified settlements were divided, giving us fourteen medium-sized, and perhaps even large, villages. It can, therefore, be concluded that more than 80% of the medium-sized villages of Western Galilee continued to exist, whereas 50% of the medium-sized and large villages in Eastern Galilee ceased to exist. It is important to point out that despite the massive flight of the Eastern Galilee inhabitants, the Jews continued to live in the region and many settlements still retained their Jewish character in the Frankish period. It can be guessed, by analogy, that in Western Galilee, where 80% of the medium-sized and large villages continued to exist, the Christian communal structure also continued to exist. It is important to note, also, that the number of villages which were preserved does not necessarily have any bearing on the size of the population. We do not know what the size of the settlements was during the Frankish period and it is possible that some of them which were very large during Byzantine times shrank in size. But some important conclusions can be drawn from the above table.

The disappearance of the rural estates and monasteries

Only 14% of the Byzantine estates and monasteries in Galilee and 18% in the region north of Jerusalem continued to exist after the early Muslim era. 86% of the estates and monasteries in Galilee and 82% of those in the area north of Jerusalem were destroyed or abandoned and not reestablished. These forms of settlement, which were characteristic of the Byzantine period, disappeared in all parts of Palestine and were not reestablished later on. This present study does not deal, it is true, with the history of those forms of settlement, which is too important a subject to be discussed perfunctorily

[14] Among Latin sources there appear at least sixteen settlements whose precise location is unknown; however, they were all apparently in the Western Upper Galilee and its coastal region. For this reason they do not appear on the map and have not been included in the number of settlements mentioned. The villages whose location is unknown include a number of fairly large villages such as Casale Album. These are the settlements: Casale Album, Aithire, Caphara, Noseoquie, Danehyle, Jubie, Bechera, Carsilia, Camsara, Deir Basta, Rapha, Ezefer, Assera, Jebetza, Bedar, and Rainemonde.

within the framework of a different subject, but in the absence of any other explanation it can be presumed that the disappearance of the estates and monasteries was connected with the emigration of the Byzantines and the more affluent members of the local Christian community. The people who remained were those without any possibility to immigrate: the local Syrian population.

The continuity of the spatial distribution of the large Byzantine villages
The degree of preservation of the Byzantine villages in Western Galilee and the region north of Jerusalem was relatively high – between at least 65% in Galilee to not more than 88% in the region north of Jerusalem. In both regions the distribution of the villages remained unchanged between the Byzantine and Frankish period. Likewise, the number of new villages established during the early Muslim period was not large in either region. It can be said that the distribution of local settlements in those regions during the Frankish period constituted a degenerated form of Byzantine settlement distribution, without almost any addition of new settlements.

The map describing the distribution of settlements in the Galilee in the Ottoman period (map 9) indicates that the number of settlements in Western Galilee continued to decline during the Mamluk period too. New settlements were established, but in far less numbers than were established in Eastern Galilee which, at the time, underwent an intensive process of sedentarization. It was not the establishment of new villages which characterized most markedly the settlement process in Western Galilee in later periods, but the creation of Muslim "suburbs" next to the Christian villages. It is also important to note that most of the new settlements which were created in the post-Byzantine period were, and still are, Muslim.

Unfortunately, because of the lack of written evidence, we cannot come to any unequivocal conclusion about the comparative size of the autochthonous Christian population of Galilee during the Frankish period. We have to be very careful, also, about drawing an analogy between the population of Galilee and that of Samaria. Nevertheless, in the absence of comprehensive historical data we cannot, in my opinion, ignore certain points of resemblance and difference between the settlement process in Samaria and similar processes in the Galilee.

(1) In both regions there was, in the Byzantine period, a large and well-established Christian population, and in both regions many Byzantine churches were built.

(2) In both regions there was a substantial Christian population both at the beginning of the Ottoman period and at the beginning of the twentieth

century. This point requires further elaboration. In three regions of Palestine there was, at the beginning of the twentieth century, a comparatively large Christian population: in the region north of Jerusalem (the district of Ramallah), in Western Galilee, and in Lower Galilee (Nazareth-Kafr Kanna). Almost all the settlements in the regions which retained their Christian population until the beginning of the twentieth century had continued to exist uninterruptedly from Byzantine times until our day. And, perhaps most important of all, Frankish castles and settlements were built in most of them. Many of these settlements are mentioned again and again in the Latin sources and in many of them, as I maintained above, there were Latin inhabitants in the twelfth century. Every available source testifies to the fact that there was a Christian population in these settlements between the sixth and the twentieth century and it can be assumed, although it cannot be proven, that the Christian population of these settlements continued to exist uninterruptedly from Byzantine times until today. It is difficult to imagine that a settlement which was Muslim during the Frankish period could have passed into Christian hands at a later stage; and even if this were feasible with respect to one settlement, it could not possibly be feasible with respect to the large Christian settlements in the whole country. It can also be assumed that many of the settlements which existed uninterruptedly from Byzantine to Frankish times and which were later abandoned were still Christian during the Frankish period.

According to the model which I try to develop here, the country was divided into three types of regions.

(1) Settlements which underwent a process of nomadization during the early Muslim period and had not become sedentarized until the beginning of modern times.

(2) Settlements which underwent a partial or complete process of nomadization in the early Muslim period and were resettled during the same period or during the Frankish or early Mamluk periods. In the regions which were completely nomadized and sedentarized in the early Muslim period, a purely Muslim community was created, with only "remnants" from the previous population; and in the regions which were only partially nomadized and sedentarized, as Eastern Galilee, there was a mixed population.

(3) In regions such as north of Jerusalem and Western Galilee, the former population was decimated and the settlements had deteriorated, but the processes of nomadization and sedentarization were marginal. The size of the Muslim population in these regions was in direct proportion to the extent of desertion and resettlement. These two processes were more extensive in Western Galilee (particularly in the area very near to Acre) than in the region

north of Jerusalem, and, therefore, the Muslim population in Western Galilee was larger than that in the region north of Jerusalem. The large Byzantine settlements, whose populations were undoubtedly Christian, continued to exist in Frankish times too, and some of them have remained in existence till this day.

It is important for the purpose of my study, which deals with Frankish rural settlement, that the Franks settled only in the third category of regions and, furthermore, that Frankish settlement was more intensive and widespread and occurred at an earlier time in the more Christian region north of Jerusalem than in Frankish Acre, despite the fact that the latter was no smaller a center and geographically more important than Frankish Jerusalem.

In the mixed Christian and Muslim settlements there was a physical division: the Christians lived in the old sections while the Muslims lived in the newer ones. That is the reason why in the districts of Ramallah, North Samaria, and Western Galilee, in which there were local Christian settlements, there was also Frankish settlement. And the Frankish settlement was dependent upon the existence of local Christian settlements.

In later times the slower process of conversion of individual Christians who lived in the Christian regions of Palestine began and it was then that the mixed settlements were created. In these settlements Muslim "suburbs," adjacent to the older Christian settlements, began to appear. The process began in places like Teqo'a already in the eleventh century and in places such as 'Abud and Shafa-'Amru apparently not before the Mamluk period.

In the light of this it would appear that the process of Islamization of Samaria and of Galilee during the early Muslim period was of the kind suggested by Vryonis and Levtzion: that is, in the regions which underwent nomadization for geographic-economic and political reasons there was infiltration of nomads whose presence led to a more rapid process of Islamization. Both Levtzion and Vryonis emphasize that this process of Islamization was more rapid than that of individuals. The latter process eventually led to the partial Islamization of the populations of Western Galilee and the region north of Jerusalem.

The Franks settled, according to this model, only in regions in which there was still a large Christian population. This can be seen from an examination not only of the regions studied by me but also of such regions as eastern Transjordan, Caesarea, the Sharon, north of Mt. Hebron, and others. The Franks did not settle in regions which were populated by well-established Muslim communities or by nomads in the process of sedentarization. This provides the explanation for the Frankish settlement in the south of eastern Transjordan where, according to both Frankish and Arabic sources, there were large concentrations of Christians, and also for the Franks' failure to conquer the more northern regions of Transjordan where, in the first half of the twelfth century, there was no real opposing military force, but also no sedentary Christian population.

CHAPTER TWENTY ONE

SUMMARY AND CONCLUSIONS

Frankish society: a frontier and migrant society

The difference between the picture presented here and the approach of the "existing model" can be summarized in the use made of the concept "Frankish settlement" as opposed to that of "Crusader settlement" which was used by Prawer and Smail. Both terms signify, in my opinion, different aspects of Frankish life in the Levant. "The Crusades" were limited both in space and in time and can be characterized by their bellicose aspects. The nature of the "Frankish settlement" was more civilian and extended over a much longer period of time. The Crusades, it is true, created the territorial expanse in which the new settlements were established and the process of Frankish settlement was a natural consequence of the military conquest but the fact that these two processes occurred consequently and influenced each other does not justify identifying one with the other. It would be more correct, in my opinion, to study each process separately as two consecutive stages in the creation of a "Settlement Frontier."

In the first stage (which is, in our case, the "Crusader" stage) of the creation of such a frontier the "vanguard" pinpoint the borders and capture them from a well-defined enemy. The enemy on the different kinds of frontiers need not necessarily be human. The enemy could also be a physical obstacle such as swamps, forests, and deserts, and the conquest does not necessarily have to have a violent, belligerent aspect. Nor does it have to be a one-time manifestation. In the process of creating a frontier there can be failures and fresh attempts at conquest.

In the second stage (which, in our case, is the Frankish settlement stage) the "frontier" is gradually filled with settlers and migrants, moved mainly by personal motives, such as individualism, flight from a common enemy, economic advantages, avoidance of competition, etc.

277

The differences between the first and second stages, and between the conquering vanguard and the settler rearguard, are stamped on the collective memory in a process which converts the former into a myth. The participants in the first stage are described in descriptive terms such as "pioneers," "conquistadores," "crusaders," "drainers of swamps," "conquerors of the West," etc., and images are selected in order to vest a mythical pantheon with an aura of idealism and self-sacrifice. The mythological symbols are selected according to the nature of the frontier: warriors (if the frontier was conquered by war), saintly figures (if the frontier is a religious frontier), and individualistic figures (in the case of the American frontier). Events in the lives of these selected images are given an idealistic mantle for the educational benefit of future generations.

It is difficult to draw an analogy between the sermonizing of the intellectuals and stark reality. Amongst the conquering vanguard there must have been many who were motivated by selfish and personal reasons, divorced from any altruistic desire to do good for the benefit of society as a whole, while the opposite was true for some of the later settlers. But the myth surrounding them does not recognize such details and regards them all as one collective figure with common characteristics.

The frontier myth is of value only if it contradicts the pioneer generation with the future generations. Every such myth has a specific and well-defined objective – the future generations, who are contemptuously dismissed as suffering from a weakness of character foreign to the pioneer generation. Migrants to the conquered frontiers and the second wave of settlers are not regarded by their contemporaries (who create the myth) as "conquerors of the frontier," "pioneers," or "conquistadors," and they gradually become ordinary mortals whose weaknesses darken their actions. It is this generation which the myths aspire to influence and educate.

The new society which arises in the frontier region sends out conflicting messages about its loyalty towards the ideals of the frontier: as this society becomes more crystalized it reveals a tendency to demonstrate to the outside world its loyalty towards the principles of the frontier myth, mainly for the purpose of receiving aid or legitimization from those societies from which it originated. In all such collective demonstrations of loyalty, the new society will emphasize that the conquest of the frontier has not been completed and that the mythical task of doing so is still in process.

On the other hand, and at the same time, a different attitude is adopted for internal consumption: the intellectual elite tend to erect a monument to the frontier myth and to enjoin and lecture the new settlers to take an example from it and follow in its footsteps instead of distancing themselves from its ideological principles. The new generation are called upon to live up to the ethical and religious standards of the frontier pioneers, which were the raison d'être for its conquest, and to continue the struggle against the human or cultural enemy. Failure to do so, they are warned, could end in disaster.

The "Crusaders," the conquerors of the country, constituted the frontier myth of the Frankish period. They were immortalized (as witness the attitude towards Godfrey of Bouillon and other Crusaders), their sacrifice was "in the name of God" and thence, so thought their contemporaries, came their strength. The immortal qualities of these first Crusaders were thought to come from their devotion to their faith and their unreserved readiness to fight and die for it. The same approach was applied also to the Crusaders of later generations such as Richard Lion-Heart or St. Louis.

An example of this Crusader myth can be found in the words of William of Tyre. In describing the events of 1174 in the Latin Kingdom of Jerusalem, William referred to the difficulties experienced by the Kingdom in withstanding the threat posed by Salah al-Din. He repeated the question "so often asked": "How did it happen that our ancestors, a mere handful, so courageously faced superior enemy forces . . . and were victorious, so glorifying the name of God?"

William divided the causes for the sorry state of the Kingdom into three. He first emphasized the fact that his contemporaries had distanced themselves from their faith, and he compared this with the religious devotion of the first conquerors of the country. These latter, he says, were unreservedly faithful to God, while the distancing of his contemporaries from their faith was at the root of their decline. William calls his contemporaries by a collective name intended to distinguish them from the first conquerors: "Populus orientalis."

The second cause, according to William, was the fact that whereas the first conquerors were trained men of war, who rushed into battle in the name of God, the "orientals" had lost all military ability because of the long period of peace they had enjoyed. They had, he asserted, lost their enthusiasm for war together with their enthusiasm for their faith. "Secunda causa nobis ex latere occurrit, quod tempore preterito, cum illi viri venerabiles, zelo ducti divino, ardore fidei interius succensi primum ad Orientales partes descenderunt, erant bellicis assueti disciplinis, preliis exercitati, usum habentes armorum familiarem, populus vero Orientalis econtrario longa pace dissolutus, rei militaris expers, inexercitatus legibus preliorum vocatione gaudebat."[1].

---

[1] William of Tyre, 21, 7, 969–970.

Only at the end of his list of causes does William return to reality. He
ascribes the unification of all the enemy armies for the purpose of waging
war against the Franks as one of the causes for the sorry state of affairs in the
Kingdom.

William, the intellectual and churchman, conscious of the existence of a
new identity, whom he dubs "people of the orient," mourns the fact that the
Franks enjoyed too many years of peace. He is not the only member of the
Frankish intellectual elite devoted to the Crusader myth. A similar opinion
about the inhabitants of Palestine and their obligation towards the Crusader
ideal was held by Jacques of Vitry. The "Crusaders," who were also "the
ancestors" and "the first pioneers" were characterized by their devotion to
their religion and their unreserved readiness to fight for it, and win.

The attempt made by proponents of the early model to regard all the settlers as "Crusaders" and to identify them with "knights living in fortresses
and fighting the battle for Christianity" is an attempt to associate them with
the myth which some of the chroniclers developed. But the modern scholar
cannot allow himself to be bound by the homilies of previous leaders and
thus ignore complex reality.

The real state of affairs can be reconstructed and even emerges from the
sermonizing itself. William of Tyre, who cultivated the frontier myth, does
not regard the Franks as "fighting Crusaders." On the contrary, he decries
the Frankish settlers' distancing of themselves from the fighting ideal and the
long period of peace, in the course of which the settlers were able to devote
themselves to other, more earthly (in contradistinction to religious) and less
bellicose pursuits. He also regrets the crystalization of a new collective setup
in the period after the "conquest of the frontier."

My book does not deal with the myths of the period. I have not dealt with
what happened to the mythical "Crusader generation." I have concentrated
on the "Crusaders" who settled in the East and on those who joined them
after the frontier regions had been conquered. I have tried to depict the
unheroic side of the picture – that of a migrant society with its daily and
hourly struggle against the hardships of agriculture in the Levant. I have had
constantly in mind those migrants who came to the Kingdom of Jerusalem
in search of a place in which to settle and a piece of land to cultivate. Many
of these migrants must have regarded the Levant with mixed feelings, weigh-
ing the advantages of settling in a new, unexploited, and holy country against
the harsh climate and difficult conditions.

At the root of Frankish migration to the Levant were the same reasons
which brought eleventh- and twelfth-century generations to seek a haven
and a piece of land somewhere in Europe. Just as there were people who

settled in Sicily or Spain immediately after they were conquered, so were there people who elected to settle in the Levant. These settlers wanted to live, raise families, build homes, acquire estates, and not merely to die in the name of God. They did not come to the East only for idealistic reasons. The land and farming claimed their time and strength, and the hardships of daily life were their challenge. The war against Islam was not always one of their priorities, both because of the long period of peace which they enjoyed (and which William of Tyre regretted) and because of the daily hardships which occupied all their attention.

The difficulty about comparing the Crusader frontier with other frontier manifestations is the result of the failure of the former. If the Franks had succeeded in retaining their settlement network over a long period of time, it would not have been difficult to understand that hand-in-hand with the "frontier conquest" went the gray and banal settlement process. The historical failure of settlement is what contributed to the historical image of the whole period and left us with the mythical, Crusader image. This may have led to the popular interpretation according to which even third and fourth generation locally born farmers were regarded as "Crusaders."

The "Crusader" image was nurtured also by the fact that the conquest of the frontiers never ended and was twice interrupted by the winds of war. There were, it is true, long periods of peace, particularly during the twelfth century, but before and after these periods the Franks had to mobilize for bloody wars. The scholars who developed the existing model based their image of the whole Frankish population on these wars and on the continued battle to complete the conquest of the frontiers, and ignored the other aspect of Frankish life which had developed at the same time.

But this other settlement aspect was not in the least insignificant. The Franks, it would appear, were very successful settlers and were not only fighters and builders of fortifications. The migrants who settled in the Kingdom of Jerusalem established a network of well-developed settlements reminiscent, in many ways, of settlements established in contemporaneous Europe. The intensive Frankish settlement included the construction of developed castra, of "rural burgi," and monasteries, of castles which served as centers for seigniorial estates, of smaller castles, manor houses, farm houses, unfortified villages, parochial systems, etc.

Frankish settlement was not expressed only in the construction of buildings. The Franks brought rural administrative skills with them and continued to develop them in Palestine. They built new roads and repaired the existing ones, they marked and parceled fields, introduced sophisticated methods of tax collection, recognized the importance of water and its proper distribution, developed systems of irrigation, constructed flour millls, built bridges, and learnt the secret of raising animals with whom they had not been previously familiar. The Frankish agricultural network was, therefore, flourishing and in no way as decrepit as the scholars tried to depict. Their claim that the Franks were completely unaware of what went on in their fields (save when it came to collecting their share of the crops), and had no contact with the local inhabitants, is not based on written or archeological sources and is certainly not accurate.

It is difficult to fix a scale for measuring the intensity of agricultural settlement in the Latin Kingdom and it is, therefore, difficult also to examine the extent of settlement in comparison with that in other regions during the same period. I think, nevertheless, that the sum total of 200 Frankish sites which appear in the list of settlements which I discussed (and many of which were even discovered) testifies to an extent of settlement which was neither limited nor marginal. In view of the short period of time during which the Frankish settlers lived in the Orient they can be said to have succeeded remarkably well in establishing extremely well-developed rural settlements, even though in regions of parallel size in Europe there was much more extensive settlement. It must be noted also that there were regional differences in the standard and density of settlement amongst the different regions of the country. For example, the settlement network in the region north of Jerusalem was shown to be more dense and intensive than the settlement network in the royal domain near Acre. It can be seen that the latter was regarded as less convenient for settlement purposes and that the new settlers who chose to live there were granted preferential rights. In the region near to Jerusalem we found types of settlement which were practically non-existent in Western Galilee. We discovered, inter alia, tens of manor houses, the like of which we did not find in Western Galilee, but which did exist in Mt. Hebron and apparently also in the Sharon.

A comparative study of the periods of settlement showed also that the Franks settled first in the hilly region between Jerusalem and Sinjil. The development of settlement in the Western Galilee began only in the middle of the twelfth century when the development of settlement in the central hill region was almost complete. The differences between settlement in the Jerusalem–Sinjil and Western Galilee regions were not due to economic deterministic reasons. The Western Galilee is most certainly no less fertile than Samaria and no less blessed with water. I tend to attribute the differences to the greater density of local Christian settlement which already existed in the Jerusalem region and to the fact that Jerusalem was the capital of the Kingdom.

This applies also to other regions in the Kingdom of Jerusalem. The impression created from the conclusions I draw in my thesis is that the distribution of Frankish settlements, their degree of intensivity, and the rate at which they were developed, is in direct proportion to the distribution, degree of intensivity, and rate of development of the local Christian settlements which still existed during the Frankish period. The Franks settled in all the regions in which there were Christian communities and did not settle in regions which had passed through a process of nomadization during the early Muslim period and had, by the twelfth century, a settled Muslim population.

That, in my opinion, is why one can find traces of many Frankish settlements in regions such as Jerusalem–Sinjil, Sebaste and its environs, southeastern Transjordan, Western Galilee, Lower Galilee (Safforie, Nazareth, and Tiberias), Mt. Hebron (between Bethlehem and Hebron), and others. And that is also the reason why there were no Frankish settlements in regions such as Central Samaria, Eastern Galilee, parts of Mt. Hebron and other regions in which, already then, there was a substanial Muslim majority or a Jewish–Muslim majority. It is possible that that was also the reason for the surprising failure of the Franks to attempt to conquer the northern parts of eastern Transjordan and to settle in the Golan.

This book, which was intended from the beginning to study only the process of settlement, does not presume to present a complete picture of the relationship between the Frankish and the local populations. Nevertheless, it can be stated that the fact that Frankish settlement was limited to "Christian" regions of Palestine did not apply only in the Kingdom of Jerusalem or in the hearts of other regions which were examined. It would appear that this pattern of settlement was common in the whole of the Levant and that the Franks conquered only those countries and geographic panhandles in which there was a large and progressive Christian population. Only in such countries and in such regions were Frankish political entities established.

From the documents dealing with the administration of rural regions a picture emerges of a mixed society, consisting of Frankish and local Christian components. The Franks occupied, in all cases, the highest ranks in the feudal or ecclesiastical hierarchy, but this was always a mixed hierarchy consisting of both ethnic-cultural elements – the Frankish and the Syrian-Christian. The documents reveal that Syrian society was also mixed and that the Syrians did not constitute a uniform mass with equal rights and obligations.

It is true that it was the Syrians who were the indentured farmers attached to the land, whereas the Frankish farmers, insofar as could be gathered from the written sources, enjoyed the status of free farmers. But one must be wary of painting an absolutely stereotyped picture. Not all Syrians were indentured farmers. On the contrary, there were different classes of persons amongst them. In the Kingdom of Jerusalem there were only minor functionaries and owners of quasi allodial lands, but in other regions of the Levant there were local Christians with nobility status (mainly Armenians). The Syrians fulfilled the functions of dragomen and Scribans, while the owners of the allodial lands had special rights which the sale of a village to a Frankish seignior did not prejudice, nor was their land sold together with the land of the village.

It can be assumed that social contacts and marriage ties also existed between equal social classes, just as the parochial churches apparently served both the Franks and the local Christians. It is important to remember, in this context, that members of the Frankish royal family repeatedly married Eastern Christians. It is reasonable to assume (even though we have no positive textual proof for it) that the Frankish farmers and burgesses also married Eastern Christian women of the same social status. On the other hand, it can also be assumed that the differences in social status between the Frankish aristocracy, the bourgeoisie, and the lower class of Eastern Christians were maintained in the Orient, just as they were in contemporaneous Europe.

This concept of a mixed Franco-Eastern Christian society can perhaps provide the reason for the fact that the Latin documents and chronicles ignore the existence of Muslim inhabitants. It would appear that the settlement and social relations map had an effect on the mental map of the Franks, with the result that it included only Christian regions and Christian inhabitants. And when the Latin documents deal with the rights of the local inhabitants (for example, the documents dealing with the judicial instance of the local inhabitants – the Rays) they refer mainly to "Syrian" inhabitants and mention only in passing other inhabitants.

I think, therefore, that it would be opportune to recall some of the elements of the previous French model which deals with the relations between the Franks and the local population, but which was rejected out of hand by the proponents of the existing model. According to advocates of the French model, a mixed society, which they called "Franco-Syrian," developed in the Frankish Orient. The Franks, they maintained, were influenced by the eastern way of life and by local customs and, in turn, brought law and order and physical protection to the local population. The French school described the relations between the Franks and the local population in glowing terms, and one of them actually suggested that the Frankish rulers could have served as ideal models for modern governments!

This idealization of the relations which existed between the Franks and the local population played into the hands of Smail and Prawer, who fiercely challenged its credibility, with some justification, as the proponents of the French model had no reason, save perhaps for their own imaginations and prejudices, for finding that the relations between the Franks and the Muslims were ideal. And as for the relations between the Franks and the local Christians, they too were not absolutely ideal.

The French model would have been far more acceptable had its proponents claimed that the "Franco-Syrian" society consisted only of Franks and Eastern Christians and did not include the Muslim component of the population. The broad generalization and the idealization of the relations led to the downfall of the French model and to the birth of the existing model, which, in turn, went to the opposite extreme, by arguing in favor of social, political, and settlement segregation.

The conclusions which I drew in my book point to a possible synthesis between the French model, developed by Dodu, Rey, and Grousset and the existing model, developed by Smail, Prawer, and others. According to my interpretation, a new social structure started to be woven in the Levant during the Frankish rule. This social structure was composed of a combination of Frankish and local Christians and was separate from the Muslim sector of the population of the country. The French model, which presupposed a combination of all the elements of the population, was at fault, in my opinion, for not distinguishing between the local Christian and the Muslim populations. On the other hand, the existing model, which suggested that there was complete segregation between the Franks and the "locals," was equally at fault for not recognizing the important geographical, political, and cultural functions of the local Christians.

The Franco-Syrian society created a frontier society which could be labeled "Christian under Frankish hegemony." It should be remembered that the basic ideology of the Crusades, as laid down by Urban at the Council in Clermont, was founded to a large extent on the idea of liberating the Eastern Christians from the Turkish yoke. In other words: the concept of frontier, which was at the basis of "Crusader" ideology, did not refer to a territorial frontier, but to a cultural one, namely the liberation of the Christians and not necessarily liberation of their lands. The objective of the frontier ideology became territorial only at a later stage and while already in the process of attaining it. This later ideology had a practical aspect too: the Turkish tribes were the only factors, at least in the twelfth century, threatening both the peace of the Eastern Christians and the territorial achievements of the Franks. Any potential danger from non-Turkish elements was insignificant in comparison with that to be feared from the Turks.

For at least fifty years, the inhabitants of the Kingdom of Jerusalem had been far distant from the war with the Turks. From the beginning of the 1120s and until the end of the 1160s no danger threatened the Franks who lived in the Kingdom of Jerusalem (as opposed to those who lived in Frankish settlements further north, in the regions of Edessa and Antioch). The Latin and Arab sources do make mention of isolated hostile incursions into the Latin Kingdom during this period, but these did not cause any material damage to the Franks. Military confrontations, to the extent to which they took place, occurred mainly on the borders of the Kingdom, within enemy territory, and usually ended in victory for the Franks.

The Fatimid threat (which originated from nothing more than a "simple" territorial struggle) decreased to a considerable extent, and perhaps even ended, at the beginning of the 1120s; while the struggle against the Turks and their allies, which was the raison d'être for all the Crusades, continued until later. One fact emerges from practically all of the descriptions of this struggle: the enemies of the Franks were almost always called "Turks" and not "Saracens" or "Muslims." The Turkish tribes, whose wave of migration into Asia Minor and North Syria had reached its pinnacle by the beginning of the twelfth century, mainly attacked the Frankish settlements which were closest to them: those of Edessa (in particular), Antioch, and Tripoli (to a lesser extent).

The threat posed by the Turkish tribes and rulers was, as already noted, more serious for the local Christians. Vryonis pointed out that the Turks caused more harm to the local Christians than any of their predecessors – a finding with which I heartily agree.

The Christian population, therefore, did not suffer from the threat of "continuous vital danger from a Muslim invasion" as Smail and Prawer would have us believe, since their real enemy, the Turks, were too far away, and if they constituted a threat at all it was against the inhabitants of the northern countries.

From what was said above it is clear that both types of danger – the external and the internal – did not constitute a real threat to the Frankish settlers and that, therefore, there was no reason for them to be incarcerated in walled cities and fortresses.

However, the fate of the Franco-Christian frontier was sealed when it clashed with a stronger, contemporaneous Turkish frontier. The widespread Turkish infiltration, which was also a frontier manifestation, was stronger and had practically unlimited sources and manpower. The Latin chroniclers, who described the battles with the Turks, returned again and again to the large hordes at the enemy's disposal. The Frankish migration could not compete with the massive numbers of Turkish tribesmen, who invaded the Levant at the time, and finally took control of all the Christian concentrations, as well as of the Frankish settlements built by the toil of their own hands.

The failure of the Frankish frontier in the Orient turned the process of settlement into a passing phase without any legendary value, unlike the more successful attempts at settlement in Spain and Sicily and East Germany, which left their mark on the collective European memory and became legends for future generations. But the Crusader myth – the myth of the generation of first pioneers – never disappeared. This myth of courageous fighters, devoted to their religious precepts, continued to be relevant in the collective memory of many generations to come as well as, so it would seem to me, in the collective memory of many scholars.

BIBLIOGRAPHY

Primary sources

Abu'l-Fida', *Taquim*	Abu'l-Fida', *Kitab Taquim al-Buldan,* ed. M. Reinaud and Mac Guckin de Slane, Paris, 1840.
Abu Shama, *Dhayl*	Abu Shama, *Tarajim Rijal al-Qarnayn al-Sadis wa'l-Sabi' al-Ma'ruf bi'l-Dhayl 'Ala al-Raudatayn,* ed. M. al-Kawthari, Cairo, 1947.
Abu Shama, *Raudatayn*	Abu Shama, *Kitab al-Raudatayn fi Akhbar al-Daulatayn,* vol. I.1–2, ed. M. H. M. Ahmad & M. M. Ziyada, Cairo, 1956–1962; vols. I and II, Cairo 1870.
Abu Shama, ed. *RHC*	*Le Livre des deux jardins,* trans. Barbier de Meynard, in *RHC, HOr,* vols. IV-V.
Albert of Aachen	Albertus Aquensis, *Liber Christianae expeditionis pro ereptione, emundatione et restitutione Sanctae Hierosolymitanae ecclesiae,* in *RHC, HOcc,* IV.
Ambroise	Ambroise, *L'Estoire de la guerre sainte (1190–1192),* ed. and trans. G. Paris, Paris, 1897; *The Crusade of Richard Lion-Heart,* trans. M. J. Hubert, Columbia University of Records of Civilization, Sources and Studies, vol. XXXIV, New York, 1941.
Anna Comnena	Anna Comnena, *Alexiad,* ed. and trans. B. Leib, 3 vols., Paris, 1937–1945; Eng. trans. E. A. S. Daws, London, 1929; Eng. trans. E. R. A. Sewter, Harmondsworth, 1969.
"Annales de Terre Sainte"	"Annales de Terre Sainte", ed. R. Röhricht & G. Raynaud, in *AOL,* 2.2 (1884), 427–461.
Anonymus I	*Descriptio Sanctorum Locorum Hierusalem,* ed. and trans. R. Hill, *Gesta Francorum,* Oxford Medieval Texts, Oxford, 1979, 98–101.
Anonymus II	*Peregrinationes ad Loca Sancta,* ed. T. Tobler, *Theodorici libellus,* Paris, 1865, 118–128.

Anonymus III — *Haec est via ad Terram Sanctam*, ed. T. Tobler, *Theodorici libellus*, Paris, 1865, 128–134.

Anonymus IV — *Iter ad Terram Sanctam*, ed. T. Tobler, *Theodorici libellus*, Paris, 1865, 134–140.

Anonymus V — *De Locis Sanctis,* ed. W. A. Neumann, "Drei mittelalterliche Pilgerschriften. Innomitatus V," *Österreichische Viertel-jahrschrift für katholische Theologie*, 5 (1866), 221–257.

Anonymus VII — *Descriptio Terrae Sanctae*, ed. T. Tobler, *Descriptiones Terrae Sanctae*, Leipzig, 1874, 100–107.

Anonymus VIII — *De Terra Ultramaria*, ed. T. Tobler, *Descriptiones Terrae Sanctae*, Leipzig, 1874, 193–196.

Anonymus, 1234 — *Anonymi auctoris chronicon ad A.C. 1234*, trans. A. Abouna with an introduction and notes by J. M. Fiey, in *CSCO*, 354 (= Scriptores Syri 154), Louvain, 1974.

Antoninus of Placentia — Antoninus of Placentia, *Antonini Placentini Itinerarium*, ed. P. Geyer, in *CCSL*, 175, 127–153; Eng. trans. J. Wilkinson, *Jerusalem Pilgrims before the Crusades,* Warminster, 1977, 78–89.

Les Archives — J. Delaville Le Roulx, ed., *Les Archives, la Bibliothèque et le trésor de l'ordre de Saint-Jean de Jérusalem à Malte*, Bibliothèque des Ecoles françaises d'Athenes et de Rome, I, 32, Paris, 1883.

Baha al-Din, ed. *RHC* — Baha al-Din, *Anecdotes et beaux traits de la vie du sultan Youssof [Salah al-Din]*, in *RHC*, HOr., III, 1–374.

Bar Hebraeus — Bar Hebraeus (Abu'l-Faraj), *Chronography*, trans. W. Budge, vol. I, London and Oxford, 1932.

Baudry of Dol — Baldricus episcopus Dolensis, *Historia Hierosolimitana*, in *RHC, HOcc.*, IV, 1–111.

Belard of Ascoli — Belard of Ascoli, *Descriptio Terrae Sanctae*, *IHC*, II, 43–49; trans. in J. Wilkinson with J. Hill and W. F. Ryan, *Jerusalem Pilgrimage 1099–1185*, London, 1988, 228–232.

Benjamin of Tudela — Benjamin of Tudela, *The Itinerary of Benjamin of Tudela*, ed. and trans. M. N. Adler, London, 1907.

Bongars — J. Bongars, ed. *Gesta Dei per Francos*, 2 pts in 1 vol., Hanau, 1611.

Burchardus de Monte Sion — Burchardus de Monte Sion, *Descriptio Terrae Sanctae*, *Peregrinatores Medii Aevi Quatuor: Brochardus de Monte Sion, Ricoldus de Monte Crucis, Odoricus de Foro Julii, Willebrandus de Oldenburg*, ed. J. C. M. Laurent, 2nd edn., Leipzig, 1864, 1–99.

Chalandon, "Un diplome — F. Chalandon, "Un diplome inédit d'Amaury I, roi de inédit"　　　　　　　　Jérusalem, en faveur de l'Abbaye du Temple-Notre-Seigneur (Acre, 6–11 avril 1166)," *ROL*, 8 (1900–1901), 311–317.

"Chartes de Terre Sainte"　　"Chartes de Terre Sainte," ed. J. Delaville Le Roulx, *ROL*, 11 (1905/1908), 181–191.

Chartes du Mont-Thabor　　*Cartulaire général de l'Ordre des Hospitaliers de St.-Jean de Jérusalem (1100–1310)*, ed. J. Delaville Le Roulx, 4 vols., Paris, 1894–1906, II, 899–914.

Les chemins et les pelerinages de la Terre Sainte　　Michelant & Raynaud, 177–200.

La citez de Jerusalem　　In De Vogüé, 1860, 436–444.

De constructione Castri Saphet　　R. B. C. Huygens, *De constructione Castri Saphet. Construction et fonctions d'un château fort franc en Terre Sainte*, Amsterdam, Oxford, and New York, 1981 (=Koninklijke Nederlandse Akademie van Wetenschappen, Afdeling Letterkunde, Verhandelingen, Nieuwe Reeks, 111).

Continuation de Guillaume de Tyr　　*La continuation de Guillaume de Tyr (1184–1197)*, ed. M. R. Morgan, Paris, 1982.

Continuation de Guillaume de Tyr, ed, RHC　　ed. *RHC.Continuation de Guillaume de Tyr, de 1229 a 1261, dite du manuscrit de Rothelin,* in *RHC*, *HOcc.*, II, 489–639.

Danishmendname　　*La Geste de Melik Danismend Gazi, étude critique du Danishmendname*, ed. and trans. I. Melikoff, Paris, 1960 (=Bibliothèque archéologique, 60=Bibliothèque archéologique et historique de l'Institut Français d'Archéologie d'Istanbul, 10, 11).

Delaborde　　H. F. Delaborde, ed., *Chartes de la Terre Sainte provenant de l'abbaye de Notre-Dame de Josaphat*, Paris, 1880.

Diya' al-Din al-Maqdisi, Hijra　　Diya' al-Din al-Maqdisi, *Sabab hijrat al Maqadisa ila Dimashq*, in Ibn Tulun, Shams al-Din Muhammad ibn 'Ali, *Al-Qalaʿid al jawhariyya fi taʾrikh alʿid al jawhariyya fi taʾrikh al Salihiyya*, I, ed. M. A. Duhman, Damascus, 1949.

Domesday Book　　*Domesday Book*, ed. A. Farley, Public Record Commision, 2 vols., London, 1873.

Eracles　　*L'Estoire d'Eracles empereur et la conquête de la Terre d'Outremer*, in *RHC, HOcc.,* I–II.

Ernoul　　*La Chronique d'Ernoul et de Bernard le Trésorier*, ed. L. de Mas Latrie, Paris, 1871.

Eusebius, *Onomastikon*　　ʿThe Onomastikon of Eusebius, trans. (with notes) E. Z. Melamed (=*Tarbiz*, XIX and XXI), Jerusalem, 1950.

De expugnatione　　*De expugnatione Terrae Sanctae libellus*, ed. J. Stevenson (RS, 66), London, 1875.

Les familles d'Outremer	C. du Fresne Du Cange, *Les familles d'Outremer*, ed. E. G. Rey, Paris, 1869.
Fretellus	*Rorgo Fretellus de Nazareth et sa description de la Terre Sainte, histoire et édition de texte*, ed. P. C. Boeren, Amsterdam, Oxford, and New York, 1980.
Fulcher of Chartres	*Fulcheri Carnotensis Historia Hierosolymitana (1095–1127)*, ed. H. Hagenmeyer, Heidelberg, 1913.
Galterius Cancellarius	*Galterii cancellarii bella Antiochena*, ed. H. Hagenmeyer, Innsbruck, 1896.
Gesta Francorum	*Gesta Francorum et aliorum Hierosolimitanorum*, ed. and trans. R. Hill, London, 1962.
Gesta Regis Henrici secundi	*Gesta Regis Henrici secundi*, ed. W. Stubbs (RS, 49), London, 1867.
Gesta Regis Ricardi	*Itinerarium Peregrinorum et Gesta Regis Ricardi*, ed. W. Stubbs (RS, 38, 1), London, 1864; trans. in *Chronicles of the Crusades*, Bohn's Antiquarian Library, London, 1848, 65–339.
Les Gestes des Chiprois	*Les Gestes des Chiprois*, ed. G. Raynaud, Geneva, 1887 (=Société de l'Orient latin: série historique, 5).
Guibert of Nogent	Guibert of Nogent, *Historia quae dicitur Gesta Dei per Francos*, in *RHC. HOcc.*, IV.
Hagenmeyer, *Kreuzzugsbriefe*	H. Hagenmeyer, ed., *Die Kreuzzugsbriefe aus den Jahren 1088–1100*, Innsbruck, 1901.
al-Harawi	al-Harawi, *Al-Isharat ila ma'rifat al-ziyarat*, ed. J. Sourdel Thomine, Damascus, 1953.
Hiestand, *Vorarbeiten*	R. Hiestand, ed., *Vorarbeiten zum Oriens Pontificius*, I: *Papsturkunden für Templer und Johanniter, Archivbericht und Texte*, II: *Papsturkunden für Templer und Johanniter, Neue Folge*, III: *Papsturkunden für Kirchen im Heiligen Lande*, Abhandlungen der Akademie der Wissenschaften in Göttingen, Phil.-hist. Klasse, series 3, vols. LXXVII, CXXXV–CXXXVI, Göttingen, 1972–1985.
Holy Sepulcher	*Le Cartulaire du chapitre du Saint-Sépulcre de Jérusalem,* ed. Geneviève Bresc-Bautier, Paris, 1984.
Hospital	*Cartulaire général de l'ordre des Hospitaliers de St.-Jean de Jérusalem (1100–1310)*, ed. J. Delaville Le Roulx, 4 vols., Paris, 1894–1906.
Ibn 'Asakir	Ibn 'Asakir, *Al-Ta'rikh al-Kabir,* 7 vols., Damascus, 1911–1932.
Ibn al-Athir, *Al-Kamil*	Ibn al-Athir, *Al-Kamil fi al-Ta'rikh*, ed. C. J. Tornberg, 13 vols., Beirut, 1965.
Ibn al-Athir	ed. *RHC Extrait de la chronique intitulée Kamel-altevarykh, par Ibn-Alatyr* in *RHC, HOr*, IV-1, 189–744; *RHC, HOr.*, IV-2a, 3–180.

Ibn al-Furat, trans. Lyons   *Ayyubids, Mamlukes and Crusaders. Selections from the Ta'rikh al-Duwal wa'l-Muluk of Ibn al-Furat*, trans. U. & M.C. Lyons, intro. and notes J. S. C. Riley-Smith, 2 vols., Cambridge, 1971.

Ibn Jubayr   *The Travels of Ibn Jubayr*, trans. R.J.C. Broadhurst, London, 1952.

Ibn al-Qalanisi   Ibn al-Qalanisi, *Dhayl Ta'rikh Dimashq*, ed. A. F. Amedroz, Leyden, 1908.

Ibn al-Qalanisi, trans. Gibb   *The Damascus Chronicle of the Crusades. Extracted and Translated from the Chronicle of Ibn al-Qalanisi*, trans. E. A. R. Gibb, London, 1932.

Ibn Shaddad   Ibn Shaddad al-Halabi, *Al-A'laq al-Khatira fi Dhikr Umara' al-Sham wa'l-Jazira*, II, pt 2, *Ta'rikh Lubnan, al-Urdunn wa-Filastin*, ed. S. Dahhan, Damascus, 1963, 225–230.

Ibn Taghri Birdi   Ibn Taghri Birdi, *Al-Nujum al-Zahira fi Muluk Misr wa'l-qahira*, 16 vols, repr. of Cairo, 1930–1956.

'Imad al-Din al-Isfahani   'Imad al-Din al-Isfahani, *Kitab al-fath al-qussi fi'l-fath al Qudsi*, ed. Carlo de Landberg, Leyden,1888. trans. H. Massé, *Conquête de la Syrie et de la Palestine par Saladin (al-Fath al-qussi fi'l-fath al-qudsi)*, Paris, 1972 (=Documents rélatifs à l'histoire des croisades, 10).

"Inventaire"   "Inventaire de pièces de Terre Sainte de l'ordre de l'Hôpital," éd. J. Delaville Le Roulx, *ROL*, 3 (1895), 44–106.

Iohannes Phochas   Johannes Phochas, *RHC, Grec*, I, 527–558.

Isho'dad of Merv   Isho'dad of Merv, *The Commentaries of Isho'dad of Merv, bishop of Hadatha*, trans. M. D. Gibson, Cambridge, 1911.

Jacques of Vitry   Jacques of Vitry, *Historia Orientalis seu Hierosolymitana*, ed. J. Bongars, *Gesta Dei per Francos*, 2 pts in 1 vol., Hanau, 1611, 1047–1124.

Jacques of Vitry, Letters   *Lettres de Jacques de Vitry (1160/1170–1240), évêque de Saint-Jean-d'Acre. Edition critique*, ed. R. B. C. Huygens, Leyden, 1960.

Jean of Ibelin   *Le Livre de Jean d'Ibelin*, in *RHC, Lois*, I, 7–423.

Khitrowo   *Itineraires russes en Orient*, trans. B. de Khitrowo, Geneva, 1889.

Klein, *Sefer Ha-yishuv*   *Sefer Ha-yishuv* (=*The Book of [Jewish] Settlement*). Jerusalem, 1939 (in Hebrew).

Kohler   "Chartes de l'abbaye de Notre-Dame de la vallée de Josaphat en Terre Sainte (1108–1291). Analyse et extraits," ed. C. Kohler, *ROL*, 7 (1889), 108–222.

Les Lignages d'Outremer	*Les Lignages d'Outremer*, in *RHC, Lois*, II, 441–474.
Livre au roi	*Le Livre au roi*, in *RHC, Lois*, I, 601–644.
Mansi	G. D. Mansi, ed., *Sacrorum Conciliorum nova et amplissima collectio*, 31 vols., Florence and Venice, 1759–1798.
al-Maqrizi, *Khitat*	al-Maqrizi, *Kitab al-Mawaʿiz waʾl-iʿtibar, fi dhikr al-khitat waʾl-athar*, 2 vols., Cairo, 1853–1854.
al-Maqrizi, *Suluk*	al-Maqrizi, *Kitab al-suluk li-maʿrifat duwal al-muluk*, ed. M. M. Ziyada & S. ʿA.-F. ʿAshur, 4 vols. in 12 pts, Cairo, 1934–1973.
Martin	J. P. Martin, "Les premiers princes croisés et les Syriens Jacobites de Jérusalem," *JA*, 12 (1888), 471–490; 13 (1889) 33–79.
Matthew of Edesse	*Chronique de Mathieu d'Edesse (962–1136), avec la continuation de Gregoire le prêtre jusqu'en 1162*, trans. E Dulaurier, Paris, 1958.
Matthew of Edesse, ed. *RHC*	*Extraits de la chronique de Matthieu d'Edesse*, in *RHC, Arm*, I, 1–150.
Mayer, St. Samuel	H. E. Mayer, "Sankt Samuel auf dem Freudenberge und sein Besitz nach einem unbekannten Diplom König Balduins V," *QFIAB*, 44 (1964), 36–38.
Michelant & Raynaud	M. Michelant & G. Raynaud, eds., *Itinéraires à Jérusalem et descriptions de la Terre Sainte rédigés en français aux XIe, XIIe et XIIIe siècles*, Geneva, 1882.
Michel le Syrien	*Chronique de Michel le Syrien, patriarche jacobite d'Antioche (1166/99)*, ed. and trans. J.B. Chabot, 4 vols., Paris, 1899–1924.
Mortet & Deschamps	V. Mortet & P. Deschamps, *Recueil de textes relatifs à l'histoire de l'architecture et à la condition des architectes en France au moyen âge, XIe-XIIe siècle*, Paris, 1911.
Müller, *Documenti*	G. Müller (ed.), *Documenti sulle relazioni delle città toscane foll' Oriente cristiano e coi Turchi fino all'anno 1531* (Documenti degli archivi toscani, 3), Florence, 1879.
al-Muqaddasi	al-Muqaddasi, *Ahsan al-Taqasim fi Maʿrifat al-Aqalim*, ed. M. J. De Goeje, Leyden, 1906.
Oliverus	Oliverus, *Die Schriften des Kölner Domscholasters, späteren Bischofs von Paderborn und Kardinalsbischofs von S. Sabina*, ed. H. Hoogeweg (=Bibliothek des literarischen Vereins in Stuttgart, CCII), Tübingen, 1894.
Paoli	S. Paoli, ed., *Codice diplomatico del sacro militare ordine Gerosolimitano oggi di Malta*, 2 vols., Lucca, 1733.
Petrus Tudebodus	Petrus Tudebodus, *Historia de Hierosolymitano Itinere*, ed. J. H. Hill & L. L. Hill, Paris, 1977.

Philip of Novara — "Le Livre de Philippe de Navarre," in *RHC, Lois*, I, 169–571.

Philip of Savona — Philip of Savona, *Descriptio Terrae Sanctae*, ed. W. A. Neumann, *Österreichische Vierteljahrschrift für katholische Theologie*, 11 (1872), 1–78.

al-Qalqashandi — al-Qalqashandi, *Subh al-a'sha fi sina 'at al-insha'*, 14 vols., Cairo, 1332–1346. AH.

Quaresmius, *Elucidatio* — F. Quaresmius, *Historica Theologica et Moralis Terrae Sanctae Elucidatio*, ed. Cypriano de Tarvisio, Venice, 1880–1882.

Raba, Russians — J. Raba, *Russian Travel Accounts on Palestine*, Jerusalem, 1986 (in Hebrew).

Raymond of Aguilers — *Le "Liber" de Raymond d'Aguilers*, ed. J. H. & L. L. Hill, *DRHC*, IX.

Ricoldus de Monte Crucis — Ricoldus de Monte Cruci, *Liber Peregrinacionis*, in J.C.M. Laurent, *Peregrinatores Medii Aevi Quatuor*, Leipzig, 1846, 101–141; in *IHC*, IV, 255–332.

Roger of Howden — Roger of Howden, *Chronica*, ed. W. Stubbs, (RS, 51), London, 1868–1871.

Röhricht *Bibliotheca* — R. Röhricht, comp., *Bibliotheca geographica Palaestinae: Chronologisches Verzeichnis der auf die Geographie des Heiligen Landes bezüglichen Literatur von andes bezüglichen Literatur von 333 bis 1878, und Versuch einer Cartographie*, Berlin, 1890.

Röhricht, *Regesta* — R. Röhricht, comp., *Regesta regni Hierosolymitani, 1097–1291*, Innsbruck, 1893; *Additamentum*, 1904.

Saint-Lazare — "Fragment d'un cartulaire de l'Ordre de Saint-Lazare en Terre Sainte" ed. A. De Marsy, *AOL*, 2 (1884), documents, 121–157.

Sawirus ibn al-Muqaffa' — Sawirus ibn al-Muqaffa', *History of the Patriarchs of the Egyptian Church, Known as the History of the Holy Chruch*, ed. and trans. A. S. Atiya, Yassa 'Abd al-Masih, O. H. E. Burmester, and A. Khater, 4 vols., Cairo, 1943–1974.

Sefer Nameh — *Sefer Nameh. Relation du voyage de Nassir Khosrau*, ed., trans. and annot. Ch. Schefer, Paris, 1881.

Sibt Ibn al-Jauzi, ed. *RHC* — Sibt Ibn al-Jauzi, *Extraits du Mirât ez-Zèmân*, in *RHC, HOr.*, III, 511–570.

Strehlke — *Tabulae Ordinis Theutonici*, ed. E. Strehlke, Berlin, 1869.

Tafel & Thomas — G. L. F. Tafel & G. M. Thomas, *Urkunden zur älteren Handels- und Staatsgeschichte der Republik Venedig*, 3 vols., Vienna, 1856–1857.

Temple — Cl. F. Albon, Marquis d', *Cartulaire général de l'Ordre du*

	Temple 1119?-1150. Recueil des chartes et des bulles relatives à l'Ordre du Temple, Paris, 1913.
Theodericus	Theodericus, *Theodericus Libellus de Locis Sanctis.* ed. Marie Luise & W. Bulst, Heidelberg, 1976.
Thietmar	*Mag. Thietmari Peregrinatio (Ad fidem codicis Hamburgensis)*, ed. J. C. M. Laurent, Hamburg, 1857.
Thomas, "Tractat"	G. M. Thomas, "Ein Tractat öber das heilige Land und den dritten Kreuzzug," *Sitzungsberichte der K. Bayerischen Akademie des Wissenschaften philos. -philologische classe*, 3, Munich, 1865, 141–169.
Tobler & Molinier	T. Tobler & A. Molinier, *Itinera Hierosolymitana et Descriptiones Terrae Sanctae lingua Latina saec. IV-XI exarata*, 2 vols., Genf, 1880.
Translatio Sancti Nicolai	*Monachi Anonymi Littorensis, Historia de Translatione Sanctorum Magni Nicolai, Terra Marique, Miraculis Gloriosi, Ejusdem Avunculi, Alterius Nicolai, Thodorique, Maryris Pretiosi, De Civitate Mirea in Monasterium S. Nicolai de Littore Venetiarum*, in *RHC, HOcc.*, Va, 253–293.
Usama, trans. Hitti	*An Arab-Syrian Gentleman and Warrior in the Period of the Crusades. Memoirs of Usamah Ibn-Munqidh*, trans. P. K. Hitti, New York, 1930.
al-ʿUmari	al-ʿUmari, *Masalik al-absar fi'l-mamalik al-amsar*, ed. A. F. Sayyid, Cairo, 1985.
al-ʿUthmani	al-ʿUthmani, *Ta'rikh Safad*, ed. B. Lewis "An Arabic Account of the Province of Safed – I," *BSOAS*, 15 (1954), 477–488.
Wilkinson	J. Wilkinson, *Jerusalem Pilgrims before the Crusades*, Warminster, 1977.
William of Tyre	*Willelmi Tyrensis Archiepiscopi Chronicon*, ed. R.B.C. Huygens, Corpus Christianorum Continuatio Mediaevalis, 63–63a, Turnhout, 1986; trans. E. A. Babcock & A. C. Krey, *A History of Deeds Done Beyond the Seas*, Columbia University Records of Civilization, Sources and Studies, 35, 2 vols., New York, 1943.
Yaqut	Yaqut al-Rumi, *Muʿjam al-buldan* (Jacut's Geographisches Wörterbuch), ed. F. Wüstenfeld, 6 vols., Leipzig, 1866–1873.
al-Yunini	al-Yunini, *Dhayl mir'at al-zaman fi ta'rikh al-aʿyan*, 4 vols., Hyderabad, 1954–1961.

Secondary references

Abel, F. M., 1907, "Document épigraphique sur le Patriarche Eustochios," *RB*, 17, 275–276.

1926, "Les deux 'Mahomerie' el-Bireh, El Quobeibeh," *RB*, 25, 272–283.

1927a, "Yazour et Beit Dedjan ou le Chastel des Plains et le Chastel de Maen," *RB*, 36, 83–89.

1927b, "Mirabel et la tour d'Aphek", *RB*, 36, 390–400.

1928, "Notes sur les environs de Bir-Zeit," *JPOS*, 8, 49–55.

1931, "Attarah et Nasbeh au moyen âge," *JPOS*, 11, 141–143.

1935, "Le castrum Feniculi," *JPOS*, 15, 325–326.

1937, "Afrabala-Forbelet et l' Ophra de Gédéon," *JPOS*, 17, 31– 44.

1938, *Géographie de la Palestine,* II, Paris.

1940, "Les confins de la Palestine et de l'Egypte sous les Ptolémées," *RB*, 49, 55–75, 224–239, pls. vii–viii.

Amiran, D. H. K., 1953, "The Pattern of Settlement in Palestine," *IEJ*, 3, 192–209.

Amiran, D. H. K., & Y. Ben Arieh, 1963, "Sedentarization of Beduin in Israel," *IEJ*, 13, 161–181.

Anawati, G. C., 1975, "Factors and Effects of Arabization and Islamization in Medieval Egypt and Syria," in S. Vryonis Jr., ed., *Islam and Cultural Change in the Middle Ages,* Wiesbaden, 17–41.

Anthymus, 1838, "Description of the Boundaries of the Apostolic See of the Patriarch of Jerusalem, in 1838," in G. Williams, *The Holy City*, London (1849), 490–495.

Arnold, T. W., 1913, *The Preaching of Islam. A History of the Propagation of the Muslim Faith*, London (repr. 1935).

Aubenas, R., 1938, "Les châteaux forts des Xe et XIe siècles," *RHDFE*, 4th series, 17, 548–586.

Avi-Yonah, M., 1934, "Territorial Boundaries in North-Western Galilee," *JPOS*, 14, 56–58.

1956, "Samaritan Revolts against the Byzantine Empire," *Eretz-Israel*, 4, 127–132 (in Hebrew).

1973, "The Samaritans in the Roman and Byzantine Periods," in J. Aviram, ed., *Eretz Shomron*, Jerusalem, 34–37 (in Hebrew).

Bagatti, B., 1947, *I monumenti di Emmaus el-Qubeibeh e dei dintorni*, Jerusalem.

1958–1962, "Relatio de excavationibus archeologicis in Monte Carmelo," *Acta Ordinis Carmelitarum Discalceatorum*, 3 (1958), 277–288; 6 (1961), 66–70; 7 (1962), 127–130.

1959–60, "Abud. 1. Le chiese," *Liber Annus*, 10, 185–196.

1971, "Gifna. Villaggio cristiano di Guidea," *La Terra Santa*, 47, 247–56.

1972, "Il Cristianesimo ad Eleuteropolis (Beit Gebrin)," *Liber Annus*, 22, 109–129.

1979, *Antichi villaggi cristiani di Samaria*, Jerusalem.

1983, *Antichi villaggi cristiani della Giudea e del Neghev*, Studium Biblicum Franciscanum, Collectio minor, XXIV, Jerusalem.

Bahat, D., 1990, "The Topography and Toponymy of Crusader Jerusalem," doctoral dissertation, Jerusalem (in Hebrew).

Barag, D., 1979, "A New Source Concerning the Ultimate Borders of the Latin Kingdom of Jerusalem," *IEJ*, 29, 197–217.

Bar-Asher, M., 1976, "Palestinian Syriac, its Sources, its Traditions and Selected Grammatical Problems," doctoral dissertation, Jerusalem, (in Hebrew).

Baratier, E., 1971, "Les communautés de Haute Provence au moyen-âge: problèmes d'habitat et de population," *Provence historique*, 21.

Barkay, R., 1987, "Four Samaritan Sarcophagi of the Roman Period," *Eretz-Israel*, 19, 6–18 (in Hebrew).

Barron, J. B., 1923, *Report and General Abstracts of the Census of 1922 Taken on 23rd of October, 1922*, Jerusalem.

Benvenisti, M., 1970, *The Crusaders in the Holy Land*, Jerusalem.

1982, "Bovaria-babriyya: A Frankish Residue on the Map of Palestine," in B. Z. Kedar, H. E. Mayer & R. C. Smail, eds., *Outremer. Studies in the History of the Crusading Kingdom of Jerusalem, Presented to Joshua Prawer*, Jerusalem, 130–152.

Ben-Zeev, Bat-Sheva, 1986, "Crusader Ports in the Northern Coast of Palestine in the thirteenth Century," MA thesis, Haifa (in Hebrew).

Ben-Zvi, Y., 1970, *Sefer Hashomronim (The Book of the Samaritans)*, Jerusalem (in Hebrew).

Beyer, G., 1940, "Neapolis (Nablus) und sein Gebiet in der Kreuzfahrerzeit: Eine topographische und historisch-geographische Studie," *ZDPV*, 63, 155–209.

1942, "Die Kreuzfahrergebiete von Jerusalem und S. Abraham (Hebron)," *ZDPV*, 65, 165–211.

1945, "Die Kreuzfahrergebiete Akko und Galilaea," *ZDPV*, 67 (1944–1945), 183–260.

1946–1951, "Die Kreuzfahrergebiete Südwestpalästinas: Beiträge zur biblischen Landes- und Altertumskunde," *Hervorgegangen aus der ZDPV*, 68, 148–192, 249–281.

Bloom, J. M., 1987, "The Mosque of the Qarafa in Cairo," *Muqarnas*, 4, 7–20.

Bonnassie, P., 1975–1976, *La Catalogne du milieu du Xe à la fin du XIe siècle. Croissance et mutations d'une société*, 2 vols., Toulouse.

1991, "From the Rhone to Galicia: Origins and Modalities of the Feudal Order," in P. Bonnassie, *From Slavery to Feudalism in South-Western Europe*, Cambridge and Paris, 104–131.

Bosworth, C. E., 1979, " 'The Protected Peoples' (Christians and Jews) in Medieval Egypt and Syria," *Bulletin of the John Rylands Library*, 62, 11–36.

Bourin-Derruau, Monique, 1987, *Villages médiévaux en Bas Languedoc. Gènes d'une sociabilité: X–XIV siècle*, 2 vols., Paris.

Boyd, Catherine, E., 1952, *Tithes and Parishes in Medieval Italy*, Ithaca.

Brett, M., 1973, "The Spread of Islam in Egypt and North Africa," in M. Brett, ed., *Northern Africa: Islam and Modernization*, London, 1–12.

Brice, W. C., 1955, "The Turkish Colonization of Anatolia," *Bulletin of the John Rylands Library*, 38, 18–44.

Bulliet, R. W., 1979a, *Conversion to Islam in the Medieval Period. An Essay in Quantitative History*, Cambridge, Mass.

1979b, "Conversion to Islam and the Emergence of a Muslim Society in Iran," in N. Levtzion, ed., *Conversion to Islam*, New York, 30–51.

Bulst-Thiele, M. L., 1974, *Sacrae Domus Militiae Templi Hierosolymitani Magistri; Untersuchungen zur Geschichte des Templerordes 1118/19–1314* (Abhandlungen der Akademie der Wissenschaften in Göttingen: Philologisch-Historische Klasse, 3 Folge 86), Gǫttingen.

Bunimovitz, Sh., 1994, "Cultural Processes and Socio-Political Change in the Central Hill Country in the Late Bronze – Iron I Transition," in I. Finkelstein & N. Na'aman, eds., *From Nomadism to Monarchy, Archeological and Historical Aspects of Early Israel*, Jerusalem, 179–202.

Bur, M., 1980, "Châteaux et peuplements dans le Nord et l'Est de la France au moyen-âge," *Flaran*, 1, 75–92.

1981, "Research on Medieval Fortified Houses in Eastern France: The Moated Sites of the Champagne," in F. A. Aberg & A. E. Brown, eds., *Medieval Moated Sites in North-West Europe*, Oxford, 87–101.

1987, *Vestiges d'habitat seigneurial fortifié en Champagne centrale*, Reims.

Bur, M., ed., 1986, *La maison forte au moyen-âge*, Paris.

Burrows, M., 1932, "Daroma," *JPOS*, 12, 142–148.

Cahen, Cl., 1934, "Indigène et croisés. Quelques mots à propos d'un médecin d'Amaury et de Saladin," *Syria*, 15, 356–360.

1940, *La Syrie du nord à l'époque des Croisades et la principauté franque d'Antioche*, Paris.

1950–1951, "Notes sur l'histoire des croisades et de l'Orient latin," II: "Le régime rural syrien au temps de la domination franque," *Bulletin de la Faculté des lettres de Strasbourg*, 29, 286–310.

1954, "An Introduction to the First Crusade," *Past and Present*, 6, 6–30.

1958, "L'Islam et les minorités confessionelles au cours de l'histoire," *La table ronde*, 126, 62–72.

1964, "Note sur l'accueil des chrétiens d'Orient à l'islam," *Revue de l'histoire des religions*, 166, 51–58.

1968, *Pre Ottoman Turkey. A General Survey of the Material and Spiritual Culture and History c. 1071–1330*, trans. J. Jones Williams, London.

1971, "Un document concernant les Melkites et les Latins d'Antioche au temps des Croisades," *Revue des études Byzantines*, 29, 285–292.

1972, "Une inscription mal comprise concernant le raprochement entre maronites et croisés," in S. H. Hanna, ed., *Medieval & Middle Eastern Studies in Honor of Aziz Suryal Atiya*, Leyden, 62–63.

1983, *Orient et Occident au temps des Croisades*, Paris.

Chapelot, J., & R. Fossier, 1985, *The Village and House in the Middle Ages*, trans. H. Cleere, London.

Chapoutot-Remadi, M., 1974, "L'Agriculture dans l'Empire Mamluk au moyen âge d'après al-Nuwayri," *Les cahiers de Tunisie*, 22, 23–45.

Charon, C. (= C. P. Korolevskij), 1908, "L'origine ethnographique des Melkites," *Echos d'Orient*, 11, 35–40, 82–91.

1911, *Histoire des Patriarcats Melkites*, III, Paris.

Clermont-Ganneau, Ch., 1888, *Recueil d'archéologie orientale*, I, Paris.

1898, *Recueil d'archéologie orientale*, II, Paris.

1899, *Archeological Researches in Palestine during the Years 1873–1874*, Paris.

1900, *Recueil d'archéologie orientale*, III, Paris.

1903, *Recueil d'archéologie orientale*, V, Paris.

Conder, C. R., 1876, "Samaritan Topography," *PEFQS*, 6, 182–197.

1881, "Mediaeval Topography of Palestine," in C.W. Wilson, ed., *Survey of Western Palestine Special Papers on Topography, Archaeology, Manners and Customs*, London, 274–280.

1889, "The Norman Fiefs in Palestine," *PEFQS*, 21, 201–202.

1897, *The Latin Kingdom of Jerusalem, 1099 to 1291 A.D.*, London.

Constable, G., 1964, *Monastic Tithes from their Origins to the Twelfth Century*, Cambridge.

Coursente, B., 1980, "Castra et castelnaux dans le midi de la France (XIᵉ–XVᵉ siècle)," *Flaran*, 1, 31–55.

Crown, A. D., 1989, "The Byzantine and Moslem Period," in A. D. Crown ed., *The Samaritans*, Tübingen, 55–81.

Dakhshleiger, G. F., 1978, "Settlement and Traditional Social Institutions of the Formerly Nomadic Kazakh People," in W. Weissleder ed., *The Nomadic Alternative*, The Hague and Paris, 361–369.

Dauphin, Cl., 1979, "A Monastery Farm of the Early Byzantine Period at Shelomi," *Qadmoniot*, 12, no. 1, 25–29 (in Hebrew).

Dennett, D. C., 1950, *Conversion and Poll Tax in Early Islam*, Cambridge, Mass.

Deschamps, P., 1933, "Deux positions stratégiques des croisés à l'est du Jourdain: Ahamant et el Habis," *RH*, 172, 42–57.

1934, *Les châteaux des croisés en Terre Sainte*, I: *Le Crac des Chevaliers*, 2 vols., Bibliothèque archéologique et historique, vol. 19, Paris.

1935, "Une grotte-fortresse des croisés au delà du Jourdain: el Habis en Terre de Suète," *JA*, 227, 285–299.

1937, "Les deux Cracs des croisés," *JA*, 229, 494–500.

1939, *Les châteaux des croisés en Terre Sainte*. II: *La défense du royaume latin de Jérusalem*, 2 vols., Bibliothèque archéologique et historique, 34, Paris.

Desports, P., 1966, "La population de Reims au XVe siècle d'après un dénombrement de 1422," *Le moyen âge*, 72, 463–509.

De Vaux, R., & A. M. Stéve, 1950, *Fouilles à Qaryet el-'Enab, Abu-Ghosh, Palestine*, Paris.

De Vogüé, Ch. J. M., 1860, *Les églises de la Terre Sainte*, Paris.

Dodu, G., 1914, *Le royaume latin de Jérusalem. Conférence donnée le 20 novembre 1913 à l'Université Nouvelle de Bruxelles*, Paris.

Dowling, Archdeacon, 1914, "The Town of Haifa," *PEFQS*, 184–191.

Drory, J., 1988, "Hanbalis of the Nablus Region in the Eleventh and Twelfth Centuries," *Asian and African Studies*, 22, 93–112.

Duncalf, F., 1916, "Some Influences of Oriental Environment in the Kingdom of Jerusalem," *Annual Report of the American Historical Association for the Year 1914*, Washington, 135–45.

Edbury, P. W., ed., 1985 *Crusade and Settlement. Papers Read at the First Conference of the Society for the Study of the Crusades and the Latin East and Presented to R.C. Smail*, Cardiff.

El-Ad, A., 1980, "Some Notes on Haifa under Medieval Arab Rule," *Studies in the History of the Jewish People and the Land of Israel*, 5, 191–207 (in Hebrew); for a résumé of the article in English, see p. x.

Ellenblum, R., 1987, "The Crusader Road to Jerusalem," in Y. Ben-Arieh, Y. Ben-Artzi, & H. Goren, eds., *Historical-Geographical Studies in the Settlement of Eretz Israel*, Jerusalem, 203–18 (in Hebrew).

1989, "Who Built Qal'at al-Subayba?," *Dumbarton Oaks Papers*, 43, 103–12.

1992, "Construction Methods in Frankish Rural Settlement," in B. Z. Kedar, ed., *The Horns of Hattin*, Jerusalem, 168–192.

1995, "Settlement and Society Formation in Crusader Palestine," in T. Levy, ed., *The Archaeology of Society in the Holy-Land*, London, 501–11.

1996, "Colonization Acitivities in the Frankish East: The Example of Castellum Regis (Mi'ilya)," *EHR*, 111, 104–122.

Ellenblum, E., R. Rubin & G. Sollar, 1996, "Kh. al-Lauza, a Frankish Farm-House in the Neigborhood of Jerusalem," *Levant*, 28, 193–202.

Enlart, C., 1925–1928, *Les monuments des croisés dans le royaume de Jérusalem. Architecture religieuse et civile*, 2 vols. and 2 albums, Bibliothèque archéologique et historique, 7–8, Paris.

Every, G., 1946, "Syrian Christians in Palestine in the Early Middle Ages," *Eastern Churches Quarterly*, 6, 363–372.

1947, "Syrian Christians in Jerusalem, 1183–1283," *Eastern Churches Quarterly*, 7, 46–54.

Fattal, A., 1958, *Le statut legal des non-musulmans en pays d'Islam*, Beirut.

Favreau M.-L., 1977, "Die Kreuzfahrerherrschaft Scandalion," *ZDPV*, 93, 12–29.

Favreau-Lilie, M.-L., 1980, "Landesausbau und Burg während der Kreuzfahrerzeit: Safad in Obergalilaea," *ZDPV*, 96, 67–87.

Finkelstein, I., 1988–1989, "The Land of Ephraim Survey 1980–1987: Preliminary Report," *Tel Aviv*, 15–16, 117–183.

Foerster, G., 1969, "Identification of Forgotten Crusader Remains in Dayr al-Asad in Central Galilee," *Teva Vearetz*, 11, 230–231 (in Hebrew).

Fossier, R., 1989, *Enfance de l'Europe, X^e–XIIe siècles. Aspects économiques et sociaux*, 2nd edn., Paris.

Fraenkel, Y., 1979, "The Penetration of Beduin into Eretz-Israel in the Fatimid Period (969–1096 C.E.)," *Cathedra*, 11, 86–108 (in Hebrew).

Frankel, R., 1980, "Three Crusader Boundary Stones from Kibbutz Shomrat," *IEJ*, 30, 199–201.

1988, "Topographical Notes on the Territory of Acre in the Crusader Period," *IEJ*, 38, 249–272.

Friedman, E., 1971, "The Medieval Abbey of St. Margaret of Mount Carmel," *Ephemerides Carmeliticae*, 22, 295–348.

1979, *The Latin Hermits of Mount Carmel. A Study in Carmelite Origins*, Rome.

Friedmann, Y., 1982, "A Note on the Conversion of Egypt to Islam," *JSAI*, 3, 238–240.

Friedman, Y. & A. Peled, 1987, "Did the Crusaders Build Roads?," *Qadmoniot*, 3–4 (79–80), 121–122 (in Hebrew).

Frye, R. N., 1984, "Comparative Observations on Conversion to Islam in Iran and Central Asia," *JSAI*, 4, 81–88.

Gaudefroy-Demombynes, M., 1923, *La Syrie à l'époque des Mamelouks d'après les auteurs arabes. Description géographique, économique et administrative*, Paris.

Gervers, M., & R. J. Bikhazi, eds., 1990, *Conversion and Continuity. Indigenous Christian Communities in Islamic Lands: Eighth to Eighteenth Centuries*, Pontifical Institute of Mediaeval Studies, Papers in Mediaeval Studies, 9, Toronto.

Gil, M., 1992, *A History of Palestine, 634–1099*, Cambridge.

Gottheil, R. J. H., 1908, "Dhimmis and Moslems in Egypt," *Old Testament and Semitic Studies in Memory of William Rainey Harper*, Chicago, I, 353–387.

Graboïs, A., 1978, "Haifa and its Jewish Community in the Middle Ages," *Studies in the History of the Jewish People and the Land of Israel*, 4, 147–159 (in Hebrew); for a résumé of the article in English, see p. xi.

Grant, E., 1926, "Ramallah: Signs of Early Occupation of This and Other Sites," *PEFQS*, 186–195.

Grousset, R., 1934–1936, *Histoire des croisades et du royaume franc de Jérusalem*, 3 vols., Paris.

1939, "Sur un passage obscur de Guillaume de Tyr," *Les mélanges syriens, offerts a M. R. Dussaud*, Paris, 637–639.

Guérin, V., 1868–1869, *Description géographique, historique et archéologique de la Palestine*, I–III, Paris.

1874–1875, *Description géographique, historique et archéologique de la Palestine*, I–II, Paris.

1880, *Description géographique, historique et archéologique de la Palestine*, VI–VII, Paris.

Haggett, P., 1965, *Locational Analysis in Human Geography*, London (repr. 1970).

Hamilton, B., 1980, *The Latin Church in the Crusader States. The Secular Church*, London.

1992, "Miles of Plancy and the Fief of Beirut," in B. Z. Kedar, ed., *The Horns of Hattin*, Jerusalem and London, 136–146.

Hayek, D., 1925, *Le droit Franc en Syrie pendant les croisades – institutions judicaires*, Paris.

Higounet, C., 1960, "Cisterciens et bastides," *Le moyen âge*, 56, 69–84.

1980, "Structures sociales, castra et castelnaux dans le Sud-Ouest aquitain (Xème-XIIIème siècles)," in *Structures féodales et féodalisme*, 1880, 109–117.

Hirschfeld, Y., 1993, "The 'Anchor Church' at the Summit of Mt. Berenice near Tiberias," *Qadmoniot*, 26, 3–4 120–127.

Hitti, P. K., 1972, "The Impact of the Crusades on Eastern Christianity," in S. H. Hanna, ed., *Medieval & Middle Eastern Studies in Honor of Aziz Suryal Atiya*, Leyden, 212–217.

Hoch, M., 1992, "The Crusaders' Strategy against Fatimid Ascalon and the 'Ascalon Project' of the Second Crusade," in M. Gervers, ed., *The Second Crusade and the Cistercians*, New York, 119–128.

Hoffman-Berman, C., 1986, *Medieval Agriculture. The Southern French Countryside, and the Early Cistercians. A Study of Forty-Three Monasteries*, Transactions of the American Philosophical Society, 76, part 5, Philadelphia.

Hubatsch, W., 1966, *Monfort und die Bildung des Deutschordensstaates im Heiligen Lande*, Göttingen.

Humphreys, R. S., 1977, *From Saladin to the Mongols*, New York.

Hütteroth, W. D., & K. Abdulfattah, 1977, *Historical Geography of Palestine, Transjordan and Southern Syria in the Late sixteenth Century*, Erlangen.

Johns, C. N., 1934, "The Crusader Attempt to Colonize Palestine and Syria," *Journal of the Royal Central Asian Society*, 21, 288–300.

1937, *Palestine of the Crusaders: A Map of the Country on Scale 1:350,000 with Historical Introduction & Gazetteer*, Survey of Palestine, Jaffa.

Kedar, B. Z., 1982, "Ein Hilferuf aus Jerusalem vom September 1187," *Deutsches Archir für Erforschung des Mittelalters*, 38, 112–122.

1983, "Palmarée: abbaye clunisienne du XIIe siècle en Galilée," *RBe*, 93.3–4, 260–269.

1984a, "Jews and Samaritans in the Crusading Kingdom of Jerusalem," *Tarbiz*, 53, 387–408 (in Hebrew).

1984b, *Crusade and Mission. European Approaches toward the Muslims*. Princeton.

1989, "The Frankish Period," in A. D. Crown, ed., *The Samaritans*, Tübingen, 82–94.

1990, "The Subjected Muslims of the Frankish Levant," in J. M. Powell, ed., *Muslims under Latin Rule*, Princeton, 135–174.

Kedar, B. Z., & M. Alhajuj, 1990b, "Muslim Villagers in Frankish Eretz Israel: Family Size and Private Names," *Pe'amim*, 45, 45–57.

Kedar, B. Z., & D. Pringle, 1985, "La Fève: A Crusader Castle in the Jezreel Valley," *IEJ*, 35 164–179.

King, E.J., 1934, *The Rule Statutes and Customs of the Hospitallers, 1099–1310*, London.

Kochavi M., ed., 1972, *Judaea, Samaria and the Golan: Archeological Survey 1967–68*, Jerusalem, (Archeological Survey of Israel, I) (In Hebrew).

Kohlberg, E., & B. Z. Kedar, 1988, "A Melkite Physician in Frankish Jerusalem and Ayyubid Damascus: Muwaffaq al-Din Ya'qub b. Siqlab," *AAS*, 22, 113–126

(=B.Z. Kedar & A. L. Udovitch, eds., *The Medieval Levant. Studies in Memory of Eliyahu Ashtor (1914–1984)*, Haifa).

Kopp, C., 1929, *Elias und Christentum auf dem Karmel*, Paderborn.

Kosminskii E. A., 1956, *Studies in the Agrarian History of England in the 13th Century*, Oxford.

Kühnel, G., 1988, *Wall Painting in the Latin Kingdom of Jerusalem*, Frankfurter Forschungen zur Kunst, XIV, Berlin.

Lagrange, M.J., 1892, "Chronique – Lettre de Jérusalem," *RB*, 1, 439–56.

  1925, "L'origine de la version syro-palestinienne des Evangiles," *RB*, 34, 481–504.

La Monte, J. L., 1938, "The Rise and Decline of a Frankish Seigneurie in Syria in the Time of the Crusades," *Revue historique du sud-est européen*, 15, 301–320.

  1946, "Three Questions concerning the Assises de Jérusalem," in *Byzantina-Metabyzantina*, I, New York, 201–211.

Langdon, J., 1982, "The Economics of Horses & Oxen in Medieval England," *Agricultural History Review*, 30:1, 31–40.

Laoust, H., 1950, *Le précis de droit d'Ibn Qudama*, Beirut.

Lapidus, I., 1972, "The Conversion of Egypt to Islam," *Israel Oriental Studies*, 2, 248–262.

Lawrence, T. E., 1988, *Crusader Castles*, new edn. with introduction and notes by D. Pringle, Oxford.

Lattimore, O., 1976, "Herdsmen, Farmers, Urban Culture," *Pastoral Production and Society, Proceedings of the International Meeting on Nomadic Pastoralism*, Paris, Dec. 1–3 Paris and Cambridge, 479–490.

Le-Goff, J., 1980, "L'Apogée de la France urbaine médiévale, croissance et prise de conscience urbaine," in G. Duby, ed., *Histoire de la France urbaine*, II, ed. J. Le-Goff, *La ville médiévale*, Paris.

Le-Goff, J., & R. Ruggiero, 1965, "Paysages et peuplement rural en Europe après le XIᵉ siècle," *Etudes rurales*, 17, 5–24.

Leiser, G., 1985, "The Madrasa and the Islamization of the Middle East. The Case of Egypt," *Journal of the American Research Center in Egypt*, 22, 29–47.

Lev, Y., 1988, "Persecutions and Conversion to Islam in Eleventh-Century Egypt," *Asian and African Studies*, 22, 73–91.

Levtzion, N., 1979, "Toward a Comparative Study of Islamization," in N. Levtzion, ed., *Conversion to Islam*, New York, 1–23.

  1990, "Conversion to Islam in Syria and Palestine and the Survival of Christian Communities," in Gervers & Bikhazi, 1990, 289–311.

Lewis, B., 1954, "Studies in the Ottoman Archives – I," *BSOAS*, 16, 469–501.

Lewis, N. N., 1987, *Nomads and Settlers in Syria and Jordan, 1800–1980*, Cambridge.

Little, D. P., 1976, "Coptic Conversion to Islam under the Bahri Mamluks, 692–755/1293–1354," *BSOAS*, 39, 552–569.

  1990, "Coptic Conversion to Islam during the Bahri Mamluks Period," in Gervers & Bikhazi, 1990, 263–288.

Lyons, M. C., & D. E. P. Jackson, 1982, *Saladin: The Politics of the Holy War*, Cambridge.

Madelin, L., 1916, "La Syrie franque," *Revue des deux mondes*, 6th series, 38, 314–358.

   1918, *L'expansion française; de la Syrie au Rhin*, Paris.

Magnou-Nortier, E., 1974, *La société laïque et l'église dans la province ecclesiastique de Narbonne de la fin du VIIIᵉ à la fin du XIᵉ siècle*, Toulouse.

Mas-Latrie, L., 1878, "De quelques seigneurs de Terre Sainte oubliés dans les Familles d'Outremer et Du Cange. Les seigneurs de St. George, du Bouquiau et de Saor," *RH*, 8, 107–120.

   1882, "Le fief de la Chamberlaine et les Chambellans de Jerusalem," *BEC*, 43, 647–652.

Mauss, Ch., 1892, "L'église de Saint Jeremie à Abou-Gôsch (Emmaus de Saint Luc et le Castellum de Vespasien) avec une étude sur le stade au temps de Flavius Josephe," *RA*, 3rd series, 19, 223–274.

Mayer, H. E., 1975, *Tabulae ordinis Theutonici*, ed. E. G. W. Strehlke, Berlin, 1869, repr. 1975, 9–81.

   1977, *Bistümer, Klöster und Stifte im Königreich Jerusalem*, Schriften der MGH, 26, Stuttgart.

   1978, "Latins, Muslims & Greeks in the Latin Kingdom of Jerusalem," *History*, 63, 175–192.

   1980, "Die Seigneurie de Joscelin und der Deutsche Orden," in J. Fleckenstein & M. Hellmann, eds., *Die geistlichen Ritterorden Europas*, Sigmaringen, (=Vorträge und Forschungen, 26), 171–216.

   1988, *The Crusades*, trans. by J. Gillingham, New York and Oxford (repr. 1991).

Mayer, J., 1964, "Es-Samariya, ein Kreuzfahrersitz im Westgaliläa," *Jahrbuch des Romisch-Germanischen Zentralmuseums Mainz*, 11, 198–202.

Mayer, L. A., 1956, "Outline of a Bibliography of the Samaritans," *Eretz-Israel*, 4, 252–253 (in Hebrew).

Milik, J. T., 1960, "Inscription araméenne christo-palestinienne de ʿAbûd," *Liber Annus*, 10, 197–204.

Miller E., & J. Hatcher, 1978, *Medieval England: Rural Society & Economic Change, 1086–1348*. London.

Montgomery, J. A., 1907, *The Samaritans*, Philadelphia (repr. 1968).

Morony, M. G., 1990, "The Age of Conversions: A Reassessment," in Gervers & Bikhazi, 1990, 135–150.

Musil, A., 1907, *Arabia Petraea, II. Edom*, Vienna.

Neumann, G. A., 1881, "La 'Descriptio Terrae Sanctae' de Belardo d'Ascoli (1112–1120)," *AOL*, 1, 225–229.

Nicholson, R.L., 1973, *Jocelyn III and the Fall of the Crusader States, 1134–1199*, Leyden.

Nicolle, D., 1988, "Ain al Habis: The Cave de Sueth," *Archéologie Médiévale*, 18, 113–140.

Noyé, G., 1980, "Féodalité et habitat fortifié en Calabre dans la deuxième moitié du XIème siècle et le premier tiers du XIIème siècle," in *Structures féodales et féodalisme,* 1980, 607–630.

Ovadiah, A., 1970, *Corpus of the Byzantine Churches in the Holy Land,* Bonn, 1970.

  1976, "The Byzantine Church in Eretz-Israel," *Qadmoniot,* 33, 6–15 (in Hebrew).

Perlmann, M., 1942, "Notes on Anti-Christian Propaganda in the Mamluk Empire," *BSOAS,* 10, 843–861.

Perrin, E., 1924, *Le droit de bourgeoisie et l'immigration rurale à Metz,* Bar-le-Duc, 1924.

Peters, E., 1979, "Romans & Bedouins in South Syria," *Journal of Near Eastern Studies,* 37, 315–326.

Poliak, A. N., 1938, "L'Arabisation de l'Orient sémitique," *Revue des études islamiques,* 12, 35–63.

Poteur, J. C., 1988, *Origine et evolution de l'habitat médiéval en Provence orientale,* Paris.

Prausnitz, M. W., 1972, "Romema (Haifa)," *IEJ,* 22, 246–247.

  1974, "Romema (Haifa)," *IEJ,* 24, 142–3.

  1975, "Rosh Maya," *RB,* 82, 591–4.

Prawer, J., 1956, "Ascalon and the Ascalon Strip in Crusader Politics," *Eretz-Israel,* 4, 231–251 (in Hebrew).

  1958, "The City and County of Ascalon in the Crusader Period," *Eretz-Israel,* 5, 224–237 (in Hebrew).

  1972, *The Latin Kingdom of Jerusalem. European Colonialism in the Middle Ages,* London.

  1975, *Histoire du royaume latin de Jérusalem,* 2 vols., 2nd edn. Paris (1st edn., Paris, 1969–1971).

  1977, "Crusader Cities," in H. A. Miskimin *et al.* eds., *The Medieval City,* New Haven and London, 179–199.

  1980a, *Crusader Institutions,* Oxford, 1980.

  1980b, "The Latin Settlement of Jerusalem," in Prawer, 1980, 85–101.

  1980c, "Colonization Activities in the Latin Kingdom," in Prawer, 1980, 102–142.

  1980d, "Palestinian Agriculture and the Crusader Rural System," in Prawer, 1980, 143–200.

  1980e, "Serfs, Slaves, and Bedouins," in Prawer, 1980, 201–214.

  1985a, "The Jerusalem the Crusaders Captured: A Contribution to the Medieval Topography of the City," in Edbury, 1985, 1–14.

  1985b., "Social Classes in the Crusader States: The 'Minorities'," in Setton, 1985, 59–115.

  1988, *The History of the Jews in the Latin Kingdom of Jerusalem,* Oxford.

Prawer, J., & M. Benvenisti, 1970, "Crusader Palestine: Map and Index," in *Atlas of Israel,* 2nd edn., Jerusalem, Sheet 9.10.

Preston, H. G., 1903, "Rural Conditions in the Latin Kingdom of Jerusalem during the twelfth and thirteenth Centuries," thesis, University of Pennsylvania, Philadelphia.

Pringle, D., 1982, "Church Building in Palestine before the Crusades," in J. Folda, ed., *Crusader Art in the Twelfth Century*, BAR, International Series, 152, 5–46.

1983, "Two Medieval Villages North of Jerusalem: Archeological Investigation in al-Jib and ar-Ram," *Levant*, 15, 141–177.

1985, "Magna Mahumeria (al-Bira): The Archaeology of a Frankish New Town in Palestine," in Edbury, 1985, 147–168.

1986a, *The Red Tower (al-Burj al-Ahmar): Settlement in the Plain of Sharon at the Time of the Crusaders and Mamluks*, London.

1986b, "A Thirteenth-Century Hall at Montfort Castle in Western Galilee," *Antiquaries Journal*, 66, 52–81.

1989, "Crusader Castles: The First Generation," *Fortress*, 1, 14–25.

1991, "Survey of Castles in the Crusader Kingdom of Jerusalem, 1989: Preliminary Report," *Levant*, 23, 87–91.

1992a, "Cistercian Houses in the Kingdom of Jerusalem," in M. Gervers, ed., *The Second Crusade and the Cistercians*, New York, 183–198.

1992b, "Aqua Bella: The Interpretation of a Crusader Courtyard Building," in B. Z. Kedar, ed., *The Horns of Hattin*, Jerusalem, 147–167.

1993, *The Churches of the Crusader Kingdom of Jerusalem. A Corpus*, I, A–K (excluding Acre and Jerusalem), Cambridge.

Prutz, H., 1883, *Kulturgeschichte der Kreuzzüge*, Berlin.

Razi, Z., 1970, "The Principality of Galilee in the twelfth Century," MA thesis, Jerusalem.

Reiner, E., 1988, "Jewish Immigration and Pilgrimage to Palestine [1099–1517]," doctoral dissertation, The Hebrew University of Jerusalem (in Hebrew).

Rey, E. G., 1866, *Essai sur la domination française en Syrie durant le moyen âge*, Paris, 1866.

1877, *Recherches géographiques et historiques sur la domination des Latins en Orient*, Paris.

1878, "Note sur le fief de St. George de Labaene en Syrie," *BSNAF*, 68–69.

1879, "La société civile dans les principautés franques de Syrie," *Le cabinet historique*, 25, 167–186.

1883, *Les colonies franques de Syrie aux XIIe et XIIIe siècles*, Paris.

Rheinheimer, M., 1900, *Das Kreuzfahrerfürstentum Galiläa*, Kieler Werkstücke, Reihe C: Beiträge zur europäischen Geschichte des frühen und hohen Mittelalters, 1, Frankfurt am Main, Berne, New York, and Paris.

Rhode, R., 1985, "The Geography of the Sixteenth-Century Sançak of Safad," *Archivum Ottomanicum*, 10 (1985) [1987], 179–218.

Riant, P., 1889, *Etudes sur l'histoire de l'église de Bethléem*, 2 vols., I, Genoa.

Richard, J., 1954, "Les listes de seigneuries dans 'Le livre de Jean d'Ibelin.' Recherches sur l'Assebebe et Mimars," *RHDFE*, 4th series, 32, 565–577.

1979, *The Latin Kingdom of Jerusalem*, trans. J. Shirley, Amsterdam, New York, and Oxford, 1979.

1980, "La feodalité dans l'Orient latin et le mouvement communnal: un état des questions," in *Structures féodales et féodalisme*, 1980, 651–665.

1985, "Agricultural Conditions in the Crusader States," in Setton, 1985, 251–294.

Riley-Smith, J. S. C., 1967, *The Knights of St. John in Jerusalem and Cyprus, c. 1050–1310*, London.

1972, "Some Lesser Officials in Latin Syria," *EHR*, 87, 1–26.

1973, *The Feudal Nobility and the Kingdom of Jerusalem, 1174–1277*, London.

1977, "The Survival in Latin Palestine of Muslim Administration," in P. M. Holt, ed., *The Eastern Mediterranean Lands in the Period of the Crusades*, Warminster, 9–22.

1978, "Peace Never Established: The Case of the Kingdom of Jerusalem," *Transactions of the Royal Historical Society*, 5th series, 28, 87–102.

1983, "The Motives of the Earliest Crusaders and the Settlement of Latin Palestine," *EHR*, 98, 721–736.

Robinson E., & E. Smith, 1841, *Biblical Researches in Palestine*, Boston.

Röhricht, R., 1887, "Studien zur mittelalterlichen Geographie und Topographie Syriens," *ZDPV*, 10, 195–344.

1895, "Karten und Pläne zur Palästinakunde aus dem VII bis XVI Jahrhundert," *ZDPV*, 18, 173–182.

1898, *Geschichte des Königsreichs Jerusalem (1100–1291)*, Innsbruck.

Rose, A. M., 1968, "Minorities," *International Encyclopaedia of Social Sciences*, X, 365–6.

Rose, R. B., 1987. "Church Union Plans in the Crusader Kingdoms: An Account of a Visit by the Greek Patriarch Leontios to the Holy Land in A.D. 1177–1178," *Catholic Historical Review*, 73, 371–390.

Rotschild, J. J., 1934, *History of Haifa and Mount Carmel*, Haifa.

1949, "Kurdaneh," *PEFQS*, 65.

Russell, J. C., 1985, "The Population of the Crusader States," in Setton, 1985, V, 295–314.

Safrai, Z., 1977, "Samaritan Synagogues in the Roman-Byzantine Period," *Cathedra*, 4, 84–112 (in Hebrew).

Saller, S. J., 1946, *Discoveries at St. John's, 'Ein Karim, 1941–1942*, Jerusalem.

1957, *Excavations at Bethany (1949–1953)*, Jerusalem.

Sartre M., 1982, "Tribus et clans dans le Hauran antique," *Syria*, 59, 77–91.

Schick, C., 1867, "Studien über Strassen-und Eisenbahn-Anlagen zwischen Jaffa und Jerusalem," Mitteilungen aus Justus Perthes geographischer Anstalt von A. Petermann, Gotha 13, 124–132.

Schneider, A. M., 1931a, "Die Kirche von et-Taijibe," *OC*, 28, 15–22.

1931b, "Das Kloster der Theotokos zu Choziba im Wadi al Kelt," *Römische Quartalschrift*, 39, 297–332.

Schneider, A. M., 1933, "Zu einigen Kirchenruinen Palästinas," *OC*, 3rd series, 8, 152–160.

Settia, A., 1979, "La struttura materiale del castello nei secoli X e XI: elementi di morfologia castellana nelle fonti scritte dell'Italia settentrionale," *Bolletino Storico-Bibliografico Subalpino*, 77, 361–430.

Setton K. M., general ed., 1955–1985, *A History of the Crusades*, 5 vols., Madison.

Bibliography

1985, *A History of the Crusades*, V: *The Impact of the Crusades on the Near East*, ed. N. P. Zacour & H. W. Hazard, Madison.

Sharon, M., 1976, "Processes of Destruction and Nomadisation in Palestine under Islamic Rule (633–1517)," in M. Sharon, ed., *Notes and Studies on the History of the Holy Land under Islamic Rule*, Jerusalem, 7–32 (in Hebrew).

Shmueli, A., 1981, *Nomadism about to Cease*, Tel-Aviv (in Hebrew).

Sivan, E., 1967a, "Note sur la situation des chrétiens à l'époque ayyubide," *Revue de l'histoire des religions*, 172, 117–130.

1967b, "Réfugiés syro-palestiniens au temps des Croisades," *Revue des études islamiques*, 35, 135–148.

Smail, R. C., 1951, "Crusaders' Castles in the Twelfth Century," *Cambridge Historical Journal*, 10, 133–49.

1956, *Crusading Warfare (1097–1193). A Contribution to Medieval Military History*, Cambridge.

1973, *The Crusaders in Syria & the Holy Land*, Ancient Peoples & Places Series, LXXXII, London.

Spinka, M., 1939, "The Effect of the Crusades upon Eastern Christianity," in J. Th. McNeil, M. Spinka, & H.R. Willoughby, eds., *Environmental Factors in Christian History*, Chicago, 252–272.

Structures féodales et féodalisme, 1980, *Structures féodales et féodalisme dans l'Occident méditerranéen (Xème–XIIIème siècles), Colloque de l'Ecole Française de Rome, octobre 1978*, Rome.

Talmon-Heller, D., 1990, "The Shaikh and the Community," Jerusalem, MA thesis, Jerusalem (in Hebrew).

Talmon-Heller, D., 1994, "The Shaykh and the Community: Popular Hanbalite Islam in 12–13 century Jabal Nablus and Jabal Qasyun," *Studia Islamica*, 79, 103–120.

Tibble, S., 1989, *Monarchy and Lordships in the Latin Kingdom of Jerusalem 1099–1291*, Oxford.

Toledano, E., 1979, "The Sanjaq of Jerusalem in the Sixteenth Century – Patterns of Rural Settlement and Demographic Trends," in A. Cohen, ed., *Jerusalem in the Early Ottoman Period*, Jerusalem, 61–92 (in Hebrew).

Toubert, P., 1973, *Les structures de Latium médiéval. Le Latium méridional et Sabine du IXᵉ siècle à la fin du XIIᵉ siècle*, Rome.

Tsafrir, Y., 1984, "The Arab Conquest and the Gradual Decline of the Population of Eretz-Israel," *Cathedra*, 32, 69–74 (in Hebrew).

Van-Berchem, M., 1902, "Notes sur les croisades. 1. Le royaume de Jérusalem et le livre de M. Röhricht," *JA*, 160, 385–456.

Vincent, L. H., 1931, "Les monuments de Qoubeibeh," *RB*, 40, 57–91.

Vincent, L. H., & F. M. Abel, 1932, *Emmaüs, sa basilique et son histoire*, Paris.

Vryonis, S., Jr., 1971, *The Decline of Medieval Hellenism in Asia Minor and the Process of Islamization from the Eleventh through the Fifteenth Century*, Berkeley, Los Angeles, and London.

Warren, Ch., & Cl. Conder, 1882–1884, *The Survey of Western Palestine*, London.
Wiet, G., 1924, "Kibt," in *EI²*, Leyden and London, II, 990–1003.
Wilson, C. W., 1880, *Picturesque Palestine, Sinai and Egypt*, 4 vols., Jerusalem
Zschokke, H., Emmaus, 1985, *Das neutestamentliche Emmaus*, Schaffhausen.

INDEX

Page numbers set in bold indicate intensive discussion of the subject.

Printed in the United Kingdom
by Lightning Source UK Ltd.
9724900001B/193-195